MW00628322

INDIGENOUS CITIES

Indigenous Cities

*Urban Indian Fiction and
the Histories of Relocation*

LAURA M. FURLAN

University of Nebraska Press   Lincoln and London

Acknowledgments for the use of copyrighted
material appear on page 221, which constitutes
an extension of the copyright page.

Library of Congress Cataloging-in-Publication Data
Names: Furlan, Laura M., author.
Title: Indigenous cities: urban Indian fiction and
the histories of relocation / Laura M. Furlan.
Description: Lincoln: University of Nebraska Press,
2017. | Includes bibliographical references and index.
Identifiers: LCCN 2017021814 (print)
LCCN 2017034458 (ebook)
ISBN 9781496202727 (epub)
ISBN 9781496202734 (mobi)
ISBN 9781496202741 (pdf)
ISBN 9780803269330 (hardback: alk. paper)
Subjects: LCSH: American fiction—Indian
authors—History and criticism. | Indians in
literature. | Cities and towns in literature. |
City and town life in literature. | Indians of
North America—Ethnic identity. | BISAC:
LITERARY CRITICISM / Native American.
Classification: LCC PS153.I52 (ebook) | LCC PS153.I52
F87 2017 (print) | DDC 810.9/897—dc23
LC record available at https://lccn.loc.gov/2017021814

Set in Scala by Rachel Gould.
Designed by N. Putens.

And Coyote blues-ing on the urban brown funk vibe
wanders
in and out of existence
tasting the brown
rusty at times
worn bitter from relocation.

—Esther G. Belin, "Blues-ing on the Brown Vibe"

CONTENTS

ILLUSTRATIONS

ACKNOWLEDGMENTS

This book was written across many geographies as I charted a course across the United States: from its beginnings in Santa Barbara, through southeastern South Dakota, to western Massachusetts, where I now make my home. I owe thanks to many people and many cafés along this route and in these locations. It has indeed been a long journey.

This book was first conceived as a dissertation at the University of California, Santa Barbara, which provided me with generous fellowship and research funding. My primary debt is to my mentors, who helped shape this project and offered encouragement at the time when I needed it most. It is a pleasure to acknowledge my gratitude to Giles Gunn, Shirley Geok-lin Lim, and Stephanie LeMenager, who served as my dissertation committee. I have Shirley to thank for feeding me, offering her home as sanctuary, keeping me on schedule, introducing me to famous writers, giving me the confidence to say something new, and believing that I could be both a poet and a critic. I am grateful to many others as well, including historian Paul Spickard, whom I was fortunate to work with while putting together the collection *Crossing Lines: Race and Mixed Race across the Geohistorical Divide*. I took an amazing class with Carl Gutiérrez-Jones and then later served as his research assistant. I learned much from Inés Talamantes in a course on Native religions. This project had its origins in a dissertation seminar led by the late Richard Helgerson, and I will forever be thankful to him. A big *wado* to my friend and fellow UCSB grad, Marc Coronado, whose kindness and generosity helped me in more ways than I can express. I also made some wonderful friends through the American Indian Student Association, including Linda Murray, who taught me so much.

I am grateful for the support of a junior research leave at the University of Massachusetts, during which I drafted the introduction to this book. UMASS has provided other research funding as well, which I have used for travel, permissions, and a graduate research assistant. I want to thank my colleagues in the English department for their collegiality, friendship, and conversation, especially Randall Knoper, Laura Doyle, Ron Welburn, and Jen Adams. Several have provided astute comments on chapter drafts as well: thank you, Jane Degenhardt, Rachel Mordecai, Asha Nadkarni, Suzanne Daly, and Donna LeCourt. A big shout-out to TreaAndrea Russworm, my writing partner extraordinaire, for her camaraderie and moral support throughout the process. I feel fortunate to have landed in a department with such helpful and supportive colleagues. I am also thankful to be a part of the community of scholars in the Five Colleges Native American and Indigenous Studies Program. Thanks also to the Institute for Teaching Excellence and Faculty Development for scheduling regular writing retreats and for their support of faculty writing. A heartfelt thanks to writing coach Cathy Luna for her encouragement and careful reading.

I have drawn upon the intelligence of many friends and colleagues in Native studies. I would especially like to express my gratitude to readers Chad Allen, Lisa Tatonetti, Susan Bernardin, Dean Rader, Meg Noodin, and Scott Andrews, who helped me work through and clarify my ideas in one chapter or another. Special thanks to Stephanie Fitzgerald and Becca Gercken for their unflagging support and for their willingness to answer all of my random questions. Thanks also to the regulars on the ASAIL listserv, a generous and wicked smart bunch of scholars and writers. I received much feedback on early versions of this work as I presented it at the Native American Literature Symposium and the Native American and Indigenous Studies Association meeting. *Wado!*

A big thanks to the writers and the artists whose work I discuss in the book, especially Susan (Mona) Power, who spoke with me about her book and graciously read my chapter; Debra Yepa-Pappan, who allowed me to interview her about her art; Richard Ray Whitman, who told me about his photographs; and Esther Belin, who talked to me many years ago about city Indians in Los Angeles. Thanks to the authors and artists who have granted me permission to reprint their words and images. You all do amazing work.

Thanks to the staff at the Newberry Library and the former Native American Educational Services College for helping me with archival research on relocation.

My sincere gratitude to research assistant Lisha Storey Daniels for her invaluable support in the final stages of manuscript preparation.

Many, many thanks to the folks at the University of Nebraska Press, especially acquisitions editor Matthew Bokovoy, for his support of this project, for pointing me in the right direction, and for helping this become a book. Thanks also to two anonymous press readers, whose suggestions made this a stronger book. Any mistakes are my own.

Lastly, most importantly, I thank my family for believing in me and for giving me the time and space to write but for always reminding me to make time for fun. They are my rock. Lisa and Miles: I waited so long to find you.

Introduction

The rerelease of Kent Mackenzie's neorealist film *The Exiles* in 2008 coincided with a renewed interest in urban Indians, surely stirred by Sherman Alexie's endorsement and extensive promotion of the release.[1] The film, begun while Mackenzie was a student at the University of Southern California, was intended to document the lives of a group of urban Natives in the Bunker Hill neighborhood of Los Angeles in the 1950s.[2] The narrative follows an unmarried couple, Yvonne Williams and Homer Nish, during the course of one Friday evening as Yvonne takes in a movie and visits with a neighbor while Homer and his friends spend the night carousing at Indian bars before ending up on "Hill X" for an after-hours gathering.[3] The 35 mm black-and-white film presents itself as a documentary of urban Indians, though, like historical Indigenous documentaries, the action and dialogue are mediated by Mackenzie, a non-Native filmmaker.[4] However, *The Exiles* is a complex text and not so easily dismissed: it is drawn from Mackenzie's research on the Bureau of Indian Affairs relocation program and fieldwork on several Arizona reservations and meant to be an exposé of relocated Indians.[5] The plot is drawn directly from interviews with urban Indians, and the film in its entirety was dependent upon the collaboration, improvisation, and spontaneous dialogue of Mackenzie's Native informants, all of whom played themselves.[6] While the rerelease has garnered much attention and critics' accolades, the original was mostly ignored and forgotten.

I begin here with *The Exiles* because it reveals many of the thematics seen in the contemporary urban Indian narratives that are the focus of this study, and it suggests a constellation of issues around which this book circulates. As Paula Gunn Allen once suggested, "One of the major issues facing twenty-first-century Native Americans is how we, multicultural by definition . . . , will retain our 'indianness' while participating in global society."[7] In other words, cultural survival in the global age has been a challenge for Native peoples. While the circulation of people, ideas, and material goods existed in the Americas long before contact with Europeans, legislated relocations and terminations in the twentieth century have brought this movement into relief, causing increased reflection on the nature of the boundaries between Indians and non-Indians, reservations and cities. Allen suggests that preserving and redefining "indianness" in the wake of histories of migration and assimilation are particularly difficult for Indians "off the reservation," a derogatory epithet for someone who has escaped, gone rogue, or gone mad that Allen seeks to reclaim.[8] Though not an unproblematic text, *The Exiles* provides a version of an off-the-reservation story from the relocation era—a story that touches on some of the inherent concerns of this study: questions of home and homeland, the relationship between people and place in the modern era, and anxiety about maintaining Indigenous identities in the urban space.

This book takes up stories that take place off the reservation, in cities specifically, contemplating how new urban Indian communities get represented in these texts, how American Indian authors imagine what it means to be "Indian" in urban spaces, how fictionalized traditions are maintained or modified in the city, how urban heroes and stories differ from reservation heroes and stories, and how conventionally perceived Indian space and urban space historically overlap. My central critical questions are these: What are the aesthetics of urban Indian writing? How are these texts reflecting the shift in Native identity in the wake of urbanization? How are they redefining relationship to place and rescripting the story of urban Indians? Finally, how do they challenge readers to reimagine the borders of reservation, city, and nation? One of the central claims of this book is that these texts reveal that political agency and cultural preservation are possible in the city. They also demonstrate the persistence of tribal and family stories and identities regardless of geographic location. Urban Indian narratives are not solely about despair and dislocation; they imagine a cultural past identified with ancestral lands and/or a reservation and a present that require the making and remaking of Native bonds and communities. Together, these authors represent a new direction in American Indian writing.

I return us briefly to *The Exiles* to consider how this film can augment early critical understandings of urban narratives. In my reading of the film that follows, I will consider how this film simultaneously presents valuable archival images from a critical era in Native history, considers the implications of urban relocation, and, perhaps inadvertently, contributes to the dominant narrative about Indians in the city. Further, I would like to suggest that we think about what gives this 1961 documentary currency today while, at the same time, we consider how our contemporary access to images of city Indians remains mediated by a non-Native lens. As Mackenzie asks us to pause to consider "the plight of the urban Indian" in the 1950s, he draws attention to issues of mobility and locationality and contested space that continue into the present. In a preliminary script, Mackenzie titled the film *The Trail of the Thunderbird*, or *Thunderbirds* for short.⁹ Intended to be both a play on the thunderbird figure found in Indigenous cosmologies and the fortified wine of the same name, the title is meant to name the group of Indian characters the "Thunderbirds," but it also invokes the Ford Thunderbird, one of the many cars that appear throughout *The Exiles*. Both the "trail" of the original title and the automobile suggest travel and mobility, the "go-go-go" that Mackenzie describes in the script. There is an abundance of movement throughout the film: from the flashing of Curtis photographs during the opening credits, to the ascent of Angels Flight (the cable car that climbs Bunker Hill), to Yvonne's perambulations through the city, to the men's constant migrations from bar to bar. Viewers are presented with repeated images that invoke the hustle and bustle of urban life while simultaneously they are compelled to consider the relocation of Native peoples from reservations to cities, of Indians in a modern space. The Thunderbird is reminiscent of Geronimo's Cadillac in the photograph that Philip Deloria calls attention to in *Indians in Unexpected Places*, and it also symbolizes the rising importance of the automobile in post–World War II American cities.[10] In Mackenzie's picture, urban Indians are not only in unexpected places, they are moving quickly and dangerously toward modernity as they simultaneously reclaim an appropriated name and symbol in the process.[11]

As the film opens, a narrative voice tells us that "a new generation" of Indians has "wandered into the cities." While this may be true for a number of Mackenzie's Indians, "wandering" does not describe the systematic removal and assimilation of peoples legislated by US government policies, particularly the relocation program begun in the 1950s, which I will discuss shortly. Even those who have left their home reservations "by choice" are affected by economic conditions that are a direct result of a history of settler colonialism. The word *wander* also seems to belie Mackenzie's use of the word *exile* in the title; as scholars like Edward Said have argued, exile implies force and prevents return.[12] Indeed, *exile* is derived from the Latin for "banishment." Not all city Indians were made to leave their homelands, and many, including those in the film, visit there on a regular basis. Even if Mackenzie imagines city Indians to be "exiles," they are not entirely downtrodden; in fact, he portrays them as rebellious in spirit. This imprecision of language calls attention to the struggle over the representation of urban Indians and I would argue doomed the film's potential success with the public. "Exile" evokes guilt and implicates Americans in the process. Early texts such as this one suggest that the urban space may be one of empowerment, but if characters are "exiles" who "wander," what agency do they possess? Thus, even as *The Exiles* provides a mediated window into the past, it allows us to "witness" a formative moment for Indian peoples. The scene on Hill X, the place where urban Indians gather after the bars have closed, offers

FIG. I. Scene from Hill X. Film still from *The Exiles* by Kent Mackenzie, 1961.

the most promising glimpse of what is to come: an intertribal community that grows out of increasing urbanization. It is a scene of claiming (and perhaps reclaiming) space, one of purposeful movement and mobility, but the potential for activism has not yet come to fruition.

I would like to invoke another early urban text here, Kiowa playwright Hanay Geiogamah's *Body Indian* (1972), which offers another version of the urban Indian experience and articulates the need for coalition in the city. *Body Indian* was first performed at La Mama Theatre in New York City by the American Indian Theater Ensemble (later called the Native American Theatre Ensemble) and featured a multitribal cast.[13] The play is set in an apartment in Oklahoma City, where protagonist Bobby Lee and his "friends" are partying with lease money from their reservation allotments.[14] We discover that Bobby Lee lost his leg during a blackout on the train tracks. During the course of the play's five scenes, his fellow Indians "roll" him—they steal his money, hidden in his pockets and shoes, even in his prosthetic leg—each time he passes out, and each time he is rolled, a train whistle sounds, and images of train tracks are projected on the stage. Throughout the play, characters become more intoxicated and fade in and out of consciousness. Geiogamah's drama is not solely about the dangers of alcohol, however; the play more clearly articulates a warning about the state of Indian community, what Geiogamah calls "Indi'n brotherhood," particularly in the city space.[15] Geiogamah's realism, as he sees it, seeks to expose "how Indians abuse and mistreat one another in a dangerously crippling way."[16]

The city as it gets imagined in *Body Indian* consists of a dingy apartment, chronic drinking, and the danger of trains, which here symbolize the movement and modernity seen in *The Exiles* but with the added historicity of railroads constructed across Indian lands in the nineteenth century. Invoking this history aligns twentieth-century relocations with prior reterritorializations of the continent as US space and property, suggesting that movement away from Indian Country participates in the loss of sovereign space; at the same time, these characters are displaced by the allotment system. The train's whistle sounds like an alarm, and the narrative reads as Geiogamah's alarm. The play makes plain that the "body Indian" or Indian body is broken in numerous ways: in addition to the obvious broken body of Bobby Lee and the destructive alcohol consumption, calling attention to the history of allotment and the leasing of Indian lands suggests a way of fragmenting the body Indian, of fracturing the tribal land base and dismembering the nations. The Indian body is also broken in terms of community; the urban space seems to hold no promise for the future of tribal peoples. This iconic play, produced just two years after the occupation of Alcatraz, an important articulation of Indigenous agency, imagines urban Indians in a bleak, disempowered way. If Indians are going to survive in the city, Geiogamah suggests, they are going to have to unite across tribal lines; they are going to have to imagine a common history and a common identity.

Together, these two early cultural productions call attention to a trajectory in the representation of urban Indians in the realist mode and establish the themes that continue in contemporary urban Indian literature, particularly those associated with relationships to self and tribe and place. Both *The Exiles* and *Body Indian* articulate displacement in the era of relocation, but they also suggest that cities are where identities are remade and where intertribal collectivity offers the greatest means of survival and resistance. Distinct tribal affiliations and histories are mostly absent from these early narratives; indeed, homelands and reservation spaces exist in memory and play secondary to the cityscape. At the same time, modes of mobility and movement mean that "home" and "away" are readily exchangeable—and that Indian bodies are not bound by state-imposed borders, even as home places remain important in terms of tribal identities and ongoing disputes over those boundaries and sites. Further, these two texts highlight the diversity of urban experience, signifying that Indians in Los Angeles in the 1950s differ from Indians in Oklahoma in the 1970s. In other words, there is not one way to be an urban Indian, as sociologists and ethnographers would have us believe. Finally, these texts rescript Native peoples into the American national imaginary— not solely located in the distant past or in remote places—on their own terms. Collectively, these early texts set the stage for a new version of Native storytelling.

This is a book about representations of urban Indian experiences, particularly those from the postrelocation era. The moment of relocation is a critical historical event for contemporary American Indians and American Indian authors, as relocation policy represents ongoing strategies of removal and assimilation. Certainly there were Indians in cities prior to relocation, but the 1950s were marked by a rise in interest in the urban Indian—an interest that lasted well into the 1970s (coterminous with the end of relocation). While the image of city Indians that dominated the public imagination was one of desperation and poverty, Native writers tell another story, one of survival and re-creation. In the literature, the shift from a reservation setting to an urban one begins to occur in the 1960s in poetry, spreading into drama and fiction in the 1970s (with *Body Indian* and Gerald Vizenor's urban trickster stories, for example).[17] Although literature set on the reservation continues to be the focus of critical discussion in scholarly circles, American Indian writers have been producing narratives about the urban experience for several decades.[18]

The texts of this study were published during a twenty-year period, from 1985 to 2005.[19] The works I have selected, by authors Janet Campbell Hale (Coeur d'Alene), Sherman Alexie (Spokane/Coeur d'Alene), Louise Erdrich (Ojibwe), and Susan Power (Dakota), are representative urban texts from a variety of geographical locations and tribal perspectives. Each city in this study brings with it its own complex history that involves both Indigenous and settler interactions; these histories are briefly detailed in each chapter as part of the story these authors provoke. Taken together, these texts demonstrate an arc that radiates from the relocation era through Alcatraz and other political actions of the 1970s, the identity politics of the 1980s, concerns about citizenship and federal recognition in the 1990s, and negotiations of nation and nationhood that continue into the present.

What I am calling urban Indian literature, writing from and about the city, reflects, among other things, a transformation in American Indian demographics and resulting identities that emerged in the wake of increased urbanization.[20] In other words, urban Indian writing articulates a radical shift in the often-discussed relationship between people and place, a shift in Indian identity—in the way people think about themselves as Indians. These texts rescript and reimagine the notion of "Indian space" as they demonstrate that any such geographic designation is complicated by (multiple) migration(s). My thesis builds on other important work in the study of American Indian literatures, particularly that concerned with *place* and *home*.[21] It is my intention that we begin to think critically about characterizations of American Indians as rooted peoples. This misconception was perhaps most clearly articulated by anthropologists like Lewis Henry Morgan and then reproduced much more recently by William Bevis, whose "homing plot" describes a tendency in Native novels for protagonists to leave the reservation for urban spaces, only to return "home" in need of reintegration and healing.[22] This rooted subjectivity stems from narratives constructed around the relationship between Indians and place, not from genuine historical stasis. American Indians are people who grew up on reservations and remain connected to their communities, or so the assumption goes. In actuality, American Indians have always been travelers and border-crossers, even before government-mandated removals and relocations. Examples of this lie in evidence of large-scale trade networks, sites like Cahokia, early Indigenous explorers, performers in Buffalo Bill's Wild West show, turn-of-the-century political activists and authors on speaking tours, and Hollywood actors of the silent-film era.[23] Today, urban Indians carry with them connections to their homelands, ties of tradition and kinship, but they also create new diasporic communities in the cities, complicating what it means to be Indian. Urban Indian narratives highlight these communities and offer a kind of tribal cosmopolitanism as a replacement for a more rooted tribal subjectivity.

Because *Indigenous Cities* challenges predominant theories of the rootedness of American Indians to place and provides new ways of recasting off-reservation Indians as cosmopolitans, it offers a counterpoint to the prevailing critical focus on nationalism in discussions of American Indian literature. Although I recognize the importance of the nation as a political entity and the sacredness of Indigenous sites, I often find the nationalist approach to be confining and incompatible with readings that focus on urban and multitribal peoples, a description that applies to many Native peoples today. My work instead suggests a more transnational reading of contemporary American Indian literature and proposes that we begin to think through the boundaries of national identity for modern tribal peoples, especially those who live away from their ancestral homelands and reservations. These texts and their inherent characters are border-crossers. Allegiance to nation is sometimes complicated by factors of geography, ancestry, and political affiliation. By crossing the imperial borders of the reservation and the conventional reservation novel—the dominant mode for more than a hundred years—urban Indian texts challenge images of Indians as savage, anachronistic peoples confined to rural, captive places and instead reimagine Native peoples as complex, cosmopolitan subjects. This reimagination of Indian Country, to use Nicholas Rosenthal's phrase, works as a reclaiming of space and, in effect, a renarrativizing of US history.[24]

We see the need for this new narrative in a scene from *The Exiles* when Homer, standing outside a liquor store in Los Angeles, reads a letter from his parents and subsequently imagines them back at home in Arizona.

The scene cuts to a man we assume is his father, who is shown shaking a gourd rattle and singing in Hualapai (a song about a rabbit hopping from place to place, according to Mackenzie).[25] The father is visited by a man on horseback, they have a conversation, and then the man traverses the vast landscape, not following the visible road but seemingly making his own path. In a monologue that accompanies this panoramic scene, Homer reveals that he is not from the reservation but from Valentine, Arizona.[26] The landscape we have just seen could easily have been a reservation space; without signs or visible reservation boundaries, this appears to be Indian Country as it is traditionally conceived.[27] What Mackenzie reveals in the juxtaposition of text and image seems to fall outside the purview of his project and demands our attention.

As Homer's monologue continues, he says, "My people wandered all over the place. Two or three hundred years ago. Before the white man came in, you know." Homer's words in conjunction with the images of this landscape and the man on the horse suggest a past in which contemporary boundaries are meaningless.[28] The histories that get revealed here suggest older migrations, a cosmopolitanism and mobility that precede US national geography. The Hualapai are known to have traded extensively with their neighbors: pottery, corn, meat, and, later, horses and European goods.[29] Their pattern of migration was used against them in at least two land claims, the second of which demanded the return of six million acres of their ancestral territory.[30] Homer confesses that he would "rather be in that time than this time." Time and place work in tandem here; he does not express a wish to go back to his homeland but to a period in time when his people "wandered all over the place," a time before the construction of modern boundaries. At the same time, Homer uses his tribe's history of mobility as the impetus for his "wandering," first to San Diego and the US Navy, then up to Los Angeles.

Another history is embedded in this scene, one that also invokes movement. Valentine, Arizona, lies on Route 66, which runs from Chicago to Los Angeles. Route 66, constructed in 1926 with the rise of the automobile in America, signifies a move that provided further unification of national space, making the West more accessible to the rest of the

FIG 2. "Reservation" scene. Film still from *The Exiles* by Kent Mackenzie, 1961.

nation. When Homer remembers his childhood interactions with tourists at the trading post, also in his monologue, he is connecting the early twentieth century with an earlier tribal history (through trading) and with later twentieth-century events (namely, urbanization), all of which invoke cosmopolitanism during the precontact, reservation, and relocation eras. When we view this scene in this way, perhaps using Wai Chee Dimock's notion of "deep time," we also see how urbanization speaks to the unfixing of bounded identities and that place knowledge extends beyond the contemporary reservation spaces, that Indian Territory is larger and more complex than the national narrative allows.[31] This way of reading reveals something about how memory and place overlap, and it informs the entirety of this book.

Indigenous Cities brings together multiple histories and geographies to propose a way of thinking about and discussing representations of urban Indians. It enacts a kind of spatiohistorical reading that suggests that both time and place are critical aspects of these textual productions.[32] It is interested in the cultural work these texts perform, what they say about urban living, and how they convey their urbanness. It is also interested in the historical complexity of cities that gets revealed in these texts: as Michel de Certeau has suggested, places have "inward-turning histories, pasts that others are not allowed to read, accumulated times that can be unfolded but like stories held in reserve."[33] *Indigenous Cities* operates on the assumptions that all US cities are Indigenous cities; that each city has a long and complex Indigenous and settler colonial history; that the city functions as a "contact zone," to borrow that phrase from Mary Louise Pratt; and that cities as cosmopolitan spaces have and do have the potential to germinate meaningful activism.[34] Before I offer some theories about the aesthetics and cultural work of urban Indian literature, I will in the remaining sections of this introduction first outline a brief history of Indians in the city and then map out the critical terms for the study.

CITY INDIANS, OR INDIANS IN THE CITY

A 1973 episode of *Bill Moyers Journal* entitled "Why Did Gloria Die?" tells the story of an Ojibwe woman who died of hepatitis in Minneapolis as a result of limited access to health care. "Like other Indians," says Moyers, "she began to die the moment she left the reservation to come to the city." The picture became clear: American Indians did not belong in the city, modernity had passed them over, they were not adaptable or assimilable, they were either invisible or the victims of prejudice, they were taxing the already struggling urban infrastructures, and they were homesick for their reservations, where they really belonged. Studies in the late 1960s and early 1970s on the "urban Indian condition" portrayed it as an alienating, degraded, oxymoronic state, focusing specifically on mental health issues and alcoholism.[35] This same view was disseminated in the mainstream media. Newspaper and magazine articles followed the Bureau of Indian Affairs' relocation program very closely, often warning mainstream Americans about the surge of Indian migrants in their cities. The press was also responsible for perpetuating a number of stereotypes about Native peoples. The *Christian Science Monitor*, for example, in its 1956 article "U.S. Faces Challenge in Relocating Indian Volunteers," explains that "the Indian" is "not concerned with time" and "shares what he has with everyone."[36] The article title itself suggests that relocation is a problem—one not *caused by* but *solved by* the government.

Despite all of the press regarding the relocation program, which saw Indians in the city as a new phenomenon, Indians have always lived in these spaces. Each city in this study brings with it its own complex history that involves both Indigenous and settler interactions. These cities—Chicago, Minneapolis, Seattle, San Francisco—like all US cities, are located on Indigenous lands, as artist Jaque Fragua (Jemez Pueblo) reminded us when he recently painted "This Is Indian Land" in giant red letters on a construction wall in downtown Los Angeles.[37] Settlement in each of these cities involved the displacement of hundreds of thousands of people. These cities have specific physical features and are situated in geographically advantageous locations near large bodies of water. Prior to contact, each one, to a varying degree, had long been a cosmopolitan center—a place of trade and abundance, inhabited and visited by people from a variety of tribal nations. This kind of cosmopolitan narrative is not often the one told about Indigenous peoples, but as we change that narrative, we begin to imagine, as the texts in this study do, that settler cities have their own cosmopolitan origins and histories. There are Native peoples who refused to leave when legislated to do so, there are people who continued to come to these urban places to do business or to visit with family, there are some sent there as a result of boarding school outing programs, there are others who removed but then returned in subsequent decades or generations to take advantage of economic opportunities such as participating in Buffalo Bill's Wild West or in the rise of the film industry in Hollywood, constructing the railroad, joining the military, or finding a job in the growing defense industry during the world wars, to name some examples. The movement in and around these cities is vastly complex and impossible to generalize.

In the chapters that follow, I attempt to locate the ways in which contemporary authors evoke these earlier urban iterations, particularly in the way that these texts layer and map these histories, as a way of acknowledging Native claims on these spaces. My use of the relocation period to frame this project is not meant to deny the existence of Indigenous peoples in cities prior to the 1950s nor to claim that the relocation program was the only means of movement to cities. It is instead to recognize the import of the relocation period—to populations, to social and political issues, to conceptions of Indian identity, to American ideas about Indians. There is no denying that relocation changed the story about urban Indians. Relocation functions as a "period of rupture" and a "critical narrative site," to borrow Stephen Cornell's terminology, the latter of which he defines as "events or sequences of events that carry rare emotional power for group members and, as critical moments in their version of their story, shape the tale that they tell."[38] Relocation policy affected hundreds of thousands of people, and it altered the narrative they told about themselves. As Walter Benjamin has suggested, the closer the historical event, the more fragmented the narrative around it.[39] Stories about relocation and the urban space took time to appear, demonstrating the critical distance needed to narrativize this period, as I will discuss further in the following section.

The acceleration of urbanization caused by the relocation program was unprecedented, and this era continues to be critical to understanding Indigenous history in the twentieth century. Begun after the Second World War and ending in the early 1970s, relocation was initially an employment program for returning Indian veterans and was designed by the BIA as an alternative to growing poverty on the reservations, which had dramatically increased after years of drought.[40] In 1956 the Senate passed Public Law 959, or the Indian Adult Vocational Training Act, which established urban and reservation training centers, though relocation had begun unofficially in 1952, supported by the first commissioner of Indian Affairs, Dillon Myer, who had orchestrated the plan for Japanese American internment during the war. Field offices were established on reservations for the purpose of attracting reservation-dwellers to move into the cities. During the first years of relocation, relocatees could be sent to Chicago or Los Angeles, then later to Cleveland, Dallas, Detroit, Denver, Oakland, San Jose, Tulsa, or Oklahoma City. They received bus or train fare, fifty dollars to use to move their household goods, a temporary room (usually at a YMCA or transient hotel), and job placement assistance, mostly as industrial laborers. Though certainly a good percentage of American Indians were living off the reservation by the Second World War, many as a result of termination policy, a measure that legally "terminated" a number of tribes in the 1950s, relocation facilitated the move to cities for thousands of Indigenous peoples. Between 1952 and 1967, nearly twenty-eight thousand Indians were employed through the program. From 1951 to 1971, more than one hundred thousand were relocated from their reservations to urban areas.[41]

The relocation program offered a new life in the city, the possibility of economic gain, and modern conveniences like washing machines and automobiles. Field offices maintained photo albums of relocatees, many posed in front of their new appliances or homes. To determine potential success, relocation officers visited the homes of relocation candidates as many as two or three times before the move. Once they arrived in the city, with an address and directions to the BIA office, relocated Indians were on their own. The program covered four weeks of lodging and meal expenses, the time allotted to find employment. Many program participants complained that the BIA failed to follow through with its promises of jobs and superior housing—advertised in the relocation brochures—and many found themselves in unstable positions as day laborers, living in lower-class neighborhoods, often in tenement buildings, in a sense, becoming a part of the urban poor.[42] A large number of participants simply left the cities and returned to their home reservations. The BIA calculated the "return rate" and conspired to relocate people farther from home to discourage their return, though historian Don Fixico reports that 70 percent of early relocatees did return to their reservations.[43] According to an early report from the Chicago Field Office of the BIA, based on interviews with relocated Natives in 1953, the reasons for return included "lay-offs," "drunkenness," "no commitment to city life," "illness," the inability to be "high class," or their belief "in old ways."[44] Some participants were found to have taken advantage of the BIA's "free trip" to the city to visit their friends and family, with no intention of relocating at all.

Relocation into America's cities happened amidst housing shortages, loss of manufacturing jobs, and flight into the suburbs, the latter of which was in large part a result of new loan programs from the Federal Housing Authority (FHA) and the Veterans Administration (VA) that allowed many veterans to buy newly constructed houses outside city limits.[45] Likewise, post–World War II cities were experiencing heightened racism and the rise of urban ghettos, into which the majority of relocated Natives were moved. In the 1950s, politicians and the media were describing urban problems as "blight." Traffic congestion, sewage issues, and pollution led to plans for downtown reconstruction projects, some of which resulted in the gentrification of warehouse districts and federal programs to redevelop urban highways. Of course, by the mid-1960s, cities were hotbeds of racial unrest. During the span of the three decades of relocation, American cities were racially segregated and economically and environmentally challenged. Relocated Indians moved into the ghettos, where they struggled to gain wage labor and satisfactory housing.

The urban space became a place of rearticulation of citizenship and belonging, as well as a locus of political movements. While there were certainly social problems that resulted from relocation, positive changes occurred as well, especially those that led to a heightened sense of activism and a new collective identity based on common experiences and common goals.[46] Naming and theorizing this identity reveal an interesting dialogue about what to call urban Indians. While Alan Sorkin describes a "neo-Indian social identity" in the urban space, focusing on the newness of the construction of this identity, Vine Deloria Jr. and Clifford Lytle call urban Indians "ethnic Indians," suggesting that Native identity off the reservation has become "a common, albeit artificial, heritage."[47] Terms like "neo-Indian," "pan-Indian," "pantribal," what Stephen Cornell calls "supratribal," and "ethnic Indian" are all attempts to describe this new identity that comes from the intermingling and merging of tribal peoples, particularly in the urban space.[48] I prefer "intertribal" over "pantribal" or "pan-Indian" to describe this new Indian identity, as the former suggests the formation of a new group, between and among, and conjures camaraderie, not necessarily the all-inclusive coalition evoked by *pan*. The "Indian" in pan-Indian also evokes the purposeful erasure of difference that Native peoples have been engaging with since contact. An even better term comes from Gerald Vizenor (White Earth Ojibwe), who describes a "new tribal consciousness" coming out of the cities.[49] "New tribal consciousness" describes both a changing identity and the kind of activism that results from this change.

Certainly, intertribalism is not new in the relocation period; Native peoples have formed relationships and coalitions throughout history, pre- and postcontact.[50] Beginning in the 1950s and 1960s, however, new American Indian community centers became places where increased interactions between different tribal peoples led to different kinds of activities—from powwows to potlucks and sporting events, as Susan Lobo describes in her collaborative history of the Oakland Intertribal Friendship House.[51] While community centers and events provided important services and social functions where tribal identities commingled and coalesced to a certain extent, very concrete tribally specific cultural practices have been transported to the urban space, as we will see in the literary productions. Urbanization has affected Indian identity, especially given the importance of place to Native peoples—and how much the reservation experience has come to define "Indianness" in the United States. Contemporary tribal cosmopolitanism challenges many such older stereotypes, but it also raises questions about Indigenous identity and the very nature of Indianness. While governmental and tribal requirements for tribal enrollment are often the standards by which identity is determined, Indian identity for many has been decided by other factors, such as participation in a Native community and acceptance by tribal members.[52] Identity issues are more complicated for urban Indians, where the community itself is very fluid, and even more so for those who are generations removed from the reservation.[53] Mi'kmaw scholar Bonita Lawrence writes, "Having a reserve to point to as a homeland, where one's family has been part of a web of relations within the community, anchors these individuals in profound ways as Native people, even if most of the actual connections they develop in their lives are within the urban Native community."[54] Here Lawrence points to the lack or gap between absent place and tribal belonging, two different types of girding dependent on each other. In other words, we need to pay attention to the ways in which the reservation (and other Indigenous geographies) continues to be an anchor for urban peoples.

The convergence of Native peoples in the urban space gave rise to a reinvigorated tribal consciousness and a new kind of political activism that sometimes united urban and reservation Indians. By the late 1960s, Indian people were participating in urban social movements, Red Power protests that included fish-ins, the Trail of Broken Treaties (1972), and what became the American Indian Movement (AIM) in Minneapolis in 1968. AIM arose in direct response to urban issues, and it set up "survival schools" to teach urban Indian students Native languages and traditional culture. The most iconic event of the era happened independently of AIM, when on November 9, 1969, fourteen Indian college students traveled to Alcatraz Island.[55] This historic moment was closely followed by the mainstream press and supported by celebrities like Jane Fonda. The occupiers used the 1868 Treaty of Fort Laramie, a Sioux treaty that they believed promised all surplus government land would revert back to Indian ownership. The plan for Alcatraz Island as Indian land—and it was once Indian land—since the federal penitentiary had been closed in 1963 included the building of an American Indian cultural center and a college for Native students.[56] The original group of occupiers, led by Richard Oakes (Mohawk), consisted of university students from San Francisco State, Cal Berkeley, UCLA, and UC Santa Cruz.[57] They were later joined by numbers of urban and reservation Natives as the months wore on and many of the students returned to class. On the island, cellblocks became temporary housing. Daily boats brought supplies and more occupiers. John Trudell's broadcast of a show called *Radio Free Alcatraz* was picked up by Pacifica Radio. The occupiers, calling themselves Indians of All Tribes, Inc., issued statements and a proclamation to the federal government, the most poignant of which enumerates the resemblance of Alcatraz to Indian reservations.[58] Famous photographs from "the Rock" are evidence of the importance of the claims: graffiti proclaims, "This is Indian land," an obvious but crucial statement. This very visible reclaiming of American space resonates in urban Indian narratives.

The Alcatraz occupation, which I will return to in chapter 1, marked a new movement, one that happened in an urban space and that was led by and achieved by *urban* Indians. At Alcatraz, Indians were visibly off the reservations, and they were collectively demanding ownership of nonreservation property. Like every other historical action that involved multiple tribes working together, the occupation made the US government anxious.[59] Even though Alcatraz Island promises very little practical use because of its isolated location and the presence of prison buildings, this kind of political action had the potential to set precedent. In the end, even though Alcatraz occupiers were forced to abandon the island, the occupation was not a failure; this momentous act of protest became a catalyst in the making of a new tribal consciousness based on common political goals and perceived commonalities that crossed tribal lines.[60] Alcatraz called attention to Indian concerns both on and off the reservation, and it led to other protests across the nation, like the Chicago Indian Village movement, which I will discuss in chapter 4. The city space may have been challenging for Indigenous peoples in this era, but it precipitated political action and coalition and community in a new way. While there were Native peoples in cities before the BIA's relocation program, this massive, directed effort to once again remove reservation Indians from their ancestral homelands provoked a widespread, organized reaction. In turn, land, location, and belonging are critical themes in this era and in the literature that describes it as Indigenous peoples appear and reconfigure themselves in the urban landscape, staking claims in the city space.

THEORIZING URBAN INDIAN WRITING

This project purposefully brings together concepts from many theoretical positions, including those from cultural studies, Native studies, global studies, postcolonial studies, border theory, and urban studies. I engage with concepts from recent work on the transnational in particular, aware of the limitations and trendiness of such an approach. This literature under examination is *urban*, and at the same time it is *diasporic, cosmopolitan*, and *transnational*, and while it differs in many ways from work that is usually described as such, it shares some common ground, particularly in relation to the tropes that get deployed, namely, those centered around notions of home and belonging. For this reason, I am proposing a way of thinking about urban Indian narratives in these critical terms and envisioning how urban Indian subjectivity can be understood in relationship to movement and travel, migrations and relocations. My goal in doing so is to engage critical thinking about the relationship between people and place not to prove that Indigenous homelands are no longer relevant but to address contemporary shifts in population that are the result of government policy, economic circumstance, and personal choice. I would like to move the conversation beyond the one that usually circulates in relationship to Indians and land: one that centers solely on loss and victimization and predicates a "natural" connection between people and their place.

One of the primary things that gets reimagined in urban Indian narratives is the relationship between people and place, a relationship that is at once historical and complex but often clichéd and misunderstood. It is commonly assumed that American Indians are people who grew up on reservations and remain connected to their communities and their tribes. This stereotype is a fairly recent one, given that the reservation system on a wide scale began during the Indian removal of the Jacksonian era, but it is an extension of earlier images of Indians.[61] Early colonists described the Native inhabitants of the Americas as roving bands of half-naked cannibals, heathens, or savages and equated them with the landscape, something that, like the land, the American Garden of Eden, needed to be tamed and conquered. As historian Robert F. Berkhofer Jr. points out, this primitivist view of Indians as children of nature, already a misnomer apparently based on Christopher Columbus's geographical error and a collective entity that did not exist prior to contact, gave way to a more romantic vision of Natives in the 1800s that was based on the idea of the vanishing race, the Noble Savage.[62]

By the late nineteenth century, white Americans had determined that "civilization and Indianness were inherently incompatible," writes Berkhofer.[63] It would follow that Indians do not belong in the city space, sites associated with the height of Western civilization, even if, as Ian Buruma and Avishai Margalit point out, the Western city is a "wicked symbol of greed, godlessness, and rootless cosmopolitanism."[64] If this is what characterizes the city, then surely Indians, communal people believed to be rooted in their tribal territories, do not belong there, even in the modern era. This again invokes Deloria's concept of "Indians in unexpected places," which in his work does not apply directly to urban Indians but might aptly do so.[65] The idea of Indians missing out on modernity can be seen in the famous 1971 Keep America Beautiful commercial: Iron Eyes Cody, dressed in recognizable "Indian" clothing, paddles a canoe in a river, a city skyline behind him and a drumbeat in the background. In the end, Cody has tears in his eyes—a response to the trash in the river and along the shore, the plumes of pollution arising from the city, and the spoiling of "his land." While that is the narrative that unfolds in this public service announcement, the divide between reservation and city was not as clear in the early 1970s as perhaps it once had been.

In *Place and Vision: The Function of Landscape in Native American Fiction*, Robert Nelson traces the relationship to the reservation space in novels of what Kenneth Lincoln calls the Native American Renaissance, begun in 1969 when *House Made of Dawn* earned Kiowa writer N. Scott Momaday the Pulitzer Prize. Nelson argues that cultural literacy for American Indians relies upon "an intimate knowledge of a particular landscape," knowledge that defines and validates identity and provides an antidote to what he describes as postmodern malaise.[66] The malaise of the Renaissance era, according to Lincoln, is a direct response to relocation and urbanization. Nelson argues, then, that the acculturation and detribalization of the modern era provoked authors such as Momaday and Leslie Marmon Silko (Laguna Pueblo) to focus on the importance of place. Indeed, seminal novels like *House Made of Dawn* (1968) and *Ceremony* (1977) contemplate the repercussions of leaving the reservation space, in both cases to serve in the US military. While both of these novels depict increased movement away from tribal homelands and contain scenes of urban locales, specifically of Los Angeles and Gallup, they locate Indian identity and wholeness within the reservation space. What Bevis has called "homing plot" is prevalent in novels of this era: protagonists leave the reservation but must return "as if by instinct" in order to be healed and reintegrated into the tribal fold.[67]

Some useful ways to theorize the relationship between Native peoples and place come from the work of renowned authors like Silko, Simon Ortiz (Acoma), and Allison Hedge Coke (Huron/Cherokee).[68] In his essay "More Than Just a River," for example, Ortiz discusses the importance of the *chunah*, or the Rio de San Jose near McCartys in New Mexico.[69] Some of the essay's vignettes focus on personal remembrances and childhood memories, some on the origin of the river itself, while others describe cultural activities that take place along the river. The river becomes part of the people's historical memory, and there are stories that get told about the river—when it is high, when it is low. Ortiz argues that the physicality of the river, which traverses Acoma land, is not as important as the human experience of the river. Silko's essay "Language and Literature from a Pueblo Perspective" makes the same claim, particularly in relationship to stories that surround an arroyo in Laguna. She tells the story of a Vietnam vet whose new Volkswagen rolls in this arroyo, an arroyo that has claimed numerous automobiles. This place, this arroyo, becomes the place where cars have been lost; it is a site of repetitive loss. The stories about this place provide a shared experience for the community, and the site itself becomes populated with these stories. For Silko, as for Ortiz, the landscape is storied with the history of the people. What is important is human history in this place, the people's memories of place—not necessarily some kind of mystical aura that is attached to place. Hedge Coke's work adds another dimension to this when she says, in relation to the Blood Run mound site on the South Dakota–Iowa border, the namesake of her poetry collection, that this "place has memory."[70] Hedge Coke's assertion allows for the land to remember the people who lived in this place—in this case, a cosmopolitan trading site that thrived until the 1700s.

Engendering the land with memory makes a case for a symbiotic relationship that requires further untangling. In his often-cited work on the Western Apache, anthropologist Keith Basso writes that before the introduction of print culture, "places served humankind as durable symbols of distant events and as indispensable aids for remembering and imagining them."[71] Place, then, not only becomes layered with the history of one's people but is a space that can be read. Further, place is essential in determining identity, as Dakota historian Angela Cavender Wilson has suggested: "Indigenous people seem to share a belief that our way of life, land, ceremonies, and language are of divine origin. That is, a divine force placed each indigenous nation, or guided us, to a specific place that would be our own, and provided us with a set of original directions about how we were to live."[72] Territory is divinely ordained and sacred, and it is often *where* people came into being, whether from the sky or up through the earth, according to tribal origin stories. Place is important, historically and spiritually, but Indian peoples do not have a supernatural connection to the land, and, as the texts I am examining demonstrate, they *can* survive away from their homelands. At the same time, the seizure of Indian land provides the backbone of US history; all of America's cities are built on stolen land. Place becomes even more important when the threat of loss looms; thus, dispossession often remains central in Native consciousness and cultural productions. The land remains contested, as Ojibwe scholar Gail Guthrie Valaskakis points out: American land has been "explored, settled, mapped, treatied, reserved, privatized, developed, idealized, contested, and imagined."[73] The land is "both territory and sacred site," both of which invoke historical political struggles.[74]

Thus, territory can be articulated as a site of creation and a site of spiritual import, but it also has meaning in terms of spatial boundaries of political community and nation. The nation still has meaning for Indigenous peoples; it is an important entity in terms of citizenship and sovereignty. Indian lands are undoubtedly important on a number of levels—historically, economically, for issues of sovereignty or people-hood, for subsistence—and my project does not in any way advocate the dissolution of Indian nationhood and mass migration to America's cities. It recognizes a danger in doing so. Nor is it meant to negate claims of Indigeneity to this land. What it is interested in is contemplating the relationship between Indian peoples and their tribal nations, particularly when they no longer reside in their home communities. It is less interested in assimilation per se and more interested in Indigenous subjects in transit (to evoke Jodi Byrd here), crossing modern and historical political boundaries and geographic space and making new homes in urban locales.[75] While discussions about Native space and place often center on dispossession, I would like to shift this conversation to think instead about new spatial encounters and *retakings* of place, for this is what happens in urban Indian texts.

The city as I imagine it is a cosmopolitan place with shifting borders and populations, with a geography that must be navigated and learned, a pace that is markedly different from that of rural communities and towns, and an economy dependent on the labor of the working classes. My thinking about the city and the way that urban space gets imagined, mapped, and navigated has been influenced by the work of a number of social geographers and urban theorists. For example, Henri Lefebvre argues that space itself is historical, and his articulation of a "spatial practice," of the construction and appropriation of space, is critical to my readings of urban texts.[76] This "spatial practice," in conjunction with Certeau's ideas about "ways of operating" and the "tactics" people use to navigate urban spaces, informs all of these chapters.[77] My argument resonates with the work of M. Christine Boyer, who writes about the way in which cities construct a past that, she argues, does not include "displaced and disadvantaged" peoples.[78] My idea of the contemporary city comes from Boyer's interpretation of the city as "spectacle"—constructed through juxtapositions and reliant on "perpetual movement"—and from Yi-Fu Tuan's description of cities as "carpentered habitats."[79] Mike Davis's *City of Quartz* informs my understanding of the built environment and the policing of public spaces, particularly with regard to the homeless, as part of a class war reminiscent of the one in Alexie's *Indian Killer*.[80] Part of this class war involved the destruction of Los Angeles's Bunker Hill, which played so prominent a role in *The Exiles* and postrelocation urban Indian lives.[81] Additionally, Edward Soja maps a Los Angeles whose landscape is racially constructed, and David Harvey suggests ways of solving social and spatial conflicts in the city.[82] I also see Soja's and Harvey's ideas about social justice in conversation with the recent work of theorist Judith Butler, who, along with Greek anthropologist Athena Athanasiou, contemplates the politics of dispossession and the power of activist bodies in space.[83] Their ideas about "the political and affective labor of critical agency" and "a politics of the performative" are helpful in thinking through the manifestations of urban collectivity and activism that occurred in the wake of relocation, evidence of which appears in each text of this study.[84] Though Butler and Athanasiou do not specifically discuss Indigenous dispossession in the United States, they offer a triangulation of *people*, *place*, and *dispossession* that I find germane to this discussion. The city may be a place where economic and racial injustice becomes manifest, but it is also a place where transformative activism is possible and productive.

Recognizing Indigenous nations as *nations*, I turn to recent work on the transnational to think through mobility, movement, and travel as related to urban spaces. I recognize that the transnational often operates on a vertical binary in terms of the Indigenous and colonizer,[85] but it also offers a useful discourse for working out the mechanisms at play for Native peoples who live in urban spaces. For example, Stephen Clingman proposes that the "nature of boundaries" may be a "defining characteristic of the transnational," pointing out that transnational fiction concerns itself with travel and movement and routes both in subject and in form.[86] Critical for me in Clingman's theorizing is the way in which he sees the transnational as merely an extension of the national—that the two are not at odds with each other. In fact, the word *transnational* seems to underscore the very existence of the nations whose boundaries are being crossed. Trans*national* lends itself to discussions of both sovereignty and nationalism—and what it means to migrate from one national space to another. I would argue, then, that the rise in movement away from tribal communities was a major culminating factor in the rise of the nationalist movement (and the focus on home in Indigenous writing).

I have found especially useful the groundbreaking transnational work being produced by Native studies scholars. For example, Shari Huhndorf offers an Indigenous perspective on the transnational as she surveys the various ways that Indigenous art and literature transcend national boundaries.[87] She argues, as I do in this project, that the global or transnational turn has "re-fashioned indigenous cultural expression along with social and political structures," that global concerns have united Indigenous peoples across national borders.[88] Chadwick Allen also challenges traditional ideas about transnationalism in his recent work. He argues that the discourse of transnationalism is arranged vertically, from colonized to colonizer, with the Indigenous always on the periphery, and that its focus is on the contemporary nation-state. His Indigenous-to-Indigenous approach proposes a way of thinking outside of popular theoretical constructions of the transnational, diaspora, and exile and moving away from transnationalism as it is currently conceived. Allen also thinks about the circulation of Indigenous texts, particularly as they are read and viewed by other Indigenous peoples. This is a really compelling way of thinking about the movement of peoples and ideas, though in this book I am more interested in the way texts are *about* crossing borders. Another formulation of the transnational critical to my project is Renya Ramirez's formulation of the "hub," a description of the way that "urban Indians occupy the center, connected to their tribal communities by social networks represented by the wheel's spokes."[89] As she points out, her concept is similar to Paul Gilroy's formulation of the black Atlantic, particularly as it challenges "ideas of diaspora that placed the 'homeland' at the center."[90] With the urban space or hub at the center, the focus shifts to contemporary constructions of identity and place making. The nations exist, but they are in the periphery in this model. The hub is another way of thinking of the city as a meeting place for Native peoples and a "collecting center" for "ideas, information, culture, community, and imagination" that circulate through the center and out through the spokes to other tribal communities.[91] The hub describes the way urban Indian peoples interact with one another and travel between places, reminding us that often the routes between city and reservation are well traveled. Ramirez sees the hub as a form of transnationalism, as a way of viewing urban Indians in "nation-to-nation relationship[s]" and recognizing their tribal citizenship in a way that coincides with national movements and sovereignty rights.[92]

Reading urban Indian writing through a transnational lens asks us to think about what connections to tribal nations mean—and about how Native peoples cross national boundaries in their everyday lives. To think more critically about ideas of *boundaries* and *borders* and *crossing*, I turn to scholars of border theory, which, as Paul Jay argues, centers on the "politics of location."[93] Border theory is concerned not only with physical borders and boundaries and interstitial spaces but also with the resulting psychological states that these borders impose. While the borders or boundaries of Indian Country, of the reservations themselves, have a set of historical, political, and jurisdictional issues different from that of the US-Mexico border, the physical crossings of these borders elicit many of the same results: distance from home and homeland, absence of support system, loss of community, changes in citizenship rights.[94] José David Saldívar asks a question critical for this study: "What changes . . . when American culture and literature are understood in terms of 'migration' and not only immigration?"[95] Authors like Sherman Alexie have employed the concept of immigration to talk about the move from reservation to city.[96] This certainly calls attention to borders, which in Indian Country are already and always contested but which now often appear invisible. Reservation borders, at once markers of containment and the limits of sovereignty, are now indicated by road signs (which call to mind histories of cultural tourism). Most of these boundaries are settler ones, and they do not define the whole of aboriginal territories. We need to remember that reservation boundaries were once intended to hold captive Native populations, to protect white Americans from (real and imagined) Indian wrath and violence. Today these boundaries hold different significance.

While some might argue that tribal traditions are protected by these borders, it is impossible to ignore the global flow of information and culture that gets circulated throughout what we consider to be Indian Country.[97] Reservations are no longer isolated, culturally pure spaces, and we need to pay attention to the way tribal cosmopolitans participate in global society: they make new homes away from their home communities; they collaborate with other Indigenous peoples in these new spaces; they travel to reservation spaces; and they preserve and adapt traditional cultural practices. I draw upon the way that anthropologist James Clifford imagines American Indians as migrants, as tribal cosmopolitans, as an "unrooted" (or, as I will argue, multiply rooted) diaspora.[98] Clifford points out that tribal groups have always practiced "older forms of tribal cosmopolitanism (practices of travel, spiritual quest, trade, exploration, warfare, labor migrancy, visiting, and political alliance)," even though popular narratives root them like trees.[99] Cosmopolitanism existed in the precontact Americas in places like Cahokia and Blood Run, trade centers where multiple tribal groups gathered and interacted. City Indians are also tribal cosmopolitans; they simultaneously maintain tribal identities and global ones as they participate in urban life. At first glance, "tribal cosmopolitanism," like "urban Indian," seems to be oxymoronic, but it signifies a useful contradiction for this project.[100] What are the possibilities for an identity that is simultaneously tied to a particular landscape and, to use Timothy Brennan's phrase, "at home in the world"?[101] Clifford's model of tribal cosmopolitanism provides useful ways for thinking about the experiences of contemporary urban Indians in terms of diaspora, particularly with his concepts of "double or multiple attachment" and "dwelling-in-displacement."[102] Clifford writes, "Diaspora cultures thus mediate, in a lived tension, the experiences of separation and entanglement, of living here and remembering/desiring another place."[103] Like other peoples dislocated from their homelands, urban Indians experience this tension between home and away, memory and desire. Contemporary theories of globalization and diaspora seem to suggest that one can be Indian outside of Indian Country as long as one has established networks, such as those that Arjun Appadurai has described. Appadurai, like Benedict Anderson, posits that the rise of print capitalism and mass media allowed for the creation of "diasporic public spheres" in which people "deploy their imaginations" in order to create "new mythographies."[104] I wonder what kinds of "new mythographies" arise in new urban Indian spaces, particularly for second- and third-generation city Indians. How do stories about reservation space become *replacements* for this space for people who grow up in cities? What are the "steady points of reference" for urban Indigenous peoples?[105]

As this work will demonstrate, new tribal consciousness does not depend on the erasure of specific tribal identities and practices; in other words, tribal cosmopolitanism is not an assimilative process but one that allows for survival. For tribal cosmopolitans, those multiple attachments can be to city spaces, to reservation spaces, to sacred sites and ancestral homelands, and to all of the spaces in between.[106] At the same time, tribal cosmopolitanism calls attention to historical interactions with other Indigenous peoples and historical movements throughout North American geographies. There are political and practical reasons for thinking beyond national boundaries in our increasingly global world. The kind of cosmopolitanism I am engaging differs in several important ways from the cosmopolitanism described by Elizabeth Cook-Lynn or Arnold Krupat as part of an ongoing debate in the field of American Indian literary studies. Cook-Lynn argues against a cosmopolitan reading practice—the use of tribal and nontribal viewpoints and theories—while Krupat sustains that such a practice is useful and preferable, that reading widely and outside the confines of the nation provides for a more sustainable, comparative discourse.[107] I do not intend my use of the term *cosmopolitan* to align with either critic's definition or prejudice, though my reading practice may certainly be called cosmopolitan in nature. Instead, I see tribal cosmopolitanism as a productive way of defining an identity that is in line with Kwame Anthony Appiah's notion of cosmopolitanism: that of multiple alliances to place and nation.[108] This version also acknowledges the futility of living as though tradition is always static and always positive and insists that although aspects of a given cultural heritage may be lost, transformed, abandoned, or replaced, such changes do not diminish a people's group affiliation or identity unless they want them to. When we think about Native peoples as cosmopolitans, we pay attention to the existence of multiple homes and homelands. We challenge geographical fixity and boundaries of empire, rethink relationships to place and nation, and rework conceptions of homogeneous Indigenous identities.

WRITING THE CITY

In 1997 Dinitia Smith of the *New York Times* described "a new group of Indian writers" who were "increasingly hard edged and urban." Unlike their predecessors, these authors were writing novels not "set on reservations and suffused with longing for the vanished coherence of the tribal world," Smith wrote. They were, instead, "taking their characters off the reservation."[109] Indeed, the trend that Smith observed began long before her article, though these earlier urban "traces" are often hiding in plain sight. In the nineteenth century, for example, Potawatomi author Simon Pokagon's "The Red Man's Rebuke" (later named "The Red Man's Greeting"), which Pokagon distributed at the World's Columbian Exposition in Chicago in 1893, evokes the precontact history of the city, when the "Red Men lived in Wigwams," as he criticized the celebration of settler colonialism that was the fair.[110] Mohawk writer E. Pauline Johnson's career ostensibly began when she recited her poem "A Cry from an Indian Wife" at a Toronto bookstore. Johnson toured and performed throughout Canada, and she traveled to the United States and London, seeking a publisher for her work. Though the urban traces of her work may not be so evident, the invocation of movement in both her poems and travel writing, sometimes manifested in the figure of the canoe, signals a life spent off the reserve. Johnson eventually retired to Vancouver, a city that claims her. In the early twentieth century, both Luther Standing Bear and Black Elk (Lakota), in *My People the Sioux* and *Black Elk Speaks*, respectively, chronicle their travels with Buffalo Bill's Wild West, including an incident during which Black Elk becomes lost in Paris, gets arrested in London, and is stranded when the show leaves without him.[111] Salish writer D'Arcy McNickle's *Runner in the Sun* (1954) travels to ancient Aztec cities, and *The Surrounded* (1936) follows Archilde Leon once he returns from Portland, Oregon, to his home reservation in Montana. We do not often think of these early texts in terms of their urbanism but instead read movement away from home and homeland in assimilative terms. Certainly, the concerns of these texts are not explicitly urban, and the city is not central.

The urban Indian voice gets stronger in the wake of relocation, as I have suggested. *House Made of Dawn* and *Ceremony* have received the most critical attention, and they are important markers in the trajectory of the urban in Indigenous writing. Because of the narrative gap between the "critical narrative site" and the telling, novels like Momaday's and Silko's imagine urban landscapes, but as other critics have noted, the city is portrayed as a destructive place where tribalism is difficult to maintain.[112]

Sean Teuton has discussed these texts as Red Power novels—novels that engage in the political momentum begun with Alcatraz—but I would like to suggest that a shift occurred *after* the publication of these novels and that the shift is important in recognizing the political power of these novels.[113] I concede that Momaday's novel envisions the potential for urban intertribal community and activism, particularly through his characterization of Reverend Tosamah and inclusion of the scene on the hill overlooking Los Angeles (reminiscent of Hill X in *The Exiles*). *House Made of Dawn* would have been a very different novel had Momaday chosen to make Tosamah the narrator and imagined the city as a place of empowerment. At the end of *Ceremony*, Tayo has recovered from war trauma and the "whiteness" of Los Angeles, but while he has been out in the world, it is in the tribal space of the reservation where he is at home. Neither Abel nor Tayo can live in the city of Los Angeles in the post–World War II era, far from their people and their homelands. As such, the reservation remains the critical center of these books.

It is not until the 1980s—some twenty-five years after relocation began—that authors do more than illustrate the chaotic nature of the city and the loss of identity for urban dwellers. They are, instead, portraying worlds in which Native peoples gain political power in collective tribal communities and attempt to reclaim portions of the American landscape. A necessity of the plot seems to be a break (sometimes historic, sometimes violent, as in the case of *Indian Killer*) with the reservation space. The protagonist creates a distance between self and place and redefines his or her identity in terms of a new subjectivity, one that is at the same time urban and Indigenous. Connecting with the urban Indian community, whether at an Indian bar or at a community center or at Alcatraz, is important to the creation of this subjectivity. It is crucial that Indian spaces exist in the cities. (In the case of *The Exiles* and *Body Indian*, these spaces are being created; for later generations, the quest is to find these spaces.) In the cities, Indian characters become what Vizenor calls "postindian warriors" who "create their stories with a new sense of survivance."[114] Vizenor's "survivance" is both "an active sense of presence" and a rejection of "dominance, tragedy, and victimry."[115] These new urban narratives are the stories of survival, of "survivance," of negotiations between cultural heritage and city life and a refusal to be confined to or contained in Indian Territory. In cities, Native characters reestablish and sometimes reclaim space in creative, occasionally subversive ways. The survival strategies that get represented in these fictions, including versions of community building and imagined intertribal activities, affect the construction of Indian identity, especially one that has been historically and culturally correlated with place.[116] In this work, urban Indian identities are a constantly changing articulation.

Thus, *Indigenous Cities* begins with Janet Campbell Hale's *The Jailing of Cecelia Capture* (1985), one of the first urban Indian novels.[117] In other words, its primary setting is a city space. Like the other texts I will discuss, Hale's does not end with the protagonist's return to the reservation; it does not follow the convention of the homing plot. Good or bad, the city becomes "home" for the major characters in these novels. The connections that characters maintain with their natal communities vary a great deal, but the primacy of the reservation as Indian space is diminished. In fact, urban Indian novels project a very different conception of home. The networks of connection, within the city and between the cities and reservations, are what are ultimately important. These stories are *about* mobility; the urban Indian subject is a traveler, a transnational, and a trickster of sorts. The routes between cities and reservations are well traveled. The reservation space is not absent in these novels; it exists in memory, in imagination, in stories, in plans to regain land that has been lost by theft and treaty, as part of the hub, perhaps in desire. Like the majority of immigrants, many urban characters first see relocation as temporary and the reservation as "home." The narratives are not confined to America's biggest cities, and they seem to emanate from very different geographic urban spaces, particularly those that were major relocation centers, in the Midwest and the West.

In the four chapters that follow, I survey representative urban texts, tracing a rough chronological trajectory according to publication date. As I track the development of urban writing, history remains central, especially in relationship to the relocation era and the political activism that followed Alcatraz. The narratives shift in tone and emphasis as they move farther away from the historical juncture I have already described, as urban Indian communities become more populated and residents become more settled and savvy in their interactions. The texts I have chosen are written by recognizable authors, some of whom are known for their engagement with the city space, others who have only made a brief foray into urban territory. The authors currently live or have lived in the cities they describe. My selection of texts attempts to provide a range in terms of tribe and location, but a study such as this one cannot be exhaustive.[118]

In the first chapter, I read Janet Campbell Hale's novel *The Jailing of Cecelia Capture* as a liberation text, one that articulates a historical and allegorical break from the reservation and configures San Francisco as a redemptive space. Hale engages with the trope of the "awakening" as she parses out a number of feminist and Indigenist concerns, particularly through a redefining of *home*. Cecelia Capture's memories of the Alcatraz occupation, which I have already described as a key event in the history of urban activism, serve to coalesce both her Indigenous identity and her determination to work for justice for her people, the Coeur d'Alene. Though critics have read this novel as assimilationist for its lack of "tradition" and "explicit Indianness," I suggest that instead we read Cecelia's moves toward self-determination in the urban space as evidence of the novel's Indigenous consciousness.

In the second chapter, I argue that Sherman Alexie's depictions of homelessness in three texts, *Indian Killer* (1995), "What You Pawn I Will Redeem" (2004), and *Flight* (2007), serve as a rethinking about place and exile and tribalism. In Alexie's early work, the absence of a home (read: reservation) community, whether physical or in memory, is detrimental to maintaining Native subjectivity, while his later work has moved away from his fundamentalism about the absolute destructiveness of the city. His homeless characters, like Carlotta Lott in *Indian Killer*, Jackson Jackson in "What You Pawn," and Zits's unnamed father in *Flight*, are very literal reminders of Indigenous dispossession—of the irony of being homeless on Indigenous land. Homeless people are so often blamed for their homelessness, but Alexie depicts homelessness as a direct result of settler colonialism. As what Dean Rader would call "engaged resistance," Alexie gives his homeless characters narrative agency, the power to tell their own stories, which develops into an urban Ghost Dance.[119] This assertion of Indigenous voice and presence in the city hinges on Chief Seattle's speech, which ends with a warning that "the dead are not altogether powerless."[120]

In the third chapter, I argue that Louise Erdrich's novel *The Antelope Wife* (1998) is a significant attempt to renarrativize Indian life by portraying the reservation as a global place and Minneapolis as a "hub" and a site with historical Indian understructure. One way she does this is by focusing on movement and exchange—of people, objects, and rituals. By extending the borders of Ojibwe territory beyond the borders of contemporary reservation designations, Erdrich reclaims both space and time in a way that collapses the very dichotomy of reservation and city. This chapter demonstrates the ways in which urban texts work to remap historical boundaries, using Minneapolis, a city with a large Native population and an important site of Indian activism (where AIM was formulated), as an example. Erdrich's release of revised editions of the novel in 2012 and 2016 (as *Antelope Woman*) works as a new claiming of space, just as her narrative revision mimics the movement and fluidity of the city and the need to retell and rescript the urban experience.

In the final chapter, I turn to Susan Power's *Roofwalker* (2002), a multigenre work of short stories and personal essays that center around the city of Chicago. Power's Chicago narratives are multiply layered with Indigenous histories as she works to construct an urban aesthetic reminiscent of LeAnne Howe's concept of "tribalography," bringing together past, present, and future.[121] This text enacts the convergences of tribal histories and alternate textualities, all of which belie an Indigenous consciousness that is dependent on an Indigenous narrative epistemology, of writing from experience via the narrative "I." Her book articulates *how* to reconstruct a place narrative as it is doing it: for example, when Power's mother demands the removal of an offensive statue from the Chicago Historical Society or when Melvin Shoestring inserts the history of Indigenous students at Yale into the tour guide's narrative. The city holds this revolutionary potential, and Power creates a cast of artist figures whose work rescripts the historical narrative to demonstrate that the urban space demands a new story.

This book is an intervention into discussions about American Indian literatures and place, urbanization, and globalization. Urban texts are set in diverse American cities, and their thematics and aesthetics reflect issues of the urban experience. Together, urban Indian literature creates a fuller imaginary of the Indigenous peoples of North America. It explores the tension between preserving the local or tribal and participating in the global, cosmopolitan world. These texts imagine a kind of trajectory: from the political awakening in Hale's novel, to an evocation of the Ghost Dance in Alexie's work, to an articulation of the hub in Erdrich's fiction, to the rescripting of memory and history in Power's text. The city is both a generative space and one where Indians are marginalized, and these urban geographies pose a significant challenge to the ways in which Native peoples have been narrated. The writers of this study are redefining or calling attention to a very different relationship to place and what constitutes "home." Urban texts formulate a new tribal consciousness, uncover a cosmopolitan Indigenous past, and remind us to—in Robbie Robertson's words—come "chanting down the street like a cannibal in Manhattan."[122]

CHAPTER I

An Indigenous Awakening

We, the native Americans, re-claim the land known as Alcatraz
Island in the name of all American Indians by right of discovery.
—"Alcatraz Proclamation," *Movement* (Indians of
All Tribes newsletter), January 1970

Hulleah Tsinhnahjinnie's (Muscogee/Diné) *Metropolitan Indian Series
#2*, a photograph taken on Yerba Buena Island in the 1980s, features a
young girl in what appears to be traditional Plains dress gazing out at a
foggy San Francisco in the distance.[1] In this image, Tsinhnahjinnie juxtaposes "city" and "Indian," which at first suggests an out-of-placeness,
the "Indians in unexpected places" that Philip Deloria describes in his
seminal book, but something else emerges from its composition. The
Bay Bridge is located on the left edge of the photograph; the girl, leaning
against a tree, provides the right edge. As art critic Whitney Chadwick
and others have noted, Tsinhnahjinnie's project revises Edward Curtis's,
particularly in the composition of Curtis photos such as *The Mother* and
Hopi Woman, which place Indigenous women on the margins of the
photograph.[2] In this image, Tsinhnahjinnie plays with the margin and
the center: if we imagine that the right is a mirror of the left, or at least
that these images provide a parallel framing, Tsinhnahjinnie is suggesting that this girl is *herself* the bridge. The model, Carol Webb, a Colville,
might as well be Janet Campbell Hale's Cecelia Capture in a scene from
the novel, particularly in the way that the city gets described: as "a magic

FIG 3. *Metropolitan Indian Series #2* by Hulleah J. Tsinhnahjinnie (Muscogee/Diné), 1984. Reproduced by permission of the artist.

place . . . rising up out of the bay."[3] Tsinhnahjinnie's and Hale's projects mesh in another important way: as art critic Theresa Harlan has argued, Tsinhnahjinnie's *Metropolitan Indian Series* "acknowledges the persistent presence of Native people in urban cities and attests to the communities that they built."[4] In other words, both assert that Indians *belong* in San Francisco, a city with an important and tumultuous Indigenous history.

In the 1980s, as Tsinhnahjinnie was taking the photographs for this series, a number of Native women writers took up urban life in their work: first, Paula Gunn Allen in *The Woman Who Owned the Shadows* (1983), followed by writers like Linda Hogan, Wendy Rose, Beth Brant, and Joy Harjo, in both poetry and short fiction.[5] Rose, the Hopi/Miwok poet born in Oakland and raised in San Francisco, writes about the "spokes," like those in Renya Ramirez's hub, in her poem "To Some Few Hopi Ancestors," when she imagines that the voices of the ancestors "follow us down / to Winslow, to Sherman, / to Oakland, to all the spokes / that have left earth's middle."[6] Important to this discussion of Hale's work is Rose's use of the word *left:* I read agency and self-determination in the migrations that Rose describes. While displacements and relocations may have been the impetus for these migrations, Rose's poem focuses on the movement. That those "that have left" are followed by the voices of the ancestors serves as evidence of the portability of Indigenous identity as well—that movement away from the homeland does not necessarily equal assimilation.

What is critical about Janet Campbell Hale's early urban novel, *The Jailing of Cecelia Capture* (1985), is that it suggests both thematically and allegorically that urbanization demanded a break from the reservation space. The story begins as protagonist Cecelia Capture has been arrested for drunk driving and welfare fraud on her thirtieth birthday. The remainder of the novel narrates Capture's memories of the events that led up to this moment—her childhood on the reservation and her decision to move to San Francisco—all from the perspective of her jail cell.[7] With this lens, Hale calls specific attention to the condition of captivity. Her protagonist knows multiple geographies: her reservation homeland in Idaho, a second reservation in Wapato, Spokane (where her husband and two children live), and the Bay Area (to which she has returned for law school). She negotiates her Indigenous identity in a city that seems bent on erasure, but she seems reluctant to join any official urban Indian community— and she especially avoids what she calls the "Sidewalk Indians."[8] What saves her from a tragic end is her memory of the takeover of Alcatraz in 1969, an event that symbolizes the possibility of Indian agency and self-determination and, as I will argue, a home in the city.[9]

Hale's novel remains important for a number of reasons: the scant attention it has received (although nominated for the Pulitzer Prize, the book has fallen into relative obscurity); its decisive break with the reservation novel tradition; its articulation of the urban experience during a formative political period, namely, 1960s San Francisco; its consideration of the intersection of gender and race; and its redefinition of Indian identity in the spaces outside the reservation. Initial reviews of the novel were mixed, and few critics since have discussed the work.[10] Though Louis Owens initially praised the novel, he later panned it, mainly for what he calls Hale's "professional victimage and romanticized self-destructiveness."[11] In *Mixedblood*

Messages, Owens names a number of signifiers that make Indian novels marketable, namely, a reservation setting, poverty, and alcoholism.[12] Taking up Owens's argument that successful Indian novels need such signifiers, critic Ernest Stromberg argues that *The Jailing of Cecelia Capture* has not received much critical attention because it lacks "explicit signifiers of 'Indianness,'" or "traces of specific oral traditions, symbols from the Native culture, and articulations of an indigenous spirituality and worldview."[13] Stromberg writes, "While the novel features an Indian protagonist, there is little else that is explicitly Indian, in ways we might identify as 'traditional,' about the novel."[14] Critic Frederick Hale argues that Cecelia Capture is "detribalized" in the city, that she has "no tribal vision."[15] Accordingly, one's physical proximity to "tribe," already a problematic word because of its primitivist connotations, determines how much "tribal vision" one might maintain. This is in direct conflict with contemporary theories of diaspora, which articulate the transportability of cultural identities, affiliations, objects, and ideas. What these comments demonstrate is the firm notion that "authentic" Indian writing must take place on a reservation.

Given the specific criticism of Hale's novel, it becomes apparent that urban Indian texts—especially an early one such as hers—pose a tangible challenge to the methodologies and expectations of theorists of American Indian literatures. In this chapter, I argue that Hale's novel is indeed "explicitly Indian," despite its urban setting and its aversion to the reservation, especially if, as Taiaiake Alfred posits, "Indian" is more than something that is attached inherently—it has more to do with actions and convictions. In other words, being Indian "implies doing."[16] Cecelia Capture's perceived individualism and "detribalization" in the city do not preclude the novel from being identifiable as "Indian"—and in fact, Capture's activism, or "new tribal consciousness," to return to Gerald Vizenor, provides evidence of her "Indianness." The critical action at the heart of this book is about crossing borders—of place, of gender, of race. Hale's novel lacks the spatial fixity of most American Indian writing, and, to be sure, her protagonist challenges the established roles for Native women in fiction. Educated, fiercely independent, and decidedly conscious of Indigenous feminist concerns, Capture is a new kind of Native subject—one who must articulate an identity and navigate the world outside of the confining spaces of the reservation.[17] Her relocation signals both liberation and self-determination. She must articulate a new home place in San Francisco—a city at once magical and historically deleterious for Indigenous peoples.

Like the other cities in this study, San Francisco and the entire Bay Area have a complicated settler colonial history, which I will briefly outline here. The Bay Area is Ohlone (a group of Costanoans) and Coastal Miwok territory, with the Miwoks in present-day Marin County to the north and east. Settler contact in California, of course, was first with the Spanish, who constructed a trail of missions up the coast and who, in 1776 under the charge of Juan Bautista de Anza, established El Presidio Real de San Francisco, a military garrison, and the Mission San Francisco de Asís (or Mission Dolores), now the oldest structure in San Francisco. The missions were intended to convert the Indigenous population but even more so to utilize their labor in the growth of the colony of Alta California. During his exploration of the Bay Area, Anza encountered "some sixty autonomous" tribal groups, writes historian Claudio Saunt, "each composed of a few hundred individuals occupying an area about ten miles in diameter."[18] Archaeological digs in the Bay Area have revealed hundreds of shell mounds and evidence of multiple village sites.[19] Seven Costanoan languages were spoken, along with seven other languages.[20] Anza's group first camped twenty miles from San Jose, then at Mountain Lake, a mile and a half from the Golden Gate Bridge.[21] The Spanish arrival intensified disagreements and competition for resources among the locals, and the Spanish brought with them a devastating number of diseases. It has been widely documented that the Spanish mistreated Indians in the missions, abuse that included violence (such as flogging and sexual assault) and forced labor.[22] As historian Robert H. Jackson has argued, the San Francisco Bay missions were far deadlier than those in the south; he attributes this to overcrowding in adobe buildings, malnutrition, and the devastating effects of cultural loss, in addition to the introduction of foreign diseases.[23] In the first thirty years of the colony, there were six hundred births and twenty-four hundred deaths at the mission.[24]

In the nineteenth century, as the mission period ended, Mexican occupation, a short-lived Russian colony, and then the gold rush continued to impact Indigenous people in the Bay Area. North of San Francisco, the Russians established Fort Ross Colony in 1812, using captive Indian labor.[25] Beginning in the 1830s, the Mexican land grant system forced populations to disperse, while documented epidemics of smallpox, malaria, and syphilis ravaged those who stayed behind.[26] Like their Spanish predecessors, Mexicans in California enforced a racial hierarchy and relied upon a system of forced and semifeudal labor, both of which would be passed on to the United States after it claimed California in 1846.[27] The Indigenous population of California declined by 80 percent between 1846 and 1873 under American rule, as the increase of gold seekers and other settlers continued what historian Benjamin Madley has called "an American genocide."[28] Brendan Lindsay similarly argues that this new democracy was, in fact, "a culture organized around the dispossession and murder of California Indians."[29] As the gold rush began, there was talk of removing and "exterminating" California Indians altogether.[30] San Francisco grew exponentially during the gold rush, from a small town of two hundred to one with thirty-five thousand residents in a matter of six years. In 1864 an executive order established the federal reservation system in California, establishing as Indian lands one-tenth of the acreage promised in a series of eighteen unratified treaties negotiated in 1851–52.[31] Forty-one of those reservations, or *rancherías*, were terminated in the 1950s under the California Rancheria Termination Act, part of US termination policy, with an additional seven losing status in 1964. A number of terminated tribes have regained federal status since then, and several have ongoing claims.

Through this long genocidal history of dispersal, relocation, forced labor, and targeted physical and legislative violence against California Indians, violence against both land and body, they have continued to declare their existence and their humanity. For example, despite the long-held belief that the Ohlones had become extinct (an idea attributed to anthropologist Karl Kroeber, who in 1925 declared them so), Ohlone people have asserted themselves politically throughout the twentieth century.[32] In coalition with Indians of California (extant 1928–64), Ohlones sued the US government for land reparations.[33] In the 1960s, Ohlones participated in the San Francisco–based activist group the American Indian Historical Society, which fought to save a mission cemetery from a freeway project in Freemont.[34] Ohlones to a large extent protested the Alcatraz occupation because it took place on their land and because protesters came from outside the region.[35] In the 1970s Ohlones again joined with local tribes to preserve a burial ground in Watsonville threatened by the construction of a warehouse.[36] The Muwekma Ohlones (enrollment four hundred), who lost federal acknowledgment status in 1927, have been working since 1989 to regain recognition—a difficult process, to be sure, one complicated by resettlement practices in California that precipitated interaction and intermarriage among tribal groups.[37] In 1989 the Muwekma group was finally successful in retrieving ancestral remains from Stanford University, which, along with San Jose State University, had excavated Ohlone sites between 1948 and 1984.[38] The Muwekma Ohlone claim for federal recognition was unsuccessful: in 2002 the Bureau of Indian Affairs denied their petition, largely because the group has not continuously lived together as a "village," an impossible criterion for tribes without land bases that have been scattered through the settler colonial process.[39] Recently, another Ohlone group, numbering two thousand, the Costanoan Rumsen Carmel tribe, located in Pomona, has demanded that a cultural center be built in San Francisco's Hunters Point.

Indigenous immigrants to the Bay Area have of course included people from other California tribes and then, at the beginning of the twentieth century, from farther away. For example, students from Sherman Institute in Riverside, California (to which Rose's poem refers), Intermountain Indian School in Brigham City, Utah, and Stewart's Institute in Carson City, Nevada, were sent to the Bay Area from the 1920s to 1938 as part of the Outing Program, which sent residential school students out into the community to work.[40] Some came to attend the Oakland Central Trade School or Merritt School of Business. Natives found work in California during the world wars, sometimes in the shipyards in Richmond, and those serving in the military passed through Camp Pendleton in Southern California or Camp Roberts in the Central Valley. Beginning in 1922,

Lagunas and Acomas came to work for the Atchison, Topeka and Santa Fe Railway and lived in Santa Fe Indian Village in an unincorporated area of Richmond. In exchange for the ability to build the railroad through tribal lands, Santa Fe promised jobs to Laguna and Acoma men. In Susan Lobo's *Urban Voices: The Bay Area Indian Community*, Ruth Sarracino Hopper describes life in the Indian Village, where people from the pueblos established their own government, built their outdoor ovens, and grew traditional crops.[41] Though studies published in the 1960s noted that tribal groups kept to themselves in the city, the San Francisco Indian community began to coalesce during this period.[42]

The first intertribal groups in the Bay Area were the Outing Club and the Yurok Club until the YWCA sponsored the Four Winds Club in Oakland, the sole organization for Bay Area Natives until the Intertribal Friendship House opened in Oakland in 1956, the same year the American Indian Center opened in San Francisco.[43] In her autobiography, former chief of the Cherokee Nation Wilma Mankiller tells the story of her family's relocation from Oklahoma to San Francisco in 1956: their weeks in a hotel in the Tenderloin district (where there is still a substantial Indian population); their home in Daly City and later in Hunters Point; and the "overt discrimination," which Mankiller links to the violent history of missions in California. Mankiller chronicles her family's relationship with the San Francisco American Indian Center and later activism during Alcatraz, both crucial to her Indian identity and her commitment to help other Indigenous peoples. She describes this time as her "period of awakening."[44] San Francisco by the late 1960s was the epicenter of the counterculture. It had a burgeoning music scene, and it had become notorious for its political activism, including the Free Speech Movement at UC Berkeley and Bay Area protests against the Vietnam War, both precursors to Alcatraz. Though many Native people were drawn to San Francisco both during and after the occupation, the city was also, along with Oakland, an official BIA relocation center. Today the Indigenous population of the Bay Area numbers approximately eighty thousand, according to the census: the Intertribal Friendship House says that it serves sixty thousand urban Natives in the seven-county Bay Area.[45]

I begin this study with Hale's early urban novel because, like *The Exiles*, it establishes many of the central concerns that we can trace through later texts—and also because it does the important work of articulating a break with the reservation, in both a physical and a literary sense, in order to make a home in the city. As I (and others) have suggested, the majority of American Indian novels in some way contemplate relationships to place—to home—often following what William Bevis has called the "homing plot": protagonists leave their reservations, become corrupted by the "outside" world, and return home in need of healing and reintegration.[46] "Home" in this sense is larger than a physical geographical place; it includes larger kinship and social networks, membership in a community that has a historical relationship to this place. As diaspora scholars have long noted, one of the certainties that has come undone in the modern world is "the notion that there is an immutable link between cultures, peoples, or identities and specific places."[47] Arjun Appadurai, for example, has accurately noted that binaries of "here" and "there" are no longer so clearly delineated; specific "flows" of people, ideas, and objects work to preclude any kind of isolation or cultural purity.[48] Likewise, Hale's work is an articulation of the tension between containment within spatial boundaries and the prevailing belief that Indian identity is predicated on reservation living. By linking Cecelia's story, one that considers living on the reservation a kind of captivity, with the urban story of relocation, Hale underscores the paradox that underlies the desire for an Indigenous homeland that is associated with histories of containment and military defeat.

In fact, Hale's novel has an antihoming plot; that is, the protagonist is desperate to distance herself from her homeland—the Coeur d'Alene Reservation—in a way that links Hale's writing to male writers and the "hero plot."[49] In the American hero plot, male protagonists leave their homes to do great things, they "light out for the territory," they win epic battles.[50] Perhaps Hale's use of this traditionally male plot structure led to some of the criticism of the novel, particularly Stromberg's charge that the protagonist asserts too much individualism to be tribal. This argument is again predicated on the notion that tribal people must physically be located on tribal lands, or, even further, that one's geographic position determines one's ethnic and/or national affiliations. It is another way of asserting ahistorical desires of containment and racial purity while also asserting that a woman's place is in the home, or at least on the reservation, and that women who leave are rogues or outlaws, to return to Paula Gunn Allen here.[51] However, as Rayna Green once pointed out, Native women writers "live utterly urban lives."[52] They live away from their reservations, but they return to them in their writing. To be sure, gender as a category has been left out of critical discussions of Hale's novel. Partly as a means of recovering this Renaissance-era novel, I will in this chapter discuss this urban text in terms of its diasporic, feminist, and Indigenist thematics, beginning with its articulations of "home."[53]

THAT PLACE CALLED HOME

In Hale's novel, we encounter Cecelia Capture as she is simultaneously constructing an urban Indian subjectivity and a "home" in the city space. "Home" is a trope often used by women writers, especially those of color, who, as Biddy Martin and Chandra Talpade Mohanty argue, "cannot easily assume 'home' within feminist communities as they have been constituted."[54] So while the feminist project as conceived by white European feminists often excludes the concerns of minority women in the United States, namely, the desire to work for gender *and* racial equality, Native writers and scholars such as Laura Tohe, Cheryl Suzack, and Kim Anderson have articulated the intersectionality of Native feminism and pointed out that the relationship between mainstream feminism and Native feminism is tenuous at best.[55] "For many activist Native women of this hemisphere," argues Inés Hernández-Ávila, "the concern with 'home' involves a concern with 'home*land*.'"[56] She continues, "For Native people, any notion of 'home' within the domestic sphere was largely and intentionally disrupted by the colonialist process."[57] "Home" evokes histories of landownership and allotment policy and disputes over boundaries and inheritance. Thus, "escape" from the reservation need not be seen as abandoning family and community but as a political act against those boundaries and that historical captivity. In other words, "home" on the reservation is not a prelapsarian world, untainted by colonization and "white ways," but it has been affected by settler patriarchy as a result mainly of Christianity and boarding schools. As Hale's novel suggests, the reservation as "home" needs to be further deconstructed in the modern era. The novel often overlaps with the concerns of mainstream feminism as well, including its evocation of "captivity" to describe the protagonist's actual physical incarceration, her failed marriage to a white professor, and her mother's troubled relationship to the reservation. Feminist consciousness, Roberta Rubenstein argues, often associates home with captivity: "Challenging deeply-imbedded cultural scripts that defined women in terms of familial and domestic roles, [feminists] viewed home not as a sanctuary but as a prison, a site from which escape was the essential prerequisite for self-discovery and independence."[58] Thus, in Hale's novel, escape from the domestic space and, relatedly, the reservation space is necessary for an Indigenous "awakening" to occur.

One of the most obvious (and perhaps most troubling) ways that Hale's novel works through issues of place is in its considerations of home in its multiple manifestations: home as homeland (or reservation), the physical space of Cecelia's family's home there, low-income housing in San Francisco, the domestic space of her married home life, her cluttered apartment in Berkeley, and the process by which the Bay Area becomes home. In order for the city space to be home, this necessary break or dero-manticization of the reservation must occur first. From the beginning of the novel, Hale connects the trope of "captivity" with notions of "home" as Cecelia's memories of the reservation, her childhood home, are revealed while she is literally being held captive in her jail cell in Berkeley. From this place of ironic captivity—given Berkeley's association with hippies and the counterculture, she conjures her childhood home: "There was the familiar feel of the snow and the sound of the wind during a blizzard as it swept across the frozen hills and echoed through the forest, and then the sound of the coyote howling."[59] This passage includes elements often associated with reservation space, but it is remarkably lacking in nostalgia. Cecelia even imagines herself buried in snow there, "her blood turned to ice."[60] The fear of being covered in white is certainly suggested in this passage (perhaps signifying assimilation), but more pertinent here is how the cold comes to mean home for Cecelia—and how her body is "contained" there. She imagines the reservation as a frozen wasteland, a sad emptiness, not capable of sustaining life. In other words, what is designated as "home" to her people, the reservation, is beset with deadly cold.

In an interesting move, Hale juxtaposes Cecelia's memories of home with her recollection of photos of the massacre at Wounded Knee, pictures of bodies in the snow, Lakota people on the Pine Ridge Reservation, their home, contained and slaughtered.[61] Wounded Knee also signifies the failure of the Ghost Dance to disappear the settlers, as well as the end of the reservation era, the closing of the frontier, and the Indian Wars. The reservation in this case is neither isolated nor safe—it is a place of trauma and defeat. Hale similarly describes the reservation as a bounded place in the passage that describes Cecelia's trip to Ford Butte with her children as she shifts back to describing the Coeur d'Alene Reservation: "She told her children that her father's father had been a young warrior in that last Indian war, fought the white people here in this very spot where they now stood. Her father's parents had been among the first Indian people *ever made to live on a reservation*."[62] This particular historical site, which is both a sacred place and a place of loss, is a site of trauma for her people. It is here that the protagonist explains to her children that her father shortened their family name, Eagle Capture, to Capture when he joined the army in World War I. Although the practice of Anglicizing names is not particular to Native Americans, it is interesting that he does so when he leaves the reservation to join the military, leaving one kind of captivity for another. Cecelia's grandfather had been named for his ability to "snar[e] wild eagles for their feathers."[63] The shortening of the family name removes the agency of capturing eagles for ceremonial reasons and suggests they are now the "captured" and not the "capturers." As the juxtaposition of these two historical sites suggests, home, for Cecelia, is not only a place of capture but also a site of historical defeat.

Instead of being taught about the sacredness of her people's homeland, Cecelia learns to be conflicted about this place from her parents, both of whom are damaged in some way by settler colonialism. Her mother,

Mary Theresa, is depicted as a mixed-blood who exhibits many signs of internalized racism.[64] Her father, Will, is a product of the boarding school system. Her mother often complains, "Damned dumb Indians. You all think you're something, don't you, you with your pitiful few acres of worthless sand and rock, Indian land that nobody wanted."[65] Cecelia's mother wishes that "they could get away from this awful, godforsaken place."[66] She provides a multilayered construction of the reservation as home—sacred land that "nobody wanted." This place is "awful," full of awe, and at the same time "godforsaken," abandoned even by God. She connects the reservation with Indian identity and calls attention to the diminished size of reservation space. Cecelia's father, on the other hand, says that he once believed that "this land belonged to him and he belonged to it," but he sells his land, which "contained the bones of countless generations of ancestors," when it became economically necessary to do so.[67] The contradiction between land as sacred and land as possession causes a psychological split for Cecelia that she cannot reconcile. She is conflicted about the land, which in her family is simultaneously venerated and hated. This sort of ambivalence about the homeland has been read by critics as an indicator of an "un-Indian" text, but Hale is clearly calling our attention to the formation of the reservation space, to its purpose and its history as a colonial construct.

This thread continues when Cecelia's later visits to the reservation are fraught with feelings of discomfort, of no longer having a "home" there. She remembers taking her children with her to show them where she grew up. Her descriptions of this place elicit both a sense of embarrassment about the poverty there and disdain for the conditions: "It was a long ways out in the country, and the road leading from the highway was all grown over with weeds. The house itself still stood, but just barely. It was faded to a dark brown, dusty color, there were no windows, and the floor was rotting away. The children toured it, amazed that their own mother had lived such a primitive life, without electricity or running water. Cecelia felt anxious and was sorry she had brought them there."[68] Hale's description of this reservation home evokes isolation and decay. In fact, the land seems to be reclaiming the very structure that was once Cecelia

Capture's home. The house becomes an allegory for Capture's life on the reservation: poor, rural, and embarrassing. It also seems telling that her children have inherited their mother's scorn for this place.

The novel's pervasive antinostalgia about the reservation is somewhat complicated by the protagonist's relationship to another reservation, the Yakima Indian Reservation. When Cecelia is thirteen years old, her mother takes her to live with Cecelia's older sister on this reservation in the town of Wapato, where Cecelia and her mother live out of a car, undeniably another example of poverty and displacement, a kind of homelessness caused by insufficient housing and tribal infrastructure. Years later, in the present of the novel, Cecelia surprisingly remembers this place with fondness: "the vineyards and the smell of the sugar-beet refinery and the odor of mint in the air. She could visualize the mountains."[69] The language here begins to sound nostalgic for the reservation, but it is a transferred nostalgia because Yakima is an adopted home place, not her ancestral homeland. When Hale writes, "She thought that it would feel good to be back home in the Valley again," she begins to assert the possibility of multiple homes and multiple homelands for Indigenous peoples.[70] Cecelia's connection to the land is not genetic or primitive; it is associative. Because Yakima is a chosen home, it evokes for Cecelia a sense of freedom. Yakima Valley suggests fertility and abundance, while the Coeur d'Alene Reservation is associated with death and poverty.

And so the protagonist's flight to the urban space does not erase her Indian identity: Cecelia Capture is cognizant of the difference between autonomy and captivity, and she chooses the big city because of its promise of freedom. Wapato still contains the inherent problems of the reservation: destitution, teenage pregnancy, poor health, and wage labor. Cecelia's ambitions for a better life are similar to those of immigrants to the United States, and in a way she becomes an immigrant when she relocates to the city. The reservation offers only "a hard and lonely life, and she would not live that way again for anything."[71] Cecelia dreams of opportunity and success, and she knows she must leave the reservation or she will turn into her mother, a captive in an unhappy marriage. Driven by poverty and an unhappy home life to migrate to the city, Cecelia breaks the pattern.

She is aware of the history of her reservation, she is a descendant of the "first" reservation captives, and she rebels against the confinement of the reservation. Ultimately, Cecelia represents the psychological dilemma about forging an identity based on a place of trauma. In other words, how does one knowingly have affection for a home/land that is fraught with historical and contemporary loss? How does one simultaneously desire to belong to one's people and yet refuse to be imprisoned in a cycle of poverty on land that is but a fraction of their ancestral homelands?

Hale's pointed criticism of the reservation space is reminiscent of the Indians of All Tribes' "Alcatraz Proclamation to the Great White Father and His People," written in 1969 at Alcatraz, an event that becomes important later in the novel.[72] In this document, protesters declare that Alcatraz is suitable as an Indian reservation "by the white man's own standards," because, like other reservations,

1. It is isolated from modern facilities, and without adequate means of transportation.
2. It has no fresh running water.
3. It has inadequate sanitation facilities.
4. There are no oil or mineral rights.
5. There is no industry and so unemployment is very great.
6. There are no health care facilities.
7. The soil is rocky and non-productive, and the land does not support game.
8. There are no educational facilities.
9. The population has always exceeded the land base.
10. The population has always been held as prisoners and kept dependent upon others.

Even though this proclamation is meant to be a satire of historical treaties, there are some complicated implications of the proclamation's assertion that reservation land is worthless, particularly when this notion gets deployed detrimentally to justify policies such as termination and relocation and to take resources from Native people.[73] Because the proclamation's assertions overlap with Cecelia's sentiments and thus Hale's depictions of the reservation, it seems critical to read this document in conjunction with the novel. Though Indian land is certainly valuable, economically, culturally, and politically, as Cecelia's mother points out in the novel, Indian land is land that no one (read: the United States) wanted (of course, until they wanted it too). Indian land is the "leftover" from the encroachment of settlers, first by brute force, then through legislation. The reservation becomes the space designated for the now-dependent Indigenous peoples, a prison even.[74] Native groups fought on the battlefield and in courts to hold onto this land, now reservation land. The reservation as it gets described is devoid of resources—schools, hospitals, jobs, clean water, infrastructure—as a direct result of settler colonialism. This proclamation thus works to ironize reservation nostalgia. As Carolyn Strange and Tina Loo have argued, these conditions at Alcatraz made it possible "to reimagine the place as the home for American Indian rebirth and self-determination."[75] If this is life on the reservation, it is no wonder Capture decides to escape. The conditions of living, coupled with the harsh reality of the central character's family life, make a "homing narrative" impossible in this novel. Even while Cecelia is aware of the history of her reservation and is a descendant of the "first" reservation captives, she rebels against confinement, and Hale makes this leaving a political act.

BIG-CITY INDIANS

In Simon Ortiz's short story "The San Francisco Indians," first published in Ken Rosen's anthology *The Man to Send Rain Clouds* (1974), an unnamed Indian man has come to the city to find his granddaughter. Outside the American Indian Center, boarded up and closed, the man encounters members of the San Francisco tribe, really a group of hippies led by Chief Black Bear, who are looking for a "real Indian" to conduct a peyote ceremony for them. They take the Indian back to their apartment in the Haight, they feed him and give him wine, but they are disappointed when he decides to give up his search and return home. What prompts the old man to go back to the reservation is his realization that "Indians are everywhere"—and that, wherever his granddaughter is, there will be other Indian people who will look out for her. The grandfather's encounter with the urban space is one of curiosity and adventure, and he is adept with his navigation skills (he finds the American Indian Center; he takes a cab back to the bus station). Ortiz's critique lies in the invisibility of Native peoples in the city: the locked door on the American Indian Center, the inability of the "tribe" to find other Indians. The complexity of this story can be seen in the juxtaposition between Chief Black Bear's statement, "There are no Indians around," and the old man's, "There are Indians everywhere."[76] The hippies do not read urban Indianness in the same way. In other words, those in the know can find Indians in the city space, despite what seems to be a dispersed population and "invisibility." In the end, the granddaughter is not "lost" to the city. This story, which describes the same period of Cecelia's relocation, also set in post-Alcatraz San Francisco, thinks about urban Indian identity and the relationship between hippies or wannabes and Indians, narrative threads that Hale's novel also picks up. Cecelia lives with hippies in Haight-Ashbury, even though they regard her as foreign and exotic. Being Indian is fashionable at this time, and Cecelia looks the part. At the same time, she senses the uncanniness of *being* Indian when those around her are *pretending* to be Indians.[77] The presence of these imposters immediately alerts Cecelia to the kind of cultural theft that exists *off* the reservation—also present in Ortiz's story—and gives her an awareness of the cachet that her Indian identity signifies in this setting.

When Cecelia Capture relocates *herself* to San Francisco, it is during the height of the relocation program, and the Bay Area already has a large and growing Indian community. She works to distinguish herself from the Sidewalk Indians she encounters in the Indian part of town—another "Indian space" that she avoids. The Sidewalk Indians depicted by Hale are straight out of the "Indians cannot survive in the city" narrative, and Hale's protagonist at first rejects them and it. However, once Capture sinks into the urban underclass when she becomes a single mother (ironically, one of the circumstances she tried to avoid by leaving the reservation), she begins to seek other Native people, first at the American Indian Center "over on Sixteenth Street" in a "skid-row section of town" and then at "an Indian bar on South Van Ness": "There were Indians there, all right, lots of Indians from all over the country, and most of them were already drunk, though it was still very early. These Indians were, it seemed to her, *hopeless, displaced people.* No longer Indian, yet not white either. Big-city Indians *talking about how great it was 'back home on the rez,'* banding together, a *band of outcasts.* They began conversations by asking what the other's tribe was. Arapahoe, Cheyenne, Navajo, Cherokee, Sioux, it didn't matter."[78] In these urban Indian spaces, Capture discovers narratives of class struggle, displacement, and loss of identity. The new urban tribe is in effect a "band of outcasts," an intertribal formation based on underclass solidarity. Recognizing her as "Indian," a man stops Capture outside the bar and says, "We're the biggest tribe of all. That's right. Us Sidewalk Indians."[79] Capture rejects the tribe of Sidewalk Indians, subaltern, hopeless, and homeless: "She preferred being alone to being one of them. She had seen such awful desperation in their Indian faces."[80] Her use of "their" makes the distinction between "her" and "them" very clear; the options for ethnic unity and loss of tribal specificity do not appeal to her. Capture is not nostalgic for "back home on the rez," as the conditions of reservation living are often harsh and romanticizing that life is counterproductive. In other words, it is more practical to focus on making a home here than to mourn a past life in captive poverty. It is also worth noting that Cecelia is unable to find a community of Native women here—though we know from Wilma Mankiller's account that she and other women found the San Francisco American Indian Center to be a "sanctuary" and a "safe place."[81]

In another interesting juxtaposition, Cecelia conjures the "fenced-in buffalo herd" in Golden Gate Park immediately after her run-in with the Sidewalk Indians.[82] Like the Sidewalk Indians, those "on Relocation," the buffalo are displaced, moved to San Francisco from South Dakota after Wounded Knee as part of a captive breeding program, and, like reservation populations, the buffalo are depicted as sad remnants of a noble species, "preserved" or frozen in time.[83] Capture takes her son to see the buffalo in the park, where she "s[its] on a bench and enjoy[s] the sunshine on her face."[84] This brightness stands in contrast with the "dark flight of stairs" of the American Indian Center or the darkness of the bar in broad daylight.[85]

Cecelia finds freedom in the open spaces of the city and distances herself from "the displaced" as a refusal to be another victim of the urban space. While this might be read as a stereotypical move to align Cecelia with nature, I would like to suggest that something else is happening, for we also get a positive description of her run-down Berkeley apartment, another "home" that gets described in this novel: "The threadbare carpet in the living room, the worn paisley-print linoleum on the floors of the other rooms, the streaked *yellowed wallpaper*, the furniture that looked as if it belonged in the lobby of a downtown transient hotel, all of it was just fine. This apartment was part of her now, for all its temporary air."[86] Her "home" displays markers of Cecelia's economic status—the "thread-bare carpet" and "worn" floor and "streaked" walls—but Hale is doing something else here. The allusion to the "yellowed wallpaper" connects Cecelia to the escape from the Cult of True Womanhood as portrayed by Charlotte Perkins Gilman in her story "The Yellow Wallpaper" (1899). Like Gilman's protagonist, Capture is a depressed young mother, protected by her husband, and on the verge of madness. Hale conjures Gilman's depiction of female captivity here to signal that Cecelia is able to break free from homemaking and the domestic. Thus she escapes from the woman's sphere, as well as the sphere designated for Indians, the reservation, once again linking her newly awakened feminist and Indigenist consciousness in the urban space.[87]

In Berkeley, Cecelia Capture is able to enact a different perspective. Unlike the captured/captive incarcerated in isolated and claustrophobic prison cells, she enjoys the view that her apartment offers. This place has a "wide-openness about it, a certain feeling of freedom: high in the sky and not closed in."[88] She seems to be attempting to reproduce the wide-openness of the rural space here, especially in the fact that she sleeps with her bedroom window open (something she learned from her father), but perhaps she is simply articulating the possibility of spatial and personal freedom in the city. Unlike the reservation, this place does not hold her captive—at least not in the same way. An open window here has a different purpose: it lets in not fresh air but city air and city noises. In other words, this open window acts as a constant reminder of Capture's geographic locality—and her freedom. A similar sentiment can be found in poet Janice Gould's (Concow) depictions of Berkeley. Gould, who grew up in Berkeley, writes in "A Berkeley Life":

> Most of my life I looked out
> over the bay, over the blue
> water and bridge
> to the white city that gleamed
> in the morning sun.[89]

This view, like Cecelia's, suggests a calmness that is provoked by this panoramic landscape, that the aesthetic of the city, the "whiteness" of it (which Cecelia also describes as "all white and beautiful"), the way that land and shore are easily defined with the eye, is both captivating and liberating in its navigability.[90] At the same time, it articulates the distance between Berkeley and San Francisco, the wider circle of the metropolitan area that includes them both, and the kind of mystique that the city holds.

An important part of Cecelia's freedom in the urban space relates to her newfound anonymity and ethnic ambiguity, and she begins to create a new persona in the city: "Carmen was what she always told men in bars her name was."[91] She is often mistaken for Mexican (a common experience for Indians in California), especially while working at a Mexican restaurant, and so she begins to "pass" as such. "Even Mexicans in California mistook her for one of them," Hale writes.[92] This is a very different kind of passing—though the majority of Mexican peoples also have Indigenous ancestry. In the ethnic landscape of California, Capture's heritage becomes vague, indistinguishable from the most visible brown people. We see an example of this when Cecelia is in jail: "Velma studied her carefully, taking her in from head to toe. Twenty-seven, she would guess, or twenty-eight or thereabouts; hard to tell. Dark skinned. Not very dark, but dark enough to show she wasn't white. Mexican, more than likely."[93] Velma tries to "read" Cecelia's ethnicity; set against the backdrop of San Francisco, she is more likely Mexican than something else. In the city, Cecelia is read as Indian only by other Indians, while in the reservation space, the protagonist is undoubtedly Indian. In San Francisco, where no one expects to encounter Indians, she can *decide* whether or not to be identified as Indian—and this indeterminacy becomes empowering. Indeed, when she overhears some fellow law students talking about how "vague" they think she is, she decides that she needs "to become a little more vague."[94] While this novel could potentially become a different kind of passing narrative, the protagonist does not *always* obscure her Indian identity and in fact chooses to be Indian for the purposes of political activism—at Alcatraz.

URBAN INDIGENOUS WOMANHOOD

Hale was one of the first Native authors to create a female protagonist, itself a groundbreaking move for Native fiction.[95] Cecelia Capture is an anomaly in a number of respects, particularly in her refusal to conform to traditional gender roles and her crossing into the male domain by leaving home. In many Native cultures, women are entrusted to be the transmitters of tradition and have been responsible for domestic work and for moving the home during periods of migration. Cecelia Capture's experience in the urban space is fully influenced by gender—from her racially coded body (which, as I have suggested, usually gets read as Mexican and which she uses sometimes to her advantage during romantic encounters) to her role as welfare mother. Historians have argued that the urban space was unusually hard on Indian women during this time period, though studies by literary critics Lisa Tatonetti and Mark Rifkin have demonstrated that Indigenous queer women in particular found refuge in cities.[96] In her work on feminism in Native American literature, Kathleen Donovan maintains that even today urban Indian women experience particularly gendered problems: "a loss of power and esteem in formerly matrilineal cultures; the trauma of psychological, physical, and sexual abuse from Native and non-Native men; prostitution; a frequent inability to care for their children, with the subsequent loss of their families to a paternalistic social-welfare system; a high rate of teen-age pregnancy and infant mortality; and, sometimes, an unmistakable, yet usually unexpressed anger, at the perceived passivity of Native men."[97] The very concept of motherhood for Native women is changed by the urban setting. For one, geographical distance from extended family places more responsibility for cultural transmission on the mother.[98] As Navajo activist Annie Dodge Wauneka explains it, "Most of us learn about our 'Indianness' from our mothers."[99] In her famous essay "There Is No Word for Feminism in My Language," Navajo poet Laura Tohe explains that the women of her tribe "passed on to their daughters not only their strength, but the expectation to assume responsibility for the family, and therefore were expected to act as leaders for the family and the tribe."[100] Though indeed Cecelia is not Navajo, we may read this same kind of responsibility here. Certainly, gender roles in the urban space, away from extended family and tribe, are substantially altered. While female friendships may be forged, we might also recall the women in Joy Harjo's "Woman Hanging from the Thirteenth Floor Window," those on the ground who are urging the title woman to jump.[101] What may appear to be a tribal camaraderie or sister-hood is canceled out by competition, jealousy, and individualist pursuits.

In Hale's novel, women are complicated moral characters, and it is not always clear where the protagonist learns how to be a Coeur d'Alene woman. In a dated history of the Coeur d'Alene Indians, Jerome Peltier curiously describes women as "faithful wives and good mothers," though Cecelia Capture's mother is far from "good."[102] Cecelia learns early on that her mother resents her for continuing her perceived captivity: "Just when I thought I was going to be free, I found out that *you* were on the way."[103] Mary Theresa despises the responsibility of motherhood because it controls her ability to have an autonomous mode of life, and she certainly does not pass along cultural knowledge nor a positive sense of self-worth. Some of this certainly relates to her racial identity: though Mary Theresa's own mother was "the chief's daughter" (of an unspecified tribe), she is described as a "light-skinned, green-eyed half-breed who didn't show her Indian blood at all."[104] In fact, we know that she is capable of passing as white; however, her marriage to Will solidifies her status as Indian, just as does her habitation on the reservation. Mary Theresa's self-loathing transfers into her hatred of Cecelia, who, like Will, has dark skin and "Indian" features. Mary Theresa compares Cecelia to her sisters and tells her that she's "not pretty like them."[105] She begins to call her a "dirty little thing" when Cecelia is only four years old.[106] Mary Theresa associates her youngest daughter with the reservation, and she reiterates the racist claim that reservation Indians are "dirty" and "useless."

Often Mary Theresa's criticism centers on Cecelia's hair, which Cecelia wanted to grow long in the traditional way—though it has become clear that her knowledge of "tradition" does not come from her mother. Cecelia remembers when she is twelve years old and fantasizing about growing it to "the long, long, past-the-waist length."[107] Her mother says, "Why don't you get it cut and put in a good perm. You look just like some old witch. You look like Geronimo. You look like some damned reservation kid."[108] The connection that Mary Theresa makes here between the "wildness" of Geronimo and Cecelia's appearance as a "reservation kid" is resounding. For Mary Theresa, "looking Indian" is a determinant of identity, and adopting a modern, non-Indian hairstyle is a denial of that identity. This passage may also vaguely refer to a traditional Coeur d'Alene puberty ceremony, during which young girls were secluded in a ceremonial house for four days, and "at the end of the four days, the community had a celebration and the girl adopted a new hair style signifying her passage into womanhood."[109] However, Hale does not mention this coming-of-age ceremony, and it's hard to say whether Cecelia or Mary Theresa is suggesting a change of hairstyle at puberty, but the issue of hair comes up again later when Cecelia's father dies. When Cecelia returns to Idaho for the funeral, her mother tells her "how awful she looked, like a California hippie with that stringy long hair."[110] It is interesting how her mother makes that connection between hippies and Indians here—but she also seems to be suggesting that Cecelia has been tainted by California in some way. Cecelia does get her hair cut, thinking to herself, "This was what her mother always wanted."[111] But Cecelia has other reasons for cutting her hair: "She didn't even bother explaining to her mother about tribal tradition—that a dead man's wife and unmarried daughters were supposed to cut their hair to show that they were in mourning."[112] This haircutting practice is performative in terms of both race and gender, but Cecelia does not learn this behavior from her mother—and, in fact, she seems to reject her mother's self-hatred.

Cecelia's mother does teach her about certain womanly duties, that "housework equals virtue, womanly virtue."[113] This sentiment does not necessarily reflect "Indian" values but is something Mary Theresa absorbed from boarding school—something akin to Virginia Woolf's "Angel in the House."[114] Because Cecelia rejects this version of womanhood early on, her mother tells her that "no man would ever have her."[115] Mary Theresa is dedicated to housewifery, and it is only during periods of separation from Will that she leaves the home to work. Cecelia's seeming inability to do housework in the present of the novel is a direct rebellion against her mother's beliefs about female domesticity and therefore non-Indian values—and against becoming a drudge or kept woman: "She kept her apartment in appalling condition, with law books and news magazines strewn about and discarded articles of clothing draped here and there over arms of chairs or the back of the couch, and stacks of empty aluminum cans that had once contained diet soda."[116] This messiness is evidence of a deliberate antidomesticity, for, unlike her mother, Cecelia learns to see a certain kind of middle-class domestic womanhood as merely another kind of captivity.

Another way Hale works through issues of gender in the novel can be seen in Cecelia's development of her body image, to think about the Indigenous body as it moves through these spaces. Cecelia is extremely self-conscious about her appearance when she is a young girl and even decides "to become as thin as a cracker, as thin as a fashion model."[117] Because she goes to an all-white school at the insistence of her father, her understanding of female beauty is based on Anglo ideals, not Native ones. As she ages, Cecelia has a heightened awareness of her dark skin: "She hated looking in mirrors. She wanted to look elegant and beautiful, but this mirror couldn't tell her whether or not she did."[118] It becomes obvious that she has internalized her mother's racism, and the low self-esteem she suffers affects how she relates to men, mostly all non-Native men: "It was through her ability to attract men that she found the assurance that she was an attractable and desirable woman."[119] Indeed, Cecelia defines herself in accordance to how she is perceived by non-Indian men. Here Hale reminds us that Native women, as Rayna Green has famously argued, have historically been oversexualized and fetishized, particularly by white men.[120] The phenomenon continues, as we see in the examples of Cecelia's relationships with two white men, Bud Donahue, who dies in the Vietnam War, and her husband, Nathan, who "told her, in the early days of their affair, that he had never experienced such passion before, except when he was a very young man and had spent a year traveling in Mexico and South America. In Guadalajara he had gone to a whorehouse, and he had imagined himself in love with a beautiful prostitute there. Her name was Lupe."[121] Nathan's association of Cecelia with prostitution is not irrelevant—and it reveals much about their relationship. It becomes obvious that Nathan regards Cecelia as his inferior, someone who he thinks is not intelligent enough to attend law school. She does eventually rebel against the captivity Nathan imposes—and what he represents: settler colonialism that can be traced back to the *Mayflower*. Cecelia's rejection of his paternalism works to reclaim the image of the Native woman as a thing of pleasure for white men. Certainly marrying a white man creates a number of quandaries for a Native woman, especially with tribal rules about blood quantum and enrollment (a topic that Hale does not broach in her novel), which could later affect their citizenship status and relationship to nation. This relationship is also the result of living in the city; she would not have met Nathan (or Bud) otherwise.

Hale's protagonist is also not a "faithful wife," and her affairs reveal more complications with off-reservation romance. Although her "stable" relationships seem to be with white men, her transgressions or affairs are with men of color: Roberto, Raul, and Running Horse. So while "ethnic" men provide a sense of decadence to Cecelia's life, she relies on Nathan, a white man, for maintaining a home and raising her children. Cecelia is, in fact, a "kept woman" due to Nathan's inability to see her as his equal. Her encounter with Running Horse—the one Native man she has slept with—adds a twist to this narrative of interracial relationships. Upon learning that she is a law student, he tells her, "There's nothing much worse than an educated squaw."[122] That an Indian man uses this vulgar word, a word so frequently used by non-Indians to describe an Indian woman as a drudge and a sex object, is doubly ironic—and it reminds me of the kind of sexism reported in the Red Power movement. Hale reminds us that Indigenous women can and do endure overt sexist behavior from both inside and outside their own communities. And yet, despite his comments, Cecelia romanticizes their encounter:

> Before there was anyone else on this continent, before Vikings, before the *Mayflower*, before the Spanish conquistadores, before the African slave ships, before Ellis Island and its famous huddled masses and all the others, before any of them, their ancestors were here, hers and Running Horse's, and maybe a thousand years ago their ancestors knew each other, a man and a woman who found each other beautiful, and maybe they slept together like this in each other's arms, a man and a woman together somewhere in a teepee on the Great Plains, covered with a buffalo robe, lying as they were now.[123]

Capture noticed that the color of their skin was nearly the same, and "she felt happy because it felt right in a way it never had been before with any other man . . . because this man, this dumb, uneducated skin, this cowboy-cum-lumberjack could understand her soul in a way no white man ever could, ever."[124] She traces the desire between Indian men and Indian women to the precontact era in what reads as a yearning for idyllic purity and cultural stasis—though this fantasy eliminates their tribal distinctiveness. There is certainly a conflicting message here. By sleeping with him, Cecelia accepts Running Horse's sexualized and insulting depiction of her. Her reimagination of the past casts them both into stereotypical roles, but the passage suggests Cecelia's naming of him as a "dumb, uneducated skin" reciprocates. Cecelia proclaims, at least mentally, her superiority to him. Is this episode a reclaiming of female power, if she gets what she wants, an intimate encounter with a Native man? And does Capture control her own body in this encounter? It also seems crucial that this passage peels back history, maybe not in the same way that city histories are getting mapped in these texts, but in a way that suggests a longing for presettler spaces. Certainly the reference to the *Mayflower*, at least, is a nod to Nathan, whose ancestors were passengers on that famous voyage.

From prison, Cecelia experiences an "awakening," of course reminiscent of Kate Chopin's protofeminist novel *The Awakening*. As Hale writes, "Her awakening, as always, was sudden and total."[125] Hale and Chopin both write novels about "making a home," the responsibilities of motherhood, and the experience of being an outsider. By deliberately engaging with this well-known text, Hale places her work in the tradition of American feminist writing. The trope of captivity in the novel—expressed in terms of alcoholism, race, gender, and marriage—culminates in the event that frames the novel: Capture's arrest for drunk driving and, subsequently, for welfare fraud. It is during this period of imprisonment that Cecelia seems to gather enough strength to break free of her other captivities, namely, her marriage to Nathan and the way he determines her worth. The only seeming contradiction to this analysis is Cecelia's determination to commit suicide near the end of the novel (though unlike Chopin's protagonist, she does not). In a maudlin scene following her release from prison, Cecelia thinks to herself, "Would she have to throw herself in front of a truck, she wondered, or jump out her apartment window, or try something else less private than a simple gun?"[126] Though this scene is perhaps one of the weaker scenes in the novel, as critics have complained, Hale is doing something interesting here: she brings her protagonist to the edge, the verge of suicide, and then she "saves" her, in a revision of Chopin's narrative. Hale's Cecelia has the power to escape the domestic captivity that Edna Pontellier cannot (indeed, Edna is likened to the caged canary that appears in the novel's first pages). What saves Cecelia, I will argue in the next section, is the memory of "Indians feeling effective" at Alcatraz.[127]

THE COLOR RED

Prior to Hale's evocation of Alcatraz, there are traces of Cecelia's Indigenist and activist propensities early in the novel. For example, when she dresses in red for a high school track meet in what she believes is a display of Indian pride, her father tells her, "None but a certain kind of woman wears red."[128] It might be difficult to ascertain whether this admonition comes from his notions of Native womanhood or from his boarding school experience, but the trope of the "woman in red" is most certainly Christian in nature, associated with sexual looseness and lasciviousness.[129] For Cecelia, the color red meant something else: "They used to say you could always tell Indians because of the color red. When they saw a rig coming or people riding horses in the distance, they would say, 'Just look for the color red, and you'll know if they're white or Indian.'"[130] Capture proclaims: "Red was always going to be her favorite color when she grew up, she thought vindictively. Her whole wardrobe would consist of nothing but red. Red coats and red dresses and red high-heeled shoes, red jeans and red nylon stockings. Even red underwear."[131] Red high-heeled shoes, stockings, and panties may seem to suggest promiscuity, as her father fears. While Cecelia believes that in choosing red she is choosing Indianness, her father is more interested in protecting his daughter's sexual purity. What is important here is that she has the choice, and she chooses red: she is enabling herself just as she will when she relocates herself to San Francisco and when she joins other Native peoples in political protest at Alcatraz, arguably another way of dressing in red.

Her father's Native identity is often ambivalent like this, which we can probably attribute to his experience at the mission school. "You learned to live like a reasonable facsimile of a white person," Cecelia says to him.[132] She continues: "Like many Indian people of his generation, her father seemed to Cecelia in some curious way ashamed of being Indian, although he would have denied it vehemently. He spoke the native language, hadn't even begun to learn English until he was twelve and went to mission school."[133] Her mother wants to be Irish, and Will becomes a "copy" of the white man. The novel's indictment of Catholicism, as represented by the "mission school," is clear here. The school seems fairly successful in "killing the Indian, saving the man," causing Will to suppress his Native identity, first by taking away his language, his words. Occasionally, his anger comes to the surface, for example, when he is jailed for a bar brawl that results after he overhears a comment about "a taste for squaws."[134] The penalty for standing up for Indian women is imprisonment, captivity. For the most part, however, Will behaves like a model American citizen, even joining the army and fighting in the

First World War: "Cecelia could not help wondering how her father had managed to feel patriotic, why he had enlisted when his father had been defeated in the Indian wars and he himself was not even a U.S. citizen at the time. Her father had taught her a little Indian history when she was small. She knew Indians weren't granted citizenship until 1924."[135] Of course, Cecelia realizes the irony of his becoming a soldier for a country that has disenfranchised him. Her knowledge of history leads her to comprehend the cognitive dissonance between colonial capture and her father's US patriotism. Partly as a result of his inner turmoil, Will becomes an alcoholic, even though his father, Eagle Capture, held that "alcohol was the single greatest enemy of the Indian people."[136] In the novel, not only Cecelia's predicament but Will's failures are blamed on the destructiveness of alcohol. Eagle Capture had encouraged Will to study law, but Will flunked out of the University of Notre Dame, where he had received a football scholarship. Will fails as an American hero and all-American athlete—just as he bemoans being unable to produce a male heir who would succeed in becoming a lawyer (which he envisions as a male pursuit). Eagle Capture instilled in Will a belief that the law (and the university system) was a tool for Indian rights:

> He was the one who had brought the white man's system of justice to the tribe. He believed that the key to survival was legal representation. If the Indian people had had adequate legal representation, there would have been no Little Bighorn or Wounded Knee. It wouldn't have been possible for the white-eyes to steal land and murder Indians. Legal representation was the key. Through the orderly system of laws the Indian people could regain much of what they had lost; they could make sure that treaties were kept, that no more land was stolen and that water rights belonged to the rightful owners.[137]

Eagle Capture argues that the only way for a colonized people to become empowered is to understand the colonizers' laws. This knowledge is needed to protect and recapture the land, to ensure that the tribe does not lose its place in the American landscape.

Cecelia inherits from her father his trust in the law, and she learns from him that "it was the duty of any Indian person able to become a lawyer to become one and then dedicate *his* professional life to helping his people obtain justice."[138] Law is instrumental in achieving any kind of ongoing activism, and this is what gives Cecelia her motivation: "Will's son would provide the Indian people with quality legal representation."[139] Cecelia becomes "Will's son" in many ways: she attends the white school because the mission school is not "academically sound," according to her father, even though her sisters had gone there.[140] Cecelia's sisters also speak their Native tongue, but Will refuses to teach it to Cecelia because he wants her to think in English. He tells her that if "you were going to compete successfully in a white man's world, you had to learn to play the white man's game. It was not enough that an Indian be *as good as*; an Indian had to be *better than*."[141] Will is the one who gives Cecelia her competitive nature, the desire to "win the game" and, I would argue, the impetus for her to pursue law in the first place.

Years later, Capture's husband, Nathan, will question her ability to study law: "He didn't think she had the kind of mind it took to succeed at studying law. She was not swift and analytical enough."[142] Nathan's statement carries racist undertones, considering the "Indian mind" to be less capable than the white. Cecelia encounters this same prejudice once she does attend law school, mostly exhibited by her white female classmates who talk behind her back and doubt her intellect. The protagonist, however, uses this antagonism to strengthen her resolve. Though critics have read Cecelia's desire to practice law as an "individual pursuit," one that is potentially whitewashing, this desire carries an activist resolve: Capture daydreams about committing suicide, but "she never daydreamed about dropping out of law school."[143] The image of *Black's Law Dictionary* holding open her apartment window, an image that is repeated throughout the novel, is an important one that works on many levels. There is the window of opportunity, there is the window from which she may jump, there is the window that is open because Will Capture teaches his daughter to leave it so for good health, and there is the window from which she can see all of the rooftops of Berkeley. The dictionary, like her father's and grandfather's political principles, is a constant presence. Cecelia Capture does not become white by studying law; she learns the white man's laws in order to protect tribal rights and assets.

Cecelia's categorical hatred of most white people is also a clue that she does not want to become one. From her father, Cecelia learns rage, "blind rage, taking possession of him, of his body and his mind and his very spirit."[144] Will Capture does not like it "when white men called him chief," and he defends himself against such mockery.[145] In fact, Will dies of a heart attack after cutting down a tree to spite his white neighbor.[146] And though Cecelia herself is also a mixed-blood, she disowns her mother's "whiteness": "Cecelia's Irish forebears were not *her* people. They were *white*, just like the redneck crackers in the little reservation towns."[147] In other words, "her people" were Indians, Coeur d'Alenes. She is conscious of physiognomy and phenotypes as well, and she acts in a very protective manner of her children's Indianness: "The Donahues were fond of telling her that Corey was 'the spitting image' of his father, and maybe he was. He showed his Indian blood only a little. His complexion was nearly as dark as his mother's."[148] While the Donahues want to see Corey's whiteness, Cecelia would rather celebrate his Indianness. Her daughter, on the other hand, seems to take after her father, Nathan: "Because Nicole was white-looking, people were startled to learn that they were mother and daughter, but Cecelia said Nicole didn't really look white, except in a 'superficial sense.' She was very light-complected and had a small, slightly turned-up Anglo-Saxon nose with a light sprinkling of freckles. But her eyes were another matter."[149] This is a reversal of Capture's experience with her own mother, who was lighter than her daughter. Cecelia sees what she believes are "Indian features" in her children, and, unlike their Anglo relatives, she is not interested in how well they can "pass" for white, though their Indianness may be invisible in the city space.

Cecelia's indictment of white people is also leveled at historical erasure. At a party with Nathan in Spokane, for example, Cecelia sits outside contemplating the whiteness of the guests, none of whom, she believes, knew about Wounded Knee. For the second time in the novel, she conjures the photographs: "She remembered the photographs of the communal grave, the long trench the soldiers dug and piled the bodies into. She had read accounts of how the white soldiers had not only taken articles of clothing and jewelry and scalps but had cut genitals and other body parts off the corpses as well, souvenirs to bring home from Wounded Knee. She drank more. . . . She hated them all."[150] Cecelia places the blame for Wounded Knee, which conjures the Ghost Dance and the desire for white people to vanish, on all white people. Not only do whites know nothing about Indian history, but they are guilty of desecrating Native bodies. Remembering Wounded Knee is empowering in the novel—as a trauma that is part of collective Indigenous memory, meant to reclaim and retell that which has been forgotten or erased. In the last scene of the novel, in the cemetery, Capture contemplates the eucalyptus trees, not native to North America, and thinks, "Why didn't they go back to where they came from? Why didn't everyone do that?"[151] Here she again expresses the sentiment of the Ghost Dance, the desire to reverse settler colonialism, and again wishes for a presettler Indigenous place. The cemetery becomes an important site in the novel, where literally layers of histories are buried. This conjuring of the Ghost Dance in San Francisco is a precursor to Alexie's version of an urban Ghost Dance (which in *Indian Killer* also ends in the cemetery), which I will detail in the next chapter.

At the end of the novel, when it seems certain that Cecelia is determined to commit suicide, what stops her is a sense of commitment—to her "self" and her people, her dedication to her ancestors and her community, despite her resistance against being confined there.[152] First, she has yet to finish law school, and she realizes she has not made her "final arrangements": "She wanted to be buried in northern Idaho in the little tribal cemetery near her dad and her two dead brothers and all the other Captures. Because that was what she was. Cecelia Capture. Cecelia Eagle Capture. But they wouldn't permit the body of a person who had taken her own life to be buried in the tribal cemetery."[153] At first glance, this seems curious, given her aversion to the reservation, but it affirms her connection to tribe and family. Wanting to live there is not the same as wanting to be buried there—many urban Indians are buried on their home reservations.[154] She even reclaims her surname prior to Anglicization, Eagle Capture. Of course, naming is important. And so, juxtaposed with this desire for repatriation and this act of self-naming, Cecelia conjures memories of Indian protest at Alcatraz Island: "She remembered going to Alcatraz during the Indian occupation of 1969. Good feelings out there then. Indians feeling effective. Even skid-row bums had gone to Alcatraz and felt as if they were a part of the Indian people."[155] This is the only mention of Cecelia's participation in the Alcatraz occupation—or having participated in any Indigenous political movement, for that matter. This is a novelistic leap to a new and very different representation of captivity. The occupation, as I outlined in this book's introduction, was carried out by a majority of college students from Los Angeles and the Bay Area who were later joined by Native peoples from many tribal nations and locales, making this a cosmopolitan and urban space and enterprise.[156] The occupation was also a place-making endeavor as graffiti and signs on the island appropriated the ownership of this space.[157] Alcatraz got renamed and reclaimed as "Indian land." In essence, urban activism in the novel serves as a counterhistory to reservation history, as Hale configures the takeover of Alcatraz as a more contemporary manifestation of the Ghost Dance. She proposes that the only way to survive loss of home place and tribal community is to invoke an intertribal consciousness, and Alcatraz signifies this new political sensibility. This shift in vision significantly alters the novel's register: leaving the reservation is not just necessary for the protagonist's personal survival; it is crucial to the possibility of activism in the urban environment.

In 2000 the San Francisco Arts Commission's Art on Market Street Kiosk Poster Series commissioned a series entitled *Re-Membering: Dismembered Memories, San Francisco Historical Circle of the Displaced.* These posters, created by René García and John Jota Leaños, depict forgotten and displaced peoples in particular "sites" throughout the city. *San Francisco Historical Monument No. 1795–6*, for example, superimposes historic photographs of Ohlone people with Mission Dolores and the text: "In 1795 a large group of Ohlone people escaped oppressive labor conditions of Mission Dolores and escaped to the East Bay. Spanish settlers were unsuccessful in hunting, capturing, and returning the Indians to the mission camp."

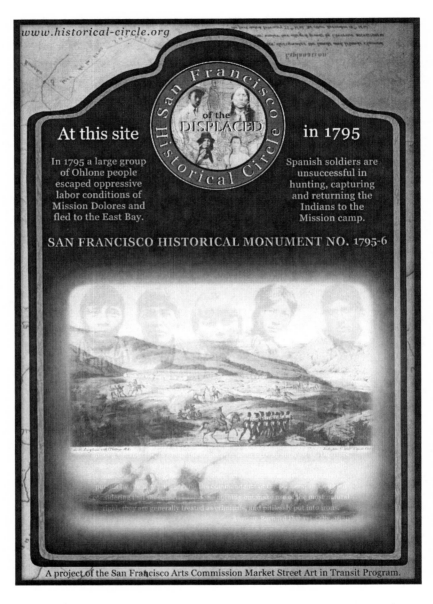

FIG 4. *Re-Membering: Dismembered Memories, San Francisco Historical Circle of the Displaced: Monument No. 1795-6* by René García and John Jota Leaños, 2000. Art on Market Street Kiosk Poster Series commissioned by the San Francisco Arts Commission. Image courtesy of the artists and the San Francisco Arts Commission.

The artists used the outline of a historic site road sign, with a shadowy old map in the background, to evoke an official history here. The renowned lithograph by Louise Choris, entitled *Tule Reed Boat* (1816), of Miwok people in tule canoes overlays the text of French explorer Auguste Duhaut-Cilly, from his *Voyage to California* (1820), who observes that the local Indians are treated "as criminals, and put pitilessly into irons." This poster sites these two peoples—the Ohlones and the Miwoks—in the space of the city during the mission period both as a recovery of that history and as evidence of a spirit of coalition and protest—the escape—that will continue to be the legacy of San Francisco.[158]

The most recognizable protest, of course, is the Alcatraz occupation, which continues to be an important memorial and activist event, although few of the protesters' demands were ever met.[159] Each year on Thanksgiving Day, a sunrise ceremony is held on Alcatraz Island.[160] This gathering commemorates the Alcatraz occupation, provides an antidote for dominant narratives about Thanksgiving, and provides a space for the urban Indians of San Francisco to gather to celebrate their survival and articulate their rights and needs. Visitors to the island (over 1.5 million annually) will still see the graffiti and slogans painted during the occupation—and in 2012 the National Park Service (which now runs Alcatraz Island) had many of the signs restored and repainted. The famous water tower has also been restored in recent years. In 2014 plans were finally drawn up for a cultural center on the island (one of the occupation's demands). The complex, designed by Haena Kim, builds upon some of the existing structures in a way that acknowledges both the past and the future of this place.[161] Plans are also under way to renovate the Alcatraz lighthouse, the oldest operational lighthouse on the West Coast. Alcatraz the island remains a visible part of the San Francisco landscape, just as Alcatraz the event remains a significant marker of an era and an articulation of Indigenous resurgence and urban activism.

Hale's inclusion of this event in her novel is a reminder of its importance in the urban Indian story of San Francisco. While early critics of Hale's novel suggest that the converging of tribes in the city space and disdain for the reservation do not display "traditional Indianness," I have here suggested otherwise: Indian identity is based on commitment, regardless of external markers of race and geography, and Indianness is not static but fluid. Identity can be complicated in cities, and thus urban texts often depict modern, cosmopolitan Native subjects who may or may not be disconnected from their home communities but who, like Cecelia, participate in Western culture, aka the university and the law. Cecelia is a law student who is disconnected by various degrees from her home community, but Hale suggests that Cecelia will use her law degree for tribal concerns. Critic Janet St. Clair has rightfully argued that Cecelia Capture claims "voice, place, kinships, and direction" at the end of the novel.[162] To be sure, Capture becomes empowered as a Native woman in the urban space. The city is where individual and collective liberation is possible. Cecelia represents a new generation of strong Indian characters who are survivors, on or off the reservation. Hale shatters the vision of the idyllic, pastoral reservation setting that fixes reservation nostalgia as a passive longing for an unreal home, and she subverts the homing plot so prevalent in novels of the Native American Renaissance. In Hale's novel, the reservation space has changed: it is not always ancestral land, and, as Cecelia points out, it is a place of defeat. By escaping from this place, Cecelia gains agency—both feminist and Indigenist agency. She dresses herself deliberately in red.

In *The Jailing of Cecelia Capture*, Hale proposes that the only way to survive loss of ancestral home place and tribal community is to invoke intertribal Indigenous activism, particularly the sort of activism that occurred at Alcatraz and that is lacking in earlier texts like *The Exiles*, *Body Indian*, even *House Made of Dawn* and *Ceremony*.[163] These efforts are a way of claiming space in the city. Indeed, Alcatraz is the critical center of Hale's book—it is the clearest marker of time and space in the novel. The spatial appropriation of Alcatraz becomes extremely significant during a time of heightened urbanization. Alcatraz, once Indian land, exists as a sort of oasis close to the urban space yet still isolated from "civilization." That Alcatraz was also a federal penitentiary makes the takeover a reclaiming of captivity itself.[164] A prison does not always have to be a prison. Indians here control their own isolation, a distinct departure from the reservation experience. The occupation also succeeded in changing official US policy from termination to self-determination— which, as Alfred points out, begins with "self."[165] Alcatraz is a marker of that self-determination, and Hale constructs her novel around this critical historical event. Self-determination is what motivates Cecelia to leave the reservation, to study law, to divorce her husband, to join or not to join with other urban Indians. Cecelia Capture fashions her own space and controls her own body in that space. She breaks free of the colonialist structure of the reservation and gains agency in the urban setting: "She *would* be free. Whatever happened to her, however her life turned out, that much was certain. She would be free."[166] The possibility of freedom in the city begins to change the narrative of relocation to one of self-determination, and this is, in the end, what marks this urban novel as an Indigenous text significant for its attention to the intersection of gender, identity, and place.

The Urban Ghost Dance

> What Would Jesus Do? He'd skip Mass, head downtown, and
> break bread with the homeless.
>
> —Sherman Alexie, July 29, 2012, on Twitter

In Sherman Alexie's prose poem "Freaks" (1993), the narrator, Victor, encounters three Indians at the Seattle waterfront.[1] The three are not named as homeless, but they are marked as such: they are "sharing a bottle of wine and a can of Spam," and the narrator asks them if they "need any change," to which they reply, "A change of clothes, a change of underwear." As Victor, undoubtedly Alexie's alter ego, gives each of them a dollar from his "wallet full of money," he thinks, "I don't feel generous or guilty, just half-empty and all lonely in this city which would kill me as slowly as it is killing these three cousins of mine."[2] The narrator is Spokane, and the homeless group includes one Lakota and two Yakamas, so they may not be actual cousins: Native people often refer to each other as "cousin" regardless of actual kinship ties. They are cousins via an imagined Indigenous community. The city space allows for these cosmopolitan connections, but it also challenges preservation of both tribal and physical self.

Alexie not only symbolically reclaims his homeless brethren across class and tribal lines in this poem but also begins to uncover the tangled Indigenous history of Seattle and to reveal his own ambiguous relationship

75

to the city. He depicts the homeless men in the social realist mode; they are drinking and downtrodden, lacking in basic human needs, like the clothing they suggest they need. At the same time, they are survivors; they possess what Certeau calls "tactics" for navigating the urban landscape.[3] Similarly, in "Transient" (1992), a poem from *The Business of Fancydancing*, a narrator describes lying "under newspapers" and "making dimes appear / in the hands of generous tourists." Alexie humanizes and embodies these transient men, and, more significantly, he gives them the agency to begin to narrate their existence. He calls attention to the homeless Indians in Seattle who might otherwise be invisible and unheard, and he asks that we consider the irony of the Indigenous homeless—especially of those who are homeless on their own aboriginal lands. In these early urban pieces, published just before he moved to Seattle, Alexie's "Transient" and "Freaks" present scenes overdetermined in their commentary on social and economic inequity, disenfranchisement, and human connection.

In this chapter, I trace the multiple urban thematics and aesthetics suggested in these early poems, paying close attention to Alexie's ambivalence toward the city through his earlier reservation-based stories to his more recent work, which is becoming more and more urban. As I will demonstrate, his engagement with homelessness serves to map his search for meaning in the urban experience—and in so doing, he repositions city space and redefines *home*. The trajectory of his depictions of the urban space follows in the wake of his own relocation to Seattle and elucidates a changing relationship with the reservation that he more clearly articulates as *prison* in recent interviews and in his young adult novel, *The Absolutely True Diary of a Part-Time Indian* (2007).[4] Yet the city, a symbol of empire built on Indigenous land, is the site of historic and contemporary dispossession—an embodied dispossession for the homeless. Particularly in *Indian Killer* (1995), "What You Pawn I Will Redeem" from the collection *Ten Little Indians* (2003), and *Flight* (2007), the three texts under consideration here, Alexie's homeless people navigate an urban space that has historically rendered them invisible and undesirable. As Jackson Jackson says in "What You Pawn," "Homeless Indians are everywhere in Seattle. We're common and boring, and you walk right on by us, with maybe a look of anger or disgust or even sadness at the terrible fate of the noble savage."[5] Indeed, they are named by their condition, by a *lack* of belonging to a place.[6] They are simultaneously *inside* and *outside* the city and nation. At the same time, Alexie's homeless Indians demonstrate how the remaking of tribal bonds enables survival in the city space—and how narrating their stories makes spatial claims. Thus, the city is always at once a generative space and one where Indians are marginalized. For Alexie, this cosmopolitan place, this place of ironic exile, is where intertribal politics must begin; this is where "collective rage," in the form of an urban Ghost Dance, can become meaningful.[7]

Alexie's motivations for writing about homelessness are not always clear. In interviews, for example, he rarely discusses his literary and literal advocacy for the homeless. He does engage with homelessness as an important social justice issue, one that affects Indigenous peoples in great numbers, evident in his three interviews with Tim Harris, director of the Seattle street newspaper *Real Change*, whom Alexie fictionalizes in the short story "What You Pawn I Will Redeem."[8] In the 1998 interview, Alexie explains that he has "a lot of relatives who have been street people at one time or another" and that he "spend[s] a lot of time talking to [the homeless]."[9] In 2003 Alexie said that he now "talk[s] about the universal condition of the poor," and in a 2015 podcast, he called himself a "class warrior."[10] Other motivations get revealed in Alexie's prose poem sequence "My Encounters with the Homeless People of the Pacific Northwest," which appeared in the literary journal *Willow Springs* in 2006. For one, Alexie writes that "ethnic guilt" is what compels him to talk to homeless Indians, even when those conversations don't go so well. He also retells a joke about a homeless man turning out to be his uncle—again, the family motive.[11] With his success as an author, class is thrown into greater relief—and homelessness certainly brings to light this disparity.[12] Alexie lives well in a city that has a long history of dislocating Native peoples—and one that continues to have a large homeless population, despite its liberal bent and socially minded tendencies.[13] Focusing on class, as Alexie did so directly in the stories in *Toughest Indian in the World* (2000), also leads to deeper questions about and a wider depiction of the Indigenous experience.[14]

As Alexie's work underscores, homelessness is a very real problem in Seattle, where there are approximately eight thousand homeless people on any given night in Seattle's King County, 5 percent of whom are Indigenous (only 1 percent of Seattle's population is Native).[15] In fact, only Los Angeles, Las Vegas, and New York have higher homeless numbers than Seattle.[16] Seattle's recent ambitious ten-year plan to eradicate homelessness in King County failed, leaving more homeless than when it began.[17] Officials cite the recession and lack of affordable housing as the root causes for this ongoing homelessness. Battles continue to rage between the city and SHARE (Seattle Housing and Research Effort) and WHEEL (Women's Housing, Equality, and Enhancement League), ally organizations that have advocated the construction of temporary "tent cities" in city parks and abandoned lots and since 2012 have closed as many as fifteen of their shelters in Seattle.[18] Meanwhile, homeless Indians continue to be served by several agencies: the Chief Seattle Club, the Seattle Indian Health Board, and the Daybreak Star Indian Cultural Center, built in 1977 and operated by United Indians of All Tribes.[19] In 2010 Seattle's homeless Indian community was brought into sharp relief with the highly publicized and protested fatal shooting of John T. Williams, a Nuu-chah-nulth First Nations woodcarver, by police officer Ian Birk for carrying a weapon (his pocketknife) and for not responding to Birk's commands. Williams, a homeless man who frequented the Chief Seattle Club, was shot four times essentially for whittling, being hard of hearing, and looking menacing. No charges were filed against Birk, though he did later resign, and Williams's family was awarded a $1.5 million settlement. In 2015 A Tribe Called Red, a well-known urban Native band from Ottawa, released "Woodcarver," a song about Williams that uses overlays of sound from police radio and news reports. This incident certainly serves as a reminder of the politics and violence of displacement.

To make sense of the homelessness in Seattle's present, we need to look to its rich Indigenous past. This was Indian space long before early settlers aggressively attempted to remove tribal peoples from the city center. As historian Coll Thrush unravels in *Native Seattle*, Seattle, or New York–Alki ("New York eventually" in Chinook Jargon), has always been global and cosmopolitan, even before Denny Party "pioneers" landed at Alki Point in 1851, and even more so once it became a city. There is evidence, both archaeological and from the oral tradition, of peoples from all over the Northwest Coast and Alaska traveling to this place, the territory of the Duwamish, Lake People, and Suquamish. Thrush charts the locations of Native peoples after Alki Point, from encampments on the waterfront, Yesler's sawmill, the Lava Beds, and Ballast Island, and the various ways in which Native peoples have been historically dislocated from these spaces both subtly and overtly. For example, in the wake of the 1855 Treaty of Point Elliott, which ceded fifty-four thousand acres of land and established several reservations, one of the first laws passed after Seattle's incorporation in 1865 was the Removal of Indians ordinance, which stated that "no Indian or Indians shall be permitted to reside, or locate their residences on any street, highway, lane, or alley or any vacant lot in the town of Seattle," though workers residing with their employers were exempt from this legislation.[20] Though the effects of this displacement led to early versions of homelessness, which continued throughout the end of the nineteenth century, one of the most famous holdouts was Chief Seattle's daughter Princess Angeline. Angeline refused to relocate according to treaty stipulations; instead, she remained in the city and took in laundry and sold baskets to earn a living. She later became the first Native subject in Edward Curtis's photographic career; reportedly, he paid her a dollar for each picture.[21] Angeline lived out her life in Seattle. She died in 1896 and was buried in Lakeview Cemetery near her long-time friend Henry Yesler.[22]

By the 1880s there was increased pressure for removal from the city even as more tribal peoples came to the city for economic reasons, to visit relatives, to stay, or to buy goods. Two fires, in 1889 and 1893, proved to be extremely detrimental to Native residents. The first accidental fire burned thirty-three blocks of the business district, which included Yesler's wharf and the Lava Beds, a neighborhood of ill repute that housed many Indians. The second fire intentionally burned several Native longhouses at Herring's House, a historically Indigenous town along the West Seattle shoreline. Those displaced by the fires moved to Ballast Island, or to the

Duwamish area of town, or to one of the nearby reservations.[23] All of this served to create a homeless population within the city confines. By the 1910s Bureau of Indian Affairs agent S. A. Eliot described nearly "one to three thousand Indians who are landless and homeless" in Seattle.[24] The city's homeless varied greatly based on migration patterns, sometimes aligned with the hops harvest on nearby farms and with ceremonial schedules. While the two world wars drew more Native workers to the city, in the aftermath, they were the hardest hit by layoffs. By the 1950s Pioneer Square, marked by a Tlingit totem pole, had turned into a place called Skid Road, where homeless Indians congregated and continue to congregate.[25] This place, Pioneer Square, clearly named in accordance with the American frontier myth, figures largely in Alexie's stories.

In Pioneer Square today, where many homeless people gather, a totem pole known as *Land in the Sky*, by Lummi carver Joe Hillaire, stands, along with the 1909 bronze bust of Chief Seattle by artist James Wehn and the *Day/Night* sculpture by Cheyenne and Arapaho artist Hock E Aye Vi Edgar Heap of Birds, which consists of two large ceramic and steel panels, one on either side of the statue of Chief Seattle, on which are written, "Chief Seattle now the streets are our home" and "Far away brothers and sisters we still remember you" in both English and Lushootseed, the language of Chief Seattle (Sealth, Seathl, or See-ahth).[26] The city of Seattle regulates this space with curfews in attempts to at least temporarily dislocate the homeless during periods of high tourism. In *Indian Killer*, Alexie argues through the consciousness of Marie Polatkin, "The powerful white men of Seattle had created a law that made it illegal to sit on the sidewalk. That ordinance was crazier and much more evil than any homeless person."[27] While Seattle projects itself as an Indigenous city with an Indigenous "place-story," it attempts to suppress the visibility of the Native homeless population.[28] Alexie's work consistently points to this irony: of Indigenous space without Indigenous people, how homeless Indians are simultaneously there and not there, of what it means to be homeless on your own land.

Homelessness in literature conjures a constellation of themes, as John Allen maps out in his book on homelessness in American literature. I

FIG 5. *Day/Night* by Hock E Aye Vi Edgar Heap of Birds, 1991. Ceramic enamel on steel. Located at Pioneer Place Park, 100 Yesler Way, Seattle. Photo collection of the artist, used with his permission. Also pictured: *Chief Seattle Fountain,* James Wehn, 1908. Cast and gilded bronze and granite. Commissioned by the City of Seattle Street and Sewer Department as part of improvements made for the 1909 Alaska Yukon Pacific Exposition. Collection: Seattle Office of Arts & Culture. Used with permission.

have already traced many of these themes in this study: alienation, escape, rebellion, the urban, travel, the Other, domesticity, and "home."[29] Alexie's work taps into these concerns by asking, Can the city be *home* for the *unhomed?* In the urban space, the homeless are what cultural geographer Tim Cresswell calls "out of place," literally living in alleys, parks, under viaducts.[30] Parks are man-made "natural" spaces designed to be recreational spaces. They are *not* meant to be living spaces; homeless people do not "belong" in them. The other "place" where homeless people congregate is on the streets—also public spaces. Some of the most important actions in Alexie's stories occur in the streets. Some actions are violent and some are celebratory, such as when Jackson Jackson dances with his grandmother's regalia in the street at the end of "What You Pawn." Homeless Indians are a visible and public reminder of poverty, as well

FIG 6. Reverse view of *Day/Night* by Hock E Aye Vi Edgar Heap of Birds,
1991. Ceramic enamel on steel. Located at Pioneer Place Park, 100 Yesler Way,
Seattle. Photo collection of the artist, used with his permission. Also pictured:
Chief Seattle Fountain, James Wehn, 1908. Cast and gilded bronze and granite.
Commissioned by the City of Seattle Street and Sewer Department as part of
improvements made for the 1909 Alaska Yukon Pacific Exposition. Collection:
Seattle Office of Arts & Culture. Used with permission.

as a disturbance of order. Above all, they are Indians in the urban space;
they have refused to stay "in their own country," on their reservations,
which I have already described as an act of rebellion.[31] In the city, they
inhabit public spaces, the in-between spaces, places where tourists visit. As
Thrush points out, homeless Indians are everywhere in Seattle, and they
are the *only* Indians that non-Natives encounter. Though the No Indians
Allowed signs have faded into Seattle's urban legend, this very real and
present dispossession (and the animosity that it seems to evoke) has not.

The engagement with homelessness in Alexie's work, particularly
in *Indian Killer*, "What You Pawn," and *Flight*, articulates a rethinking
about place and territory as multiple histories get mapped onto the space
of what is now Seattle (and in *Flight*, Tacoma). In fact, as I will argue,
Alexie's urban texts are mapped in a way that his reservation stories are

not. Further, Alexie very explicitly makes the connection between the dispossession of land and of homeless Indian peoples. "Homeless," of course, means to be without a home; metaphorically, all Indians are in some way homeless, having lost such a large portion of their homelands, as Cyrus Patell has argued in his work on *Indian Killer*. For Patell, *Indian Killer*'s strongest message is that "all American Indians are in some fundamental way homeless, victims of displacement, dispossession, and cultural damage."[32] Homelessness is part and parcel of the "structured dispossession" of settler colonialism that Glen Coulthard has so eloquently described.[33] The engagement with homelessness in Alexie's work, then, works to ironize the domestic situation of Indigenous peoples in the United States. American Indians are colonial subjects—like other colonial subjects, they have been exiled, relocated, and alienated. Talking about homeless Indians is political.[34] It is an act of resistance against the colonial projects of the United States. It calls attention to the effects of the past in the present, as homelessness is a constant and visual reminder of historic relocation(s) and displacement. Writing about homelessness, then, is a way of inhabiting, remapping, navigating, and narrating space.

Part of Alexie's project is surely a move to humanize the homeless, as Jennifer Ladino suggests in her essay on *Ten Little Indians*.[35] In his 2003 interview in *Real Change*, Alexie said, "Homeless people don't need to be romanticized and they don't need to be vilified—there's plenty of both—what they need is to be humanized. And to humanize somebody you show everything. Everything. The best of who they are and the worst of who they are."[36] Humanizing street people also makes them visible; "seeing them" is an important step in this process.[37] Alexie humanizes his homeless characters first and foremost by telling their stories—or allowing them to narrate their own lives. This works as a "muting" of "white noise," to use James Cox's derivation of Alexie's language: "The fiction writer intervenes in and rewrites the narratives of conquest by inserting Native American voices into the storytelling."[38] Giving homeless Indians voice and narrative power serves as an erasure of dominant memes that circulate around them; it gives voice to the voiceless. Alexie does not necessarily ask the reader to feel sympathy for these characters, many of whom are flawed and unlikeable human beings. But they are human beings, and Alexie asks us to show them respect by listening to their stories.[39]

Throughout his career, Alexie's work has contemplated the divide between urban Indians (homeless or not) and reservation Indians. In the title story of *The Lone Ranger and Tonto Fistfight in Heaven* (1993), for example, the narrator recalls what the "old Indian poet" says about living in the city—that Indians can reside there but can never live there.[40] This phrasing simultaneously evokes temporality, transience, and mobility. "Residing" is more impermanent than "living," and the city space does not offer stability; in fact, it seems to "consume" tribal members who move there.[41] And to take this a step further, in the city, if Indians are not living, then they may just be the ghosts of Chief Seattle's speech, a point to which I will return later in this chapter. In *Reservation Blues*, when the band Coyote Springs encounters homeless Indians in Seattle, they are "trapped by this city and its freeway entrances and exits."[42] Alexie often describes the reservation's confinement in this way, which in this novel reflects the ambivalence that comes with celebrating the reservation.[43] In some ways, the reservation symbolizes community and communal history; however, it also represents the loss of ancestral lands, "a fragment of the whole." For Alexie, particularly in his earlier work, Indianness is dependent upon living (or having lived) on the reservation.[44] Those who do not live there become either sell-outs or homeless. In the film *The Business of Fancydancing*, Seymour Polatkin returns from Seattle to the Spokane reservation—also marked with a sign—for the funeral of his old friend Mouse. Seymour's relationship to his reservation community is strained for a number of reasons (his sexuality, his success as a writer, his habit of writing about the experiences of the people close to him), but Alexie makes sure to visually mark the geographical distance as well.[45] Certainly, Seymour's cosmopolitan desires—to leave the reservation and live in the city—are at the heart of the film's conflict. At the end of the film, Seymour is doubled: one Seymour stays on the reservation, and one Seymour drives away. While one could read this as a double or split identity, that Seymour has two "selves" here, I propose that the Seymour who drives away is spectral—that urban Seymour becomes a ghost. In the city, Seymour may be ephemeral and elusive, but he is also empowered in a way that the reservation does not afford.[46] This city is not the same debilitative space of *Lone Ranger* or *Reservation Blues*. In 2005 Åse Nygren noted this change: "While in Alexie's early fiction, the reservation is a geographical space of borders and confinement, in his more recent fiction . . . the reservation changes its ontology and becomes a mental and emotional territory."[47] Alexie's own comments reveal a shift in his thinking about the urban/reservation dichotomy. In a 2013 interview with Joe Fassler in the *Atlantic*, for example, he elaborated on what he considered to be toxic and confining about the reservation setting: "Why do we make them sacred now, even though most reservations are really third-world, horrible banana republics?" The reservation system was intended to imprison, he says. In fact, Alexie now sees Adrian Louis's line from the poem "Elegy for the Forgotten Oldsmobile," "I'm in the reservation of my mind," as an articulation of reservation captivity, both psychological and literary.[48]

In this chapter, as I read three of Alexie's urban texts in chronological order, I will chart the complexity and transient nature of Alexie's urban Natives and map how homelessness overlaps with spectralization, particularly as an enactment of an urban Ghost Dance. The historical Ghost Dance, of course, was a religious movement in the nineteenth century led by messiah-figure Wovoka, a Northern Piute, which culminated in the massacre of an estimated 153 Lakotas at Wounded Knee in 1890.[49] The movement sought unity among Indigenous peoples and proposed that dancing would cause a transformation that would at once reunite them with their ancestors and disappear the settlers. Like other Indigenous messianic movements, the Ghost Dance was "born as a result of tremendous cultural change and in the midst of cultural crisis," writes historian Rani-Henrik Andersson.[50] In this case, the cultural crisis was clearly tied to the beginnings of the reservation system.[51] The Ghost Dance, as Lisa Tatonetti has argued, has "revolutionary potential" in Alexie's work, and, in fact, Alexie "uses it as an explicit metaphor for Native resistance."[52] In *Indian Killer*, for example, Alexie's first extended engagement with homelessness and the urban space, Alexie suggests that a Ghost Dance is taking place—and, I will argue, it is the city that makes it possible.[53] While the main plot centers on the eponymous "Indian Killer," a collective rage is forming in the background, a rage among the metaphorically homeless and the literal homeless people who gather in Occidental Park and under the Alaskan Way Viaduct. Homelessness here serves as the impetus for resistance, and the city serves as the space for coalition. The short story "What You Pawn I Will Redeem" is a quest narrative that follows narrator Jackson Jackson, a homeless Spokane Indian living in Seattle, on a mission to recover his grandmother's powwow regalia from a pawnshop. Jackson Jackson and his posse of homeless Indians are ghostly; they are mostly invisible in the city, and they disappear one by one. In the final scene, Jackson's celebratory dance with his grandmother's regalia registers as another kind of urban Ghost Dance—it is a reclamation of past and triumph in the present. In *Flight*, protagonist Zits is a mixed-blood foster child who has weathered many temporary homes, while his long-lost father is homeless on the streets of Tacoma. Zits meets a white boy self-named Justice, who leads him to acts of violence as retribution for the wrongs committed against Native peoples. While Zits's father himself reads as ghost, I propose also reading Zits as ghost: in one of the opening chapters, he is shot in the head during a bank robbery, which sends him on a series of historical time travels—and enacting yet another Ghost Dance.

Alexie's literary articulations of the Ghost Dance inevitably conjure ghosts, and Seattle is full of them.[54] In Seattle's Occidental Park (located in the Pioneer Square district), which Alexie says is "not much of a park, one city block filled with benches and bad publicly funded sculpture," stands a bust of Chief Seattle and, as I mentioned earlier, Heap of Birds's *Day/Night*.[55] Heap of Birds's piece refers specifically to the line "Day and night cannot dwell together," from Chief Seattle's "famous speech" in 1854, published by Dr. Henry A. Smith in the *Seattle Sunday Star* more than thirty years later. While the validity of this speech has rightfully been called into question, its message has been persistent in the American imagination.[56] Smith's version of the speech's final lines reads:

And when the last Red Man shall have perished, and the memory of my tribe shall have become a myth, these shores will swarm with the invisible dead of my tribe, and when your children's children think themselves alone in the field, the store, the shop, upon the highway, or in the silence of the pathless woods, they will not be alone. In all the earth there is no place dedicated to solitude. At night when the streets of your cities and villages are silent and you think them deserted, they will throng with the returning hosts that once filled them and still love this beautiful land. The White Man will never be alone. Let him be just and deal kindly with my people, for the dead are not altogether powerless.[57]

The Seattle/Smith text suggests that ghosts or spirits—"the returning hosts"—will continue to inhabit this space.[58] For sure, this constructed narrative is intricately linked to the myth of the Vanishing Indian. In fact, Thrush has pointed out, "It is as though the returning hosts, those phantoms prophesied in the Chief Seattle Speech, have turned out to be *nothing more than* homeless Indians."[59] Heap of Birds's panels also make an explicit connection between the "transient inter-tribal people," as his artist's statement names them, and the ghosts of the speech, as he seeks to commemorate both Chief Seattle and the many homeless or transient Indians who congregate in this very spot. As art historian Bill Anthes argues, Heap of Birds "bring[s] history into focus" and "reinserts an indigenous presence in contemporary urban spaces."[60] I want to suggest, as well, as does the last line of the Seattle/Smith speech, that the "dead are not altogether powerless"—and that Alexie's Ghost Dance is very much in conversation with these textual ghosts.

What Thrush's reading of Alexie's portrayal of homeless Indians as ghosts misses is Alexie's intended irony and the "revolutionary potential" embedded in such a portrayal.[61] Alexie uses the trope of *ghost* to think through the complicated subjectivity of homeless Indians. This is not simply an "urban parable": the homeless as ghosts are reminders of the dislocative act and evidence of Indigenous permanence in the urban space. Indeed, "ghosts are political," argues Michael Bell.[62] In Alexie's work, the homeless provide a way of remembering the past, and they reveal the anxiety about the Indigenous history of Seattle. Throughout American literary history, as Thrush himself suggests, writers have spectralized Indians, mostly in the name of vanishing and haunted places.[63] Indians are disappearing, they wrote, but their ghosts are reminders of their absence—and of the horrors of American colonization. In *Ghostly Matters*, Avery Gordon writes that "the ghost is just the sign . . . that tells you a haunting is taking place."[64] "To write stories concerning exclusions and invisibilities," she proclaims, "is to write ghost stories."[65] Haunting, for Alexie, is empowering, as is the telling of ghost stories. Ghosts, like homeless Indians, are embodiments of the dispossessed. Ghost stories recount "place-stories," write Boyd and Thrush, and these stories "highlight the ways in which knowledge of place and past are constructed, produced, revealed, and contested."[66] Further, they "illustrate the degree to which urban and Indigenous histories, rather than being mutually exclusive, are in fact mutually constitutive, and the ways in which ghost stories can provide access to very real pasts."[67] Seattle, with its history of tribal diversity and colonial displacements, has its own brand of ghosts, and Alexie's work draws upon these local stories. For this reason, my reading is predicated on the contexts of these histories and these specific geographies—and I believe that Alexie's homeless/ghosts have something important to say.

Indeed, the streets of this city are filled with its first inhabitants—homeless ones, as both *Day/Night* and Alexie's work make plain. Kathleen Brogan has suggested that literary ghosts "bridge a distance" from culture.[68] She writes, "As both presence and absence, the ghost stands as an emblem of historical loss as well as a vehicle of historical recovery."[69] Alexie's ghosts register a historical distance, and they are finely attuned to geography; they literally recover and reveal the past through their stories and mobility. Alexie's later work further challenges preconceived ideas about the relationship between Indigenous peoples and place: here they are "residing" and "living" in cities, following previously mapped routes between traditional Indian lands and the city and staking claims in ceded territory. His homeless Indians inhabit and haunt the urban space, despite legislation and policing meant to relocate them elsewhere.

In other words, Alexie turns to the trope of urban Indians as ghosts to ironize the notion of Vanishing Indians and, more importantly, to remap the city by demonstrating how it is riven with past displacements in the present. He literally empowers the disenfranchised by mobilizing a contemporary Ghost Dance in Seattle.

THE URBAN GHOST DANCE

Alexie's fictional urban shift started in 1996 with *Indian Killer*, and it is in this novel that we find his first extended depictions of homelessness. In *Indian Killer*, a murder mystery set within the space of Seattle, reservation space exists only in the periphery (in memory and in John's imagination), while the city and its multiple articulations of homelessness are at the fore. Protagonist John Smith is a tribeless Indian adopted by white parents and raised in a suburb of Seattle. Like those famous urban Indians, the Mohawks who helped to build the New York skyline, John becomes a construction worker, helping to build the "last skyscraper" in Seattle.[70] Meanwhile, a series of violent crimes is committed, and the police dub the perpetrator the "Indian Killer," namely because the killer leaves behind two owl feathers at the scene. In true crime novel fashion, Alexie leads the reader to believe that any one of the characters could be the killer—though the finger points so often at Smith that many reviewers of the book have proclaimed that he is the killer.[71] In my reading of the novel, the killings are instead being manifested by a modern Ghost Dance that has arisen on the streets of Seattle, as Marie Polatkin, college student turned activist, herself suggests near the novel's end: "So maybe this Indian Killer is a product of the Ghost Dance. . . . Maybe this is how the Ghost Dance works."[72] Marie thinks the Ghost Dance could be a response to any number of critical Indigenous issues: reservation poverty, infant-mortality rates, suicide, fetal-alcohol syndrome, and homelessness, among others.[73] Marie's list makes an interesting juxtaposition between the reservation and the urban, suggesting movement through and between, and sees homelessness as an extension of reservation problems. My spatiohistorical reading that follows will focus on the novel's articulations of location and dislocation, paying close attention to the literal and metaphoric homelessness in the novel, its spatial practices, and moments in the text where Alexie gestures toward Seattle's history of dispossession. This reading triangulates the tropes of *homeless*, *ghost*, and *place*, reading across and through the history and geography of Seattle to suggest that the urban space is what makes this Ghost Dance possible and that its "revolutionary potential" is, above all, dependent upon locationality.

Not only is *Indian Killer* set in the urban space of Seattle, but Alexie seems intent in this novel on mapping the landscape of the city and its emplacement within the Pacific Northwest.[74] While much of his earlier work is devoid of geographic detail, in this novel Alexie locates characters and scenes in particular neighborhoods, revealing specific coordinates and intersections, beginning with city streets and then panning out toward outlying areas, like the Tulalip and Hoopa Reservations.[75] The spatial practice of the novel, established very early on, gets revealed through movement, as it demonstrates the kind of mobility possible in the urban space of Seattle, as well as how Seattle fits within a network of Native spaces in the Northwest. For example, as John Smith imagines his birth in the first chapter of the novel, the narrative follows a helicopter as it "circles downtown Seattle, moves east past Lake Washington, Mercer Island, hovers over the city of Bellevue."[76] There are "skyscrapers, the Space Needle, water everywhere. Thin bridges stretched between islands."[77] Alexie begins with this aerial overview of the city, using the helicopter to create a bird's-eye view, and then works to narrate the action on the ground. As other critics have noted, the helicopter and "rescue" conjure imagery from the Vietnam War, which John could possibly remember from television and have incorporated into false memory. In this dream-like scenario, the reservation is imagined as war zone, and Seattle (or its suburbs) represents safety—quite an inversion of the usual narrative. The place-names and geographic markers continue throughout the novel, and their names are often reminders of the settler and physically altered space of this city.[78] The aerial snapshot that begins the novel reveals a changed landscape and seems to suggest the vastness of Puget Sound territory, which becomes divided only as the land comes into closer view. We see Seattle's "distinct and divided neighborhoods" in the novel as Alexie's commentary on the ways in which urban boundaries articulate racial and class difference.[79] I would argue, then, that Alexie's meticulous geography in this novel calls attention to the boundaries that get articulated not only in the city spaces but territorially, as lines between city and reservation, of the constructedness of Indigeneity as it is currently conceived.

On the ground, *Indian Killer*'s characters are in near constant movement, and even the characters who are not physically homeless are metaphorically so. For example, Marie Polatkin secretly returns to the Spokane Reservation in the middle of the night; her cousin Reggie suddenly appears at her apartment in the city—and at the end of the novel, he is on the move again, walking down "a country highway" toward another "city of white men."[80] Retired cop turned writer Jack Wilson walks his old beat. John Smith is perhaps the most mobile: he, too, steals into his parents' home while they sleep; he walks the city streets; he "returns" to his home reservation in dreams; and he travels to nearby reservations in search of his birth family. As further evidence of Alexie's mapping, the novel precisely follows John's perambulations: "He walked north along the water, across the University Bridge, then east along the Burke-Gilman Trail"; "He walked across the Fremont Bridge, north of downtown, southeast of his Ballard apartment"; "He walked up Aurora, past Big Heart's Soda and Juice Bar up on 110th and Aurora."[81] Even though John's increasing confusion and mental illness may affect his actual spatial awareness, Alexie tracks his movement through Seattle—and explicitly uses the concept of mapping to think about Indigenous knowledges of place and the settler colonialism that gets invoked by the map as part of what Mishuana Goeman calls "spatialized power dynamics."[82] The specificity of the city spaces—its neighborhoods and streets—speaks to both intimate place knowledge and the ways in which race and class are enacted and mediated by this geography.

Maps are visual reminders of the physical loss of lands, of the naming of those places, and of the narratives of those places. Contemporary Seattle on a map, for example, bears little evidence of its historical landscape, and while Indigenous names may be markers on that map, Indigenous peoples (historical and present) are rendered invisible.[83] Puget Sound, for example, named after Peter Puget, is known to local Natives as the Whulge (an anglicized version of the Lushootseed word for "saltwater").[84] The Burke-Gilman Trail, to use an example from the novel, follows an old railroad line and is named after two men from Seattle's settler history, Judge Thomas Burke and railroad man Daniel Gilman, who established the Seattle, Lake Shore, and Eastern Railroad in 1885, which served the Puget Sound logging industry.[85] Of course, the railroad was also a critical factor in the increase of the settler population at the end of the nineteenth century, and so Alexie's mention of the trail invokes this history as well. While white people in the novel carry maps, like Daniel Smith, John's adoptive father, who is obsessed with and seemingly calmed by physical maps (and perhaps by settler history and white privilege), John, in his efforts to be "Indian," eschews the map: "He knew he should carry a map because he was always getting lost, but he had just never bothered to buy one. Besides, maps were dangerous."[86] John has learned to distrust the (settler) map; he has learned the danger of those narratives—and perhaps the erasure marked out by those early colonial expeditions. Settler maps are symbolically antithetical to Indigenous knowledge about places (though, admittedly, many cartographers relied on local place knowledge), and here John forgoes the map, despite his absence of place knowledge. Here Alexie encourages us to think beyond the map, to interrogate the narrative of the map, to question the power structure that produced the map, to think about the construction of space, and to foreground Indigenous spatial knowledge, even in the urban space.

John Smith's aversions for maps make sense within the context of his failed quest for an Indigenous identity; indeed, he is but a ghost of his tribal self, as critics have noted. For example, Stuart Christie has suggested that Smith is "ostensibly cut off from his tribal story" and therefore cannot map "his own story in narrative terms."[87] Nancy Van Styvendale reads Smith's trauma specifically as "the trauma of dislocation."[88] He is aligned with the homeless Indians in the novel, and I read him as homeless; indeed, as Cyrus Patell has argued, he is "at home nowhere."[89] We find John Smith more often on city streets than at home; he often visits with homeless Indians under the Alaskan Way Viaduct, "though he never spoke more than a few words to anyone."[90] Smith longs to be a part of the tribe of urban, homeless Indians, but he cannot function as Indigenous without his origin story, without knowing his tribal affiliation or having a relationship with a homeland.[91] His unpredictable behavior (stemming from what appears to be unmedicated schizophrenia) and paranoia certainly align him with the mentally ill street people, and for this reason Marie reads John as homeless when she meets him at the student protest powwow early in the novel.[92] In so many ways, John Smith is more homeless than the homeless Indians he encounters. While they seemingly have community, John is a tribe of one: "John sat by himself, apart from a group of Indians who were singing and telling jokes. More laughter. John watched those Indians, in dirty clothes and thirdhand shoes, miles and years from their reservations, estranged from their families and tribes, yet still able to laugh, to sing. John wondered where they found the strength to do such things."[93] John has a physical home in the city (two if we include his parents' home and his apartment), but he lacks the map to his own Indigenous self, one that would lead him to the laughter of survival. It is significant that the main character of this novel is metaphorically homeless and that his dislocation is critical to his eventual demise.

As John Smith's quest takes him to Indian communities throughout the Northwest, the novel's geography extends beyond the space of Seattle, evoking larger regional networks and routes. In a significant early scene, John hitchhikes to the Hoopa Reservation in northern California to vaguely search for his birth family. Instead of making a meaningful connection here, he discovers a woman named Sweet Lu, who takes him on a "Bigfoot" tour of the reservation.[94] The tour takes them "deep into the woods, using logging roads and cattle trails. Once or twice, she simply imagined a path through the trees and followed it."[95] This kind of travel stands in sharp contrast to the urban navigations, with street names and signposts to mark the geography, and is reliant upon Sweet Lu's intimate knowledge of this place. Alexie allows for a "re-scripting," to use Chadwick Allen's term, of Indigenous space in the novel.[96] The presence of Bigfoot (or Sasquatch) here, which seems to mark the reservation space as magical or mysterious, becomes another way of Indigenizing this space.[97] Alexie is tapping into Northwest Coast stories about Bigfoot (to which Alexie refers in "The Sasquatch Poems" in *The Summer of Black Widows*), a figure prominent in a variety of tribal cosmologies. In Spokane stories, for example, the creature is named Selahtick and belongs to a race of smelly, salmon-stealing giants.[98] These stories work to map the geography of the entire coastal region: Bigfoot inhabits these woods and these spaces and is imbricated in this landscape.[99] As such, Bigfoot possesses the quintessential Indigenous place knowledge: he knows these woods, and he knows where to hide.

The Bigfoot episode works to challenge the notion of belonging and Indigeneity. Sweet Lu's Bigfoot tours are self-conscious in a humorous way: they are meant for tourists (evoking even another kind of movement), and they demonstrate her awareness that outsiders believe that Bigfoot (even in naming him so) is Indian superstition. Alexie poignantly makes John simultaneously a tourist, an outsider, and Indigenous; Sweet Lu gives him an "Indian discount," and he presumably believes in the existence of Bigfoot, but he does not belong on this reservation. Not all Indians, we see, "belong" on reservations. Sasquatch is equally as elusive as the identity of his birth parents; both are located (at least in John's imagination) on reservation land. In "The Sasquatch Poems," Alexie makes it clear that these mythical figures are female, thereby making Sasquatch and mother interchangeable here. Like John himself, they are spectral—they exist only in absence (whereas urban ghosts are very much about presence). The reservation, then, is a place of secrets and of absence, a landscape that John cannot read, with or without a map. His vision is narrowly constructed, even in his belief that he must originate from one of the Indigenous places geographically close to Seattle. This serves as a reminder that *our* vision as readers is often equally narrow, that we need a more cosmopolitan (or networked) perspective on stories, on history, on identity.

The novel travels north of Seattle as well, to the Tulalip Indian Reservation, home to a confederation of Salish tribes as designated by the Treaty of Point Elliott.[100] In the novel, Marie's classmate David Rogers travels to Tulalip to visit the casino (where he is murdered, though not by Indians), and he was raised on a farm near the Spokane Reservation, Marie's and Reggie's, and, of course, Alexie's home reservation. Again, while the city is central in the novel, it exists in correlation to these multinational reservation spaces. Tulalip gets coded as dangerous for outsiders, as a site where historical conflict gets reenacted not only on the level of possible individual Indian/white violence but as reminder of colonial dependency and racial hatred on a larger scale. This gets voiced by shock disc jockey Truck Schultz, a caricature of Rush Limbaugh, who incites violence following David's disappearance: "Well, citizens, we keep giving Indians everything they want. . . . Indians have become super citizens. . . . And we give all this to them because we supposedly stole their land from them. Indians are living a better life than they ever did before. . . . We give them everything, and yet they cannot take care of themselves."[101] Of course, Indians are not "given" anything; this land is treaty land, designated Indian space in exchange for the loss of much larger spans of land. A similar sentiment comes from David's father, who encouraged his young sons to shoot at Spokane Indians who came on their property: "Throughout his life, his only real contact with Indians happened in the middle of the night when reservation Spokanes crept onto his family's farm to steal camas root, the spongy, pungent bulbs of indigenous lilies that had been a traditional and sacred food of the local Indians for thousands of years."[102] David's father says, "This land has been in our family for over a hundred years. And those Indians are stealing from us. They're trying to steal our land."[103] This is border warfare that, like the events at Tulalip, evokes a history of territorial disputes—where the events of the past hundred years are juxtaposed with "thousands of years" of land tenure. At the same time, the ghosts of the past seem to be bumping up against the very much alive and tactical Spokanes, who refuse to be relegated to history. I would argue that this same logic is behind Truck Schultz's hate speech: the Indians in the present (in this case, the Tulalips) are surviving (and perhaps even thriving) because of their casino business, counter to the narrative of Manifest Destiny, that iteration of Indian defeat and white victory.

Alexie conjures more historical ghosts with the narrative of Jack Wilson, retired detective turned novelist who claims Native heritage in a fictional tribe, the Shilshomish. In fact, Wilson's fictional protagonist, Aristotle Little Hawk, is the "last of the Shilshomish." Wilson's alleged ancestral story goes like this: "'I'm part Shilshomish Indian,' Wilson said. 'I looked it up. There was an old medicine man named Red Fox who lived in a shack on Bainbridge Island. Back in the 1920s or something. His Indian name was Red Fox, but his American name was Joe Wilson. My dad used to say that Joe Wilson was his great-uncle.'"[104] Like John, Wilson is metaphorically homeless, raised by numerous foster families (not unlike Zits in *Flight*). Like John, Wilson creates a history for himself (whether or not based in fact or family legend). In a conversation with Dr. Clarence Mather about Wilson's vague claims to Indigeneity, Marie says, "The Shilshomish don't exist as a tribe anymore. There are no records of membership."[105] Presumably, the Shilshomish are a fictionalized version of the Shilshoolabsh (or Shilsholes), a Seattle tribe related to the Duwamish that is no longer federally recognized, although Bainbridge Island is traditionally affiliated with the Suquamish.[106] Even though Alexie chooses to fictionalize Wilson's supposed tribal affiliation, doing so conjures more history, more ghosts. Wilson's place-story reveals a number of things about Seattle. First, it narratively evokes the history of Bainbridge Island, located in Puget Sound due west of Seattle. The story about Red Fox/Joe Wilson resonates with that of Salmon Bay Charlie, or Hwelchteed, who lived with his wife, Cheethluteetsa, or Madeleine, in a shack in the town of Tucked Away Inside in the early twentieth century. Hwelchteed portrayed himself as a hereditary leader of the Shilsholes, and he and his wife frequently traveled to Ballard to sell salmon, clams, and berries.[107] Salmon Bay Charlie was legendary, known to locals and tourists, and when he was removed from his shack and resettled on the Port Madison reservation in 1915, it marked the end of an era. Though Indians had been legislated out of Seattle by that time, as we have seen, there were hold-outs like Salmon Bay Charlie. And so whether Jack Wilson is referring to Charlie by accident or false memory, or whether Alexie seeks to invoke him, Charlie is the kind of ghost that symbolizes Seattle's complicated Indigenous past. He is a ghost preserved in story, but he isn't a silent ghost. Alexie's inclusion of Red Fox's (or Charlie's) story allows the past to narrate for itself. Wilson may be an ethnic fraud, but his story reveals the persistence of Indigenous place-story and the absence of such knowledge in mainstream Seattle.[108]

The historical forces that led to Red Fox's/Salmon Bay Charlie's habitation in a shack on Bainbridge Island/Tucked Away Inside are part of the story invoked by Alexie's allusions to urban homelessness. Apparently, Salmon Bay Charlie owned ten acres on a site where three longhouses once stood. There are archival photographs of both Charlie and his famous shack, which, although fairly large in size, seems precarious in its construction.[109] In terms of place-story, there are multiple erasures at work. First, the location of Charlie's house is not indicated on any of Seattle's early maps.[110] Charlie simply disappears from this landscape. Also, there is a clear absence of community here; Charlie gets depicted as the "last of" the Shilshoolabsh, who pointedly have been removed from the area and resettled at Port Madison.[111] Indeed, a search for "Shilshoolabsh" and "Shilshole" finds very little. Shilshole Bay, which includes Ballard, seems to be all that remains of the Shilsholes. This land, like all of Seattle, was ceded in the Treaty of Point Elliott. There is legislative erasure of the Shilshoolabsh as well through the revoking of federal recognition. They are simply no longer a legal entity. In the end, Jack Wilson's story functions as a place-making narrative that recuperates Salmon Bay Charlie (and his ghost) and calls him back into existence.

More historical ghosts are conjured with the "box of recordings" that Dr. Clarence Mather finds in the basement of the anthropology building.[112] The tapes contain the stories of Snohomish, Makah, Yakama, and Spokane storytellers, "twelve hours' worth of magic," he says, "recorded by a forgotten anthropologist during the summer of 1926."[113] Mather disagrees with Reggie Polatkin, Marie's cousin, about the fate of the tapes: the professor wants to "make them public and publish an article about them," while Reggie urges him to erase them. "That's a family story," Reggie argues. "Stories die because they're supposed to die."[114] As the tapes become objects of contention, their stories once again gain currency and power in this space. When Mather becomes afraid he will be a target of the Indian Killer, he imagines that there are ghosts in the basement. While as readers we are not privy to this recorded story—or the other stories that Mather listens to in secret—they become another instance of the past intruding on the present. These stories are ghost stories, set like Red Fox's story in the 1920s. And in the present, these are home-less—or at least dislocated and disembodied—ghosts. The tapes reveal the richness of tribal diversity in this place, and as Mather argues, these elders allowed themselves to be recorded. These tapes are the product of a "forgotten anthropologist"—yet another ghost conjured here. There are three possible identities for this lost anthropologist: Erna Gunther, Thelma Adamson, and Melville Jacobs, all of whom studied with Franz Boas at Columbia University, worked with peoples of the Northwest, and taught at the University of Washington in the 1920s. Though Gunther was hired sooner, Adamson and Jacobs spent more time collecting and recording stories in and around Washington State.[115] In 1934, after having contracted tuberculosis, Adamson published her *Folk-Tales of the Coast Salish*. Mather's tapes are thus very provocative: as a collection, they "serve as the basis for Alexie's critique of cultural imperialism," according to Janet Dean;[116] they provoke questions about the ethics of ethnography, asking even larger questions about the relationship between Natives and academics; they elicit anxiety about the ownership of stories, about cultural property, as articulated by Reggie in the debate;[117] and they call attention to themselves as disembodied voices, as ghosts from the past. But while it is simple to track down the anthropologist who might have recorded these stories, it is much more difficult to recover the identities of the storytellers and the contexts of the telling. And so while Alexie signifies on the politics of knowledge production, both past and present, and suggests that the people in power (here, the academics) control the stories (symbolized by the tapes but operating on a much larger scale), he can and does allow these Indigenous ghosts to speak. Much like his homeless characters, they are empowered through voice.

A correlative story of the tapes is the one that involves Chief Seattle's bones—he who imagined this city full of ghosts. As Mather wanders the basement alone, the novel twice mentions that these bones are rumored to be hidden here somewhere. However, Chief Seattle is buried on Suquamish tribal land in a cemetery behind St. Peter's Mission Church, so why would his bones be here in the university's anthropology building?[118] Conjuring his bones calls further attention to the power structure at work here as white Seattle works to control its history. Would it be ironic for the city named after Sealth to have stolen his bones, or are his bones a mere trophy for the victors—grave looting in the name of science? To my knowledge, there are no stories about Chief Seattle's grave being robbed, though the threat may always be there. Indigenous bodies are constantly displaced, possessed and dispossessed, violated, disrespected, and co-opted.[119] In fact, Chief Seattle's grave was threatened in 1904 by plans to build an armory, but Seattleites protested and built a coping around the grave.[120] Certainly, Alexie marks anthropologists as grave robbers (and the university as an imperial institution), for there are other bones here as well: "the Indian remains in that basement," "the bones of dozens of other Indians," also called "forgotten" bones.[121] In Big Heart's Soda and Juice Bar, Reggie asks Wilson if he is going to "dig up graves."[122] In the darkness, Mather hears a "strange rattling," like the sound of "beads shaking, or sand in a shell, or bones rubbing together."[123] Listening to the stories has caused these bones to come to life, to participate in the larger Ghost Dance that is being enacted in the novel.[124] Suffice it to say that, like stories, these (homeless) bones have staying—and saying—power. Alexie evokes secret histories, and he articulates a way for Chief Seattle to be doing some of the haunting: Chief Seattle promised ghosts, and here he becomes one of them. Indeed, the bones symbolize the promise. The chief is, metaphorically, refusing to be buried in this particular historical moment. To return to Avery Gordon here, ghosts "appear when the trouble they represent and symptomize is no longer being contained or repressed or blocked from view."[125] Similarly, Slavoj Žižek writes, in reference to Lacan, that the dead return *"because they were not properly buried."*[126] Alexie's unearthing of Chief Seattle's bones and these other unnamed remains comes in the wake of the Native American Graves Protection and Repatriation Act (NAGPRA), legislation passed in 1990, and the acknowledgment of the

152,000 individual human remains interred in museums and universities across the United States.[127] As the novel participates in this larger timely dialogue, Alexie points to the university's participation in the history of desecrating graves and collecting bones. These local bones, too, "not properly buried," are a part of this Ghost Dance.

Another poignant site of ghosts in the novel is the Chapel of the North American Martyrs, where Father Duncan takes a young John Smith. Simultaneously a Jesuit and a Spokane Indian, Father Duncan literally embodies the historical violent encounters between missionary priests and Native peoples.[128] In the chapel, "John found himself surrounded by vivid stained glass reproductions of Jesuits being martyred by Indians. Bright white Jesuits with bright white suns at their necks. A Jesuit, tied to a post, burning alive *as Indians dance around him*. Another pierced with dozens of arrows. A third, with his cassock torn from his body, crawling away from an especially evil-looking Indian. The fourth being drowned in a blue river. The fifth, sixth, and seventh being scalped. An eighth and ninth praying together as a small church burns behind them."[129] This urban site memorializes Jesuit loss at the same time it represents (at least temporary) Indian victory—though these deaths occurred in the eastern United States, not in the West.[130] When John asks for Father Duncan's interpretation of these images, the priest is unable to articulate the complexity of the situation—or to reconcile his priesthood. Alexie writes, "As a Jesuit, he knew those priests were martyred just like Jesus. As a Spokane Indian, he knew those Jesuits deserved to die for their crimes against Indians."[131] He is both "bright white Jesuit" and "evil-looking Indian." Both Indian and priest get configured as ghosts, transported through time and space by the stained glass. When Father Duncan disappears at a retreat, literally "walks off into the desert," we are meant to interpret this as the result of the man's inner turmoil, of the inability of his two identities to coexist. The novel, then, like John, becomes haunted by Father Duncan and, subsequently, by settler religious history. John imagines that he is visited by the priest "in dreams" on multiple occasions, and when John is upset and confused after being physically attacked, he goes in search of the priest at a different parish. Alexie subtly suggests that John is sexually abused by the priest and in doing so recognizes the historical abuse by clergy members that has recently come to light.[132] So even while Father Duncan has disappeared from present-day Seattle, his ghost remains tethered to the city and to John. John thinks, "Father Duncan must have been on a vision quest in the desert when he walked to the edge of the world and stepped off."[133] This action gets very literally mirrored when John "step[s] off the last skyscraper in Seattle."[134] The inclusion of Father Duncan and the Chapel of the North American Martyrs functions in two ways: first, Alexie maps the conflict between Catholics and Indians (and, again, the ultimate victors provide the narrative—in this case, a visual narrative); second, he is able to insert a more local history about Catholics and Spokanes into a larger national context. The chapel provides coordinates as both a historic Indigenous site (even if the history took place elsewhere) and a contemporary conundrum for Catholic Indians. And like the university, the chapel and, by extension, the whole of the Catholic Church get implicated in their participation in the dispossession and abuse of Indigenous bodies.

Just as Chief Seattle's bones and Father Duncan evoke out-of-placeness, so do Alexie's homeless characters. In a novel that maps the story of a potentially schizophrenic adopted Indian man onto a mystery about a serial killer in Seattle, the homeless characters might easily be overlooked.[135] But homeless Indians are not in the background of the novel; they are front and center at critical moments in the plot, particularly in the scenes of violence in the latter part of the novel. Their backstories are part of the urban fabric that Alexie weaves: Alexie literally narrates them into existence.[136] *Indian Killer* begins with an epigraph from poet Alex Kuo, Alexie's poetry teacher at the University of Washington: "We are what / We have lost." Alexie charts many different forms of loss in the novel: loss of life, loss of tribal identity, loss of vision, loss of peace and order, loss of tribal languages, loss of stories. Many of his urban Indian characters have "lost" their home communities—and this, for Alexie, is the worst loss imaginable. Indeed, protagonist John Smith cannot *live* without knowledge of an Indigenous home.[137] As Marie says, the homeless "were like an Indian tribe, nomadic and powerless."[138] While homelessness conjures the underbelly, the downtrodden, Alexie's homeless Indians are also tacticians and survivors, asserting their historical place in the city of Seattle.[139] They are able to navigate the in-between spaces of Seattle—the alleys and docks and doorways—and to narrate in a way that gives them agency.[140] The novel also promotes collective action through coalition, a reminder of the possibilities of the urban space.[141] As Renya Ramirez has argued, "Movement into the cities has increased the possibility for gathering and politically organizing."[142] These homeless Indians may be the ghosts that Chief Seattle prophesied, but if, as Brogan argues, ghosts "register distance," then they also function as markers of time and of place—and of "revolutionary potential."[143]

The homeless characters represent a wide range of tribal nations and evoke a number of tribal histories. Some come from local tribes, like Carlotta Lott (Duwamish) and Cornelius (Makah) and Zera (Puyallup), while others, like Fawn, come from far away—in her case, an unnamed reservation in Montana. Their (his)stories tell us something about where they come from and how they became homeless, and their stories allow them to stake a claim in this space in spite of the official narratives and policing meant to exclude them. Alexie recounts the many reasons for their homelessness: mental illness, alcoholism, domestic abuse, veteran status, injury, systemic poverty. Near the end of the novel, Alexie gives this brief portrait:

> King, the failed college student. . . . Joseph, the recluse, who always wore a pair of nonprescription sunglasses, kept a hand drum hidden in the brush near the freeway, and would still sing old tribal songs. The newspaper man, Crazy Robert, who was a reporter for the *Seattle Times* when he was twenty-five and homeless by the time he was thirty-five. . . . Agnes, who kept a menagerie of stray dogs and scavenger birds, spoke in whispers. Green-eyed Kim, the angry one, the nurse who had spent ten years in prison for killing an abusive husband. Annie, with black hair that once flowed down to her knees, now knotted and tangled beyond repair. She used to sing standards in a Holiday Inn Lounge in Norman, Oklahoma.[144]

These are stories of loss: of employment, of health, of beauty, of family, of voice, of agency, of home. There is a glimmer of hope associated with homeless Joseph's "old tribal songs," but mostly these characters are damaged. Importantly, Alexie names these characters, an act that is both humanizing and affectionate; naming them and knowing their stories render them visible. They are visible to Jack Wilson, who as a former detective represents a kind of settler surveillance: "He walked a beat downtown and knew the names of most of the homeless Indians who crowded together beneath the Alaskan Way Viaduct and in Pioneer Square. Lester, Old Joe, and Little Joe always together, Agnes and her old man, who was simply known as Old Man, the Android Brothers, who'd come here from Spokane years earlier and were collecting spare change for bus tickets back home. Beautiful Mary, who was still beautiful, even though a keloid scar ran from the corner of her left eye to her chin."[145] Alexie does not blame his homeless characters for their lack of home and poverty, as our economic system is wont to do; in fact, he takes care to name the historical and social circumstances that are responsible for their homelessness. They are failed by a system that promised to take care of them—by treaty, even—and whose jurisdictions and powers are rendered useless in the urban space. They are failed by mainstream agencies and protections as well. However, in the world of the novel, they are not merely victims: Alexie takes care to simultaneously depict their pain and their resilience.

The story of Beautiful Mary serves as a reminder of how dangerous it is to live on the streets, particularly for women. We never know Beautiful Mary's backstory, where she came from or why she was homeless. We do know that "Beautiful Mary was a very visible member of the homeless community" and that her body is marked by that keloid scar.[146] Her story is about her murder, Wilson's arrest of her killer, and the novel that Wilson writes about her, titled *Rain Dance*.[147] Wilson refuses to allow her to be just "one dead Indian," as the lead detective calls her.[148] She is simultaneously memorialized and fictionalized by Wilson. Beautiful Mary is marked by violence, and she haunts Wilson after he finds her body: "Wedged between a Dumpster and the back wall of a parking garage beneath the Viaduct, she had been raped, then stabbed repeatedly with a broken bottle."[149] If ghosts signal an attempt to recover history, then Beautiful Mary as ghost is a reminder of her violent death, and she evokes a long history of violence against Indigenous women. This violence reenacts historical encounters between Native women's bodies and settlers, which critics like Van Styvendale have similarly noted about the imagined birth scene in the first chapter—the image of a white doctor delivering baby John.[150] Andrea Smith has written extensively about sexual violence as a tool of genocide, and the recent Missing and Murdered Indigenous Women (MMIW) movement is evidence of collective activism around the colonial violence being done to First Nations women.[151] Beautiful Mary's name calls attention to how her body is regarded, coveted, and abused by white men (even Wilson, who has a sexual encounter with her), and while the city seemingly discards her (literally, as trash), Alexie demonstrates how she has also left a mark on the white men who knew her (namely, Wilson). He remembers that she called him a name in her tribal language (a language unknown to the reader, as we never know her tribal affiliation): "She told him that it meant First Son, but it actually meant Shadow."[152] There is power in this (mis)naming: while Wilson wants the name to signify one small piece of Indigeneity that he so strongly desires, something that he can own, Mary uses language to *exclude* him and his erotic gaze from the urban tribe. She renders him "Shadow," which I read as ineffectual nuisance, as representational imitation, as phantom. While Wilson may register as metaphorical ghost, Mary is very much a real ghost in this story. Raped and brutally murdered, Mary continues to haunt the urban landscape.

In the narratives of homelessness, Seattle represents promise—the promise of escape, of fortune, of education, of employment—but the city can be an uncaring, hostile, and potentially violent place to call home. King's story begins like Marie's and Reggie's. Like many other urban Indians, they left the reservation for school: "King had left the reservation in 1980 to attend college and become a teacher. He had made it through one semester before he ran out of money. Too ashamed to return to the reservation, he'd worked on a fishing boat for a few years, then was struck by a hit-and-run driver while on shore leave. Too injured to work, without access to disability or workers' compensation, King had been homeless for most of the last ten years."[153] Without a support system in the city, King had to manage on his own, which he does until an unfortunate accident and injury. His story demonstrates how precarious urban life can be, that it is really very easy to become homeless, and that safety structures to protect workers are not as comprehensive as we have been led to believe. There is also the stigma of failing in the "white world" and a reluctance to return to the reservation when in need. In a poignant scene, we see how King becomes a ghost of himself in the city. He makes a phone call to the reservation, the Confederated Salish and Kootenai Tribes of the Flathead Nation in Montana, during a phone company promotion in Occidental Park, saying that he's "thinking about coming back home, you know?"[154] But King's desire is thwarted: "His telephone call had been a failure. He had talked to a stranger, a young boy, maybe fourteen. An Indian stranger, but still a stranger. King had dialed that number hoping to hear his sister on the other end of the line, but it was some other Indian. It was a number on the Flathead Reservation, King's rez, but it wasn't his family's number. A Flathead boy answered but did not know if any of King's relatives still lived on the reservation. Maybe all of his relatives had left. Disappeared, or died."[155] His connection to his home reservation is figuratively and literally lost. Alexie demonstrates that life on the reservation is not static and that the tribe continues, minus King. King becomes a ghost on the reservation when he leaves for college, and then he becomes one of Seattle's ghosts when he becomes homeless.[156] Jack Wilson, who is witness to the phone call, physically describes King as ageless: "Dressed in dirty clothes, shoes taped together, broken veins and deep creases crossing his face. The Indian might have been twenty or fifty."[157] This kind of ambiguity recalls the description of the Yakamas in Alexie's prose poem "Freaks" who appear to be two hundred years old, as I discussed at the opening of this chapter. Alexie aligns King (ironically named) with the Yakamas (and with the Aleuts in "What You Pawn" who are waiting for their boat to return).

The fishing industry is a critical element in Seattle's place-story, and it plays an important role in Cornelius and Zera's story, one of the most clearly developed in the novel. The two had

> been together for five years and had spent half of that time homeless. The other half, they'd shared and been evicted from three apartments. Money and jobs were seasonal. Cornelius, a Makah Indian, was a deep-sea fisherman, a job that would have kept him away for months at a time, and he just didn't want to leave Zera, a Puyallup. She was manic-depressive and simply couldn't take care of herself. So Cornelius worked as a manual laborer, losing the job whenever Zera showed up and terrorized customers and managers, or when he missed work to search for her after her latest disappearance. She'd been hospitalized three times and Cornelius had always missed her so much he couldn't sleep.[158]

First, their story is an economic one: seasonal labor, evictions, housing issues. Fishing connects Cornelius's story to King's—and to a larger history of Indigenous fishing on the Northwest Coast. Makahs are renowned for their fishing prowess, particularly for their whale hunting, which is protected by the Treaty of Neah Bay (1855). Just one year before Alexie's novel was published, Makahs declared their intention to resume whale hunting after a seventy-year hiatus, and much controversy ensued.[159] Alexie conjures this very public debate and the history of fishing rights and the 1970s "fish-ins"—Indigenous activism in this region. That neither man can no longer earn a living from fishing also suggests an irony: in a place where Indigenous peoples have long subsisted on fishing, both for consumption and, in later years, as commodity in a settler economy, they cannot participate in this traditional practice. Indeed, commercial fishing, hinted at in Cornelius's story, has replaced smaller fishing operations and individual peddlers in recent years. Suffice it to say that the industry may depend on the labor and skill of Indigenous fishermen, but it owes them nothing. King is injured but has no access to disability coverage; Cornelius cannot take family leave to take care of Zera. And this leads to a second observation: lack of medical and social services for Zera is in large part responsible for the couple's homelessness. The reduction of mental health facilities and deinstitutionalization, particularly in the 1980s, is often linked to the rise of homelessness.[160] Third, it is poignant and very human that Alexie portrays the relationship between Cornelius and Zera, that despite their economic situation, love and commitment are still possible.

Cornelius and Zera's story evokes other Indigenous place-stories as well. Alexie writes that they "had spent a year of nights" in "a doorway across the street from a Blockbuster Video on lower Queen Anne Hill."[161] Queen Anne Hill is the highest point in the city, named after the architectural style of the historic mansions built there.[162] The area is traditional Duwamish land, called baba'kwoh. In 1853 David Denny claimed 320 acres of land here and renamed it Potlatch Meadows. Today Queen Anne Hill has a higher per capita income than much of Seattle. It is not a place where many homeless people gather. And so Cornelius and Zera navigate and inhabit a space with a marked Indigenous past, and they have developed tactics for survival: "He'd always leave the empty thermos at the back door of the nearby McDonald's, and Doug, the redheaded night manager, would secretly fill it again with leftover coffee. Small kindnesses. Cornelius also had a loaf of bread he'd bought with money he'd made selling *Real Change*, the newspaper written and distributed by the homeless."[163] Cornelius procures bread and coffee, he sells newspapers and participates in the economic activity in this neighborhood. Their tactics reveal a place knowledge: a safe doorway, a back door that yields free coffee, lucrative positionalities for selling a newspaper (which means knowing patterns of travel and movement of both tourists and generous locals). When their attackers violate the safety of this space, Cornelius offers to leave, while Zera springs to action and attacks Aaron Rogers, who shouts, "Go back to where you belong, man!" and "Get the fuck out of our country, man!"[164] Here Alexie calls upon us to once again consider the irony of homeless Indians. Aaron reasserts Reggie's belief that Seattle is a city of white men and adds that Indians should remain in Indian Country—in other words, contained. However, Truck Schultz argues the opposite, that nonassimilation was the problem: "We allowed them to remain separate. In fact, we encouraged their separation from the mainstream values and culture in this country."[165] As this debate about the "place" of Indians is occurring, Alexie inserts a reference to *Planet of the Apes*, with these two characters, Cornelius and Zera (or Zira in the book and film), both chimpanzee scientists who are ultimately murdered in the third film, *Escape from the Planet of the Apes*. Alexie simultaneously demonstrates Cornelius and Zera's superiority over the "humans" with their race war, while he asks us to contemplate with him settler colonialism(s) and the struggle for power in the urban space.

The pinnacle of the debate over land tenure and homelessness comes from Carlotta Lott, a Duwamish woman, in her encounter with John Smith. Seattle, of course, is on Duwamish land, as Carlotta tells John: "All these white people think I'm homeless. But I ain't homeless. I'm Duwamish Indian. You see all this land around here. . . . All of this, the city, the water, the mountains, it's all Duwamish land. Has been for thousands of years. I belong here, cousin. I'm the landlady."[166] The idea of being homeless within her tribe's ancestral geography is impossible to her. In other words, being homeless refers less to the lack of house than it does to being landless, with no homeland—even if it is now "occupied" territory. As Renée Bergland has argued about American ghost stories, "The land is haunted because it is stolen."[167] Of course, at the heart of it, even though Seattle is Duwamish territory, the Duwamish are a landless tribe. Alexie conjures Carlotta as one of the original inhabitants of this site, eliciting with her all of the attendant debates regarding the Duwamish. I would even propose that Carlotta is a modern-day Princess Angeline, refusing to leave ceded territory. Although Chief Seattle signed the Treaty of Point Elliott on behalf of the Suquamish and the Duwamish (his Suquamish father had married Chief Seattle's Duwamish mother), most Duwamish people (like Angeline) refused to relocate to the Port Madison Indian Reservation with the Suquamish because it was in Suquamish territory. The Duwamish wanted their own reservation land, where the Black and Cedar Rivers merged, in exchange for fifty-four thousand ceded acres. After their longhouses were burned by the United States Army, many Duwamish moved to Ballast Island, where they lived in canvas tents from approximately 1885 to 1915. This place no longer exists—the Black

River has disappeared from the landscape—and the Duwamish are not a federally recognized tribe, though some tribal members live at Port Madison or Tulalip. Carlotta makes a particularly poignant spatial claim in the novel, given the Duwamish's legal struggles to regain their traditional territories throughout the twentieth century.[168] The Duwamish legally ceased to exist, though throughout the 1970s, under the leadership of Cecille Hansen (née Maxwell), they were able to garner public attention and outrage following the destruction of an archaeological site at Basketry Hat—a time frame that coincides with the beginning of the novel. Coll Thrush argues that the Duwamish were able to renarrativize Seattle's urban history in the wake of Hansen's activism.[169] As Carlotta demonstrates, Seattle has a difficult time reconciling its Indigenous past and present.

In Carlotta's encounter with John, she proposes that with a time machine, they might be able to travel back to the moment of contact and stop colonization. She gives him a small knife (a red herring in the murder mystery) and proclaims that the time machine is in her empty hand. John looks at it and nods in understanding. "Good magic, bad magic, it's all the same," she says.[170] I propose that we read this moment as a call for intertribal coalition—a call to take up arms in revolution. While it may be difficult to take this situation seriously, coming from a ranting old lady in a wheelchair and spoken to a potentially schizophrenic and/or violent man, when we read it in conjunction with the novel's suggestion that a kind of apocalyptic Ghost Dance is occurring, we just might surmise that Carlotta Lott is the one orchestrating, the one conjuring all of these ghosts (both real and metaphoric) to reclaim the city of Seattle.[171] Alexie has named her aptly: Carlotta is the Italian form of Charlotte, the female version of Charles, which in its Germanic form means "warrior." Likewise, Alexie describes the homeless as "a ragtag bunch of homeless warriors in soiled clothes and useless shoes" when the race war begins.[172] The race war becomes a way of reenacting conflict—and when the homeless become easy targets for violence, they fight back: "The Indians were weak from malnutrition and various diseases, but they kicked, scratched, and slapped with a collective rage. John wondered how those Indians could still fight after all they had been through. He had seen Indians like that before, sleeping in doorways, on heating vents outside city hall, in cardboard condominiums."[173] We might attribute this rage to their homelessness and its attendant conditions. Alexie here places the Indigenous homeless "outside city hall" as literally a portrait or vignette of colonial dispossession. Normally invisible, here they become visible. But as he does so, they are not merely victims; they are actors in a revolution. The homeless ghosts are rescripted and empowered. The eponymous killer, then, is the expression of collective memory, as an unnamed homeless Indian in a wheelchair proclaims: "This Indian Killer, you see, he's got Crazy Horse's magic. He's got Chief Joseph's brains. He's got Geronimo's heart. He's got Wovoka's vision. He's all those badass Indians rolled up into one."[174] This is not the novel's only reference to the Ghost Dance. As I suggested earlier, Marie makes the connection between the killer and the Ghost Dance in a conversation with Dr. Mather: "So maybe this Indian Killer is a product of the Ghost Dance. Maybe ten Indians are Ghost Dancing. Maybe a hundred. It's just a theory. How many Indians would have to dance to create the Indian Killer? A thousand? Ten thousand? Maybe this is how the Ghost Dance works."[175]

The historical Ghost Dance was meant to conjure ancestors, which Alexie does symbolically when he puts his novel in conversation with some quintessential Native novels from the Renaissance era, for this earlier generation of authors also contemplated ideas about place and alienation. When Daniel Smith takes to the streets in search of his son, he instead encounters a group of homeless Indians who tell him they know Loney, Abel, and Tayo, characters famously from James Welch's *The Death of Jim Loney*, Momaday's *House Made of Dawn*, and Silko's *Ceremony*, respectively.[176] While not physically homeless, Loney, Abel, and Tayo, like Alexie's homeless characters, exist in the margins of their home communities and have all experienced off-reservation life.[177] Indeed, as I discussed in this book's introduction, *House Made of Dawn* and *Ceremony* presented some of the earliest versions of fictional urban Indians. Alexie's allusion to these characters puts his own novel in conversation with these earlier books, and he maps his homeless stories onto the canon of twentieth-century American Indian literature, but he does so ironically. These downtrodden historical characters are what Daniel Smith expects to find, not the community of homeless people with such revolutionary potential. To return to Certeau here: "For to speak of the dead means to deny death and almost to defy it. Therefore speech is said to 'resuscitate' them."[178] The act of speaking their names, then, functions as a kind of summoning of these fictional "warriors," for them to join in the Ghost Dance.

Though Thrush argues that Alexie is participating in the myth of the Vanishing Indian by turning his homeless Indians into ghosts, I believe that he does so to conjure a very specific place-history and that his homeless/ghosts are literally and symbolically empowered in the city space. As Žižek suggests, "The return of the dead is a sign of a disturbance in the symbolic rite, in the process of symbolization; the dead return as collectors of some unpaid symbolic debt."[179] The "unpaid symbolic debt" in this novel is, of course, the land. As I suggested earlier, the focus on homelessness in this novel reveals a contemporary anxiety about place and belonging and land tenure—and Alexie very directly points out the hypocrisy of white, liberal Seattleites, perhaps specifically through his portrayal of Daniel and Olivia Smith, John's parents. Alexie uses the trope of homelessness to map some of the pertinent history of the city of Seattle, and he allows the individual stories of homelessness to function as place-making narratives. The novel remains cognizant that Seattle rests not only on the graves of Duwamish ancestors but on Duwamish land—and, through the character of Carlotta, that the Duwamish are connected to and stake claims in this space. The Ghost Dance in Alexie's novel, to return to the work of Lisa Tatonetti, alludes to "Native survivance in imaginative acts."[180] In *Indian Killer*, the imaginative acts include not only retribution for lost Indigenous lives and stolen Indigenous children but also territorial claims upon the city of Seattle, settled upon hereditary Duwamish land.

In the space of Alexie's novel, the Ghost Dance begins in the city. This suggests that for Alexie this cosmopolitan place is where intertribal politics must begin, this is where "collective rage" about the conditions of urban living can become meaningful.[181] In the final chapter of *Indian Killer*, "A Creation Story," we see the killer in a reservation cemetery, resting on a grave with a headstone, "its inscription illegible."[182] The killer begins to dance and is joined by other Indians, who also begin to dance: "The killer sings and dances for hours, days. Other Indians arrive and quickly learn the same song. A dozen Indians, then hundreds, and more, all learning the same song, the exact dance. The killer dances and will not tire. The killer knows this dance is over five hundred years old."[183] Of course, Wovoka's historical Ghost Dance is not "over five hundred years old," but the colonial moment is. The kind of alliance that Alexie advocates goes back to the moment of trauma, of displacement, to imagine decolonization in the present. The "illegible" text on the headstone signifies what has been lost along the way: languages, messages, stories, histories. As Marie says, the original Ghost Dance was an attempt to make the white men disappear. She tells Dr. Mather, "Don't you see? If the Ghost Dance had worked, you wouldn't be here."[184] If the Ghost Dance had worked, the streets of Seattle would not be filled with homeless Indians. If the Ghost Dance had worked, there would be no city of Seattle.

In American literature, Indian ghosts are often evidence of vanishing, but in *Indian Killer*, homeless ghosts tell place-stories about Seattle, and they are not relegated to the past. The apocalyptic message of the novel is that a renewal of a form of Ghost Dance has occurred—and will continue. If the Ghost Dance movement was a response to the conditions of reservation living, as historians have asserted, then Alexie's literary Ghost Dance is the result of urban living. As he has shown, the city is where homelessness is possible, where the disparity between white privilege and Native dispossession is all the more striking. The novel implicates the city of Seattle for its disenfranchisement of Indigenous peoples, who "haunt" both the novel and the city—not because they are dead, but because as ghosts they are empowered and united in revolution. This, after all, was Chief Seattle's prophecy: "The dead are not altogether powerless."

THE URBAN QUEST

Alexie's proclaimed "favorite story," "What You Pawn I Will Redeem," which first appeared in the *New Yorker* and then in the collection *Ten Little Indians*, has quickly become one of his best known.[185] It was included in a volume of *Best American Short Stories* in 2004, won an O. Henry Prize in 2005, and now appears in both the Bedford and Heath anthologies of American literature, though it has not received much critical attention.[186] If *Indian Killer* paints a broad picture of homelessness in Seattle, "What You Pawn," provides a more magnified view. The story's charming narrator, Jackson Jackson, is a homeless Spokane Indian living in Seattle. The plot spans twenty-four hours, during which Jackson discovers his grandmother's stolen powwow regalia in a pawnshop window and attempts to reclaim it. Jackson recognizes the regalia, a clear symbol of culture writ large, from a photograph he had once seen; in fact, he had never actually seen it. Even so, his insider knowledge of the "one yellow bead" that belies perfection proves that Jackson is telling the truth.[187] Even miles and years from his tribal community, Jackson remains connected in this important way. At the same time, Jackson Jackson is quite a skilled urban tactician. By the story's end, when he has succeeded in his quest to obtain the regalia, Jackson symbolically becomes his grandmother in the story's final line: "I was my grandmother, dancing."[188] In what could very well become a reservation homing story, with this cultural recovery at the end, Alexie has created a very urban quest; in fact, it is the city that makes this quest possible.[189] Jackson participates in the settler economy in his determination to buy back his grandmother's regalia—he needs to raise a thousand dollars while supporting himself and his addictions. In this concise and poignant story, Alexie gives us a day in the life of a homeless Indian, which serves to reclaim the homeless from the realm of absence and pity. While many of the actual homeless Indians in Seattle are ignored, sympathized with, or preyed upon, Alexie not only humanizes this narrator but makes him a hero. Read alongside *Indian Killer*, Jackson's dance at the story's end signifies as another kind of urban Ghost Dance, a performative and political act that claims Seattle's space.

In "What You Pawn," Alexie foregrounds the homeless voice via Jackson's narration. We hear Jackson's back-story in his own words: "One day you have a home and the next you don't, but I'm not going to tell you my particular reasons for being homeless, because it's my secret story, and Indians have to work hard to keep secrets from hungry white folks."[190] This picks up on the concern over the ownership of Native stories and who controls the narrative that Alexie began in *Indian Killer*. While the specifics may be "secret," we do hear the details he wants to reveal: "I grew up in Spokane, moved to Seattle twenty-three years ago for college, flunked out within two semesters, worked various blue- and bluer-collar jobs for many years, married two or three times, fathered two or three kids, and then went crazy. Of course, 'crazy' is not the official definition of my mental problem, but I don't think 'asocial disorder' fits it, either, because that makes me sound like I'm a serial killer or something."[191] Like King, Jackson flunked out of college. This is not Alexie's only indictment of the educational system, which often fails to support Indigenous students.[192] In addition, Jackson hints at work-related issues, relationship troubles, and mental illness. Alexie's lack of specificity here, with Jackson's diagnosis, with the number of times he has been married, the number of children he has, turns him into a kind of trickster. He is simultaneously there and not there, refusing to tell his story and then telling it anyway. There is even some ambiguity in his origins as well: Is he from the city of Spokane or the Spokane Indian Reservation? The two are in close proximity (about an hour's drive apart), but it matters if he grew up on the reservation or off, at least in Alexie's place-world. Or perhaps this is a new challenge to that paradigm. Jackson does identify with his reservation on a couple of occasions. He says, "I'm a Spokane Indian boy, an Interior Salish, and my people have lived within a one-hundred-mile radius of Spokane, Washington, for at least ten thousand years," and there have been "three murders on my reservation in the last hundred years."[193] Readers are compelled to make the assumption that he grew up on the reservation, but Alexie challenges this assumption—being Spokane and being from Spokane or the Spokane reservation are different things, and somehow this vagueness in his story becomes appropriate in the urban space.

The narrative structure of the story—an hour-by-hour record of the day—works as a "day in the life" of a homeless Indian man. This particular day may be ordinary, but, as in all quests, so many extraordinary things occur. Jackson buys lottery tickets (and wins a hundred dollars), sells *Real Change* newspapers, and panhandles. He eats at McDonald's. He drinks: "Thinking hard, we huddled in an alley beneath the Alaska

Way Viaduct and finished off those bottles—one, two, and three."[194] He goes to Big Heart's, an Indian bar that also appears in *Indian Killer*. He kisses Irene, a Duwamish woman, in the bathroom. He also passes out on the railroad tracks and is rescued by a policeman. His friends, "my teammates, my defenders, and my posse," Rose of Sharon and Junior, both disappear.[195] As Jackson later learns, Rose of Sharon, a Yakama, "hitchhiked back to Toppenish and was living with her sister on the reservation."[196] And Junior, a Colville, "had hitchhiked down to Portland, Oregon, and died of exposure in an alley behind the Hilton Hotel."[197] The loss of Jackson's "crew" may be both ordinary and extraordinary, ordinary for homeless Indians to simply vanish, extraordinary for them to vanish on the day of Jackson's quest. But the "tribe" of homeless Indians seems to be constantly in flux and nomadic. "Indians are everywhere," Jackson tells the pawnshop broker.[198] In other words, wherever Junior and Rose of Sharon go, they will find other Indians—and Jackson will find new friends, a new posse of homeless Indians.

The spatial practice in this story is similar to that of *Indian Killer*, and we experience Seattle mostly on foot, right along with Jackson. Jackson buys lottery tickets at a Korean grocery store in Pioneer Park, then goes to Occidental Park to scratch them. Jackson and his posse panhandle at Pike Place Market, and he finds the pawnshop nearby. He goes to the wharf, where he encounters some Aleuts. He takes them to Mother's Kitchen, "a greasy diner in the International District."[199] He goes to the *Real Change* office, not far from Occidental Park, then goes back to the wharf: "I stood near the Bainbridge Island Terminal and tried to sell papers to business commuters walking onto the ferry."[200] Big Heart's is located in South Downtown. Alexie writes, "It used to be way up on Aurora Avenue, but a crazy Lummi Indian burned that one down, and the owners moved to the new location, a few blocks south of Safeco Field."[201] This has happened since the time of *Indian Killer*, in which Big Heart's is on 100th or 110th and Aurora. Jackson awakes the next morning on the railroad tracks near the docks. With Officer Williams, he drives "through downtown," where the "missions and shelters" are located.[202] The urban landscape is named and well traveled, and Jackson demonstrates a familiarity with its geography—that is, until he tries to locate the pawnshop at the end of the story: "I looked for the pawnshop and couldn't find it. I swear it wasn't located in the place where it had been before. I walked twenty or thirty blocks looking for the pawnshop, turned corners and bisected intersections, looked up its name in the phone books, and asked people walking past me if they'd ever heard of it. But that pawnshop seemed to have sailed away from me like a ghost ship."[203] Of course, there's a mythical quality here—the disappearing pawnshop. The marine metaphor is an interesting one, given Seattle's location, waterways, and port identity. Jackson navigates these spaces and does eventually find the pawnshop again. He is "an effective homeless man," he says.[204] He negotiates the city space, and his movement claims all of these geographies.

The pawnshop in particular is a critical locale in this story. Pawnshops usually exist in economically disadvantaged urban neighborhoods, and they very literally prey on the poor, who are in desperate need of cash and are forced to part with those things that may hold market value. These items are used as collateral to secure monetary loans that must be paid back within a certain time frame or else the property will be sold. The practice has existed worldwide for centuries, and it reportedly came to the Americas during the colonial period.[205] It has even been rumored that Christopher Columbus's voyage was financed by the pawning of jewels. In Alexie's story, this idea of *pawning*, with all of its connotations, frames the entire story—is, indeed, a part of the story's title. And in this story, it is a highly regarded item of cultural patrimony (or matrimony, in this case) that has been pawned—by whom, Jackson Jackson cannot know, for the pawnbroker does not know or will not say. The item itself signifies the "worth" of Indian cultures on the market and suggests that the person who pawned it was both desperate and fully cognizant of the colonial desire for such objects. There is a way in which "pawn" takes advantage of the Indigenous practice of "trade"—here, cash is what is being offered in trade. This isn't Alexie's first consideration of pawning: in an early Alexie poem entitled "Pawn Shop," the narrator goes to an Indian bar but finds that all of the patrons have "disappeared."[206] Searching for them, he goes to a pawnshop, where he finds "a single heart beating under glass."[207] He knows "who it used to belong to, I know all of them." Pawning one's heart, in Alexie's iteration, is the cost of being a city Indian. I am reminded of another representation of the pawnshop, in Randy Redroad's film *133 Skyway* (2006), which follows Hartley, an urban street musician, as he tries to reclaim his guitar from a pawnshop in Toronto.[208] The pawnbroker in all of these texts represents the settler economy, with cash given for valuable objects, not unlike the cash payments for lands in treaty settlements. Thus, *pawn* also serves as a metaphor for displacement and perhaps as an analogue for treaties.

The Indigenous place-history that gets revealed in this story is no less specific than in *Indian Killer*. Irene Muse, like Carlotta Lott, is Duwamish, a reminder of the rightful owners of Seattle, even though their tribal recognition claim was denied in 1996.[209] But while the naming of Carlotta signifies "warrior," Irene's connotes "peace," which mirrors the Indigenous-colonial encounters in this text. The reference to Bainbridge Island conjures the Suquamish, who continued to live on the island into the twentieth century. Rose of Sharon and Junior, Yakama and Colville, respectively, represent the extended networks of tribal peoples in what is now Washington State. Jackson comments that the Colvilles are a confederation of tribes, and therefore *Colville* is not a reasonable tribal identity, but the same could be said about the Yakamas, which are now also a confederation of eleven identifiable tribes.[210] Alexie names Toppenish, which is the Yakamas' name for themselves, and spells *Yakama* in its newer formulation, changed from *Yakima* in the 1990s in order to more closely represent pronunciation in their language.[211] As I suggested in the previous section, the three Aleuts Jackson meets at the wharf are reminiscent of the three men of "Freaks": "Most of the homeless Indians in Seattle come from Alaska. One by one, each of them hopped a big working boat in Anchorage or Barrow or Juneau, fished his way south to Seattle, jumped off the boat with a pocketful of cash to party hard at one of the highly sacred and traditional Indian bars, went broke and broker, and has been trying to find his way back to the boat and the frozen North ever since."[212] Alexie's homeless characters are not disproportionately Aleuts, despite this history, though Alaska Natives get mapped into the larger Indigenous network here as well—the borders are rendered obsolete. Like Cornelius and King in *Indian Killer*, the Aleuts, who do not get named any more specifically than this, are fishermen, blue-collar workers in a profession that does not support them. The Aleuts might also be a metaphor for the Tlingit *Chief-of-All-Women* totem pole stolen from Alaska and brought to Seattle in 1899.[213] As Thrush has shown, Alaska Native cultures often historically displaced Puget Sound ones as Seattle created its place-story. In other words, as Seattle formulated its narrative about itself, it adopted an Indigenous identity that was based on Alaskan peoples and communities.

What also gets revealed in this history is movement: back and forth from the city to Indian Country, from Alaska to Seattle. There is a kind of reverse migration that gets suggested here: as settlers traveled through Seattle on their way to the Yukon during the gold rush, Native Alaskans were moving to places like Seattle to seek work. This mobility gets read as disappearance from the urban setting, and, as they do in *Indian Killer*, these disappearances turn these characters into ghosts. Rose of Sharon goes to Toppenish, Junior dies of exposure in Portland, and the Aleuts most likely drown: "I later heard that the Aleuts had waded into the saltwater near Dock 47 and disappeared. Some Indians said the Aleuts walked on the water and headed north. Other Indians saw the Aleuts drown."[214] The story of what happened to the Aleuts becomes mythical, even biblical, and their story is emplaced in a very specific geographic location, Dock 47, even if what happens is not entirely known.[215] All of these characters register as ghosts, if not in the present of the story, then sometime in the future. And it is a desire to travel, to return to a home place, that is the cause of the ghosting. The Aleuts, for example, were "lonely for the cold and snow."[216] Thus, in this story, Alexie formulates a new theory about homeless ghosts. Relocation or dislocation can cause melancholia, but it is nostalgia and longing that lead to spectralization.

It is precisely Jackson's nostalgia and longing for his lost grandmother, a symbol for his tribe and culture, that turns him into a ghost. As I have already suggested, it is in the act of recovery, when Jackson takes possession of his grandmother's powwow regalia, that he physically becomes his grandmother. In that moment, the traffic stops, the city stops to watch him dance. This is certainly another kind of Ghost Dance, and the metaphor here is a variance.[217] If in *Indian Killer* the Ghost Dance was a communal and political act, in this story it is functioning on a more individual level—ghosts do have voice and power in this scenario as well. Participating in a personal Ghost Dance allows Jackson to reconnect with family and tribe without physically traveling to the Spokane reservation. That Jackson is able to reclaim the regalia—in the city, from a pawnshop—certainly signals a shift in Alexie's thinking about the urban space from his earlier fundamentalism about the absolute destructiveness of the city.

In his earlier work, Alexie portrayed the reservation space as magical, but in "What You Pawn," there is magic in the city space as well.[218] Certainly the disappearing/reappearing pawnshop "ghost ship" is intended to be magical. One might even argue that the kindness of strangers is also magical: Jackson is aided by a number of non-Indians in his quest here. For example, Jackson is "saved" from the railroad tracks by a white policeman, Officer Williams, whom Jackson calls "a good cop."[219] Williams gives Jackson thirty dollars for his quest and lets him avoid detox. Then there is "Big Boss" at the *Real Change* office, who gives Jackson fifty newspapers "for free."[220] And finally, there is the pawnbroker, who sets the price for the regalia at $999 at the beginning of the story, then sells it to Jackson for $5 at the end. Jackson says, "Do you know how many good men live in this world? Too many to count!"[221] The triumvirate of white men is certainly different from the one in *Indian Killer*, Aaron and company, who brutally attack homeless Indians. Jackson also considers Kay, the Korean grocery store cashier, to be family. When he wins a hundred dollars, he gives her a twenty-dollar bill and says, "It's an Indian thing. When you win, you're supposed to share with your family."[222] Jackson makes up his own urban family, which becomes part of the magic of city life.

Jackson's quest is a very urban quest, one that relies upon knowledge of the city space and reveals its Indigenous past. While the grandmother to some degree represents the reservation and/or some kind of cultural past, she also turns out to be a bit more cosmopolitan: she certainly traveled to many powwows, and she was a nurse stationed in Australia during the

Second World War. Jackson recalls her story about meeting a Maori soldier and his joke about how "brown people are killing other brown people so white people will remain free."[223] This transnational moment—what Chadwick Allen would call a "trans-indigenous" moment—contradicts any kind of static association between her and the reservation. It suggests, as do the other texts in this study, that place-histories are more complicated than we assume—and, of course, that Indians are already travelers and cosmopolitans. We have seen other networks of movement in this story: Aleuts fishing their way from Alaska, Junior's journey to Portland, Rose of Sharon's return to Toppenish, now Jackson's grandmother's travels on the powwow circuit and overseas. Alexie unmoors his Indigenous characters from the reservation in this story—indeed, in this entire short story collection—in ways not always destructive or traumatic. The "disappearing" that occurs appears to be more of a result of nostalgia, but ghosting is again simultaneously empowering and transformative. If the Ghost Dance has revolutionary potential, then Jackson's dance seems to simultaneously claim an urban presence and a tribal past.

JUSTICE AND THE GHOST DANCE

Flight appeared nearly simultaneously with *The Absolutely True Diary of a Part-Time Indian*, Alexie's first young adult novel.[224] Like *True Diary*, *Flight* has the look and feel of YA fiction: it features a teenage protagonist narrator, the plot follows the arc of a bildungsroman, it is short in length, and the font size is rather large.[225] In interviews, Alexie repeatedly makes the distinction between the two; the difference is in the violence, he says. This is contemporary Alexie at his best—gritty, raw, acerbic. While *True Diary* has been banned by many schools because of a conversation young male characters have about masturbation (in a library!), *Flight* puts the reader front and center at a genital mutilation following Custer's Last Stand, a point-blank assassination in a fictionalized version of Wounded Knee II, a suicidal plane crash into Lake Michigan, and so on as fifteen-year-old Zits travels in both time and space in a way that is reminiscent of the television series *Quantum Leap*, though Alexie says that the time travel came directly from *Slaughterhouse Five*.[226] Zits retains his own consciousness during what Dean Rader has called "temporal displacements" while he inhabits the bodies of an FBI agent, an Irish Indian tracker, a pilot, a chief's young son, and a homeless man.[227] Zits is sometimes able to impose his will on his hosts, though he is unable to alter seemingly preordained events. In his final episode of time travel, Zits is transported into his homeless alcoholic father's body on the streets of Tacoma. He comes face-to-face with a rat, vomits blood, assaults two white tourists, and is pummeled by a passer-by before he realizes whose body he inhabits. Following the father episode, Zits returns to the present of the novel, in which he is or is not shooting people in a crowded bank. A foster child and a juvenile delinquent, Zits describes himself as homeless multiple times in the novel—and I would argue that for all intents and purposes, none of his foster families have provided him with a *home*. While there are many parallels between Zits and John Smith from *Indian Killer* (both have unidentified Native ancestry, for example, and they have both been failed by ICWA, the Indian Child Welfare Act), there are also some really important differences.[228] First, Zits "discovers" his father during the course of the novel; second, he is happily "placed" in a white foster family who intends to adopt him "permanently" at the end of the novel. Whereas John Smith commits suicide, Zits is redeemed by Alexie, and this certainly signals a shift in his thinking.[229]

Like *Indian Killer* and "What You Pawn," *Flight* invokes the Ghost Dance. In an early scene, Zits has a conversation specifically about the historic Ghost Dance with Justice, a self-named white boy he meets in lock-up. After Zits teaches Justice about the movement and its implications, Justice suggests that Zits should perform a Ghost Dance. Zits explains that "you need all Indians to do it" and that he does not want all white people to disappear, just the "evil foster families."[230] And even though Zits seemingly refuses, Alexie constructs another textual kind of Ghost Dance in this novel via rebellion (if we read Zits's bank shooting as rebellious act) and time travel (because traveling back in time invariably conjures actual ghosts). When Zits finally admits his belief in the power of the Ghost Dance, Justice says, "Now you can dance. . . . Now you have the power."[231] There are a number of allusions to the Ghost Dance in the bank scene in particular. In the bank, we see Zits say "a little prayer and dance through the lobby."[232] When a bank patron tells Zits that he is not real, he thinks, "Maybe all of us are ghosts," and wonders, "Can a ghost kill another ghost?"[233] As Zits begins shooting, he is himself shot by a bank guard in "the back of the head," and, as he says, "I die before I hit the floor."[234] This scene invokes Wounded Knee: the dancing, the rebellion, the public performativity, the gunfire and carnage that result. But this is also a modern Ghost Dance, located in downtown Seattle in a bank, a symbol of capitalism and greed and inequity. The rage that we see in Zits, Alexie seems to be saying, may be latent, but it is very accessible and incitable, given the right circumstances and historical knowledge.

If we take Alexie at a literal level and read Zits as ghost, which may explain his ability to time travel, the novel becomes a kind of Indigenous *Christmas Carol*, as each episode and historical moment Zits visits serves to teach him in some way.[235] Certainly the underlying message of all of them is something about the dangers of tribalism, particularly the potential for violence, and Zits learns "real" history, beyond what he has gleaned from watching the History Channel.[236] He is "transported" from the city space into these other historical spaces, some of them in what we would consider to be Indian Country. He "becomes" an FBI agent during the IRON siege in Red River, Idaho, in the early 1970s (the fictionalized version of the AIM siege at Wounded Knee, South Dakota); a voiceless young boy who witnesses Custer's Last Stand; an Irish Indian tracker named Gus who has a change of heart; Jimmy, a pilot who unknowingly trained a terrorist how to fly a plane; and lastly, then, his homeless father. In the first episode, as Hank Storm, Zits learns that his "heroes" were not always respectable, humane individuals and that history is more complicated than he realized. As a young boy whose vocal cords had been cut by soldiers, Zits witnesses the utter brutality of war and learns about the kind of violent retaliation that Indigenous peoples are/were capable of. As Gus, he experiences the effects of old age and acts of possible kindness during a violent encounter as Gus (seemingly under Zits's power) "saves" Bow Boy and Small Saint, two young survivors of an attack. Jimmy the pilot is haunted by his actions and by Abbad, the terrorist who was once his friend. Zits learns about betrayals—just as Jimmy is betrayed, he is also betrayer as he cheats on his wife. From his father, Zits learns about generational violence and the reasons why his father abandoned him. Of course, all of these stories are ghost stories. As ghost, Zits inhabits the bodies of ghosts (the boy, Gus, and Jimmy are actual ghosts; Hank Storm and his father are metaphorically so). This combination of historical moments, seemingly disparate, deromanticizes the past and forces the reader to view these events in tandem, all related, all important. As Boyd and Thrush have argued, the remembering is done through ghost stories; ghosts are anchors of history, self, and community.[237] These anchors are all filtered through Zits's consciousness—an urban adolescent consciousness—and we see what the past can teach us.

And so in a novel that is about violence and reconciliation and historical trauma, how do we read the homeless father episode? Why does Alexie include it? And why is it the one that propels Zits back into the present, where, presumably, in an alternate reality, he survives the bank shooting? Susan Bernardin argues that "Zits's final 'landing' into his estranged father's homeless body extends the novel's lessons both outward and inward, both globally and locally. With each agonizing scene of instruction in *Flight*, readers are compelled to revisit an entangled national story in all of its irreparable complexities."[238] The "entangled national story" is literally embodied by Zits, and while these histories get mapped onto his story, Zits cannot physically be in two places simultaneously. In fact, when Zits goes to the police to report himself, they discover a "blip" on the bank security footage. Zits was there, and he disappeared before the bullet hit him. Zits is saved from his own violent actions by the knowledge that he has gained through his travels. While in his father's body, Zits has access to his father's memory—even though his host body does not want to remember Zits's birth and subsequent abandonment. While we never learn his father's precise reasons for being homeless, we do learn about his difficult childhood. In this memory, we see Zits's father as a child, enduring abuse from his father, who thinks him worthless because he is not a good hunter. This abuse takes place at "home"; in other words, *home* is no sanctuary. This memory seemingly occurs "out of place";

there are no place markers, and we can only assume that it is somewhere that hunting is allowed. It is a rural space, perhaps a reservation space, though Alexie does not explicitly describe it as such. Zits's father fears the intergenerational violence implicit in this space, and he literally leaves his son because he does not want to perpetuate the abusive behavior that he has learned. With this knowledge, Zits gains empathy for his father and becomes somewhat reconciled to his Indigenous heritage. Zits does not have imaginary nostalgic longings to return to a reservation (as John Smith had), and his father is no longer the traitor; he is the victim.

It is significant that Zits's father is homeless. Of course, we can read Zits's father's story in tandem with Alexie's other homeless stories, but in *Flight* we are literally transported along with Zits into the body of an alcoholic homeless Indian. This is by far the most corporeal and visceral depiction of homelessness in Alexie's work. We are with Zits when he awakes to find a rat staring at him, he vomits blood in the alley, he smells rotting food in Dumpsters, he provokes fights with tourists Paul and Pam and with a passing businessman. As Zits slowly discovers the details of this life, so do we. At the same time, this is an anonymous life: Zits's father is never named. The bird in the businessman's story is named (strangely, Harry Potter), but the father is not. And yet, nameless, the father demands respect from passers-by, and he decides that the businessman telling him a story would give him that respect. Certainly the story of the accidental bird death is an odd story, but it does function to illuminate a glimpse of this man's life—in stark contrast with the homeless life, to be sure. This juxtaposition is about class consciousness and clashes between homeless Indians and the majority population of Tacoma, a locational shift I will address shortly. This encounter demands that we recognize a common humanity and that we see the connection between these two men, both of whom fail their families. The encounter with Pam and Paul also provides Alexie's critique of Northwest liberalism; they want to help Zits's father, but only so they have a story to tell about how they "saved" him. He says that he hates their "reflexive compassion" (otherwise known as "white guilt") and tells them that "white people did this to Indians."[239] He does not want their empathy and demands their engagement, demands that they look at him and *see* him as a denial of his invisibility. This seems to signify a shift in Alexie's conversation about homelessness: in *Indian Killer*, Marie might have suggested this sentiment, that "white people did this to Indians," and settler colonialism is subtly blamed for this homelessness; in "What You Pawn," Jackson Jackson makes reference to the "degradation of the Noble Savage," and there are various economic factors that lead to his own homelessness; but here, in *Flight*, Zits's father is allowed to articulate what Alexie has been trying to say all along. White people have historically and systemically displaced Indigenous peoples, and all of this homelessness is a direct result.

This novel's registers of movement also signal a shift in Alexie's positioning of city space. First, Zits physically *moves* in the present: he is a foster child who repeatedly runs away from foster homes. Of course, this is one of the multiple meanings of *flight*, "the act of running away."[240] He says, for example, "When I was eleven, I ran away from my first foster home and got drunk in the street with three homeless Indians from Alaska."[241] And in so doing, he *moves* throughout the city: "I walk from street to street, looking for help. I walk past Pike Place Market and Nordstrom's. I walk past Gameworks and the Space Needle. I walk past Lake Washington and Lake Union. I walk for miles. I walk for days. I walk for years."[242] These kinds of place details align the novel with the spatial practice of the previous works I have discussed, but *Flight* differs in two important ways. First, *Flight*'s movement adds movement of time to mobility in space. In other words, Zits's time traveling allows him to cross geographic borders along with temporal ones. "Flight," in this iteration, is a kind of autonomous passing through space to destinations loaded with historical meaning. While John Smith may have traveled through time and space to an imaginary reservation in *Indian Killer*, Zits's travels are embodied: he cannot speak as that little boy, he feels Gus's aging body, he feels his father's physical pain. Also, unlike John, the reservation (real or imagined) is not the locus of his identity. There is a noticeable absence of nostalgia for Indian space, just as there is no migration story for his father—we never know where he came from or how he became homeless.[243] The city space, as it is experienced, constructed, and signified, has the potential to be both a place of origin and a *home*, according to the novel's conclusion.

The second major shift in this novel is geographical, as the setting moves from Seattle to Tacoma. Zits lives in Seattle but finds his father living in Tacoma. Tacoma, reportedly named after the local name for Mount Rainier, Mount Tahoma, has its own Indigenous history. The city, just thirty miles from Seattle, is situated on Puyallup ancestral lands, ceded in the Medicine Creek Treaty of 1854. The Puyallups, unlike the Duwamish of Seattle, now have a reservation space in close proximity to the city. This makes Tacoma a very different space—and an alternate reality in terms of its Native past and present.[244] At the same time, Alexie demonstrates that, of course, Indigenous homelessness does not just exist in Seattle and that every settler colonial city has displaced its Native populations. In other words, this geographic shift that happens in *Flight* suggests, through its larger scope, that this displacement occurs on a national scale.

And so, in *Flight*, Alexie conjures historical and contemporary ghosts, aligns Seattle/Tacoma history with other more broadly known Indigenous histories, and inscribes Native peoples into the urban present. As he did in *Indian Killer*, Alexie demonstrates that the urban space is simultaneously a locus of colonial encounter and one with unlimited potential. Zits's father acts as a counterbalance to this narrative, however. While Zits may have found a home, his father's homelessness is never reconciled. Becoming his father, experiencing his displacement and abjection and pain, is what seems to save Zits in the end. Zits "returns" from this episode to discover that the bank shooting was a blip on the radar and that he has found a home with a fireman's family.[245] Unlike John Smith's adoptive parents, described as white in every way, Zits's new foster mother is potentially Indigenous, as hinted by her "big cheekbones."[246] "I wonder if she's a little bit Indian," Zits says. Her name is Mary, she's a nurse, and her first course of action is to heal Zits's zits, to make him visible again as Michael. He is a new urban Indian, historically aware and transformed by this history, and this is a new kind of Ghost Dance. In this narrative of home and homemaking, Zits's Ghost Dance ends literally in the hands of an Indigenous woman, a healer, in this city of ghosts.

In the 1970s and 1980s, Yuchi (Creek) artist and photographer Richard Ray Whitman created a series of photographs called *Street Chiefs*, thirty-six black-and-white images of homeless Indians on Skid Row in Oklahoma City.[247] The photos are "unromantic," writes W. Jackson Rushing III in the catalog for *Green Acres: Neo-colonialism in the U.S.*, a show at the Washington University Museum of Art in 1992 that included some of Whitman's photographs. Whitman intended the images to indict the histories of dislocation and relocation that led to such homelessness in Oklahoma. He befriended his subjects, including those in *Alley Allies*, a Choctaw man and a Chickasaw man who could speak to one another in their own language.[248] They are "allies" as well, according to Whitman, because they navigate the streets together and protect each other. *Street Chiefs*, which calls attention to lineage and the anonymity of "chief" as epithet, simultaneously humanizes the homeless and bears witness to dislocation in the present. In fact, these portraits convey a compassionate realism and a sense of familiarity with the subjects—like the Tsinhnah-jinnie image I discussed in chapter 1, Whitman seeks to counter Edward Curtis's distant and documentary photographs. And while Whitman's images were not taken in Seattle, where Curtis got his start, they might very well accompany and illustrate Alexie's texts. The images are human-izing and gritty and unflinching. Both Whitman and Alexie document the stark consequences of settler colonialism and the harshness of life on the streets—and they both are manifestations of what Rader calls "engaged resistance," which he defines as "a strategy of aesthetic activ-ism."[249] Similarly, Lucy Lippard has called Whitman's use of the camera an act of empowerment, that standing behind the camera is an act of resistance.[250] Whitman intended the photographs to be "political advo-cacy," to make the homeless visible.[251] In an interview with Larry Abbott, Whitman stated that the series was meant to illuminate "the idea that America is based upon and built upon displacement, displacement of indigenous people, the host people of this country," and it is remarkably similar to Alexie's project in *Indian Killer*, "What You Pawn," and *Flight*, "the contradiction of being landless in your own land."[252] In other words, "homeless means landless."[253]

FIG 7. *Alley Allies* from *Street Chiefs* series, 1980. Black-and-white photo by Richard Ray Whitman. Copyright Richard Ray Whitman. Used with permission of the artist.

In Alexie's early work, the reservation is critical to Indian identity, and urban life is destructive and impermanent. Like the "heart beating under glass" in "Pawn Shop," in "Gravity," a prose poem from *The Business of Fancydancing*, Alexie writes, "Every Indian has the blood of the tribal memory circling his heart. The Indian, no matter how far he travels away, must come back, repeating, joining the reverse exodus. There are no exemptions, no time to pull off the highway for food, gas, lodging."[254] Certainly, early Alexie is conflicted with the urban/reservation binary and is trapped in "the reservation of my mind." In his more recent work, the city is a more navigable space, where urban Indian warriors, some of them homeless, can maintain tribal identities and become historically aware and empowered. His homeless characters are, like Whitman's subjects, resisters and survivors, but, as Marie says in *Indian Killer*, "dancing and singing were valuable and important. Speaking your tribal language was important. Trees were terrific. But nothing good happens to a person with an empty stomach."[255] Of course, cultural maintenance is secondary to the concerns of poverty and hunger, and Alexie demonstrates that physical survival and cultural survival are interdependent but not necessarily equal.

In a 2003 interview in the *Guardian*, Alexie admitted that he no longer believes what he wrote in *The Lone Ranger and Tonto Fistfight in Heaven* about Indians in the cities: "I was much more fundamental then," he says. In a 2012 interview for the *Daily Beast*, he said, "White folks talk about finding the sacred in the wilderness, and I suppose it's there, but I hear the sacred in 3 a.m. traffic and 747s descending and loud music from the house down the block and the ship horns in the foggy night and the whirr, whirr, whirr of crowds. If people are sacred then the most sacred places are the ones where the most people have gathered." That Alexie finds the sacred in city spaces seems to be a radical transformation for him as an artist. As his representations of cities shift, so too does the concept of *home*. He moves from a "fundamentalist," place-based notion of identity to a retheorization of identity and place that is not tied to a site of origin. In fact, Alexie identifies an essentialist understanding of identity and of place with self-murder (as seen in the case of John Smith), while a reorientation of place as praxis, as social action (enacted using the metaphor of the Ghost Dance, the "gathering" of this declaration), becomes equated with survivance.

Tracing Alexie's thinking about the city via his depictions of homelessness charts an important shift in his views about tribe and nation and belonging. Homelessness in Alexie's work is embodied dispossession: Alexie's homeless Indians are disenfranchised and besieged. They dwell in the periphery—in bars, on the sidewalks, in Pioneer Square, under the viaducts. They have created new tribes out of necessity. Alexie is arguing for Indigenous presence in the city space, and his urban Ghost Dance both asserts this presence and counters any ideas about absence or disappearance. Here I return to Kathleen Brogan, who writes, "Ghost stories bear the message: we exist, we continue, our dead are not dead."[256] Alexie employs the trope of *ghost* to articulate the implications of Chief Seattle's words. Indeed, the ghosts of Chief Seattle's speech are not "powerless"; their very presence and visibility map and make spatial claims in and around the city of Seattle. In his usual trickster-like fashion, Alexie plays with the concepts of ghosts and haunting, the visible and invisible, and, in the end, his homeless ghosts make important claims upon this space. Like the other authors in this study, Alexie engages with the history of dispossession in the urban space and beyond, imagining and asserting an Indigenous presence in the city, mapping and rescripting the urban space, and articulating an urban aesthetic that is mindful of its place-story.

CHAPTER 3

Roots and Routes of the Hub

Always, finally, we re-tell.

—Kimberly M. Blaeser, "Sacred Journey Cycles"

The central figure of Louise Erdrich's *The Antelope Wife* (1998, 2012, and 2016), Sweetheart Calico, the antelope wife herself, comes from myth: stories about an "antelope woman" or "deer woman" are told by many tribal peoples.[1] Erdrich's poem "The Strange People," for example, cites a passage from the 1932 text by Pretty Shield, Medicine Woman of the Crows, which begins, "The antelope are strange people."[2] "They appear and disappear," she continues. The story is a cautionary tale about sexuality: young men become entranced with a deer woman, they cannot see her for what she is, and eventually they descend into madness, forsaking allegiance to their community. Erdrich's antelope woman travels from one man to another and is marked by movement; her existence is dependent upon this motion. Erdrich is not the first contemporary author to employ this figure: in Winona LaDuke's *Last Standing Woman*, Clair has a deer woman sighting; in Joy Harjo's poem "Deer Dancer," she is transformed into a woman entering a bar wearing "a stained red dress with tape on her heels"; Paula Gunn Allen's story "Deer Woman" locates the story in Oklahoma; and Carolyn Dunn's poem "Deer Hunter" relocates the deer woman to California.[3] Deer woman stories are stories of transformation, of crossing, of trading one identity for another. In *The Antelope Wife*, Erdrich uses this figure to articulate old and new migrations, new urban identities, and a relationship to place—in this case, the city of Minneapolis.[4]

In this chapter, I propose that Erdrich's first wholly urban novel reimagines how movement affects both spatiality and Indigeneity.[5] The novel encodes movement and articulates how the circulation of cultural practices and objects demonstrates the continuity of tradition, or, to take a phrase from Dean Rader, the novel "articulate[s] a discourse of survivance."[6] In other words, the city does not diminish Erdrich's characters' ability to survive as Ojibwes.[7] In her famous *New York Times* essay, "Where I Ought to Be: A Writer's Sense of Place," Erdrich writes that even through modern migrations and dislocations, "we cannot abandon our need for reference."[8] The unnamed reservation in *The Antelope Wife*, some two hours north, is a steady point of reference for her urban characters even as they travel to and through city spaces.[9] Unlike Janet Campbell Hale's text, *The Antelope Wife* does not express a violent break with the reservation; instead, the reservation space gets mapped within the network of circulation, in the hub that Renya Ramirez describes.[10] Both cosmopolitan and transnational, Erdrich's novel reformulates ideas about tribalism, citizenship, and belonging in its representation of urban Ojibwes within the hub of Minneapolis. Erdrich's Minneapolis, or Gakahbekong in Ojibwemowin, is not multitribal in the same way that Sherman Alexie's Seattle is.[11] Her fictional urban Indian community is predominantly Ojibwe, presumably from the same reservation and the same extended family. Throughout the novel, Erdrich uncovers and explores her characters' complex histories as she demonstrates the decolonizing power in remembering and recuperating this history. She underscores the continuance of Indian presence in this place, that Indians in the space of Minneapolis are not a new phenomenon. Located within a deeper sense of time, to riff on Wai Chee Dimock's term, Minneapolis is Indian Territory.[12] The urban structures "could all blow off," as Erdrich suggests in this passage: "Gakahbekong. That's the name our old ones call the city, what it means from way back when it started as a trading village. Although driveways and houses, concrete parking garages and business stores cover the city's scape, that same land is hunched underneath. There are times, like now, I get this sense of the temporary. It could all blow off. And yet the sheer land would be left underneath. Sand, rock, the Indian black seashell-bearing earth."[13] Minneapolis is new territory for Erdrich, whose literary enterprise has been built upon her fictional reservation, one that bears a great likeness to the Turtle Mountain Chippewa Reservation in North Dakota.[14] The way that Erdrich constructs this reservation locale, where her series of novels takes place, is often likened to William Faulkner's creation of Yoknapatawpha County. Erdrich's fictional space, unnamed until *The Last Report at Little No Horse* (2001), is similarly mapped and populated by a cast of recurring characters, which includes multiple generations of a handful of reservation families, across and through geographic markers, both real and imagined. The complexity of *The Antelope Wife*, with its shifts between allegory and realism, its many narrators (including a talking dog named Almost Soup), its tangled bloodlines and plots, all of which suggest different kinds of "crossing," elicited unusually tentative responses from reviewers.[15] The same could be said for *Four Souls* (2004), Erdrich's second urban novel, a sequel of sorts to *Tracks* (1988)—and, according to Erdrich, originally part of that novel—which follows Fleur Pillager into Minneapolis in the 1930s.[16] Indeed, critical response to her off-reservation novels suggests that Erdrich's forays into this unfamiliar territory have been met with mainstream reader resistance.[17]

The publication of *The Antelope Wife* eerily followed the tragic death of Erdrich's husband, writer Michael Dorris, just a year prior, and subsequently, early reviews focused on the textual parallels: in the novel, Rozin's estranged husband, Richard Whiteheart Beads, distraught over his wife's love for Frank Shawano, commits suicide.[18] This event does not appear in the revised novel, however. Whiteheart Beads, wanted for environmental crimes and living on the streets of Minneapolis, instead turns himself in to authorities before the novel's end. The new versions of the novel are, in fact, so changed that it seems worthwhile to enumerate some of these differences. Another tragic event from the first version, the accidental death of Deanna, one of the couple's twin girls, has been exorcised. Frank, Rozin's new beau, does not have cancer, and the two do not marry. Erdrich has reordered and reworked many of the chapters, adding some thirty-six pages to the novel. In an interview with the *Paris Review*, Erdrich said, "I always had a feeling it began well and got hijacked."[19] She has increased her use of Ojibwemowin in the novel and changed the spelling of extant words in line with her increasing knowledge of the language—and an increasing number of readers able to appreciate the language due to revitalization efforts, some of which she supports directly via Wiigwaas Press.[20] There is also a shift in point of view: in the 1998 version, a nineteen-year-old Cally (Deanna's sister) narrates several of the chapters, but in the revised versions, the girls are younger, and Cally does not narrate. Several names and genealogies are changed—for example, the grandmothers are Giizis and Noodin, distinguishable from Mary and Zosie, the important ancestral twins. The revision is front-loaded with history: we hear the story of Scranton Roy and his son (not grandson) Augustus in the first two chapters, and Erdrich makes it clearer that Sweetheart Calico is descended from Matilda and Blue Prairie Woman and thus related to the modern-day Roys.[21] I will discuss some of the other divergences in my following discussion along with my interpretation of the changes. My reading hinges in part on Jack Stillinger's theory of "textual instability," also used by Allan Chavkin in his essay on the first two versions of *Love Medicine*. Writing about the poetry of Coleridge, Stillinger suggests that textual instability is "the absence (or lack) of a single correct or best or most authoritative text."[22] In other words, "a work is constituted by all known versions of the work," and critics should, as Chavkin does, consider the multiple versions simultaneously, attentive to the changes the author makes.[23]

Though in many ways divergent, all three versions of the novel begin in the "deep past." Erdrich's incorporation of historical events in *The Antelope Wife/Antelope Woman*, beginning with the Union army's "blue-coat raid" in the first chapter, places this novel within the continuum of Ojibwe deep time, which I will detail briefly here. The Anishinaabeg were relative latecomers to the territory that would become Minnesota, an area already inhabited by other tribes: Dakotas, Cheyenne, and Ho-Chunks (Winnebagos). Their ancestors' migration from the East Coast occurred over a period of five hundred years, according to tribal history, beginning in approximately AD 900, landing them on Madeline Island, Lake Superior (now Wisconsin) in 1395. This migration was precipitated by a series of prophecies, one of which instructed the Ojibwes to migrate westward, to the place where food grows on water—a reference to the wild rice that would become integral to Ojibwe culture. By the time of contact, the Ojibwes were firmly established in the area that would become Minnesota, Michigan, and Wisconsin, extending northward into the Canadian territories of Manitoba, Saskatchewan, Ontario, and Quebec. Prior to reservation settlement, the Ojibwes followed the seasonal round, south in the winter, north in the summer.[24] Contact with other tribes, with fur traders and settlers, and later with the US and Canadian governments makes the Ojibwes more global than we often realize. According to ethnohistorian Harold Hickerson, dealings with the French fur traders catalyzed modern Ojibwe identity—an identity, then, constructed from exchange. The Pillager band of Ojibwes was even known for attempting to collect tolls from westward voyageurs.[25] In many ways, Ojibwe culture is a "culture in motion."[26]

The city of Minneapolis came into being through a series of complex events. Both Ojibwes and Dakotas occupied the region, and indeed it was known as a place where the two peoples met, though the city proper rests on traditional Dakota land. Contact history in Minnesota began in 1541, when Hernando de Soto planted a Spanish flag on the bank of the Mississippi.[27] In 1659 French Canadians Médard Chouart, Sieur Des Groseilliers and Pierre-Esprit Radisson, famous for establishing trade routes through the region, spent the winter in Dakota villages near Mille Lacs, and in 1679 Daniel Greysolon, Sieur du Lhut, also spent a winter among Indians in Mille Lacs and "discovered" the St. Croix River. In 1680 Franciscan priest Louis Hennepin "discovered" the Falls of St. Anthony (the future site of Minneapolis). The first treaty in the region was the 1825 Treaty of Prairie du Chen, which was meant to establish peace between the Dakotas and the Ojibwes (named the Chippewas in the treaty). In 1805, when Lt. Zebulon M. Pike visited the falls to expel British traders who had illegally allied with the Indians, he purchased two tracts of land from the Dakotas. In 1821 the US Army built Fort St. Anthony, later called Fort Snelling, at the mouth of the Minnesota River, the same year a sawmill was built on the west bank of the Mississippi, the first building on the site of Minneapolis.[28] In 1839 a large battle between the Dakotas and the Ojibwes occurred near present-day Minneapolis. The city was incorporated in 1856 after treaties with the Dakotas in 1838 had "cleared" the entire area for settlement. Eventually, Ojibwes were confined to seven reservations in the north (in Minnesota, Bois Forte, Fond du Lac, Grand Portage, Red Lake, Leech Lake, Mille Lacs, and White Earth).[29] Critics have placed the raid at the beginning of the novel during the time of Sioux starvation that led to Little Crow's War in 1862, when perhaps an Ojibwe village was mistakenly attacked.[30] In 1863 the Ojibwes signed a treaty that essentially sold all of their remaining land on the Mississippi and required removal to western Minnesota. This treaty was renegotiated in 1864 to include funds for building on the new reservation land. In 1872 St. Anthony, Minneapolis's first twin city, merged with Minneapolis.

Of course, a number of Ojibwe and Dakota people continued to occupy the Twin Cities after this "clearing," and these populations rose during the world wars. The Indian population in the 1920s, when Fleur goes to St. Paul in *Four Souls*, was less than one thousand.[31] The Meriam Report (1928, also known as *The Problem of Indian Administration*) found that recent arrivals were living in relative poverty, while longtime residents had become part of the middle class.[32] The city had always been a place to trade or get temporary work, as Erdrich makes clear in *The Antelope Wife*. Similarly, in her memoir *Night Flying Woman* (1983), Ojibwe author Ignacia Broker writes about moving to Minneapolis in 1941, when she worked in a defense plant—a reminder that patterns of migration predated the relocation era.[33] Though Erdrich makes references to relocation in the 2009 text, Minneapolis was not an official relocation city—it was too close to reservation lands—but other agencies, such as the St. Paul Resettlement Committee, which funded the relocation of Turtle Mountain Ojibwes, organized relocation efforts of their own.[34] Ojibwe writer David Treuer's novel *The Hiawatha* (1999), published just one year after Erdrich's and also set in Minneapolis, similarly portrays characters directly affected by relocation, a policy that he says "forgot the Indians in the cities."[35] With or without the official mechanism of relocation, the Indian population of Minneapolis grew. By the end of the Second World War, the Native population had risen to six thousand.[36]

In the original version of *The Antelope Wife*, Erdrich depicts characters who move to the city in the 1970s, the height of sociological studies about struggling Indians in urban centers, when the Indian population in Minneapolis had reached ten thousand.[37] Researchers gathered statistics on housing costs, levels of education and employment, where Indians shopped, how non-Indians perceived them.[38] As their studies revealed, Indians had to contend with racism, poverty, alcoholism, homesickness, and the inability to use modern appliances like stoves and telephones.[39] These city-specific reports present a fairly grim picture of what life was like for urban Indians, some relocatees, some veterans, all out of their element. Coupled with newspaper articles that reported the same sentiment—that Indians were outsiders and unable to cope with city life—these reports created the urban Indian narrative, often a narrative of drunkenness and despair. Erdrich's novel acknowledges and attempts to rewrite this narrative: it reproduces the story of the captive Native subject via Sweetheart Calico, on the one hand, but it also weaves her story into the fabric of urban life, juxtaposed as it is with alternate narratives of prosperity and survival.

Minneapolis was a hotbed of urban Indian activism in the 1960s and 1970s, made famous as the birthplace of the American Indian Movement, but as historians like Nancy Shoemaker have argued, Indigenous political organizations existed much earlier in the Twin Cities. Beginning in the 1920s, Minneapolis was home to the American Indian Association and Tepee Order Club, the Twin Cities Chippewa Council, the Minnesota Wigwam Indian Welfare Society, and the Twin Cities Indian Republican Club, the latter three associated with Frederick W. Peake, a White Earth Ojibwe graduate of the Carlisle Indian School.[40] These early associations were largely proassimilationist, though they did advocate for the maintenance of tribal citizenship, which came under fire in the 1930s and 1940s with the congressional proposal that urban Indians would no longer have tribal rights. Amabel Bulin, a Dakota woman married to a Scandinavian man, formed Sah-Kah-Tay ("sunshine" in Ojibwemowin), an all-Indian women's club in the late 1930s, which helped Indian women move from reservations to Minneapolis during the war, then later helped Indians living in the city.[41] Bulin, who in 1944 testified before a congressional committee on the state of urban Indians, was instrumental in the creation of welfare programs for Natives in the Twin Cities.[42] In the 1940s the Ojibway-Dakota Research Society, which originated as the Ojibway Research Society, was formed and began including people from other tribes, essentially making it one of the first intertribal organizations in the Twin Cities.[43] Members from the society later formed the Ojibway Tomahawk Band, which published a newsletter, the *New Tomahawk*.[44] American Indians, Inc., was founded in 1940, and the Upper Midwest Indian Center opened in 1954. Finally, the Minneapolis Indian Center was founded in 1975, right in the heart of the Indian community on Franklin Avenue in the Southside neighborhood called Phillips.

The American Indian Movement (AIM), which started in Minneapolis in 1967 to protest police brutality against urban Indians, was then an extension of these earlier organizations, developed to attend to concerns in this specific location.[45] While AIM started as a local organization, its ideas began to circulate on a national level, leading to many historically famous events: the Trail of Broken Treaties, the occupation of Wounded Knee, the Longest Walk, the Alcatraz occupation, and numerous fish-ins, frequently held in Ojibwe territory and in the Pacific Northwest. I would like to suggest that the way that the AIM platform *moved* and *traveled* through and across multiple geographies, gathering strength and cachet as it did so, might function as a metaphor for the kind of mobility and exchange that I find to be at the crux of *The Antelope Wife*. This novel reveals the networks and "connectivities" that "dismantle [our] sense of a coherent, bounded identity," to borrow a phrase from Donald Pease.[46] This focus on and articulation of movement, of the unboundedness of the urban space, is revolutionary in its reinscription of Indigeneity as something often thought to be frozen in both time and space. But as scholars like James Clifford and Chadwick Allen have argued, tribal peoples have already always been mobile. As Clifford observes, "Tribal groups have, of course, never been simply 'local': they have always been rooted and routed in particular landscapes, regional and interregional networks."[47] Allen, in his 2014 Native American and Indigenous Studies Association (NAISA) presidential address, discussed mobile Indigeneity: "I want to draw attention to how the category of the capital 'I' Indigenous is typically excluded from positive definitions of the transnational as 'flexible' and 'mobile.' Indeed, the category of the Indigenous easily becomes the binary opposite of the transnational in such formulations, representing neither flexibility nor mobility but, instead, the static, homogenous tribal, inherently backward and doomed because inherently unwilling and unable to embrace change and movement."[48] Likewise, anthropologist Robin DeLugan suggests that "contemporary global migration and attendant displacements and circulations create new experiences that continue to challenge narrow definitions of indigeneity that require geographic or cultural fixity (in the sense of immutable ties to place and tradition)."[49] In this vein, my reading of Erdrich's novel focuses on how it unhinges the notion of Indians as rooted peoples living on reservations, people with unchanging cultures, and suggests that these movements and circulations produce new versions of Indian identity. Movement is part of Erdrich's aesthetic here in both a physical and a metaphorical sense, as I will soon explain.

As I have been arguing throughout this book, urban Indian texts like Erdrich's demonstrate that it is possible to be both Indigenous and mobile, circulating in and around a city hub. In the sections that follow, I will articulate some of the ways that this book makes spatial claims (of both physical and textual space) and consider how her novel, like the others in this study, changes the narrative about Native peoples and cities. I am building on what a number of scholars of Native studies have begun to consider both the power and ramifications of this kind of mobility, particularly as it relates to transnational theory. For example, Gerald Vizenor's concept of transmotion suggests that "natural motion" is survivance, suggesting that Native artists and writers incorporate that motion as evidence of cultural survival.[50] Jodi Byrd (Chickasaw) builds on

Vizenor's definition in her creation of the "transit" when she writes, "To be in transit is to be active presence in a world of relational movements and countermovements. To be in transit is to exist relationally, multiply."[51] Movement has changed artistic expression, as Shari Huhndorf has argued: "Global—that is, transnational—movements of capital and empire . . . have re-fashioned indigenous cultural expression along with social and political structures."[52] Similarly, Ramirez writes that "travel . . . can be a purposeful, exciting way to transmit culture, create community, and maintain identity that ultimately can support positive changes for the Native American community across the country."[53] Motion, in this novel, is a cosmopolitan expression, a revelation of historical networks, a claiming of space, and an articulation of survival. As Erdrich's characters travel across and through the hub, their movement simultaneously performs a mapping of the urban space while it uncovers routes and distances and catalysts—existing "multiply," as Byrd suggests, just as this novel's versions do.

In *The Antelope Wife* we are simultaneously presented with a traveling baby tied onto a dog's back; a Quaker soldier who has gone west to escape the pains of unrequited love; a kidnapping that reads as a migration story; multiple stories of urban relocation; journeys to and from the reservation; and the movement of toxic waste from the city to the reservation—all mapped onto an even older history of tribal migration to the space of Minnesota. What gets revealed through these multiple registers of motion are what Lisa Lowe calls "the links and interdependencies" of the New World.[54] These linkages, or "intimacies," to borrow Lowe's term, provide further signs of historical crossings and exchange that allow for a reimagining of Indigenous rootedness. The intimacies in the novel include both violent and domestic encounters, as we will see, all of which result in the circulation of stories, histories, material culture, economies, and traditions. The empire does not simply impose itself upon the Natives; in surprising ways, Erdrich demonstrates, Native people in general and Ojibwes in particular have also made their mark on the settlers. These intimacies reveal the historical complexities of the city—of Gakahbekong and the land that is "hunched underneath."

Sometime in August 2015, an anonymous graffiti artist tagged a bus stop bench on Franklin Avenue with the words "YOU ARE ON INDIAN LAND" in all capitals, with the letter A in "LAND" replaced by a map of the state of Minnesota.[55] The bench is located in front of the American Indian Center, the historical center of the Native community here, perhaps a "safe space" in terms of its message. The artist's message is certainly not new; it appears in other contexts (as graffiti on Alcatraz Island, for example). It also was the title of a 1969 documentary about the conflict between the police and Mohawks on the St. Regis Reserve in Canada. Yet I find this bench intriguing for a number of reasons. First, it aligns recent activism like Idle No More with the American Indian Movement in the space of Minneapolis. It is also interesting as a bus bench, conjuring as it does movement and mapping within the urban space, maybe even calling attention to the economics of bus riding itself. We can imagine this bench within the network of people moving around and through the city hub, sometimes following the spokes out toward reservation spaces and traditional lands. Finally, I think that we need to pay attention to the way that the artist and bench are claiming space. The location of the bench makes a claim on the urban space: indeed, Minneapolis (as are all of the cities in the United States) is built on Indian lands. The artist's inclusion of the map of Minnesota expands the claim statewide, and, at the same time, it recognizes the relationship between city and state territories and boundaries. In other words, it simultaneously imagines itself within the context of urban and surrounding spaces in a way similar to Erdrich's book.

At the heart of Erdrich's hub is the city of Gakahbekong, a "trading village," and her descriptions of it consistently evoke movement and exchange.[56] Grandma Noodin and Grandma Giizis call it "Mishiimin Oodenag, Apple Town, because of the sound of the word—Minneapolis. Many Apple Us."[57] This language play functions as a renaming: it essentially changes the Dakota-based name to an Ojibwe one. The name Minneapolis is itself cosmopolitan: it literally means "water city," combining the Dakota word for "water," *mni*, with the Greek *polis*, "city." So much history is embedded in this naming as well: the struggle between the Dakotas

FIG 8. *You Are on Indian Land*, anonymous, 2015. Bus bench graffiti. Franklin Avenue, Minneapolis. Photo by Lindy Blumke, used with her permission.

and the Ojibwes over territory in what became the state of Minnesota; and the history of trade, which conjures both the role of the Hudson's Bay Company in the economic development of this region and the history of the lumber industry, wherein trees from the north were brought to the Twin Cities, processed, shipped across the country, and used to build more settler homes and towns. Erdrich focuses on this history in her novel *Tracks* and even more so in *Four Souls*, when Fleur Pillager follows railroad tycoon John James Mauser, who has swindled her out of her land and trees, into St. Paul, which she says sounds like a "great sleeping animal."[58] By the time Fleur reaches the city, her trees have been used to build Mauser's house: "Half was sold. The other, and the soundest of the wood, was processed right at the edge of the city to the specifications of the architect."[59] Erdrich does not reveal the location of this house, except to say that it sits on a tall ridge, overlooking "a brief network of lakes, flowing streams, rivers, and sloughs."[60] This was a "favorite spot for making camp in those original years before settlement" and the place where an Ojibwe woman had once given birth.[61] In other words, this place is named and located according to Ojibwe history and memory; it is experienced Indigenously. Additionally, Mauser's involvement with the railroad—the tracks of which Fleur followed east to the Twin Cities—further evokes movement and circulation and marks the accession of Minneapolis–St. Paul to an important center of commerce.[62] The railroad followed the old routes of the fur trade and was intended to move both people and resources. Minneapolis is thus a "trading village" on a larger scale, with tracks or spokes in every direction.

In the first version of *The Antelope Wife*, Erdrich provides no real clues or markers about where her characters reside, and she names few geographical details. This is in sharp contrast with Treuer's *The Hiawatha*, as I mentioned earlier, which provides intimate details of the city, including street and business names.[63] However, Treuer sets his novel outside of Phillips, a decision that has drawn criticism.[64] In the revised version of *The Antelope Wife*, almost as if to ward off similar commentary, Erdrich inserts more geographical details, specifically locating domestic spaces and physical landmarks, and she purposefully engages with the community of Phillips. For example, the duplex occupied by Richard and Rozin and their girls is on Andrew Jackson Street, just off Franklin Avenue.[65] Franklin Avenue is the main thoroughfare through the Indian community in Phillips, but curiously, there is no Andrew Jackson Street in Minneapolis.[66] There is a Jackson Street (sans Andrew) in the northeast quadrant of the city, but it does not intersect with Franklin. I think that it is safe to say that Erdrich has invented this particular street and in doing so has invoked a larger history of dislocation, connecting her urban Ojibwes to national settler patterns and legislations. The duplex was built in 1882, however, which does not coincide with Jackson's Indian Removal but occurs amidst the establishment of Ojibwe reservations in Minnesota, thus evoking another set of movements and legislations.[67]

This duplex, along with Frank's bakery (and the apartments upstairs, where Cecille and Frank each live), makes up the core of Erdrich's Minneapolis hub. Frank's bakery is where much of the important action takes place, where Cally first finds her grandmothers in the 1998 version and meets Sweetheart Calico, who sits outside looking for handouts. This is where the drunken Klaus comes occasionally to be cared for by his brother/cousin Frank, demonstrating how the family and community take care of their own. The bakery is also a place of intimacies and sensuality. Rozin and Frank consummate their relationship in the 1998 novel "out behind the bakery down the back alley to a playground field on a path barely hidden in a fringe of woods," and in the 2012 text, Frank teaches Rozin how to combine the right ingredients to make pastries.[68] This transmission of recipe and technique marks Rozin's entry into Frank's inner circle. Frank is not a metalworker or steelworker, like so many relocated Indians; he owns and operates his own business, and he is a master baker.[69] His bakery, along with the upstairs apartments, is also domestic space, symbolic of *home* in the city. The community at large patronizes the bakery, crossing through Indian space in the city, as the Ojibwe community circles around and through this space. Frank's role as *home* is further underscored when he begins to renovate Rozin's duplex after she has taken her daughters up to the reservation.

Erdrich's Minneapolis gets revealed through circulations. For example, while Richard and Klaus are out wandering the streets, pretending to be homeless to evade the authorities, they stop at a liquor store on Hennepin, and then, in search of water, "they pass the lake and [Klaus] gulps at the toxic shore until his stomach bulges. They are foraging on and on into the city, into the downtown area near the bus station, past the Irish pubs, music bars, and old buildings made of reddish purple stone dug from the northern Minnesota quarries or fawn-colored Kasota stone dug from the southern Minnesota quarries. Farther yet until they hit the river."[70] Their movement is juxtaposed with the movement of stone, another resource from traditional or sacred places.[71] Kasota, for example, is named for the Dakota village named after the stone plateau; *kasota* means "cleared-off place."[72] Beyond the acknowledgment of the traces of this stone, there also seems to be a consideration of the stone itself, as in the way that rocks, *asin*, are animate in Ojibwe cosmology.[73] In this passage, Erdrich evokes both Minneapolis scenery and history as the landscape is traveled and crossed. Richard and Klaus also pass through homeless shelters and rehab in the 1998 version, becoming part of the homeless community as they walk the line between homelessness and housed. They sleep in parks as punishment for their illegal dumping of toxic waste (carpet) on reservation land. Yet even in their homelessness, there is something admirable about the way they navigate the city. Together, they scavenge pizza from behind a restaurant "where the manager left unclaimed orders every once in a while."[74] They go looking for a Wendy's to use the bathroom.[75] They panhandle outside the museum.[76] Yet the one resource they have difficulty finding is water, or *nibi*. The fountains near the museum are not functional, so they head toward the river: "They reached the broad lawns and paths beside the river, went down the embankment and edged along the shore until they found a clump of bushes, familiar shade."[77] These two find the familiar in the city's "natural" places, almost as if they can inhabit that "hunched" space underneath the modern structures.

Sweetheart Calico's interactions with the city space are in stark contrast with Klaus's and Richard's; therefore, she provides the greatest critique of the city. Like the woman in Erdrich's poem "The Strange People," the antelope wife is captured, hunted, and taken into a strange man's home. In the novel, Klaus asks Jimmy Badger for hunting advice and then kidnaps Sweetheart Calico to remind him of the open plains. Jimmy Badger says, "Few men can handle their love ways" and emphasizes that antelope women like Sweetheart Calico are related to them—"descendants," he calls them.[78] Erdrich makes it clear that Sweetheart Calico is the woman from myth: her feet are often described as hooves, and Klaus says that he is "caught" by her.[79] Once he kidnaps her and brings her to the city, he keeps her bound, using a strip of the calico he has named her for.[80] In the city Sweetheart Calico changes her expressions and her clothes, and her front teeth are broken.[81] She does not speak until the end of the novel.

In the revisions of the novel, Sweetheart Calico's genealogy is much clearer than in the first text: she is a descendant of Matilda, Blue Prairie Woman's daughter; Matilda is the baby rescued by Scranton Roy (and breastfed by him) after the massacre that begins the novel.[82] After losing her daughter, Blue Prairie Woman is renamed Other Side of the Earth, the name that she gives Matilda when she is found. Both of these names, it seems, have geographic resonances. According to the genealogical chart included in the new version of the novel, Matilda has an unnamed daughter who is Sweetheart Calico's mother.[83] Erdrich's clearer articulation of the antelope wife's genealogy firmly establishes this character as an Ojibwe, specifically one who is related to the Roy family, though, like Lulu's sons in *Love Medicine*, she lives in Montana. This particular geography might link her specifically to Turtle Mountain, whose allotments are dispersed across North Dakota and Montana, though there are other Ojibwe/Chippewa populations in Montana, such as those at Rocky Boy.[84] These trust lands dot a landscape that was mapped out of the whole of Ojibwe territory.

Like her antelope ancestors, Sweetheart Calico is constantly on the move, even in the city space. Cally associates her with movement: "Her perfume smells like grass and wind. Makes me remember running in the summer with my hair flopping on my shoulders. Her scent is like sun on my back, like cool rain, like dust rising off a waterless, still, nowhere-leading road."[85] Sweetheart Calico is a captive urban subject, but she is simultaneously a four-legged animal with connections to the open plains. Erdrich writes, "At night, she remembers running beside her mother."[86] She "lopes crazily through the park," "but no matter how fast or how far she walks, she can't get out of the city. The lights and cars tangle her. Streets open onto streets and the highways roar hungry as swollen rivers, bearing in their rush dangerous bright junk."[87] In Ojibwemowin, "to walk" is *bimose*, or "life in motion"; *bi* marks all of the words for "motion."[88] Sweetheart Calico is constantly getting lost in strange, paved, unpredictable places, and, like the antelope, she is constantly on the move. She walks about the city in search of place, an embodiment of Ojibwe myth and symbolic of Indigenous dislocation on multiple registers.

Like Richard and Klaus, Sweetheart Calico crosses the line over to homelessness. She develops a drinking habit, and after an explosion throws her through a window, she is cared for by "street people" who take her to a shelter and dress her in "wool pants, a silken blouse off a rich lady's back, and a heavy padded jacket."[89] In the revision, the explosion has disappeared, but her connection to homelessness has not: "In the lighted shelter where the street people drag her, she curls up on a flea-funky pallet in the corner and sleeps, not forgetting all of her daughters but taking them back into her body and holding them."[90] This deployment of homelessness in the novel is minor compared to that in Alexie's work I described in the second chapter, but its presence equally invites consideration. Erdrich seems to similarly evoke the irony of Indigenous homelessness (without a home in Indigenous territory) and to highlight the *transient* nature of such a condition. As transients, these characters move through the city, reading and mapping it through an Indigenous lens—specifically, through an Ojibwe lens—"in motion," as it were.

Erdrich's city is "constantly in motion and constantly moved through," to borrow Eric Gary Anderson's description of the American Southwest.[91] Appropriately, Sweetheart Calico's exit from the city invokes motion, "from the water flowing off the edge of the world and [she] started walking due west."[92] She is understood through her wandering and longing—and eventually through her escape from the city space. She survives in the city, but she does not thrive in the same way as characters who have moved willingly to Minneapolis. Erdrich uses the deer woman figure to make it clear that there is a difference between "an emerging, mobile Indian identity," to use Anderson's words, and forced dislocation.[93] Like Ojibwe culture, the city space is dynamic, in motion, and a place where we are compelled to be mobile. Urban mobility in this case recalls the earlier motion of Ojibwe life in the woods and on the prairie; in other words, the new mobility of the city, just like its cosmopolitanism, is, in fact, quite old. Erdrich's hub gets revealed through this motion, and through revision the city comes into clearer focus.

MIIGEWEYON / SO THEN I GO HOME

In the preface to her collection *Absentee Indians and Other Poems* (2012), Kimberly Blaeser (White Earth Ojibwe) describes city Indians as "absentee Indians" who travel back to their reservations: "Another absentee Indian brings home a child. Stands this ground, the place of history. Claiming home, asks a blessing. Picks up the snatches of language. Repeats them.

Practices survival like she is learning the recipes for baking powder biscuits, venison sausage, or dill pickles. Measures by memory the distances to each rice bed, sugar camp, burial ground. The distance to the seventh generation. Names the makers, like she was writing a pathway."[94] Just as there are distances and pathways to be measured in the reservation space, so there are routes between home and away, reservation and city, and they are well traveled. Blaeser speaks elsewhere about the "fluidity" of Native life.[95] I would like to suggest that this fluidity gets translated into a contemplation of borders in *The Antelope Wife* as it navigates networks of exchange and crossings, symbolic of though not always representational of travel between reservation and city. Characters travel back and forth, sometimes on the powwow circuit; deceased characters are interred on the reservation (in the first version of the novel); and garbage is transported to the reservation for storage. The migratory nature of the Ojibwe people is carried over into the present as resistance against the confines of the reservation borders. In fact, the reservations are called "ishkonigan, the leftovers," and historically, of course, this is true: reservations are but tiny parcels of much larger expanses of Indigenous territories.[96] As Rita Ferrari has argued about *Love Medicine* and *Tracks*, Erdrich "uses the concept of the border as metaphor and narrative strategy for a newly imagined negotiation of individual and cultural identity."[97] In this section, I would like to pay attention to the spokes of the hub, as it were, and what I see as the text's relational locations, always attentive to the distances between spaces and the transmotion at work. The BIA bemoaned and calculated what it called the "return rate" as urban Indians traveled back to their home reservations, precisely for the reason that return is celebrated: city life does not inherently disrupt the connection to homeland. In fact, if this connection is what makes an Anishinaabeg an Anishinaabeg, then Erdrich's characters demonstrate how to be simultaneously *urban* and *Ojibwe* through their place connectedness.

Erdrich uses the very first episode in the novel, the massacre and subsequent events, to convey movement and to begin to mark out this territory. For example, the westward travels of Scranton Roy become representative of Manifest Destiny and the interactions that led to the reservation system. Meanwhile, the infant, Matilda Roy, who travels for days on the back of a protective and faithful dog, signifies this period before the construction of borders. In fact, the absence of geographical designations here makes it difficult to determine exactly *where* this action is taking place: somewhere between Minneapolis and Montana. In the novel, Blue Prairie Woman is renamed Other Side of the Earth by her people "for the place toward which she traveled," looking for her lost daughter.[98] As Giizis makes sense of this name for Deanna in the present, she says, "So often, our names include movement, the stirring of leaves, the glint of light on water, the trembling of color."[99] When Blue Prairie Woman dies and leaves the newly found Matilda alone in the wilderness, the antelope come to raise her: they are "always on the move."[100] This is the same sense of movement I described earlier with regard to Sweetheart Calico. The antelope are free of the borders that reservations and cities have created, and somehow Scranton Roy is able to return to the very spot where the massacre occurred and, later, to find the descendants of the old woman he killed.

In the present of the novel, the characters who exhibit the most freedom of movement, especially between the reservation and the city, are the grandmothers Mary and Zosie Roy (Giizis and Noodin in the revision). Cally says, "They spend most summers on the reservation homestead, the old allotment that belonged to their mother, a farmed patch of earth and woods and mashkeeg from which they gather their teas and cut bark for baskets."[101] As they do on the seasonal round, they summer north on the reservation and winter south in the city. When Cally moves to Minneapolis, she finds that "they never stop moving."[102] They cannot be confined anywhere: "A funeral here, bingo there, workshop up north or on an exciting Canadian reserve. From traditional to merely ordinary, they are constantly on the move. . . . For the past year they have enjoyed sending us postcards from various states, reservations, even cities."[103] They are hard to pin down, but there is no end to the amount of gossip Cally is able to extract from customers at the bakery: "I hear they live down the street, exactly where though, what address, none can remember. I hear they live in an apartment, an old folks' high-rise, with their daughter."[104] These elderly women are not only well-known travelers but also somehow mysterious like the antelope people. They cannot be confined to the reservation space—and they are constantly crossing borders, even the "medicine line," as some refer to the boundary between the United States and Canada.[105] Interestingly, in the new version of the novel, the grandmothers live on the reservation, coming down only when Rozin needs help with the girls. Of course, this movement meshes with the hub pattern, but it is a curious shift. To some degree, this revision gives the grandmothers a less prominent role in the novel and allows for more focus on Rozin (just as taking away Cally's narrative role accomplishes the same). What does not change is their role as arbiters of culture, grounded now both geographically and culturally in their reservation. Erdrich does seem to be reasserting the primacy of the reservation in the revision—perhaps as a means of aligning this novel with the others, as a set-up for future novels, to respond to criticism about advocating leaving (here I am thinking about Alexie's *The Absolutely True Diary*, which came out between the two versions of *The Antelope Wife*), or simply to reflect the reverse migration pattern that is becoming more and more prevalent.[106]

Rozin's movement between the reservation and the city has also been revised. In the original, Rozin and Richard Whiteheart Beads had left the reservation for the city when their twins were five years old and things had become "too political," which may or may not be a reference to struggles over treaty rights with regard to fishing in the 1970s. Rozin moves back to the reservation after the death of their daughter Deanna.[107] Almost ten years later, Rozin moves back to the city and marries Frank Shawano and eventually becomes a lawyer.[108] In the revision, Rozin and Richard "fell in love at an American Indian Movement protest" and "lived here and there" before settling in Minneapolis.[109] Rozin moves back to the reservation with the girls after her break-up with Richard, but only for a year or so—not ten—and she decides to go to law school when she returns to the city. In both versions, the reservation is a safe haven for Rozin, and the presence of Giizis and Noodin ensures that she has a home there. The shifting of politics from the reservation to the city is an interesting one. Erdrich removes the danger from the reservation space in a move that I see as a mythologizing of that space. Without its politics (and name), the reservation remains anonymous, protected in some way.

Even death in this novel involves travel back to the reservation. In the first version, the reservation is where Rozin buries her daughter, and she visits her often: "Rozin chose to bury her daughter in the old tradition underneath a grave house, built low and long with a small shelf at one end where food and tobacco could be placed for her to use. Sometimes Rozin goes up to the reservation on weekends, leaves a coin or two, copper, for some still believe that the water man exacts his price at the red stone gates."[110] Here there is the potential for a monetary exchange, as well as the "final crossing." The reservation as "final resting place" is also a telling designation. The repatriation or returning home of bodies is a common practice for diasporic peoples, maybe most notably for Jews returning to Israel.[111] In Minneapolis, multiple agencies offer services to urban Indians in need of burial. For example, historian Rachel Buff describes the American Indian Hearse Service, which "offers transportation for the dead, at no charge and 'with dignity,' back to the reservation of their origin or enrollment."[112] The Office of Indian Ministry also provides space for traditional all-night funerals and wakes, a funeral food shelf, and a hearse that will transport the deceased up to four hundred miles.[113] This program is called Miigeweyon, which translates to "so then I go home." The routes and mechanisms for return are in place for these reservation interments. The dead are returned *home* to their reservation communities and families, emphasizing the primacy of this space.

Even though Cally was born on the reservation (in the first version of the novel), it proves to be a dangerous place for her.[114] Her relationship to place is complicated.[115] First, she loses her *indis* (umbilical cord) on the reservation.[116] She says, "My mother sewed my birth cord, with dry sage and sweet grass, into a turtle holder of soft white buckskin. . . . I was supposed to have it on me all my life, bury it with me on reservation land, but one day I came in from playing and my indis was gone."[117] Even as a child, Cally knows that she will be buried on the reservation and that her umbilical cord connects her physically and symbolically to the homeland.[118] She blames her desire for the city on the loss of this object: "I thought nothing of it, at first and for many years, but slowly over time the absence . . . it will tell. I began to wander from home, first in my thoughts, then my feet took after, so at last at the age of eighteen, I walked the road that led from the front of our place . . . into the city's *bloody* heart."[119] In the revision, both girls lose their *indis* on the same day, and this sentence instead describes Cecille's drive from the reservation to the city, with the twins hiding in her back seat: "One road widens into two lanes, then four, then six, past the farms and service islands, into the dead wall of the suburbs and still past that, finally, into the city's *complex* heart."[120] Of course, this description of the route is significant—and, as Erdrich describes in *Books and Islands in Ojibwe Country*, this road is a former trade route—but I would like to focus instead on the significant shift in modifiers from the first to the second, from *bloody* to *complex*. The Ojibwemowin word for "city" is *odena*, from the word for "heart," *ode*, and so the city already signifies "heart."[121] The "bloody heart" of the city evokes violence and cruelty, both of which could be found in the first version of the novel. A "complex heart," on the other hand, calls to mind the complicated connections of the urban space, as complicated as the genealogies of the people who live there.

For Cally, the reservation is not only a place of loss but a place of illness. One year after the death of her twin sister, Cally becomes seriously ill with a fever reminiscent of Matilda's in the first chapter (and in the new versions, both twins become ill). Her mother and grandmothers doctor her with slippery elm and sage, but they cannot break her fever.[122] A snowstorm traps them in the house, unable to go for help. When the weather finally breaks, an ambulance takes her to the Indian Health Service hospital, where she is saved by an IV. This episode, narrated by the dog Almost Soup, would seem to argue for the necessity of modern medicine. Tradition has twice failed Cally, but, as I will later demonstrate, Cally does not give up on tradition—or the homeland. After she moves to Minneapolis, Cally admits, "In spite of how I want to curl up in my city corner, I picture everything back home."[123] Her mother hopes she will miss "the real land" and return to the reservation.[124] Even though

Cally can go back and forth, she remains connected to the reservation, despite the loss of her *indis*.

Klaus Shawano, described as a trader on the powwow circuit at the beginning of the novel, is also a frequent traveler. Klaus is a self-defined urban Indian, a "city-bred guy."[125] Klaus has a dreamlike conversation with Windigo Dog, who tells a joke about an Ojibwe dogcatcher whose dogs do not escape: "Mine are Indian dogs. Wherever they are, that's their rez. Every time one of them tries to sneak off, the others pull him back."[126] Klaus becomes indignant with the dog. He says, "My rez is very special to me. It is my place of authority."[127] Klaus's point here is key. He has lived in the city for years, he travels to many reservations to the west for powwows, but he knows the importance of home. The city is not a "place of authority," and, as a trader, he thrives on that mobility. He seems to manage a living there for years, though through the course of the novel he rapidly declines. This decline is not solely caused by urban life, however; much of it is caused by his love for Sweetheart Calico. He also becomes disillusioned with "all that dry space": "It was restful, a comfort to let my brain wander across the mystery where sky meets earth. Now, that line disturbs me with its lie."[128] Klaus recognizes that this line, the horizon, a border, has experienced some deep-rooted change.[129]

Like Susan Power in *The Grass Dancer*, Erdrich uses the powwow to signify a hybrid space, a place of exchange. Powwows, which occur on reservations and in city spaces, are important for many urban Indians. Urban Indians often travel to the reservation for powwows, like the "absentee Indians" in Blaeser's poem.[130] Because the majority of these are intertribal powwows, there is even more exchange—of songs, dances, regalia—but they can also be a way of looking for the familiar in a new space. As Tara Browner and others have argued, the origins of the powwow are complicated at best, and they have evolved to have a complex range of meaning.[131] In fact, many of the "traditions" of the powwow come out of Buffalo Bill's Wild West shows and do not reflect actual tribal ceremonies.[132] In Erdrich's novel the Montana powwow becomes a part of the social network of the hub: it is where objects are purchased and exchanged, where cultural knowledge (like the advice of Jimmy Badger) is distributed, where courting and new love relationships occur, where family and clan members reunite and catch up on the latest gossip, where mythological women steal the hearts of traders.[133]

Erdrich demonstrates the primacy of the reservation space in another example: the economy and exchange of garbage. Klaus works with Richard Whiteheart Beads for "the first Native-owned waste disposal company in the whole U.S."[134] Unfortunately, it seems as though the reservation has become a landfill: "Far up north on reservation land, there's money to be made in garbage. Disposal space."[135] Klaus says, "Used to be us Indians had nothing to throw away—we used it all up to the last scrap. Now we have a lot of casino trash, of course, and used diapers, disposable and yet eternal, like the rest of the country. Keep this up and we'll all one day be a landfill of diapers, living as adults right on top of our own baby shit."[136] This is a reverse of the logging industry, as I discussed earlier, which makes an appearance in both *Tracks* and *Four Souls*. In this kind of historical economy, trees are taken from reservation land, and garbage is sent back. Klaus's reflection on the nature of garbage also allows for a gauge of cultural transformation. In some ways, life on the reservation is not so different from life in the city. Popular culture (including that of the disposable diaper) has long permeated reservation life. The reservation is not an isolated, pure expression of Ojibwe culture: that culture is constantly changing, constantly in motion. The exchange of garbage is a poisoning, however, and Klaus, mistaken for Richard, is arrested "because of dumping practices."[137] "Things get dumped, terrible poisons in endless old wells," he says.[138] In the new novel, Richard and Klaus have filled an old barn, belonging to an absentee non-Native couple, with rolls of toxic carpet from a mall—the modern version of the trading post. This sort of trading is unacceptable and, one could argue, is what leads to the downfall of these two characters. While Erdrich certainly allows for other causes, mainly, love for an antelope woman, it seems to be the ultimate sin to pollute the homeland. This land is to be revered, not turned into a landfill. There is no foresight for the future in this act—no consideration of the seventh generation.[139] It is a selling out that cannot be forgiven.

And so this novel demonstrates the continued importance of homeland while simultaneously paying attention to the pathways or the many routes or spokes of the hub, illustrating Ramirez's observation that "urban Native Americans who travel back and forth from city to reservation can strengthen and reinvigorate their culture and identity."[140] This focus on the hub is heightened in the revision, particularly with the increased travel and with Erdrich's decision to move the grandmothers back to the reservation. Her Ojibwe characters maintain their connections to culture because they remain connected to their home reservation(s). Just as they are in motion in the city, so they travel the roads of Minnesota. About the 1998 edition David Stirrup argues that "a dissolving rather than redefining of borders, becomes one facet of the anti-colonial project of the book."[141] The multiple crossings do certainly lead to a blurring of boundaries that allows Erdrich to envision the space as Indigenous territory, its historical regions, networks, and routes intact.

CULTURAL CURRENCIES

The Antelope Wife demonstrates how difficult it is to trace the many crossings and exchanges between the cultures of Minnesota—the "intimacies" of this geography, to return to Lowe here for a moment. I propose that we think about this book in diasporic terms, paying attention to how "diaspora cultures work to maintain community, selectively preserving and recovering traditions, 'customizing' and 'versioning' them in novel, hybrid, and often antagonistic situations," to quote Clifford here.[142] The cultural signifiers, or "traveling culture," in the novel include both material culture and cultural practices, as Erdrich's book demonstrates how culture spills over boundaries and how portable culture can be. The cultural practices and culturally significant objects in the novel themselves reveal historical complexities. All of these objects and rituals are hybridized or syncretic; they are all somehow evidence of exchange between Native peoples and settlers. They also reveal global currents and currencies. The traditions that are carried into the city, including the ceremonial use of tobacco, the practice of naming, and the preparation of food, coupled with the calico and glass beads, provide a gauge for cultural adaptation that negates an assimilation narrative. They help maintain an Indian subjectivity in the urban space, but one that is dynamic, not fixed in the historical past.

My first example of traveling culture in the novel involves tobacco. Rozin uses ceremonial tobacco in the original version of the novel when she prepares a meal for the spirits of Richard and Deanna, who seem to be haunting her. She sets a table in the yard of her mothers' home ("mothers" because she does not know which twin bore her), with two place settings "at the western end because that is the death direction." They are "spirit plates, with tobacco."[143] Erdrich specifically talks about the Ojibwes' use of tobacco in *Books and Islands in Ojibwe Country*: "Spirits like tobacco. Their fondness for the stuff is a given of Ojibwe life. Tobacco offerings are made before every important request, to spirits or to other humans. Tobacco is put down by the root if you pick a plant, in the water when you visit a lake, by the side of the road when starting a journey. Tobacco is handed to anyone with whom you wish to speak in a serious manner."[144] It is used to appease the spirits, to give thanks to the Creator. Also, at Rozin's wedding to Frank, "the old people sacrificed a corner of the cake, with tobacco, for the spirits."[145] In a humorous scene with Richard and Klaus that takes place outside the art museum, presumably the Minneapolis Institute of Arts on Third Avenue, Erdrich suggests that the commercial use of tobacco has interfered with the ceremonial.[146] When a woman gives money to Richard, he tells her that he will put down tobacco for her. "That's a sacred gesture. We're still Indians," he says.[147] Klaus immediately responds, "You got cigarettes?" Richard gives him his "last cigarette," but Klaus does not smoke it. A short time later, Richard takes it back: "He unpeeled the wrapping from the cigarette and began to sprinkle the tobacco on the clipped grass. Klaus and Richard were very quiet, watching the flakes of tobacco fall to earth."[148] They leave this place and wander around the city until they reach the river:

> "We were here a while ago. I remember this place," said Richard. "We should put down some tobacco."
> "Or smoke it."
> "We just got two cigarettes left."

"Let's smoke it like an offering then."

"It don't mix with wine, not for religious purposes."

"That's true," said Richard. He slowly decided, and then he spoke. "This afternoon, let's just regard our tobacco as a habit-forming drug."[149]

Even though they are homeless by this point in the novel, seemingly disconnected from both culture and family, Klaus and Richard demonstrate their cultural knowledge surrounding tobacco, even if they are not performing the ritual properly. Commercial cigarettes might change their relationship to tobacco, but its sacred aspects do not disappear in the urban space.

There is an abundance of food in this novel, as critics such as Shirley Brozzo and Julie Tharp have noted, though their discussions do not imagine these culinary references as traveling culture.[150] Many of the cooking practices reflect regional foodways and cultural preferences. For example, before Rozin sets those spirit plates out in the yard, she spends hours cooking traditional foods for Richard and Deanna: "Into the pot, she pours an inch or so of wild rice. A fine sweet dust rises off the rice like smoke, smelling of the lake bottom, weedy and fresh."[151] This rice was the real stuff, "knocked into the bottom of Zosie's beat-up aluminum canoe last fall."[152] Of course, wild rice is a staple of the Ojibwe diet; recall the prophecy that the Anishinaabe traveled west to find the place where rice grows on water. Rozin will also make a vanilla pudding "from scratch," stewed turkey, and corn on the cob. In the revised novel, this cooking scene is transformed into Rozin's grief for her missing twins (missing because Sweetheart Calico had gotten them lost in the city). Rozin intends the food to draw the girls toward home. We also see traditional foods at Rozin's wedding: "The meats of the day were all game acquired by the brothers and uncles and prepared according to their own special methods. The moose was unearthed from a cooking pit in the backyard."[153] As Klaus says during the blitzkuchen episode, "We are people of simple food straight from the earthen earth and from the lakes and from the woods."[154] There is a tension between traditional foodways and colonial foods, as Zosie points out at Christmas dinner: "There should be no salt on this table! In the early days we had no salt."[155] The Ojibwe diet has changed, however, for, along with the moose and the wild rice and the deer sausages, there are "six types of potato salad," ambrosia, macaroni, Marshmallow Krispy Bars, and a box full of fry bread.[156] Even fry bread, thought to be a staple of an Indian diet, originated after the introduction of commodity flour on the reservation. Fry bread appears several times in the novel. Frank makes it in his bakery to sell alongside the breads and pastries. Cally says, "Frank slips in the little slabs of dough and they bob there, bubbling, reminding me of back home at powwows and sweating ladies at the fry-bread stands laughing and pushing those gold rounds at you."[157] Even health-conscious, cosmopolitan Cecille makes fry bread for the wedding.[158] Fry bread is a reminder of the colonial, sure, but it is also the making of something out of almost nothing: flour, salt, powdered milk, oil or lard. It has become a foodstuff born out of the reservation experience, and as such, it transcends (or travels across) tribal boundaries—and obviously lands here, in the city.

One food in particular, the blitzkuchen, a German cake, is the epitome of traveling culture in the novel. In the original novel, the story of the cake is tied up with the story of how Klaus got his name.[159] The German prisoner, whose name was also Klaus, was kidnapped from a state work camp to replace a brother lost in the war and is given a chance to save himself if he is able to impress the Shawano family with his baking. Even with meager ingredients, he creates the finest, most amazing cake—a cake that no Ojibwe had ever tasted. What could have ended with violence instead concludes with the blitzkuchen, literally "lightning cake," supposedly named for the quickness with which it can be made. This is the cake Frank Shawano, an unborn child during this episode, will dedicate the rest of his life trying to duplicate. Frank calls it the "cake of peace" and only realizes much later that the secret ingredient was fear.[160] This episode reveals one of the "intimacies" between Ojibwes and Germans in this region, a relationship that Erdrich also explores in *The Beet Queen* (1986) and *The Master Butchers Singing Club* (2003).[161] The German influence here is not subtle: this is most certainly a German recipe. The cake itself is representative of exchange, one that Frank continually reenacts as he tries to remake that cake in his Minneapolis bakery. It works as a metaphor for the present moment—it requires complicated ingredients, its origins are now somewhat obscured, and it cannot easily be replicated.

To think through the role of commodities or objects in the novel, I turn again to Arjun Appadurai, who has suggested that "commodities, like persons, have social lives" and "life histories"; he is especially interested in "the diversion of commodities from their predestined paths."[162] One of the commodities in the novel that has a "life histor[y]" includes the blue beads that appear in the very first chapter and are so crucial to the plot. Another commodity that I would like to focus on here is the calico after which the antelope woman is named. Both beads and calico have long and complex histories, and together they are essential components of a colonial trade relationship. In her exhaustive study on the history of beads, Lois Sherr Dubin argues that glass beads had an enormous "economic and aesthetic impact" on the Indigenous peoples of the Americas.[163] Beads were first used as gifts in the New World—glass was new and would eventually replace beads made from natural materials.[164] Glass beads were first made in Venice, but the technology soon spread throughout Europe—to Germany, the Netherlands, Bohemia, and Moravia (the Czechoslovakia in Erdrich's novel). These beads first came to the Ojibwes in the 1700s, during the early fur trade. The Ojibwes have long referred to glass seed beads as "little spirit seed[s]," or *manidominenz*.[165] Beading slowly replaced quilling, and beads were used to decorate articles of clothing, including regalia worn for powwows, moccasins, leggings, and headwear, as well as bags or satchels and saddles. Calico came to the Americas a bit later. Named after the Indian city of Calcutta, where it originated in the eleventh century, calico became popular in England in the mid-1600s but was not manufactured in America until the early nineteenth century. In 1831 three Massachusetts companies were producing over twenty million yards of calico per year, according to historian Paul Rivard.[166] Calico was traded widely, and reservation Indians in many locales made dresses from the fabric. Because it is made from unbleached cotton and is roughly woven, it was an inexpensive textile—one perfect for trading. Unlike some of the early trade cloth, however, calico was brightly dyed and patterned.

"Beads and calico" might appropriately describe the dress of American Indians during the reservation era: both goods were embraced by Native populations and became metonymic for *Indian.*

Critic Jonathan Little has argued that the bead metaphor in the novel creates "a narrative of overlapping spaces between cultures while also depicting the enduring strength and resiliency of the Ojibwe heritage," and I would add that the beads' movement is also critical to that narrative.[167] The blue glass beads in the novel, called "northwest trader blue," are from Czechoslovakia (Hungary in the revised edition) and have traveled through time and space to be in Minneapolis.[168] These blue beads, larger than seed beads, were highly prized by tribes of the Pacific Northwest and often called "Russian" beads, though they originated in Bohemia, not in Russia.[169] Blue Prairie Woman places them on the cradleboard with Matilda in the commotion of the massacre at the beginning of the novel. Matilda grows up wearing these beads, and she takes them with her when her mother comes for her.[170] The beads disappear from the plot until the end of the novel, when Zosie Roy (Grandma Noodin in the revised version) relates the story of how she came to possess those blue beads. When Zosie was a child, she met a Pembina woman who wore the beads.[171] Zosie falls in love with them because of the color, "that blue of my beads, I understood, was the blueness of time. Perhaps you don't know that time has a color. You've seen that color but you were not watching, you were not aware. Time is blue. Or time is the blue in things. I came to understand that my search for the blueness called northwest trader blue was the search to hold time."[172] That Zosie equates these beads with time, or the attempt to hold time, is interesting. The desire to stop time, to freeze it at this particular moment, postcontact, reservation-era time, is a desire to slow the process of acculturation, it would seem. This makes sense when Sweetheart Calico's silence is explained by the fact that she holds the strand of blue trade beads in her mouth. Zosie explains that she gambled with the Pembina woman to obtain those beads, but we do not know how Sweetheart Calico came to possess them.[173] They are well-traveled beads—and the mystery of their origin contains layers of historical exchange. There was an extensive bead trade in North America prior to European contact, for example, though these beads seem to reveal the linkage between the Northwest Coast and Erdrich's Minnesota Ojibwe specifically via the fur trade. Perhaps Sweetheart Calico can only speak these histories when the beads have been removed from her mouth. They have been brought to the city, this site of commerce, where they are once again traded, as Sweetheart Calico offers the beads to Cally in exchange for her freedom.[174]

Sweetheart Calico is kept silent with the beads, and she is bound by a strip of calico. Klaus uses the cloth to attract her attention at the Montana powwow on the advice of Jimmy Badger, who tells him that antelope people are curious and will "check anything that they don't understand."[175] Sweetheart Calico and her three daughters are "dressed in pale folds of calico."[176] Klaus puts a piece of calico, "white with little pink roses," on his trading table, and naturally the women are attracted.[177] When he has kidnapped the mother, Klaus ties her wrists to his with a strip of the fabric.[178] This is how he takes her to Minneapolis against her will. She is not able to escape even when she is not tied to him. Sometimes Klaus sleeps next to her, their wrists tied together. In the end, he symbolically ties the strip of cloth to their wrists when he decides to release her. By this time, the calico has become a "dirty gray": "Sweat and dirt and drunken sleeps, railroad bed, underpass and overpass, dust of the inner-city volleyball courts and frozen snirt and river water were all pressed into the piece of cloth that held the story of his miserableness and which was still—though grit scored, dirt changed, and sun faded—tensile, woven of the same toughness as the old longing."[179] They travel to the edge of the city, and he unties the cloth. To be bound by calico—a commodity, a trade item, an object of colonialism—signifies a fixed identity frozen in a particular moment, incapable of change. That the antelope wife cannot survive in the urban space is a demonstration of the danger in perpetuating the image of the Indian as a rural subject. She is held captive by the calico, this storied cloth, which in the end becomes a metaphor for the captive reservation Indian.

What film scholar Laura Marks argues about intercultural cinema, that it "is in a position to sort through the rubble created by cultural dislocation and read significance in what official history overlooks," seems particularly germane to Erdrich's project in this novel.[180] Erdrich finds significance in the things that make up urban life for contemporary Ojibwes—in the objects that hold historical significance, the rituals that keep them connected to other Ojibwes and to other Indigenous peoples, the things that remain and are transported. At the end of the original novel, when Sweetheart Calico begins to speak, she tells Cally, "I'm drowning in stuff here in Gakahbekong."[181] Stuff is important in this novel, as Clifford asks, What can "a gathered life and its possessions" tell us?[182] Both of these objects, these possessions, calico and trade beads, are reminiscent of Minneapolis's origins as a trading village and of Ojibwe participation in the fur trade. They are objects that move across and through both time and space. Erdrich shows us that Gakahbekong is a place of complex historical intimacies, a place of exchange, a place rife with global currents and currencies. The objects and cultural practices that get transported across space and time into the city reveal even further crossings and exchanges. Indeed, as Brenda Cooper has argued about material culture in African novels, objects "broker translation between cultures."[183] If beads and calico are representative of the nineteenth-century Indian, what does it mean to carry these things into the present? How do we translate them? As I have suggested, they may exist to abolish the boundary between past and present, reservation and city, rural and urban, Native and settler. They are enablers in a reclaiming of Indian history and space. These "things" are more than evidence of nostalgia for a lost past or place or identity. They are cultural signifiers in the present, a way of maintaining a continued sense of Ojibwe identity in the city space. Erdrich uses them very consciously to identify and then defamiliarize the stereotypical Indian, located in the figure of Sweetheart Calico, the mythical antelope wife, in effect rewriting the master narrative of conquest and colonization in the territory of Minnesota.

In *Books and Islands in Ojibwe Country*, Erdrich recasts borders and "implies cross-border relationships," as David Stirrup suggests.[184] The book, originally published as part of a National Geographic travel series in 2003, fittingly between the first two versions of *The Antelope Wife*, details Erdrich's travels to Lake of the Woods, territory that has been inhabited by Anishinaabe people "forever," according to Tobasonakwut, Erdrich's guide and the father of her infant daughter.[185] The journey is a pilgrimage of sorts, and the author is deliberate in the places she visits, the objects that she packs and travels with, and the kind of knowledge that she hopes to obtain along the way. As Blaeser has argued, stories of pilgrimage are never only the stories of the individual: they are "braided accounts that entwine themselves with the destinies of communities, generations, tribal nations, the ecosystem of a region, the spiritual inheritance of a people."[186] Erdrich's travel narrative crosses over and through her relationship with Ojibwemowin, her attempts to "read" sacred Ojibwe rock art, while she documents, transcribes, and maps the territory in the past and the present. It is a journey of desire and of reconciliation, a reclaiming of both history and historical relationships. For example, she invokes the Jay Treaty while crossing the Canadian border in full knowledge that as a tribal citizen she has the right to pass freely across that border, although she is still anxious about the contemporary application of treaty rights. She is in possession of eagle spikes, she worries, and she is unsure how she might "prove" that she is her daughter's mother. An inset map at the book's beginning locates Lake of the Woods—an area greatly affected by the fur trade—in the territory between and across the Canadian border, demonstrating as it does the imposition of settler boundaries on Indigenous territories, places such as this that physically transcend national borders and colonial imaginations. The author leaves her home in Minneapolis in her blue minivan and follows an "old Ojibwe trade route, heading north" to Ojibwe Country, as she names it—in a textual erasure of its other namings.[187]

In 1973 Ojibwe artist George Morrison was commissioned to create a mural on the side of the new American Indian Center in Minneapolis.[188] Morrison himself was an urban Indian, leaving Chippewa City, Minnesota, where he was born in 1919, for Minneapolis, where he studied at the Minneapolis School of Art. He went to New York City and then returned to Minneapolis, with other points between, finally settling in Grand Portage,

FIG 9. *Turning the Feather Around*, 1975, George Morrison. Cedar-block collage. Commissioned by the Minneapolis American Indian Center, 1530 E. Franklin Avenue, Minneapolis, Minnesota. Photo courtesy of the author.

Minnesota.[189] This cedar mural, entitled *Turning the Feather Around*, was funded by a $10,000 National Endowment of the Arts grant.[190] As the cedar has weathered, the contrast between light and dark wood has added to the "illusion of movement across the surface," in Morrison's own words.[191] Like many of his compositions, it centers a horizon line, much like the horizon that so disturbs Klaus Shawano in *The Antelope Wife*, the demarcation between land and sky that resonates as a marker between the wide-open spaces and the space of the city.[192] Art critic W. Jackson Rushing III suggests that Morrison's horizons "function like a visual mantra: *I am home again, I am home again, I am home again.*"[193] Morrison was an urban Ojibwe, though his story begins and ends in Ojibwe territory, a place that continued to anchor his work.

Erdrich's novel does some of the same work as it contemplates the border and tracks the circulation between reservation and city and the spaces between. "From the beginning," Erdrich says in *Books and Islands*, Ojibwes were "always on the move."[194] Her characters are travelers and border-crossers. As they journey, they reclaim both place and history. They are simultaneously rooted and mobile. They are traders, picking and choosing what is useful to their lives. In *The Antelope Wife*, the circulation of people is accompanied by the movement of objects, stories, and elements of portable culture—the beliefs, rituals, practices that are critically Ojibwe. In the process, settler boundaries become meaningless, as they cannot contain a culture—as she demonstrates in the map of Ojibwe Country. As Jonathan Little insightfully claims, "Erdrich dramatizes a vast web of interdependence brought about by the intersection of many cultures, pasts, and heritages."[195] In fact, the novel highlights a web of exchange and possession. Material culture and place are intrinsically connected, and movement around and through the hub becomes empowering as a reclamation of space and history. Culture is in motion, and Erdrich's novel challenges the notion of a fixed Indian identity rooted in the past, unable to adapt to modern living.

The Antelope Wife is a critical urban text specifically because it challenges many of the master narratives about Indians in general and urban Indians in particular. Importantly, Erdrich is interrupting and complicating a more traditional narrative of Native life that put greatest stress on the retention of purity. As participants in the multidirectionality of cultural flows, participants in the historical "intimacies" of this territory, Erdrich's Ojibwes challenge the stasis of Indian identities and places. She also demonstrates that the reservation was a global place long before the era of relocation. All of the Americas are Indian land, as the bus bench graffiti reminds us, and although boundaries and dislocations still resonate, the act of crossing and recrossing reduces their power. By viewing history through a sense of deep time, Erdrich redefines relocation, remaps the borders of Ojibwe country, and, as a result, dislodges the very essence of tribal rootedness.

In the 1998 text, Cally says the city is "where we are scattered like beads off a necklace and put back together in new patterns, new strings."[196] This might be an apt metaphor for Erdrich's revision of the novel as well, for she takes much of the same material and so dramatically reworks it as to construct a whole new design. As Ed Folsom says of Whitman, who repeatedly revised *Leaves of Grass*, "Whitman did not just *write* his book, he *made* his book, and he made it over and over again, each time producing a different material object that spoke to its readers in different ways."[197] Similarly, the concept of textual instability suggests that we consider the worth of the multiple versions and the ways in which they do different work, even if Erdrich did not have a hand in the actual production of the book.[198] And perhaps this is why the beads have changed for Erdrich— from Czech in 1998 to Hungarian in 2012—to make it clear that these are not the same beads, that these are two similar yet different inventions. Stillinger calls authors who republish their work "obsessive revisers."[199] Certainly, Erdrich has a history as a reviser of her work. Not only has she revised and republished *The Antelope Wife* (now *Antelope Woman*), but there are now three versions of *Love Medicine*, and in her interview with the *Paris Review*, she said that she "can't wait to change *Four Souls*." About *Love Medicine*, she told David Streitfeld of the *Washington Post*, "I feel this is an ongoing work, not some discrete untouchable piece of writing."[200] Chavkin has argued that the second version of *Love Medicine* (the third had not yet appeared) has a different set of political convictions and that Erdrich seems to have answered some of the criticism about the original text. We might make the same claim about Erdrich's first revision of *The Antelope Wife*.[201] Many of the changes do add a political dimension to the text: the addition of the duplex, built in the year the Turtle Mountain reservation was established; the references to relocation; the incorporation of the American Indian Movement. And then there's the cracker tin full of money: reparations for Scranton Roy's participation in the massacre that he brings to the survivor's family.[202] Her vision of Minneapolis has also changed. As Erdrich herself states, she had just moved to the city when she first wrote *The Antelope Wife*.[203]

Finally, I would like to suggest, extending Blaeser's argument that there is a link between "re-turning" and "re-telling" in Indigenous journey narratives, that the revision of the novel is another form of motion and fluidity—that Erdrich re-turned to the text and re-told the story in a new and different way. Just as language is "not static," as Erdrich states in her essay "Two Languages in Mind, but Just One in the Heart," stories (and culture, as scholars like Stuart Hall have argued) are also not static. In the author's note in the 2016 book, Erdrich writes, "After all, a book is a temporary fix on the world, a set of words, and words can change."[204] The story, the novel, has traveled and changed in the space of fourteen years.[205] Ute Lischke argues that for Erdrich, writing is "much like the process of attempting to re-create the Blitzkuchen."[206] And yet, to use Lischke's metaphor, the original cake, like the first beaded necklace, has permanence. I would like to further suggest that the process of re-visioning is also a re-taking and re-vising of the narrative of Native Minneapolis. This chapter demonstrates that Erdrich's novel articulates the possibility of multiple place affiliations, which I argue it accomplishes both thematically and textually. The urban aesthetic at work here is about motion and simultaneity: human and antelope, land and sky, city and reservation, the twins Mary and Zosie, the original text and the revised. Similarly, Ferrari argues that Erdrich's earlier work challenges binaries and displays what Rachel Blau DuPlessis has described as the "both/and vision" of women's writing.[207] Erdrich's use of "boundary-defying figures," as Rachel Lister calls them, is one of the ways these binaries begin to break down.[208] Likewise, there are moments in the text when the city ceases to be: "There are times in the city, rare times, when the baffle of sound parts. Cally and Deanna listen for those times of transitory silence. No cars. No planes' roar. No buses or distant traffic. No spatter of television noise, even people talking. Now, just as the twins define the moment by the absence of all it isn't, someone laughs, a car door slams, there is a screech of tires. It is gone, their moment of baseless peace."[209] The "transitory silence" is a reminder of another version of this place—preindustrial, presettlement, precontact Indigenous space, the land that is "hunched" under the city of Minneapolis through layers and layers of histories.

CHAPTER 4

The City as Confluence

Events spiral to memories,
linking lives to time and history.
                    —E. Donald Two-Rivers, "Indian Land Dancing"

In 2005 Chicago Alderman Mary Ann Smith commissioned a mural in
the city's 48th Ward to be located on the north and south walls of the
Foster Avenue underpass to Lake Shore Drive. Alderman Smith wanted
the art to represent the diversity of Chicago's Indian community, whose
locus is in the nearby Uptown area. Designed in conjunction with the
Chicago Arts Group, artists Tracy Van Duinen, Todd Osborne, and Cynthia Weiss, with the input of local Native artists like Debra Yepa-Pappan
and Chris Pappan, along with other members of the American Indian
community, the mosaic or bricolage that resulted depicts both historical
and contemporary Chicago Indians.[1] Named *Indian Land Dancing* after
the poem by the late Ojibwe writer E. Donald Two-Rivers, the sprawling
3,150-square-foot design, completed in June 2009, combines ceramic
tile work, mirror, acrylic paint, text, and photographs. The "memory
wall" includes photos of Two-Rivers himself, Susan Power (Gathering
of Storm Clouds Woman, the author's mother and one of the founders
of Chicago's American Indian Center), and other Chicago elders, along
with figures important to Chicago history, like Yavapai physician Carlos
Montezuma and Sauk leader Black Hawk. These images are juxtaposed

with large, colorful tiles that depict a giant ear of corn, a Native youth on a skateboard, an eagle in flight, an iron worker, and a mother figure with her arms outstretched. There are cattails and geese and an oversized street sign that compiles American Indian street names in the city. There is also a giant onion, a reminder of Chicago's real or imagined etymology.[2] There are images of a construction worker and drums and a teepee. Together, these images combine the contemporary and the historical, urban and rural, cosmopolitan and tribal, mythical and mundane. The mural is striking and impressive for its visual construction of history and for the way it seeks to unify such a multitude of stories.[3] This sentiment is underscored by the text of Two-Rivers's poem, which holds a prominent position on a large metal door, the centerpiece of the project. The poem "Indian Land Dancing" invokes a celebration during the wild rice harvest, when the narrator imagines that "all of Indian land was dancing."[4] This imaginative move, from a specific Indigenous community to an urban one, from motion to stasis, mirrors the relocation of so many to this urban space and envisions a fellowship with all Indigenous peoples. Likewise, the mural calls attention to circuits of movement, just as it conjures both the past and the present of the diverse Indigenous peoples in Chicago. Its visual narrative draws upon both communal and individual memory, and it is a spatial text: located near Uptown, designed to occupy the entire underpass, located (via actual signposts) within a network of Indigenous places.

I begin this chapter on a writer by invoking a mural because it offers a lens for placing Indigenous texts in an urban setting, and in many ways it "brings together" the Chicago community in the same way that Power's book does. Susan Power grew up in this community, and her stories are imbricated with the Chicago landscape. Her novel in progress, *War Bundles*, is set in Chicago, and *The Grass Dancer* (1994), a novel set entirely on a North Dakota reservation, features a semiautobiographical character named Pumpkin who is a Chicago Native, a talented Menominee girl with plans to attend Stanford.[5] Power uses Pumpkin to articulate the challenge of balancing the cosmopolitan and the tribal; while Pumpkin is a grass dancer and has a community of urban Indians, she says that she "stand[s]

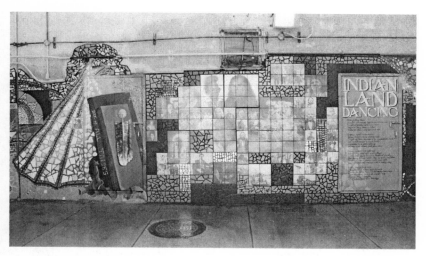

FIG 10. *Indian Land Dancing* by Tracy Van Duinen, Todd Osborne, and Cynthia Weiss, 2009. Bricolage mural commissioned by the Chicago Public Art Group. Foster Avenue underpass at Lake Shore Drive, Chicago. Photo by Todd Osborne, used with his permission. This is the centerpiece of the mural: Two-Rivers's poem and the "Book of Indians" are visible.

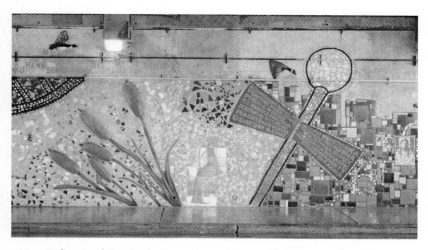

FIG 11. *Indian Land Dancing* by Tracy Van Duinen, Todd Osborne, and Cynthia Weiss, 2009. Bricolage mural commissioned by the Chicago Public Art Group. Foster Avenue underpass at Lake Shore Drive, Chicago. Photo by Todd Osborne, used with his permission. The sign at right features American Indian street names in the city.

outside" of her culture.[6] Education and knowledge from books have made it so that "she could no longer fit herself into the culture that was most important to her."[7] In her college application essay, she writes, "*I will have to put aside one worldview—perhaps only temporarily—to take up another. From what I have learned so far, I know the two are not complementary but rather incompatible, and melodramatic as it may sound, I sometimes feel I am risking my soul by leaving the Indian community.*"[8] What is striking about this statement is that the Indian community to which she refers is the one in the city; Pumpkin is just as attached to this place as someone like Harley Wind Soldier is attached to his reservation. Chicago in this novel is a generative space; it is a place of identity and wholeness. It is only when Indians like Pumpkin leave the city that they are most in danger.

Power's Chicago landscape is most clearly imagined in *Roofwalker* (2002), a collection of short stories and personal essays, which she calls "Histories."[9] As a multigenre work, this text demonstrates that the difference between story and history is difficult to negotiate.[10] In other words, the history of the city, the experiences she has there, and the stories that she tells merge in a way that makes them impossible to disentangle. Power knows Chicago. Her stories are infused with a deep place knowledge, and she maps the city's terrain in interesting and useful ways. Power's characters reflect the diversity of the Indian community—they are Lakotas, Oneidas, Winnebagos or Ho-Chunks, and Ojibwes. They experience Chicago in a myriad of ways: they work at the American Indian Center, they are activists, they are housewives, they own second-hand stores. They have come to the city for a number of reasons: for adventure, for work, to escape the politics of the reservation, to escape their own histories. Of course, Chicago has an Indigenous history of its own, and Power's text maps the layers of this history while, like the other books in this study, simultaneously locating a constellation of urban places and sites where those events took place. Chicago, for Power, is Indian Territory, even if that history has been largely obscured in the present, and she demonstrates that this space calls for a different kind of storytelling.

By some accounts, Indigenous peoples have inhabited the area that has become Chicago for the past ten thousand years, and Indigeneity is part of the past and present narrative of the so-called Windy City. Even Indigenous Chicago was cosmopolitan: Chicago proper was primarily Potawatomi territory at the time of contact, though Miamis and Ho-Chunks and Ottawas and Ojibwes also lived in the area. In fact, most Indian villages in this region were inhabited by people from multiple tribal nations. By the early 1800s, Chicago was sparsely settled by mixed-bloods and fur traders, many of them Métis from Canada. Native peoples and white settlers amicably inhabited the area, accounts show, until the Jacksonian era, when public sentiment over Indian removals shifted drastically. While the Treaty of Chicago, penned during this time period, officially purged the area of its Indigenous population, historians have now shown a persistent Native presence in the city and its suburbs.[11]

Chicago's lands were ceded in a number of treaties, beginning with the 1795 Treaty of Greenville (which relinquished one square mile at the mouth of the Chicago River) and ending finally with the Treaty of Chicago in 1833, which was formulated in light of both the 1830 Indian Removal Act and the Black Hawk War. In the 1833 treaty, Potawatomis exchanged five million acres for an equal amount of land in Missouri (later in Iowa) and received $1 million plus annuities for a period of twenty years.[12] With this final treaty, the Chicago territory was officially clear of its Indian population and open for settlement. Of some contention, however, is the ownership status of Lake Michigan's lakebed, which was never ceded in treaty. In what became known as the Sand Bar case, Potawatomi chief Simon Pokagon and later his son sought to claim the lakebed for the Potawatomis.[13] This is significant, of course, because the city's entire lakefront is built upon landfill (and therefore technically within the lake's boundaries). To some minds, Lake Michigan *is* Indian Territory.

At the center of Chicago's public memory is what has been called the Fort Dearborn Massacre or, more recently, the Battle of Chicago (1812). Fort Dearborn, situated at the mouth of the (now Chicago) River, was built in 1803, the farthest outpost in the Old Northwest Territories. During the War of 1812, the fort was evacuated and its inhabitants attacked by Potawatomis while en route to Fort Wayne. The attack took place just over a mile from the fort itself. Among the casualties were Capt. William

Wells, an Indian agent at Fort Wayne who had been raised by Miamis and was married to the chief's daughter; the fort's surgeon, Dr. Carl Van Voorhis; twenty-six soldiers; twelve militia; two women; and twelve children who rode together in a wagon. The survivors were taken captive and later ransomed at Detroit. As historian Constance R. Buckley has argued, Chicago's origin story is based on Fort Dearborn and the vernacular history written by Juliette Kinzie after the incident. Daughter-in-law of John Kinzie, a local fur trader now regarded as one of Chicago's founding fathers, Juliette wrote two versions of the "massacre": in 1844, the *Narrative of the Massacre at Chicago*, and in 1856, *Wau-Bun, the Early Day in the North-West*. Although alternative accounts of the attack were published soon after the event, it is Juliette Kinzie's, written in the mode of the captivity narrative, that has had the most lasting effect.[14]

A second Fort Dearborn was built in 1816 but was regarded as unnecessary by local residents: the Indian population had dropped, and settlers were focused on commerce. The fort was abandoned by 1823 but again reapportioned in 1828 during the Winnebago War, an antecedent to the more widely known Black Hawk War in 1832. When a garrison arrived at the fort and had to remove both squatters and refugees, a deadly cholera epidemic erupted. Fighting from the Black Hawk War never reached Chicago. The town was incorporated in 1833 and the fort finally deserted. What remained by 1871 was destroyed in the Great Fire. The fort is commemorated as the first outpost of civilization in the territory; images of the battle appear on a south-facing bridge house on Michigan Avenue, on a panel of the 333 North Michigan Avenue Building, and on an 1893 monument by Carl Rohl-Smith, which I will discuss in greater detail later in this chapter.[15] The Chicago Historical Society also preserved a portion of a tree said to mark the site of the battle. In 1939 a star was added to Chicago's municipal flag to commemorate the battle, and in 2009 the site was designated as the Battle of Fort Dearborn Park.[16]

The occasion for the creation of the Fort Dearborn Massacre monument was the 1893 World's Columbian Exposition, held in Chicago's Jackson Park. The Expo both celebrated and showcased tribal peoples as it celebrated the four hundredth anniversary of Columbus's "discovery."[17] While

Frederick Jackson Turner was presenting his essay "Significance of the Frontier in American History," declaring that the American frontier was all but closed, villages of living Lakota and Inuit peoples and other tribal exhibits populated with mannequins drew spectators—over twenty-seven million visitors in a nascent city with a population of eighty thousand.[18] While Buffalo Bill's Wild West was not officially part of the Expo—it was considered to be too low-brow—Cody set up across the street from the famous White City in a grandstand that could hold eighteen thousand people.[19] Performers from the Wild West mingled with Indigenous peoples from the exhibitions and rode the new Ferris Wheel alongside white patrons. The Expo reflected the rise of interest in anthropology and ethnography, and its collections have had a lasting effect on museums nationwide. In Chicago, the Field Museum, first called the Columbian Museum of Chicago, is evidence of this legacy.[20] For some time, the museum inhabited the building constructed for the Expo in Jackson Park, the Palace of Fine Arts, and its original collections come from the Expo itself.[21]

As Rosalyn LaPier and David Beck point out in *City Indian*, the years 1893 to 1934 in Chicago saw much activist sentiment, in line with the Progressive Era.[22] They argue that men such as Simon Pokagon, Carlos Montezuma, Francis Cayou (Omaha), and Scott Henry Peters (Ojibwe) paved the way for twentieth-century protest and were thoroughly embedded in the Chicago landscape. Pokagon's reaction to the Columbian Expo, for example, first published as "Red Man's Rebuke" and later as "A Red Man's Greeting," demonstrates these early attempts to take control of the narrative of Indigenous peoples in Chicago. Montezuma, on the other hand, is best known for his reputation as a medical doctor, but he also served as a kind of informal ambassador and concierge for Indians who visited the city—delegations on their way to Washington, students on their way to Carlisle. He also advocated for Native residents, often helping them secure employment or funds from the Office of Indian Affairs. Although Montezuma was a founding member of the Society of American Indians (SAI), a pan-Indian movement with an urban base, his relationship to the organization was a rocky one.[23] Like Pokagon, Montezuma picked up his pen—in his case, to create a newspaper called *Wassaja*—to effect change.

Chicago became one of the first cities chosen by the Bureau of Indian Affairs' relocation program, and the Native population grew rapidly: from 775 to 6,575 between 1950 and 1970, according to census records.[24] The program liked to tout its job-training initiatives, though many relocatees were failed by them.[25] BIA materials reveal that Indigenous workers in Chicago were placed in local industries, like steel mills, as apprentices, while others became file clerks, stenographers, and telephone operators.[26] Where the BIA failed, other agencies stepped in to provide much-needed social and community services. Father Peter Powell, an Episcopal priest who started St. Augustine's Indian Center, along with the All Tribes American Indian Center offered assistance with jobs, housing, health care, and meals, as well as provided spaces where Native Chicagoans could congregate for cultural and social events. The All Tribes American Indian Center—co-founded by Susan Kelly Power, Susan Power's mother, in collaboration with the BIA in 1953—in fact claims to be the first urban center in the nation.[27] Though it had its origins in the River North area, the Indian Center purchased a building in the late 1960s in the city's Uptown neighborhood, 411 North La Salle Street, where a large number of Native peoples were living.[28]

The relocation era was also one of protest, and Chicago saw its share. In particular, the Chicago Indian Village (CIV) movement was spurred by the eviction of a thirty-five-year-old Menominee woman named Carol Warrington and her six children, who had withheld rent to protest poor living conditions. The Native American Committee (NAC), a splinter group of the American Indian Center, set up a tipi across from her apartment in Wrigleyville, and numbers of tents and other protesters followed. The NAC helped Warrington retrieve her personal belongings that had been removed from the apartment.[29] Although the NAC officially backed out after a couple of days, the group that remained became the Chicago Indian Village, though it was first called the "little Alcatraz movement" by the news media, demonstrating the public's perception of Indigenous activism and the cachet of Alcatraz at the time.[30] The group demanded an Indian housing complex and adjacent cultural center, to be built in the Uptown neighborhood.

Susan Power evokes all of these histories in *Roofwalker*—from the protests over the Fort Dearborn Massacre statue, to her great-great-grandmother's dress in the Field Museum, to her mother's involvement with the American Indian Center and the community of Native peoples in the Uptown neighborhood. In "Narrating Memory," Terry DeHay describes how "Third World" American writers "need to construct alternative histories" in response to "the dominant culture's attempt to destroy and/or neutralize these marginalized cultures through the destruction or appropriation of their collective history."[31] Memory, or, more specifically, remembering, then, becomes an "act of becoming or resisting."[32] DeHay has argued that much of this writing utilizes a fragmentary or kaleidoscopic narrative style (not unlike Power's collection of fiction and nonfiction), one that challenges "unity of vision, linear progression" of the traditional narrative structure, the "singular eye or I."[33] As a result, this shifting "I" (and, I would add, the absence of chronological order) in *Roofwalker* challenges any sort of unified "truth," providing alternate versions of history. As I will demonstrate, Power constructs alternate histories through what I see as accretion—the layering of memories that make meaning when read together. Further, Power enacts a tribal mode of storytelling. Tribal epistemologies demand that one speak from experience, and in *Roofwalker*, Power demonstrates how even her fictions spring forth from the autobiographical "I."

In addition, *Roofwalker* performs the kind of convergence suggested by Choctaw writer LeAnne Howe in her theory of tribalography.[34] According to Howe, tribalography "comes from the Native propensity for bringing things together, for making consensus, and for symbiotically connecting one thing to another": "Native stories, no matter what form they take (novel, poem, drama, memoir, film, history), seem to pull all the elements together of the storyteller's tribe, meaning the people, the land, and multiple characters and all their manifestations and revelations, and connect these in past, present, and future milieus."[35] Tribalography describes the ways that authors seek to create a tribal text—one that transcends simple generic classification and the constraints of time. According to Joseph Bauerkemper in his introduction to a special *SAIL* issue on Howe's work, tribalography "denotes a dynamic process through which the apparent chaos of contradiction and multiplicity is navigated and reconfigured."[36] And while this seems to be an apt description of a book like *The Grass Dancer*, which Howe herself uses as an example, I would like to suggest that it describes *Roofwalker* as well. *Roofwalker* is an urban text, one that "brings together" a constellation of Indigenous Chicago stories that make meaning through accretion. In bringing these stories together, Power enacts a particularly urban form of tribalography to reflect the "apparent chaos" of city life. In other words, the construction of Power's text makes clear that the urban landscape and experience demand an alternate narrative mode, one that both reflects multiplicity and enacts a reclamation of place through epistemological representation.

Further, I read Power's "bringing together" the diversity of Indigenous peoples in Chicago as a cosmopolitan gesture. This community is historically and continuously multitribal, and Power constructs it through a rooted and Indigenous cosmopolitanism. Kwame Anthony Appiah writes about "rooted cosmopolitanism" in a way that is particularly useful for this discussion, naming the ways in which people are simultaneously connected to their homes and to cosmopolitan spaces.[37] Robin DeLugan has also described an "Indigenous cosmopolitanism" that "emphasizes how (individual, ethnic, national) difference and (collective, Indigenous, human) unity coexist in a framework of relatedness": "Through the idiom of indigeneity, a shared discourse recognizes that the Other, though different, is like one's self and that all people are meaningfully related to each other."[38] In *Roofwalker*, Power's stories reflect a Dakota perspective (with the inclusion of traditional stories and histories that emanate from Dakota territory) but invoke tribal diversity through her use of character and narrative voice. In fact, this multiply voiced book proves that multitribal unity is both possible and revolutionary.

In her earliest iteration of tribalography, Howe writes, "Native people created narratives that [are] histories and stories with the power to transform."[39] As *Roofwalker* maps the layers of Indigenous histories in Chicago in a kind of literary bricolage that is centered on specific places and sites, Power demonstrates how history gets constructed and reconstructed

and how the urban landscape gets rescripted and re-storied as she rein-
scribes Chicago's place-story. This reinscription is a creative act, one that
is reenacted in each story/history in the book. The book is full of the creative energies of Indigenous peoples in Chicago, and as they make, they
remake; as they create, they re-create. Power's urban aesthetic is one of
convergence: like the visual narrative of *Indian Land Dancing*, *Roofwalker*
imagines what it means to bring (hi)stories and peoples together and
how, together, they tell a new story.

(RE)VISIONING PLACE HISTORY

Historian David Glassberg argues that history and place are "inextricably
intertwined; we attach histories to places, and the environmental value
we attach to a place comes largely through the memories and historical
associations we have with it."[40] In *Roofwalker*, Susan Power demonstrates
how stories uncover lost histories in the search for place-stories, and
several of her stories are inherently *about* uncovering lost place-histories.
This articulation is best revealed in the story "First Fruits," which takes
place not in Chicago but in Cambridge, Massachusetts, another urban site
that evokes Indigenous displacement in the colonial era.[41] "First Fruits"
is the story of Georgiana Lorraine Shoestring, a Dakota girl attending
Harvard.[42] At the beginning of the story, George and her father are on
a campus tour, and they learn the popular "three lies" about the John
Harvard statue. First, the statue is not a depiction of John Harvard, for
"no likeness of John Harvard exists."[43] Second, the year on the statue,
indicating when Harvard was founded, is incorrect. Third, the college was
not actually founded by John Harvard but by a legislative body. Although
some have argued that these details are not important, that John Harvard
left half of his estate and his entire library to the new college, thereby
making him *a* founder, these discrepancies have long been a source of
contention, particularly for historians. In October 1883, for example, the
president of the Massachusetts Historical Society, the Honorable Robert
C. Winthrop, bemoaned the creation of a statue to commemorate John
Harvard, particularly given the absence of his likeness: "Such a course
tends to the confusing and confounding of historical truth, and leaves

posterity unable to decide what is authentic and what is mere invention."[44] This line between authenticity and invention gets to the heart of historiography, of how we construct historical narratives, and in Power's story, it is the Indigenous characters who are invested in discovering the "historical truth." Power mobilizes this statue as proof that public history is often wrong, that the wrong people are often commemorated, that official stories about places even as renowned as Harvard have constructed histories, and that it is our job in the present to reconstruct and rewrite these histories. Power calls our attention to the public monument itself, which commemorates Harvard's whiteness and obscures its original purpose—altogether, a kind of public art different from the mural discussed at the beginning of this chapter. Finally, she seems to be suggesting that the inauthentic history of Harvard, a foundational American institution, is a strange sort of metaphor for the many inauthentic histories of American Indigeneity, in constant need of revision.

The title of the story, "First Fruits," is a reference to a 1643 pamphlet entitled *New England's First Fruits; In Respect, First of the Conversion of Some, Conviction of Divers, Preparation of Sundry, 2. Of the Progresse of Learning, in the Colledge at Cambridge in Massacusets Bay, With Divers other Speciall Matters concerning that Countrey.*[45] *New England's First Fruits* is the first of eleven pamphlets known as the Eliot Tracts, though there is some uncertainty about whether this one was penned by the famous minister John Eliot. This is not the only questionable aspect of this document: because it was written for use in fund-raising for the Massachusetts Bay colony, it contains many misstatements and overestimations, particularly in regard to how many Indians had been converted to Christianity and how many students were matriculating at Harvard College (which, at the time of the writing, had run out of money and was nonfunctioning). These historical inaccuracies were intentional—and Power's allusion to the pamphlet functions in two important ways. First, like her inclusion of the John Harvard statue, the story's title calls attention to the persuasiveness and power of early America's writers. Second, Power contemplates the narrator's (and her own) subject position as an Indian student at Harvard. The "First Fruits" refers to those who have been converted—the "first fruits" of their labor in what would become the United States. In the story, George's father explains that the Puritans "felt that if you educated Indians, you could convert their souls."[46] "President Henry Dunster," he reads from Alden T. Vaughan's book *New England Frontier: Puritans and Indians 1620–1675*, "took seriously the statement in Harvard's charter of 1650 that the purpose of the institution was *the education of the English and Indian Youth of this Country*."[47] As Melvin Shoestring speaks, their tour guide takes notes. In this, we see a reversal of historical dictation: the Indian telling Indian history, though in this case, the history he tells comes from a groundbreaking book on Puritan-Indian relations.[48] He brings this book on the tour for the very purpose of correcting the historical narrative being told by the tour guide—the official storyteller for the institution, in this case. Melvin is concerned with the dominant narrative, just as he is concerned with the doctrine of conversion; as he leaves George at Harvard, he tells his daughter, "*Don't let them change you*."[49]

Power's story also enacts a sort of spatiohistory when Melvin Shoestring wields Vaughan's book—and he is described as holding it like a Bible—to determine the location of the original Indian College at Harvard.[50] This brick building, which stood near or behind Matthews Hall, was meant to house twenty Indian students, though Harvard was never able to recruit this number. Melvin, who is known to see ghosts, is in search of Caleb Cheeshateaumuck, a Wampanoag and the first Indian graduate of Harvard, who died of consumption a year after his graduation.[51] George says, "My father has always seen beyond the surface of things, what he calls the distracting reality."[52] Also, reminiscent of a moment in the story "Wild Turnips," "he has this telescopic, microscopic view—both large and small—peeling back layers and getting to the spirit of things."[53] These "layers" of history are not separate realities, as George later discovers. She says, "I was taught to believe that time is not a linear stream, but a hoop spinning forward like a wheel, where everything is connected and everything is eternal."[54] In other words, these moments in time exist simultaneously, and every place is simultaneously occupied by multiple narratives. She continues, "In this cosmology, I am here because Caleb came before me, and he was here in anticipation of me. We are bonded together across time, and I will recognize him when I see him."[55] Melvin encourages his daughter to search for Caleb, and during her first semester, she discovers through the act of writing about him that he does not haunt Harvard but has returned to Martha's Vineyard, where he is among his people. While Caleb's story still occupies the space of Harvard (after all, George is able to access it there), he has preserved his Indigeneity in spite of his Harvard education. "I am Wampanoag," he tells George, and she imagines that he is "letting go of the languages," the Latin, Greek, Hebrew, and English that he had learned.[56] In the story's final scene, George is teaching her roommate, Allegra, how to dance to powwow music in what becomes both a cultural affirmation and a reversal of acculturation and erasure. George's "soul" has not been converted, despite Harvard's original inclinations, and she is empowered by the recovery of the historical narrative of this place.

The historical narrative specific to Chicago in *Roofwalker* also involves a statue and a history of Indian-white relations. This statue is the *Fort Dearborn Massacre* monument, commissioned by railroad magnate George L. Pullman and created by Danish sculptor Carl Rohl-Smith, dedicated during the World's Expo in 1893. Originally placed at the corner of 18th Street and South Calumet Avenue, close to where the attack occurred, in 1931 or 1932 it was moved into the lobby of the Chicago Historical Society to "protect it from vandals," according to the *Chicago Tribune*.[57] The work depicts, in bronze, Mrs. Helm, whose account of the incident became the official narrative, along with a young child (who was not hers), as they are being saved from a hostile Indian hatchet-wielding Potawatomi leader, Black Partridge, while Dr. Van Voorhis, the fort's surgeon, lies dead on the ground. Interestingly enough, Rohl-Smith used a Lakota man, Short Bull, as a model for Black Partridge—a group of Lakota prisoners of war were being held at Fort Sheridan in the wake of Wounded Knee, further obscuring any chance at historical authenticity here.[58] At the monument's unveiling, the Historical Society's director, Edward G. Mason, located the depiction within the narrative of Manifest Destiny: "barbarians" needed to make way for "civilization" in Chicago, even though Chicago's founding did not follow in this pattern.[59] Another official statement about the monument explains the need for such a violent depiction of the event: "A massacre, perpetrated by savages, demands for full expression the portrayal of the highest degree of violence."[60]

To think about what this monument means to the city of Chicago, I turn to recent theories on the cultural work of monuments and public art. Monuments satisfy "the desire to commemorate, to mark a place, to represent the past to the present and future, to emphasize one narrative of the past at the expense of others, or simply to make the past past," write Robert S. Nelson and Margaret Olin.[61] Of course, while the *Fort Dearborn Massacre* monument represents an important historical moment in Chicago's history, it also functions to assuage white guilt: white women and children must be protected from vengeful and violent savages to make way for civilization. Indians are both "wild" and "wilderness" in this narrative. This version of the event became part of Chicago's official history; it gave the city an origin story that is sensational and satisfying, though it certainly erased Indigenous voices and perspectives. As James Young has argued about Holocaust memorials, "By creating common spaces for memory, monuments propagate the illusion of common memory."[62] The "illusion of common memory" of the Chicago monument allows the narrative of white victory to prevail, its place-story to envision conquest, and, thus, the Chicago landscape to become devoid of its Indigenous inhabitants.

Of course, dominant memorials such as this one can "become sites of conflict and contestation," writes archaeologist Dacia Viejo-Rose.[63] In 1973, some forty years after the *Fort Dearborn Massacre* was moved to the Historical Society, where it sat under a banner that read "Indian: Friend or Foe?," a protest was staged by members of the American Indian community demanding the statue's removal.[64] The monument is offensive in a number of ways: for its depictions of Indians as inevitably violent; for its emphasis on the "victims"; for its perpetuation of the "massacre" moniker; for the way it alters the truth of Chicago's origins, which were much more multicultural than this narrative allows; for its oversimplification of history; and for its memorialization of conflict. The monument was finally removed from the Historical Society in 1987, when it was relocated to a park on Kedzie, and then it was moved once again in 1997 when that park was renamed for Hillary Clinton. It now resides in a storage facility maintained by the Chicago Park District, though historians such as Ann Durkin Keating and Robert Klein Engler would like to see it back on public view.[65]

This statue makes a brief and poignant appearance in *Roofwalker*, specifically in the essay entitled "Museum Indians," a title that suggests that the only Indians Chicago recognizes are museumized: dead or frozen in the past. In this piece, Power recites her mother's relocation story (she came to Chicago at the age of sixteen for work, and she had never been on a train) and illustrates her mother's relationship to the city. Power's mother introduces Chicago to the young narrator, and she takes her to the museums: the Historical Society, the Art Institute, and the Field Museum of Natural History. According to Power, her mother repeatedly protests the statue at the Historical Society until it is removed. While it is curious that the 1973 protest is absent from her narrative, her sentiment echoes that of the protesters. Susan senior says, "This is the only monument to the history of Indians in this area that you have on exhibit. It's a shame because it is completely one-sided. Children who see this will think this is what Indians are all about."[66] The conflation of her mother's protest with one staged by the larger community turns the mother's narrative into an official history for Power, and this becomes important to the book: that her mother is the source of Power's stories—and that from her mother Power has learned to protest.

As an example of these competing versions of history, we can compare the way the protest was reported in the media and in Power's story (and, alternatively, in the one told by Two-Rivers in his play *Chili Corn*).[67] While in Power's version, her mother single-handedly protests the monument and is able to have it removed, the news media reveals that there was a protest of fifty to seventy-five activists on a particular day in November 1973, and Two-Rivers is cited as the group's spokesperson.[68] Two-Rivers writes that his play is "loosely" based on true events; in 1973 he and two friends "organized to have [the statue] removed" after experiencing the effects of its message: young children were being frightened by Indian people. According to Benny in the play, the director of the local American

Indian Movement (AIM) chapter, the statue "incites hate against Indians" and is "a symptom of institutional racism."[69] In the play, members of AIM are planning to bomb the statue when it is suddenly moved. The newspapers reported that tobacco and fruit were left at the statue, along with a note, and that the protest occurred in Lincoln Park, not at the Historical Society proper. These discrepancies, in addition to the rather large time gap between the protest and when the statue is removed (some ten plus years), make for a confused history, but the power is in the telling, the articulation of the defeat of the dominant narrative that the statue represents.

By juxtaposing "First Fruits" and "Museum Indians," it becomes clear that the parent's role as both storyteller and archivist is important, perhaps even more so in the urban space. Power's mother may be indirectly uncovering Chicago history (and family history, which I will soon demonstrate) in the same way that Melvin wields Alden Vaughan's book to recover Harvard's Indian past. Both pieces seek to know the history of a geographical place in order to understand one's relationship to that place. Both seek to undermine the dominant narrative and to insert Indigenous history into the record—in other words, both stories are about writing and *re*writing those histories. Of course, in both cases, gaps get revealed. For instance, "Museum Indians" details young Susan's visits to the Field Museum with her mother to visit her great-grandmother's blue beaded buckskin dress. Her mother says, "I don't know how this got out of the family."[70] They are connected to this dress, a family heirloom, but cannot complete the story of how it ended up in the Field Museum.[71] Even so, the story of the dress, a family story, is mapped onto and alongside the history of the Field Museum and her mother's relocation to Chicago, which is aligned with the taxidermic buffalo at the museum that they also visit. Through the confluence of histories, they are still connected to Dakota culture and land. "You don't belong here," her mother tells the buffalo. "This crazy city is not a fit home for buffalo or Dakotas."[72] For Dakotas, the buffalo (or bison) is a relative, and to see him imprisoned here in the museum is disheartening.[73] Of course, the buffalo also symbolizes the history of expansionism, extermination, and colonial defeat. These visits to the museum are thus solemn occasions, not necessarily ones of blatant protest, though Power says elsewhere that her mother was always plotting how to break into the museum and steal back this dress.[74] Power writes, "We stand before the glass case as we would before a grave."[75] She creates a visual image near the end of essay, one that demonstrates the power of re-storying so prevalent in this collection: "We leave our fingerprints on the glass, two sets of hands at different heights pressing against the barrier."[76] Young Susan and her mother make their mark on this space, however slight—not unlike the mark that George inevitably makes at Harvard or the mark that Melvin makes on future visitors to Harvard by reinserting Indigenous history into the narrative. Likewise, Susan takes possession of Chicago in the way that George claims the space of Harvard.

HISTORICAL CONVERGENCE

In her 2013 book, *Mark My Words: Native Women Mapping Our Nations*, Mishuana Goeman uses Doreen Massey's language to conceptualize space as a "meeting-up of histories," which is an apt description for the way Susan Power writes Chicago.[77] We often think of rural spaces, like the frontier, as contact zones, as places where histories intersect, but what makes Power's stories useful here is how they locate histories in urban settings. Two short stories in *Roofwalker* in particular hinge on the confluence of histories: the title story and "Beaded Soles." Both are set in Chicago in the early 1970s, and both circulate around the American Indian Center. "Roofwalker" is narrated by a young Dakota girl in Chicago named Jessie whose Grandma Mabel, according to "family legend," comes down from the Standing Rock Reservation in North Dakota for her birth and ostensibly to protect Jessie's mother from sterilization—a common fear on the reservation, especially in those days.[78] Mabel brings Jessie a star quilt (given for births and other celebrations) and an explanation for the girl's red hair: Vikings.[79] Mabel's knowledge about the Vikings and their alleged interactions with the Dakotas comes from legend, from the oral tradition, and in this way, she is a figure not unlike Melvin and Susan's mother. Mabel says, "Hundreds of years ago, long before Columbus and his three boats got lost and stumbled upon our land, those Vikings came down from the North country, where it's always cold . . . and . . . [t]hey married into our tribes."[80] This story decenters an American history that begins with Columbus and simultaneously privileges an Indigenous narrative, one that is being gradually confirmed by mainstream science.[81]

Mabel becomes Jessie's source of Dakota culture and history during Mabel's visits to Chicago and their telephone conversations in between. Jessie learns about Iktome the trickster and the roofwalker, a "Sioux spirit, a kind of angel," according to Mabel.[82] The roofwalker "was born out of misery, right after the Wounded Knee massacre, where so many of our people were killed for holding a Ghost Dance."[83] He lives "to eat dreams, and when he feasted on the dream of his choice, it always came true."[84] The story about the roofwalker is passed down by Mabel's *tunkasila*, her grandfather, to Jessie. Mabel is convinced that the roofwalker has followed her to Chicago and that he'll "get lost and never find the Dakotas again."[85] She then locates him within the city's geography: "He'll choke over those steel mills or fly straight into that John Hancock Building."[86] It is particularly telling that the story *can* be transported to the urban space, that Power (like Alexie) invokes the Ghost Dance in the city, and that the story comes to mean something new in this location.

In the title story, relocation history mingles with the history of star quilts and the Ghost Dance and Wounded Knee and forced sterilization and the Vikings. These stories get (re)mapped and (re)told within the urban space, where they become the quilt that Jessie wraps herself in. They are the stories that teach her what it means to be Dakota. When Jessie sees the roofwalker, a physical manifestation of Dakota culture and historical trauma, outside her bedroom window, she is reassured that an urban Dakota existence is possible, and she is empowered by this figure. She notes that the roofwalker resembles her father, who has recently abandoned the family to return to "dangerous" Pine Ridge, thereby linking the legend back to Wounded Knee and other histories of broken families. Jessie thus transforms the roofwalker story to give it both a contemporary meaning and historical resonance.

The overlap of historical memory and family story is equally apparent in "Beaded Soles." In this story, Maxine Bullhead recalls relocating to

Chicago in hopes of escaping what she calls the sins of her ancestors: her great-grandfather, Lt. Henry Bullhead, is renowned for being the Indian police officer to have shot and killed Sitting Bull during his arrest.[87] Invoking the idea of "blood memory," Maxine says, "On the reservation, memory is a sap that runs thick and deep in the blood. The community memory is long, preserving ancient jealousies, enmities, and alliances until they become traditional."[88] Power makes another direct connection between memory and blood: "In my family, memory was a soldier's navy blue tunic, stiffened on the left side with a spatter of sacred brown blood."[89] This blood, Sitting Bull's, soaks the coat and enters the wound of Lieutenant Bullhead, "poisoning his wound."[90]

Maxine imagines that she can escape these memories, this terrible history, by leaving the reservation. After giving birth to a stillborn son five years into their marriage, Maxine gets "Relocation fever," even though she sees through the false advertising of the glossy BIA brochures. She convinces her husband, Marshall Azure, to leave Standing Rock for Chicago. She says, "Chicago would never know I was a Bullhead. The ancestors and *heyoka* spirits with their long memories would never see me in Chicago."[91] Of course, the "Roofwalker" story demonstrates that this is not true. Marshall becomes the night watchman at the Indian Center, and Maxine becomes homesick. One night, Maxine receives a box of *wasna*— balls of ground chokecherries and corn meal—from her mother, and she walks over to the Indian Center to share them with her husband. Maxine finds Marshall in the arms of a white woman, and she stabs him in the heart. His last words to Maxine, in Dakota, are "we should never have left," meaning they never should have left the reservation; however, we see that the "curse" transcends geographical boundaries.[92] In the end, Maxine sits in prison, beading moccasins for Marshall, imagining that he is now dancing with their son and Lieutenant Bullhead and Sitting Bull.

Power's message in this story is similar to that of *The Grass Dancer*: the historical past is not truly past but continues to have relevance in the present in a convergence of both time and place.[93] Here it is the story of Sitting Bull, the renowned and revered Hunkpapa leader killed by his own people, that has historical resonance. History, like memory, runs in the blood of the Bullhead family "as if it was packaged in our genes."[94] Maxine describes the bloodied uniform that is kept in her family's closet—literally, a proverbial skeleton in the closet, but also an artifact from a critical historical moment for Lakota/Dakota people.[95] This uniform was witness to this event, and it remains in Indigenous possession; in other words, while it would seem possible that an item such as this would be on display in some American museum (the Smithsonian, for example), it is instead museumized in the Bullheads' home at Standing Rock. Certainly, other Sitting Bull memorabilia has been coveted: his cabin on Grand River was transported to Chicago in 1893 for the Columbian Expo; the Custer Battlefield Museum in Montana has a plaster Sitting Bull "death mask"; and his supposed remains were moved from Standing Rock to Mobridge, South Dakota, in 1953 in a battle over possession of his legacy.[96] Maxine visits Sitting Bull's grave at Standing Rock before she leaves as she attempts to extricate herself from his story.[97] It is important, in terms of cultural survival, that Dakota history and memory are mobile and inescapable.

This history in "Beaded Soles," then, like that in "Roofwalker," reveals some interesting linkages between Wounded Knee and relocation. It is in this story that Power most clearly articulates the draw of the city during relocation in order to think about why Indians might have accepted the BIA's offer to relocate them to the cities. Maxine Bullhead leaves her reservation to escape—the trappings of memory, public scorn, heartache over the loss of her son, and inheritance, in her case the inheritance of bad luck or poison. "I surrounded myself with Chicago's promises," she says, citing the brochures of Chicago, "The City Beautiful."[98] Maxine's expectations for the city, that her family's story/history will not have power in this space, are thwarted when she connects both her husband's philandering and his subsequent murder to "the sudden weight of sin."[99] Instead, we see them in a web of connection both to the Dakota people and to their history: Maxine's mother sends *wasna*, they speak Dakota to each other, Marshall's body is taken back to Standing Rock for burial, and Maxine imagines him to be dancing in Dakota heaven. Stories about relocation and Marshall's murder at the American Indian Center are returned to Standing Rock as this history is added to that of Sitting Bull. In other words, that history gets extended into the present of "Beaded Soles": it is Bullhead's great-granddaughter who has killed Marshall Azure, after all.

The American Indian Center plays a central role in both of these stories, "Roofwalker" and "Beaded Soles."[100] The center functions as a "hub," to return to Renya Ramirez here for a moment. As a hub, the community center is a "collecting center," with spokes that branch out to its tribal communities.[101] The American Indian Center is literally, then, the center or the heart of this community, not an outpost for a diasporic population. The center is depicted as a place of community and support and identity: members help Maxine get the materials she needs to make death moccasins for Marshall, for example.[102] It is more than a coincidence that both Marshall and Jessie's father in "Roofwalker" are employees at the center. Marshall is the night watchman, while Jessie's father "wrote proposals for the Indian community."[103] In both stories, the families live close enough to the center to walk there, and both depict it as a multitribal place. In "Beaded Soles," Power describes its physicality, evoking its structure and not just what happens inside, when Maxine says, "The building covered half a city block and was five stories high."[104] She liked having the key to the center, she says, "pretending the building was mine to be divided into large apartments for all the Indian people living in Chicago."[105] Of course, this key is important to the plot: it is how Maxine is able to enter the building and discover her husband having sex with another woman. Her desire to turn the building into housing calls attention to the unifying history of the center, along with its present and potential existence as Indian space in Chicago. This imagined reallocation and redesign of building space is also a glimpse of the creative acts that occur in other parts of this book. Its history gets evoked by its inclusion—and the need for better housing for relocatees, or the economic difficulties they experienced, is also suggested in the process.

The family history that is implied through mention of the American Indian Center and the fictional family history that drives the plot of "Beaded Soles" become explicit in the penultimate essay, "The Attic," though it is not set in Chicago. "The Attic" is about Power and her mother uncovering forgotten histories in her Grandmother Power's attic in Albany, New

York, shortly before her grandmother's death. "The Attic" follows Power as she learns about her paternal history, much of which was unknown to her due to her young age at her father's death. Power's mother wants to be sure that Susan knows about this side of her family as well, her white side, which can trace its origins in America to the *Mayflower*. Power says that she could feel the attic "pressing down on the rest of the house, burdened with the family archives and memories, a museum gone to ruin."[106] This family history stands in sharp contrast to her mother's history: it is partially revealed through the very existence of written documentation versus the oral stories, but also through the ownership of that history. In "Museum Indians," that family legacy is manifested in the Field Museum dress, as I have already suggested, and in "Reunion," Power says that her mother "recite[s] the history of my ancestors without pause."[107] In the Power household, these objects and histories are corporeal, and the author suggests that they are a "burden." They uncover "letters, treasured mementos, faces in tintypes, names in bibles, unread books"; her mother "was overwhelmed by the stories and artifacts."[108] Literally, the written word is overwhelming.

The role of Power's mother in this story is once again as archivist, and this becomes a story of historical recovery and reframing. As Power says, "The Indians were prowling through the attic on a voyage of discovery, exhuming my dead Pilgrim fathers."[109] During their attic search, Susan and her mother discover a compelling ancestor, Josephine Parkhurst Gilmore, who married Power's great-great-grandfather and wrote a trove of letters to him. They later visit her grave, where Power imagines that her mother tells Josephine stories about what was happening to Dakota people during Josephine's lifetime: "She could have lectured the girl, telling her that on September 3, 1863—just three days before Josephine Parkhurst Gilmore penned her last letter—the peaceful village of my great-great-grandfather, Chief Two Bear, had been attacked by Generals Sibley and Sully, and our Yanktonnai band nearly wiped out."[110] This event is the White Stone Massacre, though Power does not name it as such here, when 150–300 Dakotas were killed at White Stone Hill, between the James River and the Missouri River. Power says that her mother "has described the scene so vividly I sometimes think she must have been there."[111] Josephine here gets reframed by Dakota history—and the act of doing so is a way of bringing them together. Power and her mother find Josephine's history compelling, documented as it is in her letters, but certainly it is overshadowed by the story of Dakota loss. The year 1863 also locates this story during the Civil War in a kind of interesting triangulation of history. While the Civil War may dominate the narrative about 1863, Power suggests this confluence with Indigenous and personal histories that are happening simultaneously.

Josephine's story is also a story about women and the relationship with her mother: a woman in ill health, away from home, who desperately longs for her mother's help. That this story was compelling to Power and her mother is no mystery. They cannot imagine their lives without mothers. In this essay, Power also envisions that her two grandmothers meet through her as another instance of the convergence of Dakota and white American history, that she is literally an embodiment of such history, the embodiment of both her mother's oral stories and her father's archives. In these instances, white American history gets reframed from a Dakota perspective, and in the spirit of tribalography, Power demonstrates the simultaneity of histories, how American history is also Indigenous history, and how the past is always present.

ALTERNATE TEXTUALITIES

In "The Story of America: A Tribalography," LeAnne Howe cites a lecture in which Susan Power declared that Indians have been "the transformers" in American history.[112] Specifically, Power meant that Indians have been both agents of history and the tellers of tribal histories. Howe declares that Power is reclaiming American history in her work, and I would take this a step further: Power is also demonstrating the process by which counterhistories are created and disseminated.[113] In *Roofwalker*, she presents numerous versions of artist figures—creators—who challenge the status quo and use artistic expressions to tell a new story, a creation story. Like the protagonist's aunt in Ella Deloria's *Waterlily*, who is skilled in porcupine quill embroidery, Power's figures seem to draw upon Dakota myths about Double Woman, a supernatural and sacred artist figure who taught the first woman to make art.[114] She thus calls attention to the creative act and to the ability of storytelling to rescript the historical record, which is, in a sense, what Power herself is doing in this book—particularly as she shows how the landscape of Chicago gets re-storied—in the same way *Indian Land Dancing* allows for an Indigenous reconstruction of history.

Traditional thinking about artist figures—or "artist-heroes," to use Maurice Beebe's term—in fiction insists that these characters, godlike in nature, are inherently autobiographical; they are always versions of the author himself (or herself, in this case).[115] However, here I am suggesting that we pay more attention to the recurrence of artist figures in *Roofwalker* in their multiple manifestations than in whether or not they have autobiographical origins, though I do submit that the projects or creations of these figures do somehow mirror Power's project in this text. I am also less interested in what artist figures mean in mainstream settings; instead, I want to think about the role of traditional Native artists and artisans in their own communities and how Indigenous arts tell stories—like the way Haudenosaunee artists and writers "engage and conceptualize wampum traditions—oral, visual, and otherwise—as a way of organizing narrative and theoretically undergirding the aesthetics and poetics of their creations" that Penelope Kelsey writes about, or the way Mohegan baskets have discursive power, as Stephanie Fitzgerald has demonstrated.[116] Together Fitzgerald and Hilary Wyss have argued that Native "forms of material culture constitute 'texts' that can and should be read within a Native context."[117] Like Momaday's Arrowmaker or Diane Glancy's Basket Maker, Power's Indigenous artists use the creative process for cultural survival and adaptation—even if they are not always creating "traditional" Indigenous arts.[118] Their creation performs narrative reconstruction in the way Power's stories do, if we read them as texts.

To think about the role of artists in *Roofwalker*, I will first return to the fictional story "First Fruits." I have discussed how George's father, Melvin, precipitates the recovery of lost histories, those of the first Indian graduate of Harvard and the location of Harvard's Indian College. Melvin here is a creative figure. A musical composer, Melvin does research at the Newberry Library for each new album, the current one being *First Fruits*, a reference to the 1643 pamphlet "printed to promote Harvard's cause," a religious practice involving the first of a harvest, and, significantly, the title of Power's story.[119] Each of Melvin's albums focuses on a "different moment in Indian history," and *First Fruits* is about "Puritan and Indian encounters in the seventeenth century."[120] Melvin is an artist whose works retell Indigenous history, a creative historiography of sorts—not simply as archivist but as designer. And this is not a commonplace pairing, music and history; music is not often used to tell history.[121] The act of reclaiming and repurposing the title, "First Fruits," is a way for Power to demonstrate this history-in-motion. While for Harvard in the seventeenth century, the title signifies a plan for assimilation, a Puritan document, for Melvin, it is Dakota perspective on early American settler history; for Power, it is a reflection on her own experience as an Indian at Harvard. She (and her semiautobiographical character, George) vows to keep her Indigenous identity intact, and they become agents of change at Harvard—evident at the end of the story, when George teaches her white roommate how to dance to powwow music.

In the story "Angry Fish," Power makes it explicit that writing is a creative act, one that "plot[s one's] place in the world."[122] "Angry Fish" is the story of Mitchell Black Deer, an older Winnebago-Lakota man, a retired construction worker who is in love with Lena Catches, a Menominee widow who runs a second-hand store in the Uptown neighborhood of Chicago. Mitchell helps sort through boxes of donations, and one day he finds an animated, talking statue of Saint Jude, who compels Mitchell to take him home and to help him compile a book of poetry. Mitchell complies but soon grows tired of Jude, whose world purview does not allow room for Indigenous beliefs. Mitchell soon takes Jude to a nearby Catholic church, and Jude sings a song in Lakota—one he had overheard on Mitchell's language tapes—as Mitchell walks away. Mitchell himself is an amateur poet—he once published a poem in *Akwesasne Notes*.[123] This makes all three characters in this story creative figures: in addition to Jude's and Mitchell's poems, Lena keeps a scrapbook of UFO sightings and maps them in a *Rand McNally Road Atlas*, in effect creating her own visual history and archive.

Mitchell tells a multitude of histories in his story: he narrates his parents' experience at Carlisle Indian School, where they met; he reveals his story of going to Chicago on relocation; and he evokes the history of Indians in construction.[124] "I am at least partially responsible for that Lake Michigan skyline," he says, which calls attention to the ways that Indigenous peoples have marked the space of Chicago (in a very physical way).[125] Power explicitly equates this act of creation (though construction is not often considered to be a creative act) with writing and Lena's scrapbook. Mitchell says, "I stayed in construction, but at night I practiced writing, trying to plot my place in the world as neatly as Lena Catches plotted close encounters on her maps."[126] It is here that Power most clearly articulates the relationship between writing ("plot") and geography ("place"). Mitchell also shows Jude photographs of his ancestors, whose images also conjure creative processes: "men in buckskin breeches wearing single eagle feathers rising from their deer tail headdresses, women with long silver earrings and thick strands of wampum around their necks wearing silk applique dresses."[127] Mitchell offers these photographs to counter Jude's version of history in his poems. The text of Mitchell's poem appears in the story, while Jude's poems do not, save for a portion of the last one, entitled "Angry Fish," that is recited by Mitchell and therefore filtered through his consciousness. What appears as pastiche allows for the Indigenous voice, significantly taken from *Akwesasne Notes*, the "voice of Native America," to prevail. Lastly, the song at the end of the story that Jude and then Mitchell sing is about "two brothers reunited after a battle," which I read as a battle of histories, a battle of perspectives, perhaps a battle of archives.[128] In the end, Mitchell's archive is simultaneously written, oral, and visual and decidedly more compelling than Jude's.

Lena's archive on UFO sightings calls attention to the making of a historical record—aliens as historiography.[129] She clips articles from newspapers like the *National Enquirer*, which she also cites, itself an act of retelling, and then compiles them into what Mitchell calls her "UFO scrapbook." Calling it a *scrapbook* calls to mind the acts of collecting, preserving, remembering, retelling, which seem to conjure the Gramscian figure of an organic intellectual creating an unofficial historical record and also "bringing things together," to return to Howe.[130] It is significant that she uses her "red pen to plot the sighting," calling attention to geographic location and to the act of inscribing—with a "red" or Indigenous pen or perspective, she is literally tracking history.[131] Mitchell says that she "attacked the page as if the act of reading made her angry" in a way that reminded him of the way his father, educated at Carlisle and with a precarious grasp of English, also read newspapers.[132] This anger toward the dominant narrative, represented by both the boarding school and the media here, is what compels Lena to create her own narrative. Lena becomes an active agent in the telling of history, collecting and mapping stories onto place, as Power does in this book, and she creates a record and an archive, one that, unbeknownst to her, rivals Jude's compilation.

In two autobiographical essays, "Reunion" and "Stone Women," the creative act is specifically one of the imagination. In "Reunion," Power recalls an incident from her childhood, when she imagined that she introduced her parents to one another, long before they actually met. They are an unlikely couple: a young Dakota girl and a fraternity boy whose ancestors traveled on the *Mayflower*. In this imaginary meeting, her father traveled to Standing Rock and encountered her mother at Sitting Bull's grave. This becomes an act of rewriting history—one that Power herself calls "playing God."[133] This episode reveals for me the author's revisionist compulsion, even as she tries to make sense of her mixed heritage. This imaginative act is repeated in "Stone Women," a story about her maternal grandfather, Colvin Kelly, who lost his leg in a train accident while running away from boarding school. As the essay begins, Colvin Kelly is hiding from the police in a hole under the kitchen table. Colvin is guilty of purchasing and consuming alcohol on the reservation—illegal until 1955 there. Power attributes his need for alcohol to the effects of boarding school and the ongoing pain of his leg. She imagines that she could make him a Ghost Dance shirt that "will heal his leg and cure his taste for liquor."[134] She envisions that she will "paint the history of our family on its front and back," including her "ancestors' vision of the coming intruder," their "move from the East to the West," "the battles of White Stone Hill and Little Big Horn," chiefs "Gall, Sitting Bull, Crazy Horse, Two Bears," the "White Buffalo Calf Woman," Wounded Knee, World War I, and "her grandfather slipping under the train."[135] With imaginary paint, Power constructs a narrative that places her grandfather's story within the context of Lakota/Dakota history. The medium by which she creates this historical narrative is the Ghost Dance shirt, itself an item of great historic significance. The Ghost Dance shirt, which Black Elk in *Black Elk Speaks* claims to have invented, was meant to protect Ghost Dancers from bullets. The shirt, both imaginary and historical, becomes an Indigenous visual text that brings together tribal and family history—and a way for Power to insert herself into that history and transport it to the city.

The creative act of Indigenous beading appears in "Watermelon Seeds," which tells the story of a teenage girl of Mexican-Polish descent named Lois who has become pregnant by her much older Chippewa (Ojibwe) boyfriend, Donald, a Vietnam veteran who never saw combat. Donald teaches Lois to do beadwork, which he sells as his own, "Indian made," making them both artists. Lois is secretly beading a scene of Donald with his two Lakota buddies, Glen and Edsel, about the three together in Vietnam, "just like Donald's fantasy."[136] In the beadwork, "they're wounded and waiting for help. Donald is between Glen and Edsel with his arms around their shoulders."[137] Lois inserts Donald into Glen's and Edsel's Vietnam experiences as a way of solidifying their imagined brotherhood, not unlike Jude's song at the end of "Angry Fish," "we are singing together." This beadwork, then, is an example of reconstructed memory—of the ways in which stories can be altered and retold. The beadwork, like the wampum in Power's novel *Sacred Wilderness*, has discursive power.[138] This episode is complicated by the fact that Lois is non-Native, though one might argue that Donald himself might be responsible for her creations. In fact, Lois says that she is no longer in control of the scenes she creates, making it possible that she is doing his bidding even in this instance.

The creative acts in *Roofwalker* are creation stories. They are assertions of Indigenous story and history—and often negations of dominant colonial discourse. They are also artistic confluence: their creators are beading or telling or painting or plotting new articulations of history, "construct[ing] alternate histories," to use DeHay's language, in the urban space.[139] "Writing history," Nancy Peterson has argued in relation to Erdrich's *Tracks*, "has become one way for marginalized peoples to counter their invisibility."[140] In this book, Power asks readers to pay attention to the multiple ways that Native (his)stories get told as she demonstrates that tribal "texts," particularly urban ones, come in many forms. As visual and written articulations of tribalography, these works of art provide a way of making one story from many, another way of reflecting the diversity of stories in this place. Further, Power's artist figures echo the ways in which art can change narrative. In other words, in Power's world, artists are creating a revolution.

DESTABILIZING BORDERS

In Chicago artist Debra Yepa-Pappan's (Jemez Pueblo and Korean) *L Series*, she superimposes photographic images of Chicago Transit Authority (CTA) trains with a young faceless female figure dressed in traditional Pueblo clothing, a *manta*.[141] The girl is the artist's daughter, and the photograph records the young girl's first dance at Jemez. What is striking about this work is that Yepa-Pappan simultaneously celebrates Indigeneity (and her daughter's choice to participate in the dance), family history, the urban setting of Chicago, the particular neighborhood in which the artist lives, and the train itself: "How many people stop and actually think about how wonderful the train is?" she asks.[142] Her *L Series*, which is a play on the name for Chicago's train, the El, so named for its elevated tracks, transforms the city into sacred space. This particular piece visually erases the boundaries of geography by mapping her daughter's image onto the Chicago landscape. There is a kind of physical simultaneity or a confluence of place that makes for an interesting pairing with Power's work: the subject is both *there* and *here*. I read Yepa-Pappan's piece as a visual manifestation of Appadurai's argument that identity doesn't have to be "spatially bounded," that we carry those identities with us to new spaces and sites.[143]

FIG 12. *There and Back Again* by Debra Yepa-Pappan, 2012. Digital print on antique ledger paper. Reproduced by permission of the artist.

One piece in Yepa-Pappan's series, *There and Back Again* (2012), is set against a backdrop of a CTA map, and all three of the pieces in the series, *There and Back Again*, *En Route*, and *transit*, are digitally printed on antique ledger paper.[144] Yepa-Pappan's use of ledger paper is a means of bringing the past and present together, both through her method, the digital print, and her subject, urban Indians in Chicago. I would also argue that this work cuts across genres: it is simultaneously photography, digital art, cartography, and ledger art. Like the productions of Power's artist figures, Yepa-Pappan's work is transformational as it articulates the movement of urban life and the routes of the city and at the same time recalls the movement between spaces, specifically Chicago and Jemez Pueblo in New Mexico. This "bringing together" of geographic space is at once Indigenous and modern; like all of the texts in this study, her work challenges this dichotomy that pervades the dominant narrative.

Like Yepa-Pappan, Power seems to be invested in erasing or destabilizing borders: between history and memory, between reservation and city, between past and present, between Indigenous and Western knowledge, between public and private, between fiction and nonfiction.[145] While I have been thus far distinguishing between the fictional "stories" and autobiographical "histories" in *Roofwalker*, in this final section I will suggest that where the book succeeds as an urban Native text is in its form and its confluence of story. The book brings together previously published essays (mostly commissioned) and short stories, though the publication details are absent from the book.[146] In its current form, the fictional and autobiographical are separated, but the book as Power conceived it had the two intermingling.[147] As she explains in a *Ploughshares* interview, the editor suggested the division by genre to avoid reader confusion. It would certainly be a very different book if the histories and stories were interspersed. Power had imagined that this book would demonstrate how life informs her work, how the "seeds" of her fiction are found in her own life story.[148] This aligns with an Indigenous aesthetic—for naming and claiming the origin of stories, as I suggested earlier: in other words, *This is who I am and where I come from, and these are my stories*. The autobiographical is epistemological, whether or not it is segregated in the text.

Like so many Native authors, Power writes in multiple genres.[149] As critics such as Kimberly Blaeser (Ojibwe), Eric Gary Anderson, and Dean Rader have argued, Native writers are, in fact, creating new genres by refusing to conform to classical Western genres—they "qualify, question, dismiss, leapfrog over, [and] revise" these genres, according to Anderson.[150] Anderson suggests that we should be suspect of generic classifications in the first place, that they "are forms of identity imported from outside Native cultures and at times imposed on them."[151] Rader claims that American Indian poetry in particular "explodes traditional notions of genre."[152] Rader continues, in a vein similar to Howe, "Traditionally, Native Americans succeed like no other culture in uniting divergent strains of just about anything into a collective entity."[153] Native writing, he contends, has a way of problematizing diverse genres through their blurring of boundaries.[154] Howe herself has famously suggested that it hardly matters what *shape* or *form* a story takes: "I came up with the term 'tribalography' because I didn't agree that American Indians tell strictly autobiographical stories, nor memoir, nor history, nor fiction, but rather they tell a kind of story that includes a collaboration with the past and present and future."[155] In fact, Howe's configuration of tribalography as the "propensity to bring things together," to combine elements of stories in multiple genres, provides another way to think about the multigenre nature of *Roofwalker*.

Silko's *Storyteller* is a frequently cited example of a multigenre text, and in her well-known essay "Language and Literature from a Pueblo Indian Perspective," Silko argues that stories are stories, that all stories are important, and that Indigenous peoples traditionally did not categorize them the way anthropologists insisted they do (as family stories, as sacred stories, and so on).[156] *Storyteller* contains poems, short stories, and photographs, and part of the text's power comes from its juxtapositions and lack of adherence to a linear chronology. Blaeser looks to Silko's description of Pueblo expression as a spider's web to articulate both that "aesthetic form . . . has a cultural origin" and that "meaning and design are linked," and as such, texts such as *Storyteller* reveal "essential clues to reading."[157] Similarly, Rader suggests that "embedded into the architecture of Native poetry is its own theory for reading."[158] My reading of *Roofwalker* thus far has attempted to uncover its theoretical underpinnings as they are revealed in the thematic and metaphoric implications of confluence, and here I am proposing that the book's structure offers further "essential clues" for reading.

Like *Storyteller*, *Roofwalker* works to erase generic classification. In keeping with my tribalographic reading, I would like to suggest that this erasure has meaning on a metalevel; in other words, that genre crossing first functions to signify the crossings of urban life: the migration from reservation to city (seen in Power's mother's story but also in Mitchell's in "Angry Fish" and the Azures in "Beading Soles"), temporal crossings (for example, the invocation of Chicago's Indigenous history and "critical historical moments," to use Rader's phrase, of Dakota history), and the diverse alliances within the American Indian community. A lack of chronological plotting is a technique frequently used by ethnic writers, Amritjit Singh argues: they "often deny the validity of the linear progression of the traditional narrative—which implies a unity through a beginning, middle, and end—or at the very least, reorient our experience of it."[159] Not only does *Roofwalker* evade a traditional linear progression, but the majority of it seems to exist outside of time, without any reliable or steady time markers. Thus, physical, temporal, and genre boundaries are transgressed, crossed, and rendered ineffective in this text. Finally, Power's book erases the boundaries of story. In other words, her stories overflow and overlap their beginnings and endings—they cannot be contained within a single essay or short fiction.

To demonstrate how the convergence of genre functions metaphorically in the text, I will first turn to Power's depictions of a quintessential feature of the Chicago landscape: Lake Michigan. The lake is Chicago's boundary to the east; the city pushes up against the lake, and the lake pushes back. The lakefront is forever changing, by both "nature" and landfill (and everything east of Michigan Avenue is built on landfill), and Power's descriptions of Lake Michigan focus on this territorial struggle. "The lake is monolithic," Power said in an interview. "It asserts its power. The city thinks it controls it, but the lake swoops back over and takes back territory. It remembers where its territory used to be. The lake will get the last word."[160] The final essay of the book, "Chicago Waters," begins, "My mother used to say that by the time I was an old woman, Lake Michigan would be the size of a silver dollar."[161] Power writes, "I learned to squint at the 1967 shoreline until I had carved away the structures and roads built on landfill, and could imagine *the lake and its city* as my mother found them in 1942."[162] This relationship between the lake and "its city" is one of unpredictable boundaries and convergence. Power here is highlighting the destabilization of borders with this geographic example that is the ultimate expression of fluidity. Borders are forever changing as that great lake pushes up against the city and the city struggles to push it back.

The lake in *Roofwalker* is also an entity that transcends the borders of time: the lake existed before people inhabited this place, and it will continue far beyond human habitation. Power calls it "ancient."[163] Yet there are critical historical moments in the history of the lake. For example, the efforts to reconstruct the lakefront coincided with the beginnings of the settlement of Chicago, with its relationship with the railroad (namely, the Illinois Central Railroad, which was given a large parcel of land near what is now Grant Park for a rail yard). Also, much of the landfill came from debris from the Great Fire in 1871. The city burned, and during its reconstruction, further efforts were made to expand the coastline. Lastly, the issue of landfill conjures the Sand Bar case, which I mentioned at the beginning of this chapter: the efforts of Simon Pokagon and later his son, Charles Pokagon, to claim the lakebed for the Potawatomis. As John Low's work now argues, the Potawatomis are Chicago's first urban Indians—and so, through another kind of triangulation, Power acknowledges this in her text.[164]

The lake is a critical site in both *Roofwalker* and *The Grass Dancer*, where two near drownings occur. In the fictionalized version, in *The Grass Dancer*, Pumpkin is physically marked by her encounter with the lake: a hook-shaped scar is a reminder of her first time swimming in the lake. "She remembered it as the day she broke her fear apart," Power writes.[165] This scene suggests a double crossing over: Pumpkin breaches the border between land and water while simultaneously leaving behind a more fearful version of herself. She does not drown, as she fears; instead, she gets hooked by a fisherman. Even so, she gathers strength from this trial by water, from the lake itself. In *Roofwalker*, Power writes, "I learned that the lake did not love me or hate me, but could claim me."[166] Swimming alone on a particularly stormy day when she was fifteen, Power nearly drowns, until she dives deep "to the bottom of the lake, where the water was a little quieter."[167] She remains "on the lake floor" until she reaches "shallow waters."[168] Of course, according to the Pokagons' Sand Bar claim, she is on Indian land down there at the bottom of the lake.

The way Power's story provides the autobiographical seed for Pumpkin's incident is one of the ways her stories exceed the boundaries of each text. In *Roofwalker*, another one of these seeds is a house fire on Standing Rock. In "Stone Women," Power writes that the cabin her mother grew up in on the reservation had burned down.[169] This is the cabin located near Sitting Bull's grave, as I discussed earlier in this chapter. This is also where young Susan imagines her parents meeting in "Reunion" and where her grandfather hides beneath the kitchen table in "Stone Women." The house fire reappears in two stories, "Beaded Soles" and "First Fruits."[170] In "Beaded Soles," Maxine says that their cabin "burned to the ground in 1939, when I was nine years old."[171] *Heyoka* spirits are blamed for other misfortunes, all stemming from the curse of Lieutenant Bullhead's "sin," but the house fire is not specifically linked to *heyokas*. In "First Fruits," George's family home on Standing Rock burned down with her mother inside. This manifestation of personal story to fiction not only demonstrates how the author uses autobiographical details to inform her work, as she intended, but also provides evidence of how a story transcends the imagined boundaries of genre. Because it is also a traumatic story, I would argue that the retellings also function in a healing way, that each time the story is repeated, the grief lessens. It is not unlike the way Power and other Native writers utilize historical antecedents in their work; there is a modicum of historical truth by way of tribal history, and the fictions are built up around these historical moments. Similarly, Rader argues in his discussion about the "epic lyric" that Native writers constantly engage with both personal and "historical moments."[172] The historical moment of the fire, located as it is in the text, in 1939 on the Standing Rock Reservation, provides resonance and a broader cultural meaning as it gets repeated throughout these stories. Power returns to this event, the fire, as a symbol for the loss of home that her mother experienced, first through her relocation to Chicago, then the fire, and then the Oahe Dam.[173] This dam, part of the Pick-Sloan Plan, was constructed north of Pierre, South Dakota, and created a large reservoir, Lake Oahe, that flooded fertile lands on the Standing Rock and Cheyenne River Reservations when it was opened in 1962. Over 220,000 acres were flooded; Standing Rock lost close to 56,000 acres, forcing 25 percent of its population to relocate.[174] "Goddamn that Oahe Dam!" Power's mother says.[175]

This repetition of the fire perhaps functions in even another way. In Power's most recent novel, *Sacred Wilderness*, Candace has a dream in which Jigonsaseh tells her, "You don't remember how a single word had fifty meanings behind it, each one with a story like a hidden seed. What you see as repetition is another version and still another version—each of them older and deeper, each of them taking you closer to the truth."[176] These ideas of word-stories and versions of stories that get at truth are attributed to an Indigenous epistemology (this one Haudenosaunee, but Dakota words also have stories).[177] In both "First Fruits" and "Wild Turnips," Power describes these story layers: Melvin sees through the layers of things, and the narrator in "Wild Turnips" imagines being "peeled . . . like an egg," the layers stripped away.[178] In "First Fruits," George says that their house—lost to fire—was an "artifact." What, then, does it mean to lose this artifact? To get "closer to the truth"? George loses her mother in the fire, but the autobiographical Susan does not. The loss of this house signifies trauma over the mother's death, the mother herself an archive—a keeper of the historical record and cultural knowledge (as Susan's mother is in this text). Power seems to be suggesting through these versions that her mother did experience a metaphorical death when she lost her childhood home, and certainly the author feels this loss as well.[179] Her mother's stories about this cabin have survived, but the physical absence of this place marker heightens their disconnect from "home." It makes sense to conflate loss of home and home place. Readers do not know the details surrounding the fire, its cause, how old Susan's mother was at the time (though maybe, like Maxine, she was nine), whether emergency services were deployed, whether there was adequate tribal infrastructure to fight the fire, whether anyone was hurt. We do assume total loss—loss of household goods, along with family heirlooms and photographs. This puts Susan's mother's experience in "The Attic" into greater relief: being overwhelmed by the archive and historical record of her husband's family when it becomes a reminder of the loss of hers. We see this as a broken link to the past and to place. The fire reverberates, then, even in the story of the lost dress in the Field Museum; its loss is felt more deeply with the loss of the cabin and its contents.

To return to the question of the generic divide between autobiography and fiction, the emotional impact and historical significance of the fire are not lessened in the fictional versions; in fact, I would argue that they are amplified in each successive version, just as Jigonsaseh suggests. The order in which the versions appear is also relevant to its impress. We first encounter the fictional: "Beaded Soles," then "First Fruits," before we learn about the autobiographical fire in "Stone Women." These pieces also appear nearly in successive order—only a very short story, "Indian Princess," disrupts this succession. The loss of the cabin is exacerbated by the flooding of the Oahe Dam: "The log cabin where my mother lived as a child burned down long ago but she has taken me to its location. We can't walk near the foundation or scratch in the dirt of the old yard because it is ten feet underwater, flooded by the government's construction of the Oahe Dam."[180] In other words, the cabin fire becomes inextricably linked with the structural violence involved in the historical damming of the Missouri River. The site has become inaccessible and unreadable; the daughter literally cannot retrace her mother's steps nor stand where the house once stood.

The language that Power uses to describe the dam is reminiscent of her descriptions of the lake. She writes, for example, "I dream that the Oahe Dam has a wide mouth and chunky teeth, its lips rasp like paper as it eats our reservation."[181] There is a way in which this hungry body of water, created by the damming of the river, one that has exceeded its boundaries, is likened to the way that Lake Michigan cannot be contained despite human efforts to do so. And through deep time, we might connect the reservation fire to the Great Fire, particularly in the way that they are both now underwater. This comparison may seem like a stretch, but it allows for a kind of transference or convergence of the Missouri River and Lake Michigan (which, I am aware, does not happen in a geographic sense). This representational convergence allows Power and her mother to transfer the sacredness of the river to the lake, to allow the lake to make Chicago a home place, to feel acutely what the changing of borders and boundaries inflicts. Power's mother tells Susan that she needs to respect the power of Lake Michigan; inherently, she is teaching her daughter about the importance of water in the natural world—no matter where they may live.

Another representative place that transcends the boundaries of both story and book is the boarding school—which, one might argue, was meant to erase boundaries, in terms of assimilation, between whites and Indians but which often only served to reinforce them. Arguably, residential schools removed Native peoples from reservation spaces and made it difficult for them to return, even years after their schooling. Susan's mother and her grandparents are products of boarding schools, and in the beginning of "Stone Women," we learn that her grandfather lost his leg in a train accident at the age of eleven while running away from school, as I discussed earlier.[182] Power links both his injury and his alcoholism, along with his conversion and use of English, to the boarding school experience. Further, she demonstrates the significance of this event, as she proposes to represent it on his Ghost Dance shirt along with Little Big Horn, Wounded Knee, and World War I. Her mother also attended boarding school, and she tells Susan about Sister Michael, who "brought them to the maternity ward so they would understand the consequences of sin."[183] Her mother's experience has more religious underpinnings than her grandfather's, and yet both of these family stories become the "seeds" for Power's fictional versions of boarding school.

In *The Grass Dancer*, Margaret Many Wound's husband, Charles Bad Holy McLeod, is the one who attended Carlisle Indian School. He came back "wearing a white man's suit" with "a head full of education," but "he didn't remember one story about his own tribe."[184] This is reminiscent of Power's description of her grandfather, who "speaks old-time Dakota but looks more like a white man."[185] Margaret says the "reservation agent had taken him away at age four and let Pennsylvania keep him until he was twenty-one."[186] Sadly, Charles dies from tuberculosis just two years into their marriage. In *Roofwalker*, the elderly narrator of "Wild Turnips," arguably a version of Power's grandmother, met her husband, Percy, at boarding school. She tells her roommate Gertrude, "They took both of us from our families when we were just little. I didn't see my parents for seventeen years."[187] This is the same length of time that Charles McLeod is away, coincidentally. While this may simply be the number of years of schooling available, I would argue that this detail reveals the imprint of Power's grandparents' experiences in each of these books. There is one more fictional boarding school story in *Roofwalker*: in "Angry Fish," Mitchell's parents were both products of Carlisle, where they met. And though "Winnebago was his [father's] first language," "he didn't like to think in English."[188] In "Stone Women," Power poses this question about her grandfather: "Does he speak English or Dakota in his mind?"[189] Tracing the "seeds" of Power's stories in this way reveals much about her creative process as a writer: we see how her fictions are in a dialogue with critical moments from her family's history. While some of the details change (for example, changing tribal affiliation from Dakota to Winnebago, which seems to serve another purpose), Power shows us how her grandfather's story here (and her mother's story about the house fire) are formative traumatic events that are grounded in truth. In other words, even her fictional versions of these stories have a clear historical basis.

For a multigenre writer like Power, stories are more than mere tales—they are themselves modes of histories; they cannot be contained by genre, secure within the pages of a book. *Roofwalker* is a warehouse of crossing borders: Grandma Mabel journeys to the city in the title story; Donald relocates to Chicago in "Watermelon Seeds"; Mitchell moves from Green Bay to Chicago (and his father goes to Carlisle); "Wild Turnips" returns to South Dakota; the Azures move to Chicago in "Beaded Soles" (and Marshall's body is sent back to the reservation); in "First Fruits" George and her father travel to Chicago and to Harvard, and Caleb travels to Harvard and back to Martha's Vineyard; Power's grandfather escapes from boarding school; Power goes to Standing Rock to see the Stone Woman; tourists visit Sitting Bull's grave; Sitting Bull's remains are relocated; Susan's mother leaves the reservation; Power and her mother travel around Chicago; Power imagines her father coming to the reservation in "Reunion"; her father's ancestors traveled to America; Power visits Josephine's grave and Grandmother Power's home in Albany with her mother. Stories move geographically as well. For example, the roofwalker story gets transported to the city, and the story of the Oahe Dam gets mapped onto Lake Michigan. And stories cross boundaries into other stories: the fire, the boarding school, the near drownings in Lake Michigan, the dress in the Field Museum, and Herod Small War, a character from *The Grass Dancer* who appears in "Beaded Soles." This border crossing, as I have been arguing, functions both thematically and aesthetically in this text as a "bringing together" of people and place.

Next to the text of Two-Rivers's poem in the mural *Indian Land Dancing* is a collage of photographs and a large painting of a book entitled *Book of All Tribes* that leans on a yellow tiled tipi. Certainly the wall itself is a constructed text to be read, a point the artists seem to be making clear with this image of a book. Chicago's *Book* is being told here through image and juxtaposition and communal storytelling. The photos appear to be randomly placed and in no obvious chronological order. They are also tiled and of inconsistent sizes. Two-Rivers is next to Black Hawk; below them on the left is a photograph of a production by the Black Hawk Performance Company; and to the right there is a much larger image of a fancy dancer. The aesthetics here, as I have already suggested, are tribalographic and highly dependent on convergence. The story that is being told is an urban Indian story, one that reconstructs the history of Indigenous Chicago through the communal memory of its members. It is not hard to see the connection between this work and Susan Power's (even beyond the fact that a picture of her mother is also on this wall). These are Indigenous voices engaged in the telling of the Chicago Indigenous experience.

Neal McLeod (Cree), in "Coming Home through Stories," writes, "Every time a story is told, every time one word of an Indigenous language is spoken, we are resisting the destruction of our collective memory."[190] These are "wordarrows," to use Gerald Vizenor's term, as McLeod does, that counter an "ideological diaspora," or "alienation from the voices and echoes of the ancestors."[191] In *Roofwalker*, Power uses these wordarrows to reconstruct and narrate the collective story of Indigenous Chicago. Storytelling for Power is what Stuart Hall would call an "act of cultural recovery."[192] Her book enacts the multiple convergences of tribal histories and alternate textualities, all of which belie an Indigenous consciousness that is dependent on an Indigenous narrative epistemology. In *The Practice of Everyday Life*, Michel de Certeau writes that stories contain "strategic discourses" that "frequently reverse the relationships of power."[193] Similarly, Leanne Simpson (Ojibwe) suggests that "storytelling is at its core decolonizing, because it is a process of remembering, visioning and creating a just reality."[194] Power challenges the dominant narrative about Chicago as she demonstrates how public memory vis-à-vis the Battle of Fort Dearborn as origin story is flawed. As Red Dress tells Harley at the end of *The Grass Dancer*, reminiscent of Two-Rivers's sentiment in "Indian Land Dancing" and Alexie's recurrent Ghost Dance, "*You are dancing a rebellion.*"[195]

In the exhibition catalog for *First People, Second City*, the UK exhibition of Debra Yepa-Pappan's and Chris Pappan's work, Max Carocci writes, "Together they remind us that urban life is highly heterogenous, multi-layered, historically-located, and most significantly, political."[196] Likewise, both thematically and aesthetically, Power's book reflects the urban environment. The city is a place with a confluence of histories that get mapped and juxtaposed in a variety of ways in her stories. Her work demonstrates the resistance of colonial erasure through Native epistemological practices, showing how the creative process (like the book itself) has revolutionary potential, how telling stories can, as Craig Womack has suggested, "actually cause a change in the physical universe."[197] The city, then, for Power, is a revolutionary space where borders can be at best unreliable. The crossings of borders occur textually, symbolically, and repetitively. The multigenre nature of her book is part and parcel of her urban aesthetic. Like the "Roofwalker" story itself, *Roofwalker* demonstrates how narratives emerge to fulfill a need. By connecting past, present, and future, her stories celebrate the diversity of the urban experience. I close this book with a contemporary text to demonstrate that these gaps are still being filled, that urban stories are still emerging, that cities like Chicago—once thought to be devoid of its Indian peoples—have rich Indigenous histories, that we are still reconciling and understanding the geographic shifts in the modern era and what they mean for our Native communities.

Epilogue

Like *The Exiles*, Pamela J. Peters's 2014 documentary *Legacy of Exiled NDNZ* opens with a series of Edward Curtis photos, along with the promise that "displacement from our homelands has not caused the Indian to disappear." In *Legacy*, Diné photographer and filmmaker Peters presents the narratives of seven Indigenous people in Los Angeles who describe their (or their families') relocation experience. Interspersed with their stories are clips of Kent Mackenzie's film, which Peters claims "did the history of her people justice."[1] Peters's film is dedicated to and in the style of Mackenzie's—her Native subjects even appear in early 1960s period dress and are located in similar Bunker Hill sites. In conjunction with the fourteen-minute film, Peters created a photo series, also called *Legacy of Exiled NDNZ*, which presents a visual narrative of these "relocated" Indian subjects, and she plans to expand the short film into a full-length documentary.[2]

I began this book with a reading of Mackenzie's *The Exiles*, a film that attempted to tell the story of urban relocation as it was happening, and it seems fitting to end with Peters's documentary to bring this analysis full circle in one sense but also to demonstrate how the urban narrative is still being constructed and reconstructed, retold and revised. As the number of urban texts grows, we get a fuller and more complex articulation of the urban Indigenous experience. The way we read these texts, as I have suggested throughout this book, should take into account both time and place via what I have been calling a spatiohistorical practice, one that considers the layers of history—or "deep time"—of each specific city as new stories get mapped onto that space. These local histories are critical to understanding the "place" of these narratives, but equally important are the transnational networks that get revealed—that each Indigenous city operates as a "hub" of people, ideas, and things. By articulating here how Peters specifically revises Mackenzie, I hope to reveal that this revisioning also serves as a reclaiming of Indigenous story and that it performs a spatiohistory similar to the other texts in this study in the way it charts the current generation onto the era of relocation and evokes the Indigenous history of this site, history that precedes the founding of Los Angeles.

As the film's tagline asserts, "We are part of the history of Los Angeles, California." The narrative aspect of this film, the filling in of historical gaps, works to combat the erasure of urban Indians and their stories. Like the other texts in this study, *Legacy* asserts that these stories are important for understanding contemporary Native lives, and, as I have been arguing, this narrative act is an activist one. Telling the stories of relocation, whether they are from the 1920s or the 1950s or the 2000s, makes both historical and spatial claims. These stories confirm that Indigenous people have not disappeared, that they exist in the present—signified in the film by the text of the *We Are Still Here* mural, painted by Shepard Fairey in 2013.[3] Peters uses this location, in addition to nearby Bunker Hill sites and Union Station, in the film. The mural is located in Indian Alley, or Winston Street, in Los Angeles, which was also the site of the United American Indian Involvement Center, Inc., from the 1970s to 2000. UAII, a rehab center that now provides a wider variety of health and social services, offered a safe space for Los Angeles Natives, many of them homeless, who had come to the city on relocation. *Legacy* evokes this history with its inclusion of both the mural and the faux Indian Alley street sign—and coincidentally, Peters's photo series was exhibited at a

FIG 13. *We Are Still Here* by Shepard Fairey, 2013. Mural in Indian Alley, Los Angeles. Based on Aaron Huey photograph of the same name, 2012. Courtesy of SHEPARD FAIREY/OBEYGIANT.COM. Photo by Stephen Zeigler, used with his permission.

gallery in the former UAII building. Telling *their* stories—signified by the NDNZ in the title, a slang word created by the community to describe themselves—is an assertion of identity, a self-naming that comes from the urban space.[4]

The film also represents a significant move toward self-representation. As I discussed in this book's introduction, *The Exiles* is an important historical archive that developed from Mackenzie's aim to document and expose the lives of urban Indians affected by relocation policy. Native people—both in front of and behind the camera—helped to shape the film in many ways, but these images were mediated by a non-Native lens, a lens informed and colored by a long history of documentary film about Indigenous peoples. That is, while Mackenzie's intent may have been honorable and justice-minded and he may have given his actors and crew a good amount of creative freedom in the process, he created and secured the funding for this project—a thesis project at that. Peters's film conveys that *The Exiles* is valuable for its archival footage, clips of which she includes in her film, while at the same time, she makes it clear that hers is an Indigenous cultural production, one that reclaims and retells the story of urban Indians in LA. A headline from the LA *Observed* claims that Peters "modernizes" Mackenzie's film, and in a sense this is true: Peters does update the urban Indigenous story by using the narratives of contemporary Native people, many of whom are second- and third-generation Angelenos.[5] However, there is more to this project than that: I would argue that the way Peters reclaims and recasts Mackenzie's narrative recalls the way photographers like Hulleah Tsinhnahjinnie "retake" Curtis's pictures, as I discussed in chapter 1 (and, like Mackenzie's film, Peters's film opens with Curtis images in a way that marks this intentional revision). This project, then, also speaks to the work that the texts in this study are doing: rescripting the narrative of urban Indians. Peters's decision to put her informants in period dress, for example, signifies that she intends her film to be this kind of rescripting; it consciously puts her filmic text and her subjects in conversation with Mackenzie's text, just as it maps them very visually onto the era of relocation. In addition to this wardrobe choice, the way that Peters juxtaposes images/clips from *The*

Exiles with her subjects, who sometimes appear in the same locations in Los Angeles, forces a comparison and dialogue with the earlier film. What gets revealed in these juxtapositions is a deliberate shift in tone between the films: the tension and hopelessness suggested in the darkness of Mackenzie's film are noticeably absent from *Legacy*. This tonal shift is also evident in Peters's revision of the film's final iconic scene, which has been revised to include all of the actors, not just those who have presumably been out carousing all night.

I would also like to suggest that *Legacy* calls attention to the movement of the city in a similar way that I described in my analysis of *The Exiles*—maybe sans Thunderbird and tunnels, though in Peters's film, the actors do visit the base of Angels Flight, the famous Bunker Hill cable car. However, in both the still photographs and her film, Peters utilizes Union Station in a way that Mackenzie never did. The setting of Union Station works on a number of levels, the most important of which reveals the *mode* by which many Native peoples traveled to Los Angeles, particularly those who came as part of the relocation program. Peters's subjects are also depicted as travelers, pictured with suitcases in the train station. In this way, her Los Angeles becomes the hub that Mackenzie's is not: Mackenzie's subjects, downtrodden and lost in the city, long for their reservation homes. Peters's subjects tell stories about traveling back and forth between reservation and city. Union Station serves as a reminder that many Indigenous city-dwellers remain connected to—and travel back to—reservations, that there is movement around and through the city space. The lines between city and reservation, foreign and familiar, modern and traditional have become unsettled, or, to return to Paula Gunn Allen's *Off the Reservation*, "boundaries have grown permeable, wide open spaces abound."[6]

Relocation continues to be an important part of the Indigenous story, though there are many new reasons and pathways for Native peoples to live in cities. *Legacy* tells the "origin stories" of how American Indians came to LA; as Peters suggested in an interview with *Pasadena Monthly*, migration is the "untold story."[7] The film confirms that the relocation era continues to signify an important historical juncture, a critical event

FIG 14. *Welcome to Los Angeles* from *Legacy of Exiled NDNZ*, © 2014 by Pamela J. Peters. Reproduced by permission of the artist.

whose narrative is still being constructed. The continued construction and rescripting of the relocation narrative is at its core an act of activism, for what the relocation program set out to do was to disrupt and dislocate Indigenous lives. Peters's film returns to relocation to parse out what it means to contemporary urban Natives, allowing them to understand their families' migration stories and "paying tribute to the first generation of Relocated (exiled) Indians," in Peters's words.[8] A similar project is under way in San Francisco, as the activist group Urban Native Era has set out to make *Stories of Survival: Relocation and the Untold Stories of Native America*, a project to record relocation stories from community elders. This oral history video project has a goal of educating younger generations about urban Native lives.[9] Relocation stories are epic stories of bodies in motion, stories of survival and discovery, stories about old places and new, stories about traditional and new urban identities, stories to be remembered and passed on. They are historically minded but cognizant of the present and future—to invoke LeAnne Howe's concept of "tribalography" again here.[10]

I end *Indigenous Cities* with a reading of *Legacy* for what it tells us about the importance of urban Native *stories*—plural—for there is no one way to *be* or to *become* an urban Indian. My aim in this book has been to assess the aesthetics and cultural work of a growing body of urban narratives, to articulate the ways in which these narratives are different from reservation narratives, though not any less "Indian." In other words, urban Natives are still Native: urbanization and legacies of assimilative policies have not erased Indigenous identities. Relocation and other migrations in the twentieth century have, however, altered the story that we tell about Indigenous peoples in the United States. In 1973 Bill Moyers called urban Indians "rootless nomads in a strange new world."[11] But he was wrong. The stories of urban Natives are stories of survival, about how Native peoples migrate, adapt to new surroundings, find and redefine community, and maintain and redefine Indian identity. We find stories like Coyote's in Diné poet Esther Belin's poem, cited in this book's epigraph, who is "blues-ing on the urban brown funk vibe" as he navigates Los Angeles, weary from so many relocations but crafty with his shape shifting and narrative. As I have suggested throughout this book, we cannot talk about Native people and place in the same way. Urban Indian literature is the literature of diaspora; it is a way of writing the nation(s) *away* from the nation(s). It often invokes the reservation space in memory while at the same time embraces the city space and the collectivity of peoples there. Individual tribal nations and tribal identities remain important; however, the promise of intertribal political collectivity gets imagined as well. Land is always part of the story, even when the story is about the urban space. Relationship to place, to self, to family, to tradition, to language, a mode of being in the world—all of these things get unsettled by relocation. As I have demonstrated through my readings, cosmopolitanism and urbanization are not necessarily new things for Indigenous peoples, but these texts demand that we pay attention to this demographic shift—that their stories are essential to our understanding of the contemporary Indigenous experience.

SOURCE ACKNOWLEDGMENTS

"Blues-ing on the Brown Vibe" is from Esther G. Belin's *From the Belly of My Beauty* (Tucson: University of Arizona Press, 1999). © The Arizona Board of Regents. Reprinted by permission of the University of Arizona Press.

An earlier version of chapter 1 first appeared as "'Look for the Color Red': Recovering Janet Campbell Hale's *The Jailing of Cecelia Capture*," *Intertexts* 14, no. 2 (2010).

The epigraph for chapter 2 appears courtesy Sherman Alexie.

An earlier version of chapter 3 first appeared as "Remapping Indian Country in Louise Erdrich's *The Antelope Wife*," *Studies in American Indian Literatures* 19, no. 4 (2007).

The epigraph for chapter 3 comes from Kimberly M. Blaeser's "Sacred Journey Cycles: Pilgrimage as Re-turning and Re-telling in American Indigenous Literatures" (*Religion and Literature* 35, no. 2 [Summer 2003]) and appears with permission of the author.

The epigraph for chapter 4 comes from E. Donald Two-Rivers's "Indian Land Dancing" in *Fat Cats, Pow Wows, and Other Indian Tales* (Lawrence KS: Mammoth, 2009) and appears courtesy Denise Low.

INTRODUCTION

1. I use the words "Native," "Indigenous," "Indian," and "American Indian" interchangeably throughout this project, as there is no general consensus on this terminology. I refer to individual tribal nations when appropriate.

2. The film was submitted as part of Mackenzie's master's thesis at USC in June 1964. It was filmed over the course of three years, from 1958 to 1961. It was shown at a few film festivals but never gained wide release.

3. Yvonne is San Carlos Apache, and Homer is Hualapai.

4. I am thinking here of the work of Robert Flaherty, which Mackenzie studied in preparation for this film.

5. Mackenzie says in his thesis that he was enraged after reading Dorothy Van de Mark's "Raid on the Reservations" in *Harper's Magazine* (1956) and set out to make this film.

6. This speaks to Michelle H. Raheja's *Hollywood Reelism* in terms of Native collaboration in films made by non-Native directors, which she argues occurred with Flaherty's *Nanook of the North* and in many early Hollywood films. This is not to say that everything in the film was "real." The fight scene at the end was staged, and Yvonne and Homer were not actually a couple. See Austin, "*The Exiles*: Finding the Story."

7. Allen, *Off the Reservation*, 6.

8. Allen, *Off the Reservation*, 6. Allen writes that someone "off the reservation" is

"someone who doesn't conform to the limits and boundaries of officialdom, who is unpredictable and thus uncontrollable. Such individuals are seen as threats to the power structure. They are anomalies: mavericks, renegades, queers. Seen in its historical context, designating someone 'off the reservation' is particularly apt. Originally the term meant a particular kind of 'outlaw,' a Native person who crossed the territorial border, called a reserve or reservation, set by the United States or a state government. In those days 'the reservation' signified a limited space, a camp, to which Native people of various nations were confined. Those who crossed the set borders were deemed renegades. They were usually hunted down, and most often, summarily shot" (6).

9. The preliminary script, the funding proposal, the final script, and the master's thesis are included on the 2006 DVD release of the film. Other early titles were *The Night Is a Friend*, *A Long Way from Home*, and *Go Ahead On, Man*. See Mackenzie, "Description," 100.

10. See Deloria, *Indians in Unexpected Places*, 136–38. As Deloria explains, Indians in cars are in "unexpected places" because Indians in the American imaginary belong firmly fixed in the past, not traveling toward a mobile and technologically advanced future.

11. The thunderbird figure can be found in numerous tribal cosmologies throughout the Southwest, Northwest Coast, Great Plains, Great Lakes, and Southeast.

12. See Said, "Reflections on Exile." Exile, writes Said, "is the unhealable rift forced between a human being and a native place, between the self and its true home" (173). He also argues that "anyone prevented from returning home is an exile" (181).

13. Geiogamah is explicit in an author's note that it should be obvious that characters come from different tribes, though which ones in particular is not important to the plot.

14. Darby estimates that the monthly income on eighty acres of land in 1969 (a typical allotment) would have been approximately $400. See Darby, "People with Strong Hearts," 161.

15. See Geiogamah's interview with Kenneth Lincoln in *MELUS* (1989).

16. Quoted in Darby, "People with Strong Hearts," 160.

17. Early urban poetry came from writers like Simon Ortiz, Joy Harjo, Wendy Rose, and Maurice Kenny. See McGlennan, *Tribal Alliances*, on urban poetics.

18. Significant criticism that focuses on urban Indian literature has appeared as well. See especially Rader, "I Don't Speak Navajo"; Ruppert, "The Urban Reservation"; Miller, "Telling the Indian Urban"; and Rifkin, *When Did Indians Become Straight?*

19. These dates are not meant to be inclusive of the production of urban Indian literature, which continues to be written in the present.
20. Two-thirds of the Native population in the United States now reside off-reservation in urban areas. See Fixico, *The Urban Indian Experience*.
21. See, for example, Nelson, *Place and Vision*; Wilson, *Writing Home*; Hafen, "Indigenous People and Place"; and Clark and Powell, "Guest Editors' Introduction."
22. See Morgan, *Ancient Society*; and Bevis, "Native American Novels."
23. See, for example, Raheja, *Hollywood Reelism*; and Pauketat, *Cahokia*.
24. Rosenthal, *Reimagining Indian Country*. Rosenthal writes, "Much of this book is about how American Indians themselves have long been actively reimagining and defining an Indian Country that includes cities, towns, rural areas, and reservations" (3).
25. Mackenzie, "Description," 105.
26. See Shepherd, "At the Crossroads," for a history of the Hualapais' relationship to their reservation, which grouped thirteen decentralized bands into one tribe in the middle of their aboriginal homelands. The reservation population grew in the 1950s and 1960s, despite the relocation program.
27. Mackenzie calls this "the reservation scene" in his notes, so it's unclear whether this scene takes place in Valentine or on the Hualapai Reservation. The confusion is somewhat revealing: for Mackenzie, the city-reservation dichotomy holds.
28. The Hualapai Reservation, created in 1883, consists of one million of the original five million acres of the Hualapai ancestral homeland. See McMillan, *Making Indian Law*; and Shepherd, "At the Crossroads."
29. McMillan, *Making Indian Law*, 4.
30. Shepherd, "At the Crossroads." Shepherd argues that the Hualapais' claims reveal their "resistance to hegemonic notions of space and place because they rejected propaganda that they had to remain fixed on the reservation and passively accept the status quo" (32).
31. Dimock's "deep time" suggests that we consider time and space simultaneously, that place contains echoes of earlier events. See Dimock, "Deep Time."
32. This methodology is usually associated with the field of history, like Stanford University's Spatial History Project, directed by Zephyr Frank.
33. Certeau, *The Practice of Everyday Life*, 108.
34. See Pratt, *Imperial Eyes*.
35. Some of these include Wax and Buchanan, *Solving "The Indian Problem"*; Stanbury, *Success and Failure*; Sorkin, *The Urban American Indian*; and Guillemin, *Urban Renegades*.

36. Mildred Weiler, "U.S. Faces Challenge in Relocating Indian Volunteers," *Christian Science Monitor*, December 1, 1956, K3.

37. For more information about this graffiti, see John Converse Townsend, "This Native American Artist's Street Art Reminds LA Residents Who Was There First," *Fast Company*, August 24, 2016, www.fastcoexist.com/3063111/this -native-american-artists-street-art-reminds-la-residents-who-was-there-first.

38. Cornell, "That's the Story of Our Life," 45; Cornell, "Discovered Identities," 116.

39. See Benjamin, "The Storyteller."

40. Fixico reports that there were twenty-five thousand Native veterans from World War II and ten thousand from the Korean War. See Fixico, *The Urban Indian Experience*, 19.

41. See Fixico, *The Urban Indian Experience*, 19.

42. Burt, "Roots of the Native American Urban Experience," 90.

43. Burt, "Roots of the Native American Urban Experience," 91; Fixico, *The Urban Indian Experience*, 5.

44. The BIA Chicago Field Office archival documents I discuss are located at the Newberry Library.

45. See Bauman, Biles, and Szylvian, *The Ever-Changing American City*.

46. See Peters and Andersen, *Indigenous in the City*, for a global perspective on urban Indigenous identities.

47. Sorkin, *The Urban American Indian*, 132; Deloria and Lytle, *The Nations Within*, 236.

48. See Cornell, "Discovered Identities."

49. Vizenor, *Wordarrows*, 17.

50. An amazing example of this is happening as I write in 2016: the coalition of tribes protesting the construction of the Dakota Access Pipeline under the Missouri River near the Standing Rock Sioux Reservation in Cannonball, North Dakota. More than three hundred tribes are represented at the Oceti Sakowin (or Oceti Oyate) Camp, and even more have passed resolutions and sent letters of support to the tribe for their act of protecting the water. The entrance to the camp is lined by flagpoles that bear the flags of those nations in support.

51. Lobo, *Urban Voices*. For other city-specific studies, see Carpio, *Indigenous Albuquerque*; Thrush, *Native Seattle*; Straus, *Native Chicago*; LaGrand, *Indian Metropolis*; Weibel-Orlando, *Indian Country, L.A.*; and Rosenthal, *Reimagining Indian County*.

52. For discussions of Indian identity, see, among others, Weaver, *That the People Might Live*; Revard, *Family Matters, Tribal Affairs*; Allen, *Blood Narrative*; Nagel,

American Indian Ethnic Renewal; Jackson, *Our Elders Lived It*; Garroutte, *Real Indians*; and Lawrence, *"Real" Indians and Others*.

53. In recent years, a number of new books have been written on the subject of urban Indians in addition to the city-specific ones already mentioned, including Fixico, *The Urban Indian Experience*; Lobo and Peters, *American Indians and the Urban Experience*; and Jackson, *Our Elders Lived It*.

54. Lawrence, *"Real" Indians and Others*, 196.

55. See Fortunate Eagle, *Alcatraz! Alcatraz!* and *Heart of the Rock*; Smith and Warrior, *Like a Hurricane*; and Johnson, Nagel, and Champagne, *American Indian Activism*.

56. I discuss Alcatraz Island as Indian land further in chapter 1.

57. The number of Native college students had risen after the Second World War with the GI Bill, and universities also became places where people from very different geographical locations united as activists.

58. I discuss this further in chapter 1.

59. I will again here invoke the Dakota Access Pipeline protest. On August 19, 2016, North Dakota governor Jack Dalrymple declared a state of emergency and blocked main highways that lead to the site, drones and military aircraft were patrolling the camp, North Dakota state police, along with police from six neighboring states and the National Guard, were on location in armored vehicles and riot gear, arrests had been made, and protestors had been described as "armed" and "threatening," according to both social media reports and news outlets.

60. The occupation also led to policy changes, as I will discuss further in chapter 1.

61. The origins of the reservation system can be dated to 1796, when Congress drew "an eastern line of separation" intended to stand as a boundary for Indian Country, though it may be traced back even farther, to 1637, when a number of Pequots were forced onto a twelve-hundred-acre parcel. See Berkhofer, *The White Man's Indian*, 152.

62. Berkhofer, *The White Man's Indian*, 29.

63. Berkhofer, *The White Man's Indian*, 29–30.

64. Buruma and Margalit, *Occidentalism*, 21.

65. Deloria writes in *Indians in Unexpected Places* that "Indian people, corralled on isolated and impoverished reservations, missed out on modernity" (6).

66. Nelson, *Place and Vision*, 8.

67. Bevis, "Native American Novels," 598. Bevis's dependence on a kind of essentialist instinct is somewhat problematic here, as it reduces agency and historical context to natural urges, an unexplainable and mysterious connection to a place, and an assumption that Natives cannot thrive in the modern world,

with its transformed urban existence, an assumption that many contemporary novelists such as those in this study are countering.

68. N. Scott Momaday, Peter Nabokov, Jerry H. Gill, and Patricia Clarke Smith, among others, have also attempted to articulate the relationship between Native people and place.

69. Ortiz, "More Than Just a River."

70. Hedge Coke discussed this idea explicitly in a radio interview with South Dakota Public Radio in 2007, but it appears more implicitly in *Blood Run* itself.

71. Basso, *Wisdom Sits in Places*, 7.

72. Wilson, "Reclaiming Our Humanity," 74.

73. Valaskakis, "Indian Country," 151–52.

74. Valaskakis, "Indian Country," 156.

75. See Byrd, *The Transit of Empire*. I will return to Byrd's idea of "transit" in chapter 3.

76. Lefebvre, *The Production of Space*, 166.

77. Certeau, *The Practice of Everyday Life*, xi.

78. Boyer, *The City of Collective Memory*, 2.

79. Tuan, *Topophilia*, 47, 75.

80. Davis, *City of Quartz*, 232.

81. See Davis, *City of Quartz*, especially 72–74 and 230–32.

82. See Soja, *Postmodern Geographies*; and Harvey, "Social Justice."

83. See Butler and Athanasiou, *Dispossession*.

84. See Butler and Athanasiou, *Dispossession*, ix, x.

85. See Allen, "A Transnational Native American Studies?"

86. Clingman, *The Grammar of Identity*, 2.

87. See Huhndorf, *Mapping the Americas*. Scholars in Native studies have recently begun to engage with theories of the transnational. For example, recent issues of *American Quarterly* (edited by Lindsay Claire Smith) and the *Journal of Transnational American Studies* (edited by Hsinya Huang, Phil Deloria, John Gamber, and me) have focused on the transnational in Native studies.

88. Huhndorf, *Mapping the Americas*, 2.

89. Ramirez, *Native Hubs*, 2.

90. Ramirez, *Native Hubs*, 11.

91. Ramirez, *Native Hubs*, 2.

92. Ramirez, *Native Hubs*, 23.

93. Jay, *Contingency Blues*, 168.

94. Citizens of Indian nations are still able to vote in tribal elections when they are off-reservation.

95. Saldívar, *Border Matters*, 8.

96. Thanks to my graduate student Darren Lone Fight for his ruminations on Alexie and immigration.

97. I evoke Appadurai here.

98. See Clifford, *Routes*. Other scholars have noted that Indigenous identity is increasingly cosmopolitan. For example, see DeLugan, "Indigeneity across Borders"; and Biolsi, "Imagined Geographies."

99. Clifford, *Routes*, 254. See, for example, Betty, *Comanche Society*; Duff, *Western Pueblo Identities*; and Ray, *Indians in the Fur Trade*.

100. For more on tribal cosmopolitanism, see Forte, *Indigenous Cosmopolitans*.

101. See Brennan, *At Home in the World*.

102. Clifford, *Routes*, 6, 254.

103. Clifford, *Routes*, 255.

104. Appadurai, *Modernity at Large*, 4–6.

105. Appadurai, *Modernity at Large*, 44.

106. Chris Teuton suggests that there are three spaces at work in Native narratives: the Symbolic Center, the Symbolic City, and the Symbolic Reservation, pointing out that the reservation space does not always encompass originary and sacred sites. See Teuton, "The Cycle of Removal and Return."

107. See Cook-Lynn, "The American Indian Fiction Writer"; and Krupat, *Red Matters*.

108. See Appiah, *Cosmopolitanism* and "Cosmopolitan Patriots."

109. Smith, "The Indian in Literature Is Growing Up," *New York Times*, April 21, 1997, C11–C12. The authors Smith includes in the "new generation" are Sherman Alexie, Greg Sarris, Joy Harjo, Aaron Carr, David Treuer, and Susan Power.

110. Pokagon, "Red Man's Rebuke," 1.

111. Black Elk's text was written by Nebraska poet John Neihardt, who, as Raymond DeMallie has demonstrated, altered and constructed the holy man's story. In fact, it is interesting that Black Elk named these cities in the transcript (Omaha, Chicago, New York), while Neihardt changed each to "a very big town" (173). Black Elk's response to the city, "I was surprised at the big houses and so many people," is also not in the transcript (Neihardt, *Black Elk Speaks*, 173).

112. Carol Miller asserts that Momaday depicts the city as "a site of ultimate exile" ("Telling the Indian Urban," 37); while David Rice argues that for Silko the urban space "does not provide the necessary cultural story that will enrich its people" ("Witchery," 121).

113. See Teuton, *Red Land, Red Power*.

114. Vizenor, *Manifest Manners*, 4.

115. Vizenor, *Manifest Manners*, vii.

116. In *When Did Indians Become Straight?* Rifkin describes how Beth Brant's *Mohawk Trail* (1985) demonstrates that "ongoing participation in kinship and clan networks" allows for the continuation of Mohawk citizenship in the urban space (258).

117. Paula Gunn Allen's *The Woman Who Owned the Shadows* appeared two years prior.

118. Other urban Indian texts include Paula Gunn Allen, *The Woman Who Owned the Shadows* (1983); Gerald Vizenor, *Wordarrows: Indians and Whites in the New Fur Trade* (1978) and *Dead Voices* (1994); Anna Lee Walters, *Ghost Singer* (1988); James Welch, *The Indian Lawyer* (1990) and *The Heartsong of Charging Elk* (2000); Silko, *Almanac of the Dead* (1991); Lee Maracle, *Ravensong* (1993); A. A. Carr, *Eye Killers* (1996); E. Donald Two-Rivers, *Survivor's Medicine* (1998); Keith Egawa, *Madchild Running* (1999); David Treuer, *The Hiawatha* (1999); and Thomas Yeahapu, *X Indian Chronicles* (2006).

119. Rader, *Engaged Resistance*, 1. This reading, as I will detail further in the chapter itself, draws upon the work of Lisa Tatonetti. See "Dancing That Way, Things Began to Change."

120. I realize that there are many textual problems with this speech and that these words probably never came from Chief Seattle himself. I will discuss this further in chapter 2.

121. See Howe, "Blind Bread," "The Story of America," and "Tribalography."

122. From Robertson's "Rattlebone," which I do not have the permission to cite more extensively. The ironic out-of-placeness of this image embodies the sort of politicized recuperation of Native identity that I see occurring in the literary works that I examine in this project. Famous for his work with the Band from the late 1960s through the 1970s, Robertson, whose mother was raised on the Six Nations Reserve in Ontario, Canada, and then moved to Toronto, began to create music with specifically Native American themes in the 1990s. See his 2016 memoir, *Testimony*, for a narrative account of his musical career. This song comes from *Contact from the Underworld of Redboy* (1998), the unofficial soundtrack of *Indigenous Cities*, and it was where this project began.

I. AN INDIGENOUS AWAKENING

1. Ojibwe photographer Nadya Kwandibens's series *Concrete Indians* (2011) similarly captures urban Indian subjects in Vancouver.

2. Chadwick, "Reflecting on History as Histories," 36. Another photographer who has responded to Curtis's photographs is Zig Jackson (Mandan/Hidatsa/Arikara), whose images of himself in a headdress with the San Francisco skyline as a backdrop are part of his *Entering Zig's Reservation* series (1998).

3. Hale, *Jailing*, 134.

4. Harlan, "Indigenous Visionaries," 192.

5. Allen's novel, as well as Momaday's *The Ancient Child* (1989), is also set in San Francisco.

6. Rose, *Lost Copper*, 2.

7. In his review of the novel, Owens calls this a "vision quest disturbingly appropriate to modern urban Indians" (56).

8. This was also the title of Mel Ellis's 1974 novel for young adults, which details the adventures of Charley Nightwind, a young urban Indian who "escapes" to his home reservation. Ellis was a non-Native nature writer from Wisconsin.

9. Though some have argued that the takeover of Alcatraz was a decidedly male-dominated pursuit, a number of accounts point out that women played a very important role in 1960s and 1970s political activism. See, for example, Boyer, "Reflections of Alcatraz"; Hightower-Langston, "American Indian Women's Activism"; Mihesuah, *Indigenous American Women*; and Mankiller, *Mankiller*.

10. For example, in the *New York Times Book Review* Wolitzer argues that "the prose feels flat" (14). In the *Ms. Magazine* review, Cole writes, "One hopes that Hale herself will release her talents more freely in her next outing" (16). Owens's review in *Western American Literature* calls the novel "a valuable addition to the panorama of contemporary Indian life in America" (376). In her review, Manyarrows briefly discusses the depictions of racism and sexism in the novel. See also Berner's review in *American Indian Quarterly*. Sean Teuton and Dennis have also discussed the novel: Teuton sees it as an extension of the Red Power novel tradition that he outlines, and Dennis describes it as an antihoming, feminist *Bildungsroman* (94). See Teuton, *Red Land, Red Power*; and Dennis, *Native American Literature*.

11. Owens, *Mixedblood Messages*, 72.

12. Owens, *Mixedblood Messages*, 71–72.

13. Stromberg, "*The Jailing of Cecelia Capture* and the Rhetoric of Individualism," 102.

14. Stromberg, "*The Jailing of Cecelia Capture* and the Rhetoric of Individualism," 103.

15. Hale, "The Perils of Native American Urbanization," 52, 61.

16. Alfred, "Warrior Scholarship," 98. However, Alfred also argues that the most "authentic" Indigenous peoples remain in their home communities—the reserves.

17. Finnegan discusses the trope of captivity in Hale's memoir, *Bloodlines: Odyssey of a Native Daughter*, in "Refiguring Legacies."

18. Saunt, *West of the Revolution*, 76. Saunt's book investigates historical events

in the western United States that were coterminous with the American Revolution in 1776.

19. Nelson, "San Francisco Bay Shellmounds," 144.

20. Saunt, *West of the Revolution*, 76.

21. Saunt, *West of the Revolution*, 77.

22. Madley, *An American Genocide*, 27–31.

23. Jackson, "The Dynamic of Indian Demographic Collapse," 146, 153.

24. Saunt, *West of the Revolution*, 87. He is citing Milliken, *Time of Little Choice*, 266.

25. Madley, *An American Genocide*, 36.

26. DeLuca, "The Indian Attempt," 5.

27. Madley, *An American Genocide*, 38, though Madley points out the difference between "the Hispanic tradition of assimilating and exploiting indigenous peoples and the Anglo-American pattern of killing or removing them" (50).

28. Madley, *An American Genocide*, 3. Madley is not the first to suggest that genocide had been committed in California. See Lindsay, *Murder State*; Madley, *An American Genocide*, 6–8. Lindsay also cites the work of Shelburne F. Cook, Jack D. Forbes, and Robert F. Heizer. He points to William Coffer as the first to use the term *genocide* in connection with California Indians in 1977 (5). Estimates are that three hundred thousand people flocked to California during the gold rush.

29. Lindsay, *Murder State*, 2. Lindsay makes a very interesting claim about how genocide in California was fueled by sensational stories about Indians and that settlers to California had no prior real experience with Indians (24–25).

30. Madley, *An American Genocide*, 65. Madley cites a statement from San Francisco's newspaper, the *Californian*, which stated, "We desire only a white population in California, even the Indians amongst us, as far as we have seen, are more of a nuisance than a benefit to the country; we would like to get rid of them" (66). Lindsay also argues that this sentiment can be found in "numerous letters, petitions, reports, and newspaper articles" of the time (*Murder State*, 2).

31. DeLuca, "The Indian Attempt," 6.

32. Ramirez discusses Kroeber in *Native Hubs*, 110.

33. Bean, introduction, xxiv.

34. Bean, introduction, xxiv; Ramirez, *Native Hubs*, 105.

35. Johnson, *The Occupation*, 162. Specifically, in a January 22, 1970, letter, the Ohlones state, "The Ohlone people discovered, owned, and occupied the land from Pleasanton in the East Bay to the Coast, and southerly to Monterey, including the islands along the coast, Alcatraz and Yerba Buena among the others" (cited in Johnson, *The Occupation*, 162).

36. Bean, introduction, xxv; Ramirez, *Native Hubs*, 113. Ramirez writes that after this incident, Ohlone descendants were often contacted during major construction in the San Jose area and that in 1984 the California legislature formalized the process with Senate Bill 297.
37. Ramirez, *Native Hubs*, 107.
38. Ramirez, *Native Hubs*, 112.
39. Ramirez, *Native Hubs*, 123. This case is ongoing. Appeals to the US District Court have been successful, and the Ohlones may be allowed to forgo the recognition process. See the Muwekma website for updates: www.muwekma .org/tribalhistory/recognitionprocess.
40. Willard, "Outing," 30.
41. Cited in Lobo, *Urban Voices*, 14.
42. See Ablon, "American Indian Relocation" and "Relocated American Indians," for example. These studies done by urban anthropologists often underestimated the amount of intertribal activity.
43. Willard, "Outing," 31, 32.
44. Mankiller, *Mankiller*, 201.
45. US Department of Commerce, Census Bureau, 2000.
46. See Bevis, "Native American Novels."
47. Lavie and Swedenburg, "Introduction: Displacement," 1.
48. See Appadurai, *Modernity at Large*.
49. Dennis also makes this observation; see *Native American Literature*, 94–95.
50. Bevis discusses this tradition as well, but he does not apply it to any texts written by Native authors.
51. Allen, *Off the Reservation*, 6.
52. Green, *That's What She Said*, 6.
53. "Renaissance" is Kenneth Lincoln's term for the period of writing that follows N. Scott Momaday's Pulitzer Prize for *House Made of Dawn* in 1969. See Lincoln, *Native American Renaissance*.
54. Martin and Mohanty, "Feminist Politics," 192.
55. In "Land Claims, Identity Claims," Suzack argues that a number of Native women writers "articulate an alternative political grounding for their work, one that might best be understood as *indigenous feminist* in conceptual orientation" (187). See also Anderson, "Affirmations," and Huhndorf, "Indigenous Feminism." For more on Indigenous women and place, see McGlennan, *Tribal Alliances*; Goeman, "Notes"; and Fitzgerald, *Native Women and Land*.
56. Hernández-Ávila, "Relocations," 492.
57. Hernández-Ávila, "Relocations," 492.
58. Rubenstein, *Home Matters*, 2.

59. Hale, *Jailing*, 9.

60. Hale, *Jailing*, 9.

61. The Wounded Knee massacre was the culmination of the 1890 Ghost Dance. Most of the famous photographs of Wounded Knee were taken by photographer George Trager, a German immigrant living in Chadron, Nebraska. The photos depict frozen corpses lying in the snow, many in gruesome "death poses." Others show a burial party placing bodies in a mass grave. Many of the victims were stripped of clothing, taken as souvenirs by troops and reporters.

62. Hale, *Jailing*, 51 (emphasis mine). The Coeur d'Alene reservation was established by an executive order of President Ulysses Grant in 1873, following a peace treaty in 1858. The reservation is 345,000 acres. I think Hale is referring to Steptoe Butte in this passage, named for Lt. Col. Edward Steptoe, who was defeated by a coalition of one thousand Coeur d'Alenes, Spokanes, and Palouses at the Battle of Pine Creek in 1858. Steptoe Butte, located in Rosalia, Washington, is adjacent to the Coeur d'Alene reservation and has long been considered to be a sacred place. Hale mentions it in her title poem "Custer Lives in Humboldt County": "Wild grass grows again at Little Big Horn, / at Steptoe, at Wounded Knee" (3).

63. Hale, *Jailing*, 52.

64. The chapter "Daughter of Winter" in Hale's memoir, *Bloodlines*, is quite revealing about her relationship with her mother. Although in "Autobiography in Fiction," another chapter, Hale warns readers against linking autobiographical details to her fiction, the similarity is too exact to overlook.

65. Hale, *Jailing*, 83.

66. Hale, *Jailing*, 80.

67. Hale, *Jailing*, 60, 105.

68. Hale, *Jailing*, 53.

69. Hale, *Jailing*, 149.

70. Hale, *Jailing*, 150.

71. Hale, *Jailing*, 53.

72. The proclamation was published in January 1970 in the *Movement*, the newsletter of the Alcatraz occupation.

73. Both Chadwick Allen and Dean Rader have written about this document. Allen calls it a "parodic treaty" (*Blood Narrative*, 162–63). See also Rader, *Engaged Resistance*, 9.

74. Indeed, the Yavapai physician Carlos Montezuma called the reservation a "demoralized prison" in an 1898 speech, printed as "Our Treatment of the Indians from the Standpoint of One of Them" in the *Saturday Evening Post*, quoted in Maddox, *Citizen Indians*, 112.

75. Strange and Loo, "Holding the Rock," 60.

76. Ortiz, "San Francisco Indians," 12.

77. Both Green and Deloria discuss the phenomenon of wannabe Indians, who today seem to align themselves with the New Age movement. See Green, "The Tribe Called Wannabe;" and Deloria, *Playing Indian*.

78. Hale, *Jailing*, 111, 112 (emphasis mine). In *Indian Killer*, Alexie also describes urban Indians as a tribe of outcasts. On October 10, 1969, the San Francisco Indian Center on Valencia burned down under suspicious circumstances. Its replacement was a Masonic lodge in the Mission district—though an impetus for the occupation was to rebuild the center on the island.

79. Hale, *Jailing*, 112.

80. Hale, *Jailing*, 112.

81. Hale, *Jailing*, 111.

82. Hale, *Jailing*, 112.

83. As of the end of 2016 there were twelve or thirteen bison in the enclosure.

84. Hale, *Jailing*, 112–13.

85. Hale, *Jailing*, 111.

86. Hale, *Jailing*, 14 (emphasis mine).

87. According to Alfred, "Indigenism brings together words, ideas, and symbols from different indigenous cultures to serve as tools for those involved in asserting nationhood. It does not, however, supplant the localized cultures of individual communities. Indigenism is an important means of confronting the state in that it provides a unifying vocabulary and basis for collective action. But it is entirely dependent on maintenance of the integrity of the traditional indigenous cultures and communities from which it draws its strength" ("Warrior Scholarship," 88).

88. Hale, *Jailing*, 14.

89. Gould, *Earthquake Weather*, 34.

90. Hale, *Jailing*, 134.

91. Hale, *Jailing*, 34.

92. Hale, *Jailing*, 33.

93. Hale, *Jailing*, 6.

94. Hale, *Jailing*, 31.

95. The first novel written by a Native American woman is believed to be Callahan's *Wynema: A Child of the Forest* (1891). Johnson (Canadian Mohawk) frequently created female protagonists in her short fiction, as did other early Native American women writers, but the majority of protagonists in early twentieth-century novels were male. See Johnson, *The Moccasin Maker*; Zitkala-Ša, *American Indian Stories*; and Parker, *The Sound the Stars Make*.

96. Fixico discusses some of these gender inequities in *The Urban Indian Experience in America*. Some women, for example, were afraid to leave their homes in the cities, they became much more dependent on their husbands, and they often experienced more racial prejudice than did their male counterparts (176). Tatonetti and Rifkin cite Gould's and Brant's work, respectively. See *The Queerness of Native American Literature* and *When Did Indians Become Straight?*

97. Donovan, *Feminist Readings*, 18.

98. Joe and Miller, "Cultural Survival," 186.

99. Cited in Joe and Miller, "Cultural Survival," 187.

100. Tohe, "There Is No Word," 103.

101. Harjo, *She Had Some Horses*.

102. Peltier, *A Brief History*, 18.

103. Hale, *Jailing*, 74.

104. Hale, *Jailing*, 61.

105. Hale, *Jailing*, 91.

106. Hale, *Jailing*, 47.

107. Hale, *Jailing*, 54.

108. Hale, *Jailing*, 54–55.

109. Walker, *Indians of Idaho*, 125.

110. Hale, *Jailing*, 153.

111. Hale, *Jailing*, 156.

112. Hale, *Jailing*, 157–58.

113. Hale, *Jailing*, 93.

114. Woolf, "Professions for Women," 235–42.

115. Hale, *Jailing*, 91.

116. Hale, *Jailing*, 15.

117. Hale, *Jailing*, 56.

118. Hale, *Jailing*, 15.

119. Hale, *Jailing*, 5.

120. Green, "Pocahontas," 19.

121. Hale, *Jailing*, 165.

122. Hale, *Jailing*, 183.

123. Hale, *Jailing*, 185–86.

124. Hale, *Jailing*, 186.

125. Hale, *Jailing*, 13.

126. Hale, *Jailing*, 191.

127. Hale, *Jailing*, 199.

128. Hale, *Jailing*, 57.

129. Just as evil deeds are "red affairs," red suggests danger, and red hair signifies witchery.
130. Hale, *Jailing*, 59. The color red can signify a warring Indian, but it is also a sacred color for many Native peoples. Of course, the color red is associated with the Red Power movement.
131. Hale, *Jailing*, 59.
132. Hale, *Jailing*, 93.
133. Hale, *Jailing*, 59.
134. Hale, *Jailing*, 71.
135. Hale, *Jailing*, 59–60.
136. Hale, *Jailing*, 60.
137. Hale, *Jailing*, 67–68.
138. Hale, *Jailing*, 69 (emphasis mine).
139. Hale, *Jailing*, 58.
140. Hale, *Jailing*, 58.
141. Hale, *Jailing*, 58.
142. Hale, *Jailing*, 164.
143. Hale, *Jailing*, 16.
144. Hale, *Jailing*, 72.
145. Hale, *Jailing*, 71.
146. Hale, *Jailing*, 155.
147. Hale, *Jailing*, 81.
148. Hale, *Jailing*, 141.
149. Hale, *Jailing*, 52.
150. Hale, *Jailing*, 167.
151. Hale, *Jailing*, 198.
152. Sean Teuton concurs: "In recalling this Red Power vision, however, Cecelia ultimately discovers a means to persevere as a colonized Native woman in the city" (223). See Teuton, *Red Land, Red Power.*
153. Hale, *Jailing*, 199.
154. I will discuss this again in chapter 3.
155. Hale, *Jailing*, 199.
156. The occupation began November 20, 1969, and ended June 11, 1971. Organizers used the 1868 Treaty of Fort Laramie, which promised that unused federal land would revert to Indian land. As Troy Johnson points out, the Ohlone people were as a whole opposed to the occupation because Alcatraz was Ohlone/Costanoan land. See Johnson, *The Occupation*, 162.
157. Rader reads the semiotics of this graffiti. See Rader, *Engaged Resistance*, 28–46.

Rundstrom argues that the graffiti works as "placemaking" on the island. See Rundstrom, "American Indian Placemaking," 189.

158. I gather from the "SFHC Controversy Statement," posted on John Leaños's website, that the posters, which appeared during a period of gentrification protest, were not all well received by the people of San Francisco. According to the statement, "The project was received with contradictory sentiment, from e-mails denouncing us as 'racist' to letters and comments praising the work." See www.leanos.net.

159. Though, as Kotlowski details, it did influence policy changes. See Kotlowski, "Alcatraz, Wounded Knee, and Beyond."

160. This has been occurring since 1975. There is also a sunrise ceremony on Columbus Day—renamed Indigenous Peoples' Day in many locales.

161. See www.behance.net/gallery/13714781/Alcatraz-History-Museum-Cultural -Center and www.nps.gov/alca/alcatraz-historic-preservation-projects.htm.

162. St. Clair, "Fighting for Her Life," 157.

163. Rundstrom has argued that the occupation intended "to create an Indian place in which a sense of pan-Indian ethnicity could be renewed" ("American Indian Placemaking," 190).

164. See Rundstrom, "American Indian Placemaking," 206; Madley, *An American Genocide*, 345. Local tribes traveled to Alcatraz Island to gather food and for isolation, later to escape the mission system. It was established as a US army fortress in 1850, and during the Civil War, Indians who had sided with the Confederacy were imprisoned here. Then in 1873 six Modocs were jailed there for killing an army general. In 1895 nineteen Hopis were imprisoned for resisting government relocation efforts. In 1907 it became a prison for military personnel and in 1934 a maximum-security penitentiary. It was declared surplus federal land in 1964.

165. See Kotlowski, "Alcatraz, Wounded Knee, and Beyond."

166. Hale, *Jailing*, 75.

2. THE URBAN GHOST DANCE

1. Alexie, *First Indian on the Moon*.

2. Certainly Victor Joseph from *The Lone Ranger and Tonto Fistfight in Heaven* is one of Alexie's alter egos. Alexie told Tomson Highway in a 1996 interview that Thomas, Victor, and Junior are the "unholy trinity of me" (*Conversations*, 28).

3. Certeau, *The Practice of Everyday Life*, xix.

4. Banka, "'Homing' in the City," 35. Banka suggests that Alexie's evolving depictions of the urban space are meant to mirror the "adaptation to city life" for Indigenous peoples.

5. Alexie, "What You Pawn," 170.

6. In Seattle-speak, they are called *unhoused*.

7. Indeed, Frisch and Gymnich suggest that *Indian Killer* "exemplif[ies] 'the new ghost dance literature' that Vizenor envisions" in *Manifest Manners* ("Crime Spirit," 221). Mariani suggests that "even the most oppressed and unfortunate of urban Indians are able to assert some degree of control over their destinies," though he does not connect their "collective rage" as "political act" to the Ghost Dance ("From Atopia to Utopia," 587–88). James, on the other hand, describes this book as a "reverse captivity narrative" in which urban Indians such as John are being held captive in the city; see "Indians Do Not Live in Cities" and *Literary and Cinematic Reservation*.

8. The fact that Alexie has consented to so many interviews with this publication speaks to his concern for the homeless. I am indebted to Tim Harris for furnishing me with copies of these interviews.

9. "Where There's Smoke," *Real Change News*, July 1998.

10. "Seriously Sherman," *Real Change News*, May 29–June 11, 2003. This was in the June 10, 2015, episode, "Back to Spokane," of his podcast, *A Tiny Sense of Accomplishment*, recorded live in St. Paul with host Kerri Miller from Minnesota Public Radio.

11. Alexie, "My Encounters," 19.

12. Alexie often jokes about his wealth and his sons' subsequent privilege (one of whom he has nicknamed "Little Privilege"), as in the May 27, 2015, episode of his podcast.

13. For example, in 2014 Seattle officially changed Columbus Day to Indigenous Peoples' Day. However, Alexie is ever critical of the hypocrisy of neoliberal Seattleites.

14. Fazio discusses class and homelessness in *Indian Killer* specifically. The novel, she writes, "confronts the impact globalization has on local communities, emphasizing the precarious relationship and unequal power relations between individuals and the capitalist system" ("Homeless in Seattle," 142).

15. According to the Seattle/King County Coalition for the Homeless (SKCC). See www.homelessinfo.org/. Chief Seattle Club, a center for homeless and "at-risk" Native people, is currently building a new facility in Seattle. The club serves 741 members, according to *Indian Country Today*, many more than the estimate of 400 homeless Indians (or 5 percent of 8,000).

16. In March 2015 KUOW 94.9 FM reported extensively on the homeless population in Seattle. These numbers come from US Housing and Urban Development.

17. See *Seattle Times* editorial, November 12, 2013, and KUOW story by John Ryan, "After Ten-Year Plan, Why Does Seattle Have More Homeless Than Ever?"

(March 3, 2015), http://kuow.org/post/after-10-year-plan-why-does-seattle-have-more-homeless-ever.

18. See Jessica Lee, "Dozens of Homeless Camp Out at County Building after SHARE Closes Its Shelters," *Seattle Times*, March 31, 2016.

19. Bernie Youngbear led an occupation of Fort Lawton to establish a land base for urban Indians in Seattle. The result was a twenty-acre site on which the cultural center was built. See Reyes, *Bernie Youngbear*, 111–16.

20. The Treaty of Point Elliott was signed by Chief Seattle, for the Duwamish and Suquamish, along with representatives from several other tribes. The treaty ceded fifty-four thousand acres; established the Suquamish Port Madison, Tulalip, Swinomish, and Lummi reservations; and guaranteed fishing and hunting rights. See Seeman, "The Treaties of Puget Sound." See also Thrush, *Native Seattle*, 54.

21. Curtis would take more pictures of Angeline, along with other photos of Indians in Puget Sound, including *Homeward, The Clam Digger*, and *Evening on the Sound* (1898). See Gidley, *Edward S. Curtis*; and Makepeace, *Edward S. Curtis*.

22. See Bagley, "Chief Seattle and Angeline," for an account of Angeline's life.

23. Thrush, *Native Seattle*, 86. A proposed reservation for the Duwamish south of the city never materialized.

24. Cited in Thrush, *Native Seattle*, 90.

25. The *Chief-of-All-Women* totem pole was stolen from a Tlingit village in 1899 by some of the town officials. A mock trial was held, and the city paid $500 to the village. The pole was a victim of arson in 1938 and was replaced by a commissioned totem pole in 1940. See Thrush, *Native Seattle*, 113–15.

26. Wehn's first sculpture was of Angeline, in 1905. Wehn also created the full-length sculpture of Chief Seattle in 1907, based on the only known photograph, that taken by L. B. Franklin in 1864. This statue is located in Tilikum Place, in the Belltown neighborhood. See Bierwert, "Remembering Chief Seattle," for a history of Chief Seattle imagery in the city. The *Day/Night* sculpture was commissioned as part of the 1991 In Public art festival and in 1998 was purchased by the Seattle Arts Commission. It is the only entry that remains today in Seattle. Anthes writes that Heap of Birds intended the piece to be a "temporary intervention," to provide "a new critical context" for the Chief Seattle bust, which is often photographed by tourists, but the city embraced the work. See Anthes, *Edgar Heap of Birds*, 54.

27. Alexie, *Indian Killer*, 146.

28. This is Thrush's term.

29. Allen, *Homelessness*, 13.

30. See Cresswell, *In Place*.

31. Recent documented violence against homeless people in Albuquerque, for example, cites police officers who tell Native transients to "go back to their reservations." See articles in *CounterPunch* and *Indian Country Today*. Of course, this conjures the historical purpose of the reservation—to divide, keep separate, and imprison—and recalls the policing of those borders.

32. Patell, "The Violence of Hybridity," 3.

33. See Coulthard, *Red Skin, White Masks*.

34. While Alexie eschews the categorization of his work as "political" writing, he does write in "One Little Indian Boy," "Every Indian is born political" (54). I am also thinking here about critics like Gloria Bird and Elizabeth Cook-Lynn, who have famously criticized Alexie for his failure to engage with political issues in his work. See Bird, "The Exaggeration of Despair"; and Cook-Lynn, "The American Indian Fiction Writer."

35. Ladino writes that the city becomes a place of "empathetic boundary crossing and community building" ("'A Limited Range of Motion?,'" 38).

36. Alexie, "Seriously Sherman," 18.

37. Alexie, "Seriously Sherman," 18.

38. Cox, "Muting White Noise," 53.

39. There are two instances in which Alexie directly connects the telling of stories with gaining respect. First, in "The Search Engine," Corliss shows a homeless man respect by listening to his stories; and second, in a scene in *Flight*, Zit's father demands that a passer-by show him respect by telling him a story, a scene I will discuss later in this chapter.

40. Alexie, *Lone Ranger and Tonto*, 187. This "old Indian poet" is Carroll Arnett. Other critics, like James and Patell, have similarly discussed this line. I might add that this line is where this chapter began for me.

41. Alexie has since recanted this belief. See the *Guardian* interview.

42. Alexie, *Reservation Blues*, 150.

43. "Ambivalence" is from James, *Literary and Cinematic Reservation*, 9. James describes this ambivalence as "the irony of trying to give a positive identity to an imposed, restricted space."

44. Alexie, *Reservation Blues*, 283. According to Louis Owens, Alexie expressed this sentiment in a listserv conversation on April 19, 1997, under the pseudonym "lester." Alexie writes, "When I read a poem about rez life written by Adrian C. Louis, I know that he lives on a rez and can trust that he has seen what he's talking about" (qtd. in *Mixedblood Messages*, 74).

45. Here I am thinking about the driving sequences, particularly those that highlight the urban landscape.

46. Like Alexie himself, the protagonist of *True Diary* is also empowered by leaving the reservation.

47. Alexie, "A World of Story-Smoke," 150–51.

48. In his 2012 *Atlantic* interview, Alexie said that the reservation is limiting: "There is always this implication that in order to be Indian you *must* be from the reservation." The line from Louis's poem "also . . . calls to mind the way we tend to revisit our prisons," he says. In his 2005 interview with Nygren, Alexie said, "Very few of the top 30 or 40 Native writers publishing now grew up on the reservation, and yet most Native literature is about the reservation. So there is a nostalgia for purity: a time when we were all together and when our identity was sure, and when our lives were better" (154). In his *Atlantic* interview, Alexie pointed out that "almost all of [our literature] is reservation-centric. So our entire literature is in the reservation of its mind."

49. Wovoka was influenced by the Dreamer movement in the 1870s and the Shaker movement in 1881. An earlier ghost dance movement, in 1870, led by Northern Paiute Wodziwob, also affected Wovoka's doctrine. See Andersson, *The Lakota Ghost Dance*, 26–27; see also Hittman and Lynch, *Wovoka and the Ghost Dance*; Kehoe, *The Ghost Dance*; and Smoak, *Ghost Dances and Identity* for more on the history of the Ghost Dance.

50. Andersson, *The Lakota Ghost Dance*, 23.

51. Andersson, *The Lakota Ghost Dance*, 24.

52. Tatonetti, "Dancing That Way," 10, 2.

53. I would like to note that other critics, such as Van Styvendale, have made the connection between the killer and the Ghost Dance. See Van Styvendale, "The Trans/Historicity of Trauma."

54. I am not intending to argue for the existence of ghosts. As Buse and Stott have argued, "While proving or disproving the existence of ghosts is a fruitless exercise, it is more rewarding to diagnose the persistence of the *trope* of spectrality in culture. Spectrality and haunting continue to enjoy a powerful currency in language and in thinking, even if they have been left behind by belief" ("Introduction: A Future," 3).

55. Alexie, *Indian Killer*, 228.

56. The language of the speech, for example, mimics Smith's own Victorian poetry, the speech does not appear in the official record, and the occasion of the speech has even been called into question. See Furtwangler, *Answering Chief Seattle*. No fewer than seven altered versions of the speech appeared in the second half of the twentieth century: the 1971 script by Ted Perry for a film on ecology entitled *Home*; an abbreviated version of Perry's script for distribution at the 1974 Spokane Expo; a 1975 adaptation by William Arrowsmith

published in *American Poetry Review*, read by the author at the first Earth Day celebration in 1970; an anonymous revision in Joseph Campbell's 1989 video series *Transformation of Myth through Time*; a poetic adaptation in the *Midwest Quarterly* (1990) entitled "Chief Seattle Reflects on the Future of America, 1855"; *Brother Eagle, Sister Sky* (1991), a children's book; and the Nature Company's 1992 booklet, *Chief Seattle's 1854 Speech*. See Biewert, "Remembering Chief Seattle"; Furtwangler, *Answering Chief Seattle*; Kaiser, "Chief Seattle's Speech(es)"; and Krupat, "Chief Seattle's Speech Revisited."

57. Smith, "Scraps from a Diary," 10.
58. The only official record of Chief Seattle's words is from a January 21, 1855, treaty council meeting, in which he does not mention ghosts nor vanishing.
59. Thrush, *Native Seattle*, 9 (emphasis mine).
60. Anthes, *Edgar Heap of Birds*, 56.
61. Thrush writes, "Even Seattle resident Sherman Alexie, the Spokane–Coeur d'Alene Indian author rightly lauded for the complicated humanity of his Native characters, slides effortlessly into this urban parable" (*Native Seattle*, 9).
62. Bell, "The Ghosts of Place," 832.
63. For a discussion of this literary history, see Bergland, *The National Uncanny*. I would add popular culture references like *The Amityville Horror* (1979) and Stephen King's *Pet Sematary* (1989).
64. Gordon, *Ghostly Matters*, 8.
65. Gordon, *Ghostly Matters*, 17.
66. Boyd and Thrush, "Introduction: Bringing Ghosts," ix.
67. Boyd and Thrush, "Introduction: Bringing Ghosts," xxiii.
68. Brogan, *Cultural Haunting*, 36.
69. Brogan, *Cultural Haunting*, 29.
70. The "last skyscraper" is a play on the trope of "lasts" in American consciousness—*Last of His Tribe*, *Last of the Mohicans*, etc.—which of course connotes the expectation of extinction. It also seems to signify something about the growth of the city itself: the ending of skyscrapers might signal slow economic growth or a change in urban planning, from concentrated downtown centers into more dispersed economic and residential areas. Fazio discusses this in "Homeless in Seattle."
71. Krupat, *Red Matters*, 99. Here I agree with Krupat: the mystery remains unsolved at the end of the novel, and it's certainly not clear that John is the killer.
72. Alexie, *Indian Killer*, 313.
73. Alexie, *Indian Killer*, 314.
74. In his 2005 interview with Nygren, Alexie discussed his "strong Northwest

identity" and said that he believed "Indian identity is more regional than it is tribal" and that he "strongly identif[ied] with salmon people" (155).

75. Alexie himself said in an interview with Bellante that there is not much landscape in his work (*Conversations*, 4). Fazio argues that the geographic detail works to demonstrate the divide between poor and affluent neighborhoods in Seattle and that the streets "appear as sites of resistance and struggle for power" ("Homeless in Seattle," 145).

76. Alexie, *Indian Killer*, 7.

77. Alexie, *Indian Killer*, 7.

78. Today's Seattle would be unrecognizable to early settlers, Thrush has argued: "Where four rivers once joined to becomes the Duwamish, now only one flows; Lake Washington empties to the west instead of the south and is shallower; other lakes, creeks, and beaches have been filled, dredged, culverted, and bulkheaded." At end of the nineteenth and early in the twentieth centuries, the city "turned hills into islands, straightened one river and obliterated another, and reshaped entire watersheds" (Thrush, *Native Seattle*, 93, 94).

79. Alexie, *Indian Killer*, 112.

80. Alexie, *Indian Killer*, 409.

81. Alexie, *Indian Killer*, 30, 195, 199.

82. Goeman, *Mark My Words*, 2. Of course, there are Indigenous mapmaking practices as well. See G. Malcolm Lewis in *Cartographic Encounters*. Goeman also reminds us that many of these western maps were dependent on Indigenous knowledge of the land vis-à-vis Indian guides. See Goeman, *Mark My Words*, 24.

83. Licton Springs is an example from Thrush, *Native Seattle*. *Licton* refers to red pigment used for ceremonial purposes. The naming of this residential area used symbolic Indigeneity to lure settlers to live here (92). The other obvious example is the city's name itself, but there are others: the Sammamish River, for example.

84. Puget Sound, or Puget's Sound, is named after Peter Puget, a Huguenot on the Vancouver Expedition (1791–95). The expedition explored the sound in the spring of 1792. Elliott Bay (also known as Duwamish Bay and Seattle Harbor) was named during the 1841 Wilkes Expedition. Seattle's earliest maps date from 1841, 1854, and the mid-1870s. These maps focused on waterways; later maps were created for the purpose of real estate.

85. This history comes from www.seattle.gov.

86. Alexie, *Indian Killer*, 134.

87. Christie, "Renaissance Man," 5. I should add that Christie reads John's schizophrenia as a metaphor for his "mixed-blood madness," a reading that I disagree

with (3). There is no textual indication that John is a mixed-blood character. Christie also argues that the novel "solidifies racial purity as the guarantor of authentic American Indian experience" (2). While the novel is certainly essentialist in many ways (Alexie himself has called it "racist," in fact), I would argue that Christie is mistaken on this account as well: John lacks Indianness and therefore any kind of "blood memory" within the space of the novel, despite the fact that he has Indian blood. Therefore, there is no biological basis of Indian identity in this case.

88. Van Styvendale, "The Trans/Historicity of Trauma," 217.

89. Patell, "The Violence of Hybridity," 4.

90. Alexie, *Indian Killer*, 143.

91. I am not going to make the assumption, as many critics do, that John Smith was actually born on a reservation. I don't read Smith's desire for that origin narrative to be the truth of his story. It is his expectation because it is the reader's expectation. He was born in the late 1960s, in the midst of the Sixties Scoop, and he could just as likely have been born in Seattle as he could on the Spokane Reservation or at Pine Ridge. I give Alexie the benefit of the doubt when I assume that Smith is Indigenous at all: this could very well be an imagined identity, but this would make this a very different novel—and would take away the implications of a "Lost Bird," an adoptee who has been removed from his culture and community. We want to solve this ambiguity, just as we want to know the identity of the killer in the end.

92. Alexie, *Indian Killer*, 145.

93. Alexie, *Indian Killer*, 144.

94. See Paulides, *The Hoopa Project*. Apparently, Hoopa has been a productive place in terms of Bigfoot sightings. Paulides claims that Hoopa is a hotbed of Bigfoot activity, with hundreds of sightings dating back to 1940. The reservation is large in area and remote. Nonresidents have restricted access on reservation property (thus making tours like Sweet Lu's necessary and profitable). The famous 1967 footage of an alleged female Bigfoot was shot by Roger Patterson and Robert Gimlin near Bluff Creek, a few miles from the Hoopa reservation. The town of Willow Creek, south of Hoopa, hosts Bigfoot Days each year over the Labor Day weekend. Many of the eyewitness sightings in Paulides's book come from Hupa people.

95. Alexie, *Indian Killer*, 129.

96. Allen, "Re-scripting," 127.

97. And while "Sasquatch" might *sound* "Indian," the term was coined in the 1920s by J. W. Burns, an anthropologist collecting local legends in Canada, to describe an amalgam of similar creatures whose characteristics and names

varied between tribes. The word comes from the Halkomelem (or Coast Salish) *sasq'ets*. See Meldrum, *Sasquatch*.

98. In the nineteenth century, Elkanah Walker, a missionary among the Spokanes, described beliefs about Selahticks: "They [i.e., the Natives] believe in the existence of a race of giants which inhabit a certain mountain, off to the west of us. . . . They say their track is about a foot & a half long. They frequently come in the night & steal their salmon from their nets, & eat them raw. If the people are awake, they always know when they are coming very near, by the smell which is most intolerable" (Drury, *Nine Years*, 122–23).

99. A fascinating resource on the web is Tom Dailey's www.coastsalishmap.org, which contains a clickable map linking tribal stories with specific geographic locations. Dailey used Arthur Ballard's *Mythology of Southern Puget Sound* (1999) and an undated work by T. T. Waterman from the National Anthropological Archives, entitled *Puget Sound Geography*, to create his interactive map.

100. *Tulalip* means "small-mouthed bay" in Salish, according to the Tulalip website, https://www.tulaliptribes-nsn.gov. The tribes include Snohomish, Snoqualmie, Skykomish, Skagit, and other allied tribes and bands.

101. Alexie, *Indian Killer*, 208–9.

102. Alexie, *Indian Killer*, 62.

103. Alexie, *Indian Killer*, 65.

104. Alexie, *Indian Killer*, 158.

105. Alexie, *Indian Killer*, 67.

106. This fictionalizing of Shilshoolabsh sounds like other local tribal names, for example, the Duwamish, Suquamish, Snohomish, Swinomish. Linguistically, these are Lushootseed or Coast Salish tribes. Thrush explains the relationship between the Duwamish (People of the Inside Place), the Hachooabsh (Lake People), and the Shilshoolabsh (People of Tucked Away Inside), named for their settlement at Salmon Bay (*Native Seattle*, 23).

107. See Thrush, *Native Seattle*. See also Paul Dorpat's series on Salmon Bay Charlie in *Pacific*, the Sunday *Seattle Times* magazine, accessible on www.pauldorpat.com.

108. Cox, *Muting White Noise*, 189. Cox suggests that Alexie names Red Fox after an "apparently fraudulent autobiography," *The Memoirs of Chief Red Fox* (1971). Giles connects Red Fox to Redd Foxx, the African American actor and comedian. See Giles, *Spaces of Violence*, 140.

109. The photographs of Salmon Bay Charlie's home were taken in 1898 by Anders B. Wilse and in 1903 by Ira Webster and Nelson Stevens's studio. The former now appears in the Prosch Seattle Views Collection and the latter in the American Indians of the Pacific Northwest Images collection in the University of Washington's digital archives.

110. Dorpat makes this point: early maps were created to sell real estate, not to preserve historical geographies.

111. According to Thrush, "a dozen Shilshole families" still lived at Salmon Bay in the 1850s. By the 1910s, though, few Indigenous people remained in the city (*Native Seattle*, 76, 98).

112. Alexie, *Indian Killer*, 136.

113. Alexie, *Indian Killer*, 139, 136.

114. Alexie, *Indian Killer*, 137.

115. Gunther was hired in 1921, Adamson not until 1929. See Garfield and Amoss, "Erna Gunther"; and Seaburg, "Whatever Happened?"

116. Dean, "The Violence of Collection," 31. Dean argues that these stories are just one articulation of collecting in the novel, one that figuratively reflects the "violence *of* history" and the power structures at work in the archives (44). The appropriation of these stories "is part of the mechanism of racial and cultural erasure," just as much as are the collections of human remains in the basement (42). She writes, "The collected object in particular defines subjectivity, because collections consist of objects removed from their utilitarian or social context and made relative to the identity of the collector" (36). In this way, collections say more about the collector than the objects themselves.

117. There is much recent work on Indigenous intellectual property. For example, see Anderson, "Indigenous Knowledge"; and Brown, *Who Owns Native Culture?*

118. Bierwert, "Remembering Chief Seattle," 289. Biewert says that he was buried in a Christian ceremony on land that was his former home.

119. See Redman, *Bone Rooms*.

120. Bierwert, "Remembering Chief Seattle," 289. This is reported by Bierwert, who cites a 1914 article in the *Seattle Post-Intelligencer*. It is interesting how Seattle rallies around the preservation of its "patron saint."

121. Alexie, *Indian Killer*, 139–40.

122. Alexie, *Indian Killer*, 369.

123. Alexie, *Indian Killer*, 140.

124. This scene reminds me of Walters's *The Ghost Singer* (1985), set in the Smithsonian. In her novel, anthropologists are being murdered by the collected bones in the archives.

125. Gordon, *Ghostly Matters*, xvi.

126. Žižek, *Looking Awry*, 23.

127. NAGPRA regulates the disposition of human remains and cultural objects and provides tribes a process through which they can recover such items from museum and university collections. The Smithsonian is exempt from NAPRA regulations.

128. It is an interesting choice for Alexie to have made Father Duncan a Spokane. Like Marie Polatkin and Reggie Polatkin, the other Spokanes in this novel, Father Duncan is unmoored from his tribe.

129. Alexie, *Indian Killer*, 13–14 (emphasis mine).

130. The eight martyrs died in the 1600s at the hands of Iroquois, Mohawks, and Hurons in Canada and upstate New York. There is no local history here.

131. Alexie, *Indian Killer*, 15.

132. This is the line that subtly suggests something inappropriate in their relationship: "As John grew older, Father Duncan would tell him secrets and make him promise never to reveal them" (Alexie, *Indian Killer*, 13). One of the most publicized cases involves Rev. Clarence Vavra, who molested young boys at Rosebud in the 1970s, but there are hundreds of others. The Canadian Truth and Reconciliation Commission links this abuse to residential schools and estimates that the frequency of abuse could be as high as 75 percent. Alexie has made other references to such sexual abuse. In 2011, in a piece in the *Wall Street Journal* in response to the banning of *Absolutely True Diary*, Alexie writes that "I was the child and grandchild of men and women who'd been sexually and physically abused by generations of clergy" and also indicates that he himself was the victim of sexual abuse.

133. Alexie, *Indian Killer*, 16–17.

134. Alexie, *Indian Killer*, 411.

135. Indeed, most of the criticism on the novel scarcely mentions homelessness. The exceptions are Fazio, Mariani, and Patell. For other discussions of the novel, see Christie, Cooper, Cox, Dean, Giles, Fritsch and Gymnich, James, Krupat, Stokes, and Van Styvendale.

136. Fazio rightly argues that the homeless stories reveal a class narrative about capitalism and inequity. Her reading of the novel as working-class literature explores the history of labor protest in Seattle and suggests that Alexie's novel serves as a critique of "U.S. neoliberal economics" and the effects of globalization on "local communities" ("Homeless in Seattle," 142).

137. In his interview with Nygren, Alexie says that for John Smith "there's no redemption there; there's no healing, there's no talking cure" (165).

138. Alexie, *Indian Killer*, 146.

139. Christie argues that John Smith's mental illness is "a hard truth . . . (and seemingly inevitable) consequence for urban Indians in white supremacist America" ("Renaissance Man," 8)—though this does not take into account the fact that so many mentally ill people have been released from institutions, a point to which I will return later in this section.

140. Indians dwell in the periphery—in bars, on the sidewalks, in Pioneer Square,

under the viaducts. Mariani calls this space the *interstice*, "a place that is not a place in the traditional sense of the word," and therefore homeless Indians are "interstitial figures" ("From Atopia to Utopia," 583, 585). Stokes points out that *Indian Killer* "calls attention to stories as stories," the "absence of stories," the homeless people's stories, the oral stories on tape, Jack Wilson's novels ("Was Jesus an Indian?," 44, 45).

141. Similarly, in a very brief essay, Banka argues that *Indian Killer* "comments on urban Indian solidarity which manifests itself through a multitribal community formation" ("'Homing in the City,'" 37).

142. Ramirez, *Native Hubs*, 2.

143. Brogan, *Cultural Haunting*, 36. Also, Fritsch and Gymnich argue that ghosts are a common element in detective novels and that in Native American novels like *Indian Killer*, they are intricately connected to dreams and dreaming ("Crime Spirit").

144. Alexie, *Indian Killer*, 376–77.

145. Alexie, *Indian Killer*, 158.

146. Alexie, *Indian Killer*, 159.

147. Alexie, *Indian Killer*, 162.

148. Alexie, *Indian Killer*, 160.

149. Alexie, *Indian Killer*, 159.

150. Van Styvendale, "The Trans/Historicity of Trauma," 216.

151. See Smith, *Conquest*. In 2014 a report from the RCMP revealed that between 1980 and 2012, upward of 1,181 First Nations women and girls went missing or were killed. According to the report, Indigenous women make up 4.3 percent of the population yet have accounted for 16 percent of the murder victims during the past thirty years. A 2015 report by the Truth and Reconciliation Commission links this violence to mandatory residential schools. A United Nations committee, groups of Indigenous activists, along with the victims' families have called for a federal inquiry into this ongoing gendered, colonial violence and have been met with resistance from Canadian officials, including the minister of Aboriginal affairs, Bernard Valcourt, who has famously refused to call for a national investigation. Missing and Murdered Indigenous Women (known as #MMIW on social media), No More Silence, Stolen Sisters (named after the 2004 Stolen Sisters Report by Amnesty International), and Sing Our Rivers Red are some of the protest movements that have arisen in recent years. Some of these organizations, including Sing Our Rivers Red, are calling attention to violence against Native women in both Canada and the United States.

152. Alexie, *Indian Killer*, 159.

153. Alexie, *Indian Killer*, 233.

154. Alexie, *Indian Killer*, 233.

155. Alexie, *Indian Killer*, 233.

156. Alexie uses this same technique at the end of *The Business of Fancydancing* when Seymour leaves the reservation after Mouse's funeral. Seymour is doubled: one Seymour drives away, and one Seymour waves to him. The way I read this, with Bell's "The Ghosts of Place" in mind, is that the ghost of Seymour's former self is what stays behind.

157. Alexie, *Indian Killer*, 229.

158. Alexie, *Indian Killer*, 212.

159. See Miller, "Exercising Cultural Self-Determination;" and Van Ginkel, "The Makah Whale Hunt," on the history of Makah whale hunting, halted in the 1920s and resumed in 1999.

160. See Torrey, *American Psychosis*. In the 1980s forty thousand beds in state mental hospitals disappeared. The National Institute of Mental Health determined in 1988 that 125,000 to 300,000 mentally ill patients were homeless. Current estimates are that one-third of homeless people have mental illness.

161. Alexie, *Indian Killer*, 212.

162. See Queen Anne Historical Society, www.qahistory.org.

163. Alexie, *Indian Killer*, 212–13.

164. Alexie, *Indian Killer*, 215.

165. Alexie, *Indian Killer*, 209.

166. Alexie, *Indian Killer*, 251.

167. Bergland, *The National Uncanny*, 9.

168. In 1971 Duwamish tribal members were awarded $64 each in exchange for tribal lands, but in 1979 they lost fishing rights (due to a break in political leadership from 1916 to 1925). Krupat suggests that the novel begins in 1968–69 (*Red Matters*, 105).

169. Thrush, *Native Seattle*, 194–99; Duwamish Tribal Services, www.duwamish tribe.org.

170. Alexie, *Indian Killer*, 254.

171. As I will argue in chapter 3, Erdrich's novel *The Antelope Wife* reveals that Indian land lies beneath the city, that the city is only temporary.

172. Alexie, *Indian Killer*, 374.

173. Alexie, *Indian Killer*, 374–75.

174. Alexie, *Indian Killer*, 219.

175. Alexie, *Indian Killer*, 313.

176. Alexie, *Indian Killer*, 220.

177. While Abel and Tayo lived for a time in Los Angeles, Loney lives in Harlem,

Montana, a small town on the Highline near the Fort Belnap reservation. Loney's girlfriend, Rhea, plans to move to Seattle, however, and asks him to join her. See Welch, *The Death of Jim Loney*, 44.

178. Certeau, *The Writing of History*, 47.

179. Žižek, *Looking Awry*, 23.

180. Tatonetti, "Dancing That Way," 12.

181. Krupat has called this "red rage" (*Red Matters*). Fazio reads this as "revolutionizing" the homeless in their anger against the capitalist system but does not connect it to the Ghost Dance ("Homeless in Seattle," 149).

182. Alexie, *Indian Killer*, 419.

183. Alexie, *Indian Killer*, 420.

184. Alexie, *Indian Killer*, 313.

185. Page numbers in this section refer to the short story as it appears in *Ten Little Indians*.

186. Cline has written a brief essay on the story; Banka and Ladino discuss it within the context of *Ten Little Indians*. See Cline, "The Hero of the Modern Mock Epic"; Banka, "'Homing in the City'"; and Ladino, "'A Limited Range of Motion?'"

187. Alexie, "What You Pawn," 172.

188. Alexie, "What You Pawn," 194.

189. Ladino makes a similar assertion, though she argues that it is the "polycultural" nature of the city that allows for the alliances that allow Jackson Jackson to succeed ("'A Limited Range of Motion?,'" 45). Ladino focuses more on Indian identity in the story.

190. Alexie, "What You Pawn," 169. Of course, the assumption here is that the reader/listener is one of these "white folks."

191. Alexie, "What You Pawn," 169. This is another link to *Indian Killer*: Jackson as serial killer.

192. This is one of the through lines in *Indian Killer*, with both Marie Polatkin and Reggie Polatkin, who drops out of college. In *The Business of Fancydancing*, Aristotle drops out of school to return to the reservation, and in *The Absolutely True Diary of a Part-Time Indian*, Junior is critical of the reservation school, though he excels in the public school off-reservation.

193. Alexie, "What You Pawn," 169, 188.

194. Alexie, "What You Pawn," 171. The number 3 frequently appears in Alexie's work, as trios, trinities, or triumvirates.

195. Alexie, "What You Pawn," 170.

196. Alexie, "What You Pawn," 174.

197. Alexie, "What You Pawn," 181.

198. Alexie, "What You Pawn," 193.

199. Alexie, "What You Pawn," 191. In reality, Mother's Kitchen is the name of a charity that serves breakfast to Seattle's homeless once a month.

200. Alexie, "What You Pawn," 177.

201. Alexie, "What You Pawn," 181–82.

202. Alexie, "What You Pawn," 187.

203. Alexie, "What You Pawn," 193.

204. Alexie, "What You Pawn," 170.

205. For a history of pawnshops in the United States, see Woloson, *In Hock*.

206. Alexie, *The Business of Fancydancing*, 79.

207. Alexie, *The Business of Fancydancing*, 79.

208. Like Jackson, Hartley relies on his posse and on the kindness of a pawnshop employee during his quest.

209. This was briefly overturned in 2001 during the Clinton administration, only to be reversed again in 2002 on a technicality. "What You Pawn" was published in 2003.

210. The 1855 treaty that established that Yakima reservation was signed by representatives of fourteen tribes, though many refused to relocate there. See Ruby and Brown, *A Guide*.

211. This, according to the Yakama Nation's website, www.yakamanation-nsn.gov/.

212. Alexie, "What You Pawn," 175.

213. Thrush, *Native Seattle*, 113.

214. Alexie, "What You Pawn," 192–93.

215. Ladino reads this as invisibility ("'A Limited Range of Motion?,'" 55n7).

216. Alexie, "What You Pawn," 191.

217. Ladino calls this a "ceremony" ("'A Limited Range of Motion?,'" 46).

218. In *Reservation Blues*, for example, Alexie writes that "the reservation still possessed power and rage, *magic* and loss, joys and jealousy" (96 [emphasis mine]).

219. Alexie, "What You Pawn," 185.

220. Alexie, "What You Pawn," 177.

221. Alexie, "What You Pawn," 194.

222. Alexie, "What You Pawn," 181.

223. Alexie, "What You Pawn," 179.

224. In fact, Alexie said in the NPR interview that he wrote *Flight* in the middle of writing *The Absolutely True Diary*.

225. On his June 10, 2015, podcast, Alexie said he wrote *Flight* in three days.

226. In fact, *The Absolutely True Diary* topped the American Library Association's "Top Ten List of Frequently Challenged Books" in 2014. See Alexie's article in

the *Wall Street Journal* for his response to this widespread banning. See the NPR interview for Alexie's explanation of the time travel aspect of the novel. *Quantum Leap* ran on NBC for five seasons (1989–93). Scientist Sam Beckett gets lost in time and body jumps, or "quantum leaps," into the past. Of course, there are some differences between *Flight* and *Quantum Leap*: for one, Zits retains his own memory while in his hosts' bodies. In *Slaughterhouse Five*, Billy Pilgrim becomes unstuck in time, and his time travels are evoked by trauma.

227. Rader, *Engaged Resistance*, 86. Rader calls this a novel of "Indian invention," as opposed to science fiction.

228. A long history of boarding schools and the abundance of Indian children being adopted out of their tribes led to the passage of the Indian Child Welfare Act in 1978, which provides tribal jurisdiction over Indian child welfare proceedings and defines children as "cultural resources." The Indian Adoption Project (September 1958–December 1967), a coordinated effort between the Bureau of Indian Affairs and the Child Welfare League of America, placed 395 Indian children from 11 states in non-Indian households (Simon and Alstein, *Transracial Adoption*, 57). ICWA states: "(a) In any adoptive placement of an Indian child under State law, a preference shall be given, in the absence of good cause to the contrary, to a placement with a (1) member of the child's extended family; (2) other members of the Indian child's tribe; or (3) other Indian families." See also Jones, *The Indian Child Welfare Act Handbook*.

229. Alexie has said in interviews that he knows that Zits should die at the end of the novel and that the ending went through numerous rewritings. In an NPR interview, he said, "And so, you know, I wrote it a number of ways, the ending, and I did write it, you know, tragically ending and not tragically ending and more ambiguous; and in the end, the most honest feeling for me was to end it with at least some sense of hope. So I did it."

230. Alexie, *Flight*, 31.

231. Alexie, *Flight*, 34.

232. Alexie, *Flight*, 35.

233. Alexie, *Flight*, 35.

234. Alexie, *Flight*, 35.

235. Rader also makes this comparison. See *Engaged Resistance*, 87.

236. This message about tribalism can be found in all of Alexie's post-9/11 work. He has spoken about this in many interviews.

237. Boyd and Thrush, "Introduction: Bringing Ghosts," xiii.

238. Bernardin, "Alexie-Vision," 53.

239. Alexie, *Flight*, 136.

240. This kind of flight also describes his father's abandonment (though he describes

his movement in the present as "shambling") (Alexie, *Flight*, 135). There are, of course, actual airplane flights in the novel—namely, Abbad's and Jimmy's fateful flights—and bird flights, especially Harry Potter's fall/flight into the pot of boiling water. "Flight" in Seattle also conjures Boeing, the aircraft manufacturer, whose roots in the area go back to 1910. Boeing was built along the Duwamish River on land that had been owned by a Tlingit man, Ralph Young. See Thrush, *Native Seattle*, 153.

241. Alexie, *Flight*, 161. This, of course, recalls the three Aleuts from "What You Pawn."

242. Alexie, *Flight*, 162.

243. This makes sense to me if Alexie wrote *Flight* in the midst of *Absolutely True Diary*, which celebrates his own departure from the reservation.

244. The Puyallups were active in the 1960s and 1970s in asserting their treaty fishing rights. They also won a settlement that went to the United States Supreme Court in 1984 regarding twelve acres of tidelands that had been taken by the Port of Tacoma in 1950. The Puyallups were awarded $162 million, to be paid by the federal government, the Port of Tacoma, the state of Washington, private businesses, and local governments. See Ruby and Brown, *A Guide*.

245. Rader remarks on both the "Native circular narrative" and trickster narrative at work here. He reads both Zits and Alexie as trickster. See *Engaged Resistance*, 87.

246. Alexie, *Flight*, 175.

247. Whitman started taking photos near the Greyhound station in Oklahoma City starting in 1968, when he first came to the city. The photographs changed after he himself lived on the streets in 1973–74. A fire in his studio destroyed all of the negatives, along with Whitman's notes and photograph permissions. Whitman, telephone interview.

248. Whitman, telephone interview.

249. Rader, *Engaged Resistance*, 1.

250. Lippard, *Mixed Blessings*, 216.

251. Rushing, "Street Chiefs and Native Hosts," 28.

252. See www.britesites.com/native_artist_interviews/rwhitman.htm.

253. Rushing, "Street Chiefs and Native Hosts," 29.

254. Alexie, *The Business of Fancydancing*, 80.

255. Alexie, *Indian Killer*, 331.

256. Brogan, *Cultural Haunting*, 20.

3. ROOTS AND ROUTES OF THE HUB

1. I will refer to these editions as *The Antelope Wife* and *The Antelope Wife: New and Revised Edition*. The 2016 text, *Antelope Woman*, is nearly identical to the

2012 edition. Along with a new title, it includes an author's note and new cover art drawn by her daughter, Aza. "Deer woman" stories may have originated among southeastern tribes, as some have suggested, but there are also Ojibwe, Lakota, and Crow versions. See Evers, "Notes on the Deer Woman," 36. The "antelope woman" stories come from the Crow, thereby connecting Ojibwe and Crow cultures. Kleiner and Vlaicu discuss Erdrich's use of Ojibwe myths in the novel, particularly the trickster hero cycle. See "Revisioning Woman in America."

2. Erdrich, *Jacklight*.

3. LaDuke, *Last Standing Woman*; Harjo, *In Mad Love and War*; Allen, "Deer Woman"; Dunn, "Deer Hunter."

4. Van Dyke has suggested that Erdrich's use of this figure from Dakota stories is evidence of cultural exchange with the Dakota, with which, of course, the Anishinaabeg or Ojibwe have had much contact historically. See Van Dyke, "Encounters with Deer Woman," 168–88. Jacobs has argued, "The antelope people are transformational beings who become a part of Chippewa mythology once the Ojibwe establish themselves on the plains" (*Novels of Louise Erdrich*, 169). This argument works as well if the figure is Crow, not Dakota.

5. While earlier novels like *The Beet Queen* (1986) and *The Master Butchers Singing Club* (2003) take place off the reservation in the fictional town of Argus, North Dakota, *The Antelope Wife* is the first set almost entirely in an urban space. In *Love Medicine*, Marie's children come home "from Minneapolis and Chicago, where they had relocated years ago" (249), and in *The Bingo Palace*, Lipsha Morrissey has returned from Fargo. *Shadow Tag*, a more recent novel, also takes place in Minneapolis. With regard to how movement affects both spatiality and Indigeneity, Noodin writes in "Megwa Baabaamiiaayaayaang Dibaajomoyaang," "As our language teaches us, to live is to be in motion," and that story is "memory of motion" (175).

6. Rader, *Engaged Resistance*, 1.

7. In this chapter, I follow Erdrich's lead in the spelling of the term *Ojibwe*, an alternate spelling of *Ojibwa* or *Ojibway*. However, in earlier novels Erdrich uses *Ojibwa*, *Chippewa*, and *Anishinaabeg* to describe the tribal affiliation of her characters.

8. Erdrich, "Where I Ought to Be."

9. Of course, all of the Ojibwe reservations in Minnesota are north of Minneapolis. White Earth, Leech Lake, and Fond du Lac are in the two-hour range. I do believe that the reservation in the novel is a fictionalized amalgam of these Minnesota Ojibwe nations.

10. Ramirez, *Native Hubs*.

11. Spelled Gakaabikaang in *The Antelope Wife: New and Revised Edition*. The word comes from *gakijiwan*, or "waterfall," and *-abik* to indicate "stone"; in Minneapolis there are falls that go over stone. Erdrich's spelling changes reflect a lessening of regional dialect that is accompanying language revitalization (Noodin, personal communication). Noodin says in *Bawaajimo* that "spelling is still evolving and can be considered a matter of preference" (8–9). Like Alexie's, Erdrich's literary move mirrors her own relocation to the city, which happened in 1999, a year after the novel was first published.

12. In "Deep Time," Dimock suggests that deep time "produces a map that, thanks to its receding horizons, its backward extension into far-flung temporal and spatial coordinates, must depart significantly from a map predicated on the short life of the US. For the force of historical depth is such as to suggest a world that predates the adjective *American*. If we go far enough back in time, and it is not very far, there was no such thing as the US" (759). The novel itself, which begins "deep in the past," suggests such a methodology (Erdrich, *The Antelope Wife*, 3; *The Antelope Wife: New and Revised Edition*, 3).

13. Erdrich, *The Antelope Wife*, 124–25. A slightly different version of the passage appears in *The Antelope Wife: New and Revised Edition* (241).

14. There are ways that the fictional reservation resembles Turtle Mountain, particularly in terms of their specific histories. Scholars have "mapped" Erdrich's fictional spaces, pointing out the inconsistencies from novel to novel that make her geography even more difficult to pin down. For example, see Beidler and Barton, *A Reader's Guide*.

15. Ferrari argues that Erdrich's use of multiple narrators in her other novels (namely, *Love Medicine* and *Tracks*) is a "narrative technique that dissolves the boundaries" and "critique[s] any master narrative or totalizing viewpoint" ("'Where the Maps Stopped,'" 146). For example, Thomas Curwen in the *Los Angeles Times* writes that the novel is "sometimes overwritten, sometimes mismanaged." Dan Cryer of the *New York Newsday* finds Almost Soup, the dog narrator, "cloyingly cute" and the familial relationships too confusing. Mark Shechner of the *Buffalo News* insists that "you need a computer program to stay on top of them all." Wingate Packard writes in the *Seattle Times* that the novel "seems like a baggy catch-all for too many discrete little pieces." In the *Washington Post*, Tamsin Todd writes, "The large pattern of the novel may be stunning, but the detail leaves something to be desired." In *World Literature Today*, Howard Meredith says that the novel "lacks the verve of Erdrich's previous novels" and that "frustration hangs over the book." In "'Patterns and Waves Generation to Generation,'" Alanna K. Brown also writes about the complicated genealogy of the book.

16. Beidler and Barton, *A Reader's Guide*, 56. Beidler and Barton claim that Erdrich originally intended to republish an expanded version of *Tracks* but was persuaded to turn the material into a new novel, which became *Four Souls*.

17. Data from Amazon.com bear this out. The 1998 paperback of the novel ranks at 2,694,179 on the Best Sellers Rank; the 2012 paperback is listed at number 606,646 (though 33,515 in the literary fiction category). For comparison, the 2009 paperback revision of *Love Medicine* ranks at 29,937 (or 3,837 in literary fiction). The 2014 printing of *Tracks* ranks 36,861 (4,490 in literary fiction). *The Round House*, probably Erdrich's most popular book to date, ranks 4,619 in paperback (89 in political fiction and 392 in coming-of-age fiction). Data accessed on July 15, 2015.

18. Richard's story caught the attention of most reviewers, including Postlethwaite, Curwen, and Cryer, who wanted to see the parallels between Erdrich's real life and her fiction. Erdrich claims Dorris had read several drafts of the novel. See the *Star Tribune* article dated April 12, 1998. Matchie also reads the novel biographically; see "*The Antelope Wife*: Louise Erdrich's 'Cloud Chamber.'"

19. Erdrich, "The Art of Fiction No. 208."

20. Wiigwaas Press, co-founded by Louise Erdrich and her sister Heid Erdrich in 2010, publishes books solely in Ojibwemowin. In a 2011 interview with *Indian Country Today*, Heid says, "We have a responsibility to help the language live."

21. Beidler and Barton made this connection in their *Reader's Guide*, but the genealogical chart in the 1998 text does not. The revised version of Beidler and Barton's book does not treat the 2012 text, nor does any of the extant criticism. For analysis of the first version, see Barak, Brown, Van Dyke, Herman, Gamber, Korpez, Matchie, Lischke, Bouzonviller, Riche, Stirrup, and Kleiner and Vlaicu.

22. Erdrich is hardly the first writer to rewrite and republish work; in addition to Coleridge and Wordsworth, Whitman famously published multiple versions of *Leaves of Grass* (six or nine, if different printings of a version are included). See Folsom, *Walt Whitman*; Stillinger, *Coleridge and Textual Instability*, vi.

23. Stillinger, *Coleridge and Textual Instability*, 132.

24. Meyer discusses the seasonal round in "'We Cannot Get a Living as We Used To.'"

25. Hickerson, *The Chippewa and Their Neighbors*, 62–64. Gutiérrez-Jones uses this information to argue that Erdrich is a literary pillager, taking bits and pieces from several traditions; see *Critical Race Narratives*, 103. The historical Pillagers were from Leech Lake, though a group of Pillagers moved to the plains in the 1800s. See Jacobs, *The Novels of Louise Erdrich*.

26. In *Ojibwe Singers*, McNally uses this phrase in reference to Ojibwe hymns.

27. Much of this history comes from Baldwin's chapters in Atwater, *History of the City of Minneapolis, Minnesota*.

28. This history comes from Atwater, *History of the City of Minneapolis, Minnesota*.

29. Many of the treaties were made in Minnesota and Wisconsin Territories, and the Lake Superior bands are still viewed as distinct from the other bands. Also, several bands were not assigned any land and earned recognition much later. The US government wanted to put all of the Ojibwes at White Earth, but the plan failed. For more information on the history of Ojibwes in Minnesota, see Warren, *History of the Ojibway People*; Aby, *The North Star State*; Treuer, *Ojibwe in Minnesota*; Adams and VanDrasek, *Minneapolis–St. Paul*; and Kugel, "'To Go About on the Earth.'"

30. In this year, the Santee Sioux were moved to a reservation across the Missouri River. When they did not receive money and food as promised, they began attacking towns and forts. Col. Henry H. Sibley led forces west from Fort Snelling, defeating the Sioux and taking many prisoners, thirty-eight of whom were simultaneously hanged in Mankato, Minnesota. See Atwater, *History of the City of Minneapolis, Minnesota*. As Beidler and Barton point out, the date of this war "do[es] not fit precisely with the other information in the novel" (*A Reader's Guide*, 40). They propose that the massacre in the novel takes place in the 1880s or 1890s, though there is no clear historical evidence of such an event during this time period. Another clue that leads us to Little Crow's War and the Sioux starvation comes from Almost Soup, the dog narrator in the novel, who makes jokes about the danger of being eaten by the Sioux. Erdrich does say the Ojibwe village was "mistaken for hostile" (*The Antelope Wife*, 3). Jonathan Little suggests this massacre "bears a striking resemblance" to Wounded Knee ("Beading the Multicultural World," 502).

31. This number is from Shoemaker, "Urban Indians."

32. Shoemaker, "Urban Indians," 433.

33. Broker, *Night Flying Woman*, 3.

34. This reference to relocation comes from Almost Soup: "There was a new government policy designed in the kindest way to make things worse. It was called Relocation and helped Indians move to cities all over the country. Helped them move away from family. Helped them move away from their land. Helped them move away from their dogs. But don't worry. We followed them down to Gakaabikaang, Minneapolis, Place of the Falls." And later, "Relocation is the main reason fewer Indians now live on reservations than in cities." And "Damn Relocation!" Klaus thinks. There is an assumption that many of these characters moved to the city because of Relocation (*The Antelope Wife: New and Revised Edition*, 79, 129, 130). Buff makes the claim that

Minneapolis was not an official relocation city, as does Fixico, though others, such as Anton Treuer, argue that Ojibwes were indeed affected by relocation. See Buff, *Immigration*; Fixico, *The Urban Indian Experience*; Treuer, *Ojibwe in Minnesota*. For information on the St. Paul Resettlement Committee, see Shoemaker, "Urban Indians," 443.

35. Treuer, *The Hiawatha*, 62.

36. This number comes from Ebott and Rosenblatt, *Indians in Minnesota*.

37. This number comes from Adams and VanDrasek, *Minneapolis–St. Paul*. The 2000 census reported that of 382,452 residents in Minneapolis, 8,378 identified as Indian. This number rises to 12,683 when mixed-bloods, or those reporting two or more races, one as Indian, are included.

38. Many of the studies of urban Indians in Minneapolis were written by Arthur M. Harkins and Richard G. Woods under the auspices of the Training Center for Community Programs at the University of Minnesota.

39. In fact, Fixico claims that cities in closer proximity to reservation spaces demonstrate a heightened animosity toward Native peoples. See Fixico, *The Urban Indian Experience*.

40. Shoemaker, "Urban Indians," 436.

41. Shoemaker, "Urban Indians," 443.

42. Shoemaker, "Urban Indians," 442–43.

43. Shoemaker, "Urban Indians," 444.

44. Shoemaker, "Urban Indians," 444.

45. In *Like a Hurricane*, Paul Chaat Smith and Robert Warrior locate AIM's founding on July 28, 1968, by a group of Ojibwes (including Dennis Banks and Clyde Bellecourt) "out of concern for the way police were treating Indian people in the Franklin Avenue Neighborhood of the city" (114–15). Russell Means, a Lakota, later joined the AIM leadership. Alan Velie argues that AIM was "largely an organization of urban detribalized Indians even less traditional than mixed-bloods from the rez" ("The Rise and Fall," 6). Smith and Warrior write, "Some were born and raised in cities, but most were from the reservations a few hours to the north and west. For many, the trip between their reservations and the cities seemingly never ended; a cycle of returning home for weddings, funerals, ceremonies, and wild rice festivals, and in another few days or weeks or months, returning to the city for jobs or for the excitement the reservations lacked" (*Like a Hurricane*, 128). This sounds like the hub pattern in *The Antelope Wife*.

46. Pease, "Introduction: Re-mapping," 4.

47. Clifford, *Routes*, 254.

48. Allen, "2014 NAISA Presidential Address," 10.

49. DeLugan, "Indigeneity across Borders," 83.

50. In *Fugitive Poses*, Vizenor writes, "Native transmotion is survivance, a reciprocal use of nature, not a monotheistic, territorial sovereignty. Native stories of survivance are the creases of transmotion and sovereignty" (15). See also Vizenor, "Literary Transmotion."

51. Byrd, *The Transit of Empire*, xvi–xvii.

52. Huhndorf, *Mapping the Americas*, 2.

53. Ramirez, *Native Hubs*, 2.

54. Lowe, "The Intimacies of Four Continents," 192.

55. According to U.S. Bench, the company that owns and maintains benches throughout the city, this was an act of vandalism, and a police report has been filed. For this reason, I will not here advance my thoughts on the identity of the artist. A spokesman for the company told me that it would never allow a message like this one to appear on a bench ad.

56. Erdrich, *The Antelope Wife: New and Revised Edition*, 241.

57. Erdrich, *The Antelope Wife: New and Revised Edition*, 152. Everyone calls Minneapolis Mishiimin Oodenag or Mishiiminiodena—this is not Erdrich's creation. Noodin, personal communication.

58. Erdrich, *Four Souls*, 3.

59. Erdrich, *Four Souls*, 6.

60. Erdrich, *Four Souls*, 4. It is probably located in Summit Hill in St. Paul, where the James J. Hill House (built in 1891) is located. See http://sites.mnhs.org /historic-sites/james-j-hill-house/history.

61. Erdrich, *Four Souls*, 4.

62. The Great Northern Railroad (owned, in part, by James J. Hill) began operations in Minneapolis in 1862. There are many parallels between Mauser and Hill, though Hill's house was constructed long before Mauser's.

63. Critics bemoan this aspect of *The Hiawatha*. "Scarcely a page goes by without a reference to a Twin Cities street name, building, or neighborhood hangout," writes Amy Weivoda. Mark Anthony Rolo claims the novel "misrepresents the Native people of Minneapolis. Treuer settles his Indian family in a small south Minneapolis neighborhood that probably had very few Indians. . . . He does not explore the infamous Indian bars along Franklin Avenue." Even more scathing is the charge that "Treuer falls for the current perception that Indians who live in urban America are out of their place and consequently quite messed up."

64. Of course, Treuer is famously critical of Erdrich—for what he sees as her extreme focus on culture and for her inaccurate use of Ojibwemowin. See Treuer, "Smartberries"; "Reading Culture"; and *Native American Fiction*. For

example, he writes in "Reading Culture," "Ojibwe words have been lifted out of their own element and hosted in English, and not hosted very well" (54). For a more positive exploration of Erdrich's use of Anishinaabemowin, see Noori, *Bawaajimo*.

65. The duplex seems to be located in the Phillips neighborhood near the housing complex Little Earth of United Tribes. In this area, old boardinghouses have been turned into low-income housing and social services. Also, there are several bakeries on Franklin and Lake Streets that Erdrich's could be modeled after.

66. The Phillips neighborhood has become more diverse in recent years, with a large Somalian population, for example.

67. In 1854 the Fond du Lac and Grand Portage reservations were established. In 1855 Leech Lake and Mille Lacs were created. In 1863 the Red Lake reservation was created. In 1866 Boise Forte was established, and in 1867 White Earth. In 1882, the same year the duplex is constructed, the Turtle Mountain reservation was established after the General Land Office had opened their land for white settlement. This "was tantamount to an eviction notice" (Camp, "Working Out Their Own Salvation," 21).

68. Erdrich, *The Antelope Wife*, 40; *The Antelope Wife: New and Revised Edition*, 234.

69. Van Dyke identifies Frank as a Deer Man who "catches" Rozin ("Encounters with Deer Woman," 178).

70. Erdrich, *The Antelope Wife: New and Revised Edition*, 172.

71. The way that Erdrich "reads" this stone reminds me of her readings of rock art. See Erdrich, *Books and Islands*, 50.

72. Upham, *Minnesota Geographic Names*, 301.

73. Erdrich discusses this in her *New York Times* essay "Two Languages in Mind, Just One in the Heart."

74. Erdrich, *The Antelope Wife*, 97.

75. Erdrich, *The Antelope Wife*, 95.

76. Erdrich, *The Antelope Wife*, 94, 96.

77. Erdrich, *The Antelope Wife*, 97.

78. Erdrich, *The Antelope Wife: New and Revised Edition*, 90.

79. Erdrich, *The Antelope Wife: New and Revised Edition*, 91.

80. She is otherwise nameless—a move that I believe contributes to her mythical nature.

81. Erdrich, *The Antelope Wife*, 31; *The Antelope Wife: New and Revised Edition*, 92. In the second version, she breaks just one tooth.

82. In "'Waiting Halfway in Each Other's Bodies,'" Riche connects the breastfeeding

episode to traditional Ojibwe stories about relationships between humans and dogs.

83. The hardcover version of the 1998 novel did not include a genealogical chart; however, the paperback edition did. A quick comparison of the two charts reveals Erdrich's massive revisioning of the relationships in the novel. For example, in the first edition, Rozin has a twin sister named Aurora, who is not included in *The Antelope Wife: New and Revised Edition*. Frank and Klaus are brothers in *The Antelope Wife*; in *The Antelope Wife: New and Revised Edition*, they are cousins.

84. There are also a small number of Turtle Mountain parcels in South Dakota. In Montana, there were 149 allotments. See Camp, "Working Out Their Own Salvation," 30.

85. Erdrich, *The Antelope Wife*, 107–8.

86. Erdrich, *The Antelope Wife: New and Revised Edition*, 98.

87. Erdrich, *The Antelope Wife: New and Revised Edition*, 98.

88. Noodin, personal communication.

89. Erdrich, *The Antelope Wife*, 51.

90. Erdrich, *The Antelope Wife: New and Revised Edition*, 98.

91. Anderson, *American Indian Literature*, 4.

92. Erdrich, *The Antelope Wife*, 229.

93. Anderson, *American Indian Literature*, 18.

94. Blaeser, *Absentee Indians*, xi.

95. Blaeser, "'Like Reeds,'" 557.

96. Erdrich, *The Antelope Wife*, 239.

97. Ferrari, "'Where the Maps Stopped,'" 145.

98. Erdrich, *The Antelope Wife*, 14.

99. Erdrich, *The Antelope Wife: New and Revised Edition*, 263.

100. Erdrich, *The Antelope Wife*, 20.

101. Erdrich, *The Antelope Wife*, 198. *Mashkeeg* is "swamp," literally, "strength from the earth." Noodin, personal communication.

102. Erdrich, *The Antelope Wife*, 102.

103. Erdrich, *The Antelope Wife*, 108.

104. Erdrich, *The Antelope Wife*, 108.

105. See LaDow, *The Medicine Line*.

106. This set-up for future novels is one of the things that Erdrich accomplished with the revision of *Love Medicine*: an additional chapter that provided a necessary connection to *The Bingo Palace* (1994). According to her editor, Marian Wood, "New things were taking shape that she felt needed a beginning [in the first novel]" (qtd. in Devereaux, *Publishers Weekly*). The ability to go home is

of course complicated for mixed-bloods who have lost status. There are many urban Natives who have no connection to a reservation home.

107. Erdrich, *The Antelope Wife*, 84.

108. This is something she has in common with Janet Campbell Hale's Cecelia Capture.

109. Erdrich, *The Antelope Wife: New and Revised Edition*, 147.

110. Erdrich, *The Antelope Wife*, 191. The "water man" Erdrich refers to is Misshepeshu from Ojibwe cosmology. This water creature is supposed to have saved Lipsha Morrisey from drowning in Erdrich's *Love Medicine* (also recounted in *The Bingo Palace*).

111. This speaks to the larger practice of returning human remains and objects that was mandated by the passage of the Native American Graves Protection and Repatriation Act (NAGPRA) in 1990. In other words, repatriation is also political.

112. Buff, *Immigration*, 3.

113. The Office of Indian Ministry is part of the St. Paul and Minneapolis Catholic archdiocese. See the article in the *National Catholic Reporter* from February 25, 1994. In addition, the nonprofit Indian Burial Assistance Project in Minneapolis offers low-cost funeral services and hearse transportation.

114. This reminds me of Susan Power's *The Grass Dancer*, in which Pumpkin, a bright, promising, young, urban Indian loses her life in a car accident while on the summer powwow trail.

115. In "Transcending Binary Divisions," Pirjo Ahokas argues that Cally's "hybrid" subject position is due to her mixed-race identity *and* her urban residence. Cally takes "symbolic journeys to the historical locations of [her] families' experience of colonization and migration" (116).

116. Erdrich, *The Antelope Wife*, 86.

117. Erdrich, *The Antelope Wife*, 101. This practice became less common in the twentieth century with the increase of hospital births. This makes Cally's indis a rare occurrence. Noodin, personal communication.

118. In one of Luci Tapahonso's poems, "It Has Always Been This Way," she describes the Diné practice of burying the umbilical cord in the yard near the house so that the child does not wander far from home.

119. Erdrich, *The Antelope Wife*, 101–2 (emphasis mine).

120. Erdrich, *The Antelope Wife: New and Revised Edition*, 204–5 (emphasis mine).

121. Noodin, personal communication.

122. Erdrich, *The Antelope Wife*, 90.

123. Erdrich, *The Antelope Wife*, 103.

124. Erdrich, *The Antelope Wife*, 103.

125. Erdrich, *The Antelope Wife*, 26.

126. Erdrich, *The Antelope Wife*, 224. Erdrich tells a similar joke in *The Bingo Palace*. Lyman Lamartine uses the analogy of a bucket of crawfish to describe how difficult it is to leave the reservation (102).

127. Erdrich, *The Antelope Wife*, 224.

128. Erdrich, *The Antelope Wife*, 21.

129. This resembles the phenomenon in Silko's *Almanac of the Dead*, the "rapture of the wide-open spaces" that occurs when horses or dogs that have been confined are set free (545).

130. Not all powwows take place on reservations, however. Many urban centers and universities now host annual powwows for the large population of Indians in the cities. These events become part of the circuit and are therefore attended by many reservation Indians.

131. See Browner, *Heartbeat of the People*.

132. They might be described as what Hobsbawm calls an "invented tradition," or "a set or practices, normally governed by overtly or tacitly accepted rules and of a ritual or symbolic nature, which seek to inculcate certain values and norms of behaviour by repetition, which automatically implies continuity with the past" ("Introduction: Inventing Traditions," 1).

133. Tourists purchase jewelry and trinkets, while Indians buy beads and other cultural materials that are hard to find in mainstream locations or on reservations.

134. Erdrich, *The Antelope Wife*, 44.

135. Erdrich, *The Antelope Wife*, 39–40.

136. Erdrich, *The Antelope Wife*, 44.

137. Erdrich, *The Antelope Wife*, 48. For an extended discussion of toxicity in this novel, see Gamber, *Positive Pollutions*.

138. Erdrich, *The Antelope Wife*, 50.

139. See Patty Loew's book, *Seventh Generation Earth Ethics*, for a discussion of Ojibwe Seventh Generation philosophy, which suggests that all decisions be made with the next seven generations in mind.

140. Ramirez, *Native Hubs*, 2.

141. Stirrup, *Louise Erdrich*, 119.

142. Clifford, *Routes*, 263.

143. Erdrich, *The Antelope Wife*, 188.

144. Erdrich's "traditional" tobacco is probably *kinickinick*, a mix of bearberry, red willow, and a variety of leaves and barks. Noodin, personal communication. Erdrich, *Books and Islands*, 14.

145. Erdrich, *The Antelope Wife*, 179.

146. This scene is identical in the 1998 and 2012 novels.

147. Erdrich, *The Antelope Wife*, 93.

148. Erdrich, *The Antelope Wife*, 95.

149. Erdrich, *The Antelope Wife*, 97.

150. See Brozzo, "Food for Thought"; and Tharp, "Windigo Ways."

151. Erdrich, *The Antelope Wife*, 187.

152. Erdrich, *The Antelope Wife*, 187.

153. Erdrich, *The Antelope Wife*, 170.

154. Erdrich, *The Antelope Wife*, 138.

155. Erdrich, *The Antelope Wife*, 202.

156. Erdrich, *The Antelope Wife*, 170–71.

157. Erdrich, *The Antelope Wife*, 113.

158. Erdrich, *The Antelope Wife*, 157.

159. There are many revisions to this scene. First, the episode comes much sooner in the novel (p. 60 vs. p. 132) and has a third-person narrator. The kidnapped German is meant to replace a "war brother," not a real brother. Also, the German is not from a state work camp but came over after the war to work in timber (*The Antelope Wife: New and Revised Edition*, 60). Frank is only mentioned at the end, as a toddler who had tasted the cake (*The Antelope Wife: New and Revised Edition*, 70).

160. Erdrich, *The Antelope Wife*, 114.

161. Lischke argues that the blitzkuchen story is a "commentary on the significance of meeting grounds, which include cross-cultural gender relations, peaceful interactions and conflicts that have complicated the relationship between Euro-Americans and 'Indians'" ("'Blitzkuchen,'" 68). She also reads the story as a captivity narrative.

162. Appadurai, *Social Life*, 3, 41, 26.

163. Dubin, *The History of Beads*, 261.

164. See Dubin, *The History of Beads*; and Francis, *Beads and Discovery*. The earliest known bead in North America, found in Tule Springs, Nevada, has been dated to 11,000 BC. Beads made of shell, pearl, copper, wampum, pipestone, and other materials were almost entirely replaced by glass seed beads. Columbus is credited with starting the bead trade (Francis, *Beads and Discovery*, 32). Beads were exchanged as gifts, as acts of friendship, and to impress, and they eventually were bartered and became a commodity (33).

165. Erdrich, *The Antelope Wife*, 91.

166. Rivard, *A New Order of Things*, 72.

167. Little, "Beading the Multicultural World," 499.

168. See Erdrich, *The Antelope Wife: New and Revised Edition*, 263, 264, for this change from Czechoslovakia to Hungary. This revision does not appear to

be for historical accuracy alone, as it is difficult to determine the origin of many trade beads. Both Bohemia and Moravia, which made many early glass trade beads, now belong to the Czech Republic, so Erdrich's use of Czech is not inaccurate. Hungary itself was not known for its production of glass beads, though Moravia was part of the Austro-Hungarian Empire in the late nineteenth century, which might explain Erdrich's Hungarian beads (perhaps Moravian). Records from the United States Bureau of Foreign Commerce indicate that glass beads were imported from Austria-Hungary (also from Italy, Great Britain, Egypt, India, Belgium, and France) in 1884, to choose one year from the reservation era. See United States, Department of State, Bureau of Foreign and Domestic Commerce, *Commercial Relations*, 307. Francis argues that "beads often traveled long and circuitous paths within the cultural sphere of Native Americans" once they arrived in the New World, making it "difficult to precisely identify many of the beads traded in America" (*Beads and Discovery*, 28). The reference to the beads traveling through time and space to be in Minneapolis is in Erdrich, *The Antelope Wife*, 214.

169. They may have been Venetian or Bohemian in origin and may have been obtained by the Russians in China or Hong Kong or brought over by English merchants in the Canadian fur trade. See Dubin, *The History of Beads*, 274–75. According to Francis, Powhatan wanted blue beads, Verrazano gave "crystal of azure color" to Natives in New York Harbor in 1524, and Lewis described blue and white beads traded along the Columbia River (*Beads and Discovery*, 35, 36, 45).

170. Erdrich, *The Antelope Wife*, 16.

171. Pembina is an Ojibwe band name and the name of a town, a valley, and a river in North Dakota. There are Pembinas at both Turtle Mountain and White Earth Reservations. See Camp, "Working Out Their Own Salvation," 24.

172. Erdrich, *The Antelope Wife*, 215.

173. This story is part of Zosie's/Noodin's naming dream for Cally, who is named Blue Prairie Woman. In the 1998 text, the Pembina woman takes out "Sioux marked plum pits" for gambling; in the 2012 novel, they are simply "marked plum pits" (Erdrich, *The Antelope Wife*, 216; *The Antelope Wife: New and Revised Edition*, 266). This detail seems to suggest that the beads came to the Ojibwe via the Lakota, but this transmission gets erased in the revision.

174. Erdrich, *The Antelope Wife: New and Revised Edition*, 268.

175. Erdrich, *The Antelope Wife*, 27.

176. Erdrich, *The Antelope Wife*, 25.

177. Erdrich, *The Antelope Wife*, 27.

178. Erdrich, *The Antelope Wife*, 30.

179. Erdrich, *The Antelope Wife*, 227.
180. Marks, *The Skin of the Film*, 28.
181. Erdrich, *The Antelope Wife*, 219. This line does not appear in the new version.
182. Clifford, *Routes*, 9.
183. Cooper, *A New Generation*, 7.
184. Stirrup, *Louise Erdrich*, 202.
185. Erdrich, *Books and Islands*, 49. According to Erdrich, archaeological evidence demonstrates that the area has been inhabited since 2000 BC.
186. Blaeser, "Sacred Journey Cycles," 85–86.
187. Erdrich, *Books and Islands*, 14.
188. Shortly after the completion of this mural, Morrison designed another one for the Daybreak Star center in Seattle. See Morrison and Galt, *Turning the Feather Around*, 154.
189. Before returning to Minneapolis, Morrison lived and taught in Duluth, Dayton, Ithaca, Providence, and Philadelphia. See Rushing and Makholm, *Modern Spirit*; and Morrison and Galt, *Turning the Feather Around*.
190. *Turning the Feather Around* is also the title of George Morrison's 1998 biography. While the mural is often referred to as *Untitled*, according to the Minneapolis American Indian Center and his biography, he always intended it to be called *Turning the Feather Around . . . a Mural for the Indian*. Turning the Feather Around, or Gwe-ki-ge-nah-gah-boo, is also reportedly one of Morrison's Ojibwe Names. In 2001 the AIC raised funds to restore the mural. The grant is mentioned in Morrison and Galt, *Turning the Feather Around*, 151.
191. Morrison and Galt, *Turning the Feather Around*, 152.
192. In fact, Makholm calls the horizon line Morrison's "signature mark" and "an obsession" (Rushing and Makholm, *Modern Spirit*, 6). Morrison himself talks about the horizon in *Turning the Feather Around* (169).
193. Rushing and Makholm, *Modern Spirit*, 6.
194. Erdrich, *Books and Islands*, 82.
195. Little, "Beading the Multicultural World," 500.
196. Erdrich, *The Antelope Wife*, 220.
197. Folsom, *Walt Whitman*, 3.
198. However, the 2013 Harper Perennial Modern Classics reprints of her books, including *Love Medicine*, *Tales of Burning Love*, and *The Plague of Doves*, feature artwork by her daughter, Aza Erdrich, as do the first paperback edition of *The Round House*, the 2014 reprint of *Books and Islands in Ojibwe Country*, and the 2016 *Antelope Woman*.
199. Stillinger, *Coleridge and Textual Stability*, 107.
200. Streitfield, "Book Report," *Washington Post*, February 13, 1994.

201. Herman considers the seemingly apolitical nature of the 1998 text. See Herman, *Politics and Aesthetics*.
202. Erdrich, *The Antelope Wife: New and Revised Edition*, 28. The tin contains $438.13. Scranton and Augustus Roy carry it to the place where the massacre occurred in search of the old woman's family. In the 1998 text, this event takes place in the final chapter of the novel, sans cracker tin, and Augustus accompanies his grandfather, not his father (*The Antelope Wife* 238).
203. Erdrich, *Antelope Woman*, x.
204. Erdrich, *Antelope Woman*, ix.
205. Eighteen years now with the third version.
206. Lischke, "'Blitzkuchen,'" 70.
207. Ferrari, "'Where the Maps Stopped,'" 159; DuPlessis, *The Pink Guitar*, 6.
208. Lister, "'Power from the In-Between,'" 223.
209. Erdrich, *The Antelope Wife: New and Revised Edition*, 165.

4. THE CITY AS CONFLUENCE

1. The project was sponsored by Alderman Smith, Chicago Public Art Group, Alternatives Inc., and After School Matters. See Debra Yepa-Pappan's interview with Alexandra Kelstrom, Asian American Art Oral History Project, DePaul University, 2012, for a historical narrative of the project. Some of this information also comes from the project's "Information Sheet" and "Final Report," which the lead artists shared with me. Alderman Smith assembled a steering committee, and after months of meetings with the community, the artists came up with three design proposals. Community members and apprentice artists participated in the installation of the mural.
2. Chicaugua or Chekagou is supposedly a corrupted version of the Miami-Illinois or Fox word for "wild leek," which has been misunderstood as "onion." The name Shikaakwa was recorded in French explorer René-Robert Cavelier, Sieur de La Salle's 1679 memoir. It has also been suggested that the name comes from Ojibwe for "skunk place."
3. This was expressly one of the goals of the project: to reclaim and retell Chicago's Indigenous history from an Indigenous perspective. "Project Information Sheet," 2.
4. Two-Rivers, *Pow Wows*, line 25.
5. *War Bundles*, which has also been called *The Strong Heart Society* in interviews with Power and elsewhere, is the same book. Her former publisher changed the name for marketing purposes, but Power has returned the book to its original name (though it has been tabled for now). Power, interview, January 8, 2015. Power is, of course, not Menominee, and she attended Harvard, not

Stanford. Most importantly, while Pumpkin in *The Grass Dancer* dies in a car accident, Power is very much still alive.

6. I am not suggesting that grass dancing is traditionally Menominee, and certainly Pumpkin is challenging tradition by performing a predominantly male dance. Power, *The Grass Dancer*, 16.

7. Power, *The Grass Dancer*, 16.

8. Power, *The Grass Dancer*, 17.

9. I would like to point out that there is no extant criticism on this book, and only a handful of articles have been published about *The Grass Dancer*—all of which focus on what critics call her "magic realism" (a description that Power herself detests). See Schweniger, "Myth Launchings and Moon Landings"; Wright, "Visitors from the Spirit Path"; and Roland, "Pan-American (Re)Visions."

10. I will discuss the multigenre nature of this work at length in the final section of this chapter.

11. See Peterson, "The Founding Fathers"; Straus, "Founding Mothers"; and Lowe and Holley, "Treaty of Chicago."

12. See Keating, *Rising Up from Indian Country*, for a detailed account of this treaty.

13. The Sand Bar case went to the US Supreme Court in 1916, where it lost due to a lack of "continuous habitation" on said land and because this area was not considered land at the time of the treaty. See LaPier and Beck, *City Indian*, 30.

14. Buckley's study details the differences between the 1844 and 1856 texts and describes her theory on the narratives' staying power.

15. Entitled *The Defense*, this image on the south-facing bridge house on Michigan Avenue is a relief by Henry Hering. The 333 North Michigan Avenue Building, built in 1929, has fifteen panels on the fifth story by Fred M. Torrey "depicting the historical significance of the locale." See Riedy, *Chicago Sculpture*, 68.

16. Other stars represent the Great Chicago Fire, the Columbian Expo, and the Century of Progress Expo.

17. *War Bundles* includes the story of a Dakota woman on display at the Columbian Expo. Power, interview, January 8, 2015.

18. Patricia Limerick, among others, has objected to many of Turner's claims, particularly his failure to give Native peoples agency in the process and his negation of Native claims to the land. See Limerick's "The Adventures of the Frontier."

19. So named because the buildings were made of imitation marble.

20. In 1894 the name was changed to the Field Columbian Museum, and in 1905 it became the Field Museum of Natural History.

21. The building the Field Museum currently occupies was built between 1914 and 1921, when it was opened to the public.

22. *City Indian* joins a growing number of books about Indigenous Chicago, including the collection *Native Chicago* and LaGrande's *Indian Metropolis.*

23. LaPier and Beck, *City Indian*, 41.

24. See Waddell and Watson, *The American Indian in Urban Society*; and Neils, *Reservation to City*, for early accounts of relocated Indians in Chicago. Census numbers for Indians are usually underreported due to nonparticipation.

25. A telling account by Ed Goodvoice, in his BA thesis at the Native American Educational Services College (NAES) entitled "Indian Life on Skid Row in Chicago" (1991), reveals his experience with the Relocation Office, unemployment, and eventual life on Skid Row (on Madison Avenue). Goodvoice, who relocated to Chicago from the Rosebud Sioux Reservation in 1957, writes, "Skid Row was a sort of home to many Indians who had originally come to Chicago on the infamous federal Relocation program" (190). An abbreviated version of Goodvoice's narrative appears in Straus's *Native Chicago.*

26. These records are held in the Ayer Collection at the Newberry Library.

27. Though, as Rosenthal argues, the Los Angeles American Indian Center started in the 1930s. See Rosenthal, *Reimagining Indian Country*, 111.

28. Since the 1990s, the gentrification of the Uptown area has caused a decline in Indian residents, though, as the *Indian Land Dancing* project demonstrates, the neighborhood is still important to the Indigenous community. In 2017 the American Indian Center moved to a new location in Albany Park, out of the Uptown neighborhood.

29. LaGrand, *Indian Metropolis*, 232.

30. Wilson, "The Chicago Indian Village, 1970," 212.

31. DeHay, "Narrating Memory," 26.

32. DeHay, "Narrating Memory," 26.

33. DeHay, "Narrating Memory," 43.

34. Howe's ideas first appeared in "Tribalography: The Power of Native Stories" and then in "The Story of America: A Tribalography" and her book *Choctalking on Other Realities*. Also, a special issue of *Studies in American Indian Literatures* (2014) focused on the practical applications of Howe's methodology.

35. Howe, "The Story of America," 42.

36. Bauerkemper, "Introduction: Assessing," 4.

37. Appiah, *Cosmopolitanism*, xv.

38. DeLugan, "Indigeneity across Borders," 92, 86.

39. Howe, "Tribalography," 118.

40. Glassberg, "Public History," 17.

41. Even though the story takes place at Harvard, it crosses through Chicago (via

the Newberry Library—renowned for its Native history collections) and the Standing Rock Reservation (where their house burned down).

42. While this is one of the fictional stories, it has an autobiographical bent as well. Power is also currently writing a novel called "Harvard Indian Séance" that picks up this story line.

43. Power, *Roofwalker*, 112.

44. Massachusetts Historical Society, *Proceedings*, 349.

45. Melvin's current musical project is also entitled *First Fruits*, an album about seventeenth-century Puritan-Indian encounters (the reason why he has done all of this research on Harvard). I will refer to this "creative act" later in the chapter.

46. Power, *Roofwalker*, 114–15.

47. Power, *Roofwalker*, 115.

48. Vaughan's book has become the "standard authority on Puritan-Indian relations," according to William C. Kiessel's review in *American Historical Review*.

49. Power, *Roofwalker*, 135.

50. Physically, this book in its original trade edition from Little, Brown and Company does resemble a Bible in size and aesthetic. The cover is beige linen, devoid of images save for the ornate ornamentation above and below the title and its author. Of course, the connection between Puritans and the Bible is apparent. Vaughan's book includes an illustration of the Indian College building, reprinted from Samuel Eliot Morison's *Harvard College in the Seventeenth Century* (1936). The building was demolished in 1693.

51. According to Vaughan's research from Harvard records, Cheeshateaumuck is the only Indian graduate; three others "did not complete the course" (*New England Frontier*, 284).

52. Power, *Roofwalker*, 126.

53. Power, *Roofwalker*, 126.

54. Power, *Roofwalker*, 127.

55. Power, *Roofwalker*, 127.

56. Power, *Roofwalker*, 131–33.

57. The corner of 18th Street and South Calumet Avenue is the location of Dearborn Park, which was part of the Fort Dearborn Addition, meant to "forever be vacant of Buildings." Cited in Buckley, *Searching for Fort Dearborn*, 230. See "Statue Goes Back Home," *Chicago Tribune*, May 6, 1987.

58. LaPier and Beck, *City Indian*, 2.

59. Cited in Keating, *Rising Up*, 239.

60. Chicago Historical Society, *Ceremonies*, 21–22.

61. Nelson and Olin, *Monuments and Memory*, 2.

62. Young, *The Texture of Memory*, 6.

63. Viejo-Rose, "Memorial Functions," 466–69.

64. The protest took place on November 24, 1973. Riedy suggests that there were seventy protesters present. Articles in the *Sun-Times* and *Daily Reader* cite the number as fifty and seventy-five, respectively.

65. The monument is in a warehouse at Roosevelt Road and Wells Street and is covered by a tarp. See Kass, "City Keeps Statue and Controversy under Wraps," *Chicago Tribune*, August 12, 2012. See Keating, *Rising Up*.

66. Power, *Roofwalker*, 162.

67. *Chili Corn*, which appears in the collection *Briefcase Warriors* (2001), was performed twice in 1997, directed by Dan Zellner and produced by Red Path Theatre, a company founded by Two-Rivers and run through Truman College. See Two-Rivers, "Red Path Theatre," 335–36.

68. This was the *Daily News*.

69. Two-Rivers, *Briefcase Warriors*, 106.

70. Power, *Roofwalker*, 163.

71. I have contacted the Field Museum regarding this dress, and I have searched the catalog of Yanktonai Sioux collections published in *Fieldiana*. It may be part of George Dorsey's collection for the World's Expo collection, though I have been unable to confirm this.

72. Power, *Roofwalker*, 164.

73. Her mother says, "We honor you . . . because you are a creature of great endurance and great generosity. You provided us with so many things that helped us to survive. It makes me angry to see you like this" (*Roofwalker*, 164).

74. This dress also appears in *The Grass Dancer*, specifically in the chapter "Moonwalk." As Margaret Many Wounds is preparing to die, she tells her grandson Harley about her grandmother's dress in the Field Museum. She visited it once, she says: "I stood there all day practically, trying to figure out how I could get that dress back" (114).

75. Power, *Roofwalker*, 163.

76. Power, *Roofwalker*, 164.

77. Goeman, *Mark My Words*, 5.

78. Power, *Roofwalker*, 5. Also see Smith, *Conquest*, 82–83. Smith describes a history of forced sterilization of Indigenous women, particularly the Indian Health Service (IHS) campaign during the 1970s. The General Accounting Office's 1976 report concluded that 5 percent of Native women in four service areas had been sterilized between 1973 and 1976, though estimates from activist groups suggest that this number is 25 percent and as high as 80 percent in some locales.

79. Medicine, "Lakota Star Quilts," 113. Medicine discusses the history of star quilts, which originated during the reservation era, when trade cloth was quickly replacing hides for clothing and bedding. The quilts, she writes, "have long been a critical element in giveaways, and, from birth to death, the life-cycle events of Sioux peoples." They are symbols "of prestige, sentiment, and 'belongingness.'"

80. Power, *Roofwalker*, 6. Of course, this kind of claim also subtly challenges the validity of a blood quantum system. Jessie says, "As far back as anyone in my family could remember, both sides were Indian—full-blood Sioux on my mother's side and full-blood Sioux on my dad's," but of course Vikings make this untrue. Power posits that while stories of Viking encounters exist among the Three Affiliated Tribes (where red hair is common), no such stories are told among the Dakotas. Power, interview, January 8, 2015.

81. See Kolodny, *In Search of First Contact*, which examines Indigenous narratives of Norse encounters as early as AD 1000.

82. According to Power, the use of the word "Sioux" is historically authentic for the time period. In the 1960s and 1970s, she says, Dakotas still called themselves Sioux. In the title story, for example, Jessie's father's VW bus has a bumper sticker that reads "Sioux Pride." Power, *Roofwalker*, 24.

83. Power, *Roofwalker*, 23–24.

84. Power, *Roofwalker*, 24.

85. Power, *Roofwalker*, 24. Not unlike the buffalo in "Museum Indians."

86. Power, *Roofwalker*, 24.

87. Sitting Bull sustained two gunshot injuries during his arrest on the Standing Rock Reservation: Bullhead's shot struck Sitting Bull in the chest, and Red Tomahawk's struck him in the head. See Mooney, *The Ghost Dance Religion*.

88. Power, *Roofwalker*, 85.

89. Power, *Roofwalker*, 86.

90. Power, *Roofwalker*, 86.

91. Power, *Roofwalker*, 103.

92. Power, *Roofwalker*, 109.

93. This is also recurrent in *Sacred Wilderness*, particularly when Candace imagines the umbilical cord as a "rope the children could use to climb back into their history" (177). Also, Binah refers to her "usual dog and pony show about how the past isn't really the past but still impacting us today" (192).

94. Power, *Roofwalker*, 87.

95. Most importantly, Sitting Bull's death is a precursor to the events at Wounded Knee, just fourteen days later.

96. Susan Kelly Power's family lived near Sitting Bull's grave, and as a child, she

was sent out to protect it from potential looting by tourists. The grave is mentioned in "Stone Women" and "Reunion" (154, 166). The Standing Rock tribe maintains that Sitting Bull's remains are still in North Dakota, that Mobridge removed the bones of an unknown woman.

97. Power, *Roofwalker*, 105.
98. Power, *Roofwalker*, 102–3.
99. Power, *Roofwalker*, 96.
100. Of course, the American Indian Center played a central role in the author's life as well.
101. Ramirez, *Native Hubs*, 2.
102. Power, *Roofwalker*, 84.
103. Power, *Roofwalker*, 9.
104. Power, *Roofwalker*, 107.
105. Power, *Roofwalker*, 106.
106. Power, *Roofwalker*, 172.
107. Power, *Roofwalker*, 170.
108. Power, *Roofwalker*, 174, 176.
109. Power, *Roofwalker*, 176.
110. Power, *Roofwalker*, 187–88.
111. Power, *Roofwalker*, 188.
112. Howe, "The Story of America," 44.
113. Howe, "The Story of America," 45. The concept of counterhistory comes from Foucault, *Society Must Be Defended*, 79.
114. See Gardner, introduction; and Walker, *Lakota Belief and Ritual*.
115. Beebe, *Ivory Towers*, 4–5.
116. Kelsey, *Reading the Wampum*, xi; see also Fitzgerald, "The Cultural Work."
117. Fitzgerald and Wyss, "Land and Literacy," 245.
118. Momaday tells the Arrowmaker story in both "The Man Made of Words" and *The Way to Rainy Mountain*. The Arrowmaker is saved by language, by the power of words, as Momaday argues, but he is also saved by the arrow, his creation. In *Pushing the Bear*, Diane Glancy's novel of the Trail of Tears, the character of the Basket Maker unpopularly announces that his or her baskets will reflect the new territory and tell new stories.
119. Power, *Roofwalker*, 115.
120. Power, *Roofwalker*, 117.
121. Of course, there are exceptions, though these are mostly songs—not entire albums.
122. Power, *Roofwalker*, 59.
123. The Mohawk newspaper, published from 1969 to 1996 on the Cornwall

Indian Reserve in Rooseveltown, New York, purported to be the "voice of Native America." There is a reference to poems in *Akwesasne Notes* in the story "Roofwalker" as well.

124. Power, *Roofwalker*, 58. This is a nod to the famous Mohawk ironworkers.
125. Power, *Roofwalker*, 59.
126. Power, *Roofwalker*, 59.
127. Power, *Roofwalker*, 68.
128. Power, *Roofwalker*, 71.
129. Of course, aliens can also function as an allegory for urban Indians. In *American Indian Literature and the Southwest*, Eric Gary Anderson traces the infamous Roswell case and "states of alienation" in literature of the Southwest.
130. Gramsci, "The Intellectuals," 3–23; Howe, "The Story of America," 43.
131. Power, *Roofwalker*, 56.
132. Power, *Roofwalker*, 57.
133. Power, *Roofwalker*, 170.
134. Power, *Roofwalker*, 149.
135. Power, *Roofwalker*, 148–49.
136. Power, *Roofwalker*, 45.
137. Power, *Roofwalker*, 45.
138. This is the wampum that Jigonsaseh gives Maryam to commemorate their talks and confirm their mutual respect for each other's beliefs. Jigonsaseh says, "We treasured these small shell beads of white and deep purple and used them to create designs that *traced history*: commemorating important events, forging a contract" (157, emphasis mine). Also, see Kelsey's *Reading the Wampum* for an extended discussion on wampum as text.
139. DeHay, "Narrating Memory," 26.
140. Peterson, "History," 983.
141. Yepa-Pappan trained at the Institute of American Indian Arts and at Columbia College.
142. Yepa-Pappan, interview, July 24, 2014.
143. Appadurai, *Modernity at Large*, 183.
144. Yepa-Pappan, interview, July 24, 2014. Yepa-Pappan borrowed this technique from her husband, artist Chris Pappan (Osage/Kaw/Cheyenne River Sioux), who draws and paints on ledger paper. She takes this a step further, she says, by digitally printing on it, even further contemporizing her work. Their work appeared together in a Bristol, UK, show in 2014 entitled *First People, Second City*.
145. I borrow this phrase from Archuleta, who uses it to describe Silko's project, particularly in *Almanac of the Dead*, to "destabilize" the US-Mexico border.

Archuleta writes, "Silko's conclusion creates a path to healing because indigenous peoples reestablish and reclaim the ancient roads their ancestors traveled, and they are roads without borders. Furthermore, her erasure of borders and her creation of an indigenous network affirm the significance of relationships with peoples south of the border and with the environment" (Archuleta, "Securing Our Nation's Roads," 131–32).

146. For example, "Stone Women" appeared in *Iowa Woman* and *Going Where I'm Coming From: Memoirs of American Youth* (1995), "Dakota Woman" in *Riding Shotgun: Women Write about Their Mothers* (2008), "Roofwalker" in *Grand Mothers: Poems, Reminiscences, and Short Stories about the Keepers of Our Traditions* (1994), and "The Attic" in *Home: American Writers Remember Rooms of Their Own* (1997).

147. See *Ploughshares* interview. Power says, "I noticed that even when I thought I was writing a story that had nothing to do with me or my life, there was a thread of connection to memory, to lived experience, once I paid careful attention. I'd written a handful of essays about my family history, and thought it might be interesting to have a collection where a person could read a short story, then read an essay that featured the seed of actual experience which was later spun into fiction. I meant for the book to have these pairings move back and forth between fiction and non-fiction, but my editor thought it would be confusing for readers—a good point, so we created two sections instead. I think we are always writing our story to some degree."

148. She now concedes that perhaps an introduction would have helped to articulate this purpose. Power, interview, January 8, 2015.

149. Some others include Silko's *Storyteller*; Momaday's *The Way to Rainy Mountain*; Carter Revard's *Family Matters, Tribal Affairs* and *Winning the Dust Bowl*; Alexie's *The Business of Fancydancing* and *War Dances*; Eric Gansworth's *Breathing the Monster Alive* and *A Half-Life of Cardio-Pulmonary Function*; Marilou Awiakta's *Selu: Seeking the Corn-Mother's Wisdom*; Gordon Henry's *The Light People*; Elizabeth Cook-Lynn's *Then Badger Said This*; Linda Hogan's *Dwellings: A Spiritual History of the Living World*; Deborah Miranda's *Bad Indians: A Tribal Memoir*; Nora Naranjo-Morse's *Mud Woman: Poems from the Clay*; Jim Northrup's *Walking the Rez Road*; Louise Owens's *I Hear the Train: Reflections, Inventions, Refractions* and *Mixedblood Messages*; Ray A. Young Bear's *Black Eagle Child*; and Luci Tapahanso's *Saanii Dahataat: The Women Are Singing*, *Blue Horses Rush In*, and *A Radiant Curve*.

150. Anderson, "Situating American Indian Poetry," 35–36.

151. Anderson, "Situating American Indian Poetry," 35.

152. Rader, "The Epic Lyric," 126.

153. Rader, "The Epic Lyric," 127.

154. Rader, "The Epic Lyric," 137–40.

155. Howe, "Blind Bread," 333.

156. Silko, "Language and Literature," 160–61.

157. Blaeser, "Like 'Reeds,'" 266–67.

158. Rader, "The Epic Lyric," 141.

159. Singh, introduction, 19.

160. Power, interview, January 8, 2015.

161. Power, *Roofwalker*, 190.

162. Power, *Roofwalker*, 190 (emphasis mine).

163. Power, interview, January 8, 2015.

164. Low's forthcoming book is entitled *Chicago's First Urban Indians: The Potawatomi.*

165. Power, *The Grass Dancer*, 27.

166. Power, *Roofwalker*, 191.

167. Power, *Roofwalker*, 192.

168. Power, *Roofwalker*, 192.

169. Power, *Roofwalker*, 150.

170. Power, *Roofwalker*, 87, 123.

171. Power, *Roofwalker*, 87.

172. Rader, "The Epic Lyric," 134.

173. Oahe Dam is named for Oahe Mission, established in 1874, about eight miles upstream from the present site of the dam. "Oahe" translates to "a foundation" or "a place to stand on."

174. See Lawson, *Dammed Indians.*

175. Power, *Roofwalker*, 150.

176. Power, *Sacred Wilderness*, 219.

177. For example, Albert White Hat Sr.'s teachings on the Lakota language reflect this as well. See *Reading and Writing the Lakota Language.*

178. Power, *Roofwalker*, 126, 82.

179. Power says that her North Dakota family seems "plagued by fires." In addition to this fire, an aunt had several house fires, including one in which she lost two daughters. Power admits to being "deathly afraid" of fires. Power, email message to author, March 23, 2015.

180. Power, *Roofwalker*, 150.

181. Power, *Roofwalker*, 150.

182. Power, *Roofwalker*, 147.

183. Power, *Roofwalker*, 156.

184. Power, *The Grass Dancer*, 106–7.

185. Power, *Roofwalker*, 148.

186. Power, *The Grass Dancer*, 107.

187. Power, *Roofwalker*, 73.

188. Power, *Roofwalker*, 57.

189. Power, *Roofwalker*, 148.

190. McLeod, "Coming Home through Stories," 31.

191. McLeod, "Coming Home through Stories," 19.

192. Hall, "Ethnicity," 19.

193. Certeau, *The Practice of Everyday Life*, 23.

194. Simpson, *Dancing on Our Turtle's Back*, 33.

195. Power, *The Grass Dancer*, 332.

196. Carocci, *First People, Second City*.

197. Kelsey writes about Native epistemological practices in *Tribal Theory in Native American Literature*. This last phrase comes from Womack, *Red on Red*.

EPILOGUE

1. Peters discusses *The Exiles* in an interview with Lisa Napoli that appears on the KCRW blog dated January 1, 2014. See http://curious.kcrw.com/2014/01/the-modern-native-american-experience-through-a-young-navajo-photographers-lens.

2. The film premiered at the LA Shorts Fest and has also screened at the Durango Independent Films Festival, the San Diego American Indian Film Fest, the San Francisco American Indian Film Festival, and the Montreal First Nations Film Festival, among others.

3. This mural was inspired by a photograph taken by Aaron Huey for a photo essay in *National Geographic* that appeared in 2012. Neither Fairey nor Huey are Native, but they are both involved with social justice issues for Indigenous people via the Honor the Treaties organization.

4. Peters discusses this in the KCRW interview.

5. Roderick, "Modernizing 'The Exiles.'"

6. Allen, *Off the Reservation*, 7.

7. *Pasadena Monthly*, January 28, 2014.

8. This is from the project's website, www.exiledndnz.com.

9. See www.urbannativeera.com for more information about the project and organization.

10. See Howe, "Blind Bread," "The Story of America," and "Tribalography."

11. This is from the film *Why Did Gloria Die?*

MANUSCRIPTS AND ARCHIVES

Community Archives of NAES College, Chicago (now held at the Special Collections Research Center, University of Chicago Library; accessed at NAES)

 Goodvoice, Edward E. "Indian Life on Skid Row in Chicago." BA thesis, 1991. Native American Educational Services. Student Field Projects, box 10, folder 2, Special Collections Research Center, University of Chicago Library.

 Native American Educational Services. Chicago Community Agencies. Records, box 3, folder 30, Special Collections Research Center, University of Chicago Library.

Hooley, Matt. "Natives Writing Home: Minneapolis and the Rise of Native Literary Modernism." PhD diss., University of Wisconsin, Madison, 2011.

Kugel, Rebecca Anne. "'To Go About on the Earth': An Ethnohistory of the Minnesota Ojibwe; 1830–1900." PhD diss., UCLA, 1986.

Mackenzie, Kent Robert. "A Description and Examination of the Production of *The Exiles*, a Film of the Actual Lives of a Group of Young American Indians." MA thesis, University of Southern California, 1964. Included on *The Exiles* DVD.

Magoulick, Mary. "Coming to Life: Native American Cultural Renewal and Emerging Identity in Michigan Ojibwe Narratives and in Erdrich's *The Antelope Wife*." PhD diss., Indiana University, 2000.

Newberry Library, Chicago

D'Arcy McNickle Center for American Indian and Indigenous Studies
Chicago American Indian Oral History Project
Edward E. Ayer Manuscript Collection
Bureau of Indian Affairs Indian Relocation Records

Stromberg, Ernest. "'As Distant from Myself as a Hawk from the Moon': Representation and Authenticity in the American Indian Novel." PhD diss., University of Oregon, 1996.

PUBLISHED WORKS

Ablon, Joan. "American Indian Relocation: Problems of Dependency and Management in the City." *Phylon* 26, no. 4 (1965): 362–71.

———. "Relocated American Indians in the San Francisco Bay Area: Social Interaction and Indian Identity." *Human Organization* 23, no. 4 (1964): 296–304.

Aby, Anne J., ed. *The North Star State: A Minnesota History Reader*. St. Paul: Minnesota Historical Society, 2002.

Adams, John S., and Barbara J. VanDrasek. *Minneapolis–St. Paul: People, Place, and Public Life*. Minneapolis: University of Minnesota Press, 1993.

Adams, Rachel. *Continental Divides: Remapping the Cultures of North America*. Chicago: University of Chicago Press, 2009.

Ahokas, Pirjo. "Transcending Binary Divisions: Constructing a Postmodern Female Urban Identity in Louise Erdrich's *The Antelope Wife* and Zadie Smith's *White Teeth*." In *Sites of Ethnicity: Europe and the Americas*, edited by William Boelhower, Rocío G. Davis, and Carmen Birkle, 115–29. American Studies 119. Heidelberg: Universitätsverlag Winter Gmbh, 2004.

Albers, Patricia, and Beatrice Medicine. *The Hidden Half: Studies of Plains Indian Women*. Washington DC: University Press of America, 1983.

Alcatraz Proclamation. *Indians of All Tribes Newsletter* 1, no. 1 (January 1970).

Alexie, Sherman. *The Absolutely True Diary of a Part-Time Indian*. New York: Little, Brown and Company, 2007.

———. "Author Sherman Alexie Talks 'Flight.'" Interview with Rebecca Roberts. *Talk of the Nation*. National Public Radio. KUOW, Seattle. April 11, 2007.

———, dir. *The Business of Fancydancing*. Outrider Pictures, 2002. DVD, 103 minutes.

———. *The Business of Fancydancing: The Screenplay*. Brooklyn: Hanging Loose, 2003.

———. *The Business of Fancydancing: Stories and Poems*. Brooklyn: Hanging Loose, 1992.

———. "Confessions of a Blasphemer: Sherman Alexie Talks New Book, Indian Humor and More." Interview with Jane Ciabattari. *Daily Beast*, October 17, 2012. www.thedailybeast.com/articles/2012/10/17/confessions-of-a-blasphemer-sherman-alexie-talks-new-book-indian-humor-and-more.html.

———. "A Conversation with Sherman Alexie by Diane Thiel." Interview. *Crossroads: The Journal of the Poetry Society of America* 61 (2004): 4–7. Reprinted in Peterson, *Conversations with Sherman Alexie*, 135–40.

———. *First Indian on the Moon.* Brooklyn: Hanging Loose, 1993.

———. *Flight.* New York: Black Cat, 2007.

———. *Indian Killer.* New York: Atlantic Monthly, 1996.

———. Interview with Steve Paulson. *Sound Focus.* National Public Radio. KUOW, Seattle. January 23, 2009.

———. *The Lone Ranger and Tonto Fistfight in Heaven.* New York: Atlantic Monthly, 1993.

———. "My Encounters with the Homeless People of the Pacific Northwest." *Willow Springs* 58 (2006): 18–22.

———. "One Little Indian Boy." In *Edge Walking on the Western Rim: New Works by 12 Northwest Writers*, edited by Mayumi Tsutakawa, 52–65. Seattle: Sasquatch, 1994.

———. "The Poem That Made Sherman Alexie Want to 'Drop Everything and Be a Poet.'" Interview with Joe Fassler. *Atlantic Online*, October 16, 2013. www .theatlantic.com/entertainment/archive/2013/10/the-poem-that-made-sherman -alexie-want-to-drop-everything-and-be-a-poet/280586/.

———. "Redeemers." Interview with Matt Dellinger. *New Yorker Online*, April 21, 2003. www.newyorker.com/magazine/2003/04/21/redeemers. Reprinted in Peterson, *Conversations with Sherman Alexie*, 121–27.

———. *Reservation Blues.* New York: Warner, 1995.

———. "Seriously Sherman: Seattle's Favorite Pissed Off Poet Talks about Truth, Terror, Tradition, and What's So Great about America Anyway?" Interview with Timothy Harris. *Real Change News*, May 29–June 11, 2003: 1+. Reprinted in Peterson, *Conversations with Sherman Alexie*, 128–34.

———. *Smoke Signals: A Screenplay.* New York: Hyperion, 1998.

———. "Spokane Words: Tomson Highway Raps with Sherman Alexie." Interview with Tomson Highway. *Aboriginal Voices* 4, no. 1 (January–March 1997): 36–41. Reprinted in Peterson, *Conversations with Sherman Alexie*, 21–31.

———. *The Summer of Black Widows.* Brooklyn: Hanging Loose, 1996.

———. *Ten Little Indians: Stories.* New York: Grove, 2003.

———. *Toughest Indian in the World.* New York: Atlantic Monthly, 2000.

———. *War Dances.* New York: Grove, 2009.

———. "What You Pawn I Will Redeem." *New Yorker*, April 21 and 28, 2003, 168–77.

———. "Where There's Smoke . . . : An Interview with Timothy Harris." *Real Change News* 5, no. 7 (July 1998): 9+.

———. "Why the Best Kids' Books Are Written in Blood." *Wall Street Journal*

Speakeasy Blog, June 9, 2011. http://blogs.wsj.com/speakeasy/2011/06/09/why
-the-best-kids-books-are-written-in-blood/.

————. "A World of Story-Smoke: A Conversation with Sherman Alexie." Interview
with Åse Nygren. *MELUS* 30, no. 4 (Winter 2005): 149–69.

Alexie, Sherman, and Jess Walter. "Back to Spokane." *A Tiny Sense of Accomplishment*.
Episode 21. June 10, 2015. *Infinite Guest Network*. Podcast.

————. "Live with Kerri Miller." *A Tiny Sense of Accomplishment*. Episode 20. May
27, 2015. *Infinite Guest Network*. Podcast.

Alfred, Taiaiake. "Warrior Scholarship: Seeing the University as a Ground of Contention." In *Indigenizing the Academy: Transforming Scholarship and Empowering
Communities*, edited by Devon A. Mihesuah and Angela Cavender Wilson,
88–99. Lincoln: University of Nebraska Press, 2004.

Allen, Chadwick. "2014 NAISA Presidential Address: Centering the 'I' in NAISA."
NAIS 2, no. 1 (2015): 1–14.

————. *Blood Narrative: Indigenous Identity in American Indian and Maori Literary
and Activist Texts*. Durham NC: Duke University Press, 2002.

————. "Rere Ke: Moving Differently: Indigenizing Methodologies for Comparative
Indigenous Literary Studies." *Studies in American Indian Literatures* 19, no.
4 (Winter 2007): 1–26.

————. "Re-scripting Indigenous America: Earthworks in Native Art, Literature,
Community." In *Twenty-First Century Perspectives on Indigenous Studies*, edited
by Birgit Däwes et al., 127–47. New York: Routledge, 2015.

————. *Trans-Indigenous: Methodologies for Global Native Literary Studies*. Minneapolis: University of Minnesota Press, 2012.

————. "A Transnational Native American Studies? Why Not Studies That Are
Trans-Indigenous?" *Journal of Transnational American Studies* 4, no. 1 (2012):
n.p. http://escholarship.org/uc/item/82m5j3f5.

Allen, John. *Homelessness in American Literature: Romanticism, Realism, and Testimony*. New York: Routledge, 2013.

Allen, Paula Gunn. "Deer Woman." In *Grandmothers of the Light: A Medicine Woman's
Sourcebook*, 185–94. Boston: Beacon, 1991.

————. *Off the Reservation: Reflections on Boundary-Busting, Border-Crossing Loose
Canons*. Boston: Beacon, 1998.

————. *The Sacred Hoop: Recovering the Feminine in American Indian Traditions*.
1986. Reprint, Boston: Beacon, 1992.

————. *The Woman Who Owned the Shadows*. 1983. Reprint, San Francisco: Aunt
Lute, 1992.

Anderson, Benedict. *Imagined Communities: Reflections on the Origin and Spread of
Nationalism*. London: Verso, 1991.

Anderson, Eric Gary. *American Indian Literature and the Southwest: Contexts and Dispositions*. Austin: University of Texas Press, 1999.

———. "Situating American Indian Poetry: Place, Community, and the Question of Genre." In *Speak to Me Words: Essays on Contemporary American Indian Poetry*, edited by Dean Rader and Janice Gould, 34–55. Tucson: University of Arizona Press, 2003.

Anderson, Jane. "Indigenous Knowledge, Intellectual Property, Libraries, and Archives: Crises of Access, Control, and Future Utility." *Australian Academic & Research Libraries* 36, no. 2 (2013): 83–94.

Anderson, Kim. "Affirmations of an Indigenous Feminist." In *Indigenous Women and Feminism: Politics, Activism, Culture*, edited by Cheryl Suzack et al., 81–91. Vancouver: University of British Columbia Press, 2010.

Andersson, Rani-Henrik. *The Lakota Ghost Dance of 1890*. Lincoln: University of Nebraska Press, 2008.

Anthes, Bill. *Edgar Heap of Birds*. Durham NC: Duke University Press, 2015.

Appadurai, Arjun. *Modernity at Large: Cultural Dimensions of Globalization*. Minneapolis: University of Minnesota Press, 1996.

———, ed. *The Social Life of Things: Commodities in Cultural Perspective*. Cambridge: Cambridge University Press, 1986.

Appiah, Kwame Anthony. "Cosmopolitan Patriots." In *Cosmopolitics: Thinking and Feeling beyond the Nation*, edited by Pheng Cheah and Bruce Robbins, 91–114. Cultural Politics, vol. 14. Minneapolis: University of Minnesota Press, 1998.

———. *Cosmopolitanism: Ethics in a World of Strangers*. New York: Norton, 2006.

Archuleta, Elizabeth. "I Give You Back: Indigenous Women Writing to Survive." *Studies in American Indian Literatures* 18, no. 4 (Winter 2006): 88–114.

———. "Securing Our Nation's Roads and Borders or Re-circling the Wagons? Leslie Marmon Silko's Destabilization of 'Borders.'" *Wicazo Sa Review* 20, no. 1 (Spring 2005): 113–37.

Arndt, Grant P. "The Nation in the City: The Ho-Chunk Nation's Chicago Branch Office and the Ho-Chunk People of Chicago." In Straus, *Native Chicago*, 337–41.

———. "Relocation's Imagined Landscape and the Rise of Chicago's Native American Community." In Straus, *Native Chicago*, 159–72.

Arnett, Carroll. *Night Perimeter: New and Selected Poems, 1958–1990*. Greenfield Center NY: Greenfield Review Press, 1992.

Arnold, Kathleen R. *Homelessness, Citizenship, and Identity: The Uncanniness of Late Modernity*. Albany: State University Press of New York, 2004.

Atwater, Isaac, ed. *History of the City of Minneapolis, Minnesota*. New York: Munsell, 1893.

Austin, Ron. "*The Exiles*: Finding the Story." *Image* 67 (2010): 70–82.

Awiakta, Marilou. *Selu: Seeking the Corn-Mother's Wisdom*. Golden CO: Fulcrum, 1993.

Bagley, Clarence B. "Chief Seattle and Angeline." *Washington Historical Quarterly* 22 (1931): 243–75.

———. *History of Seattle: From the Earliest Settlement to the Present Time*. 3 vols. Chicago: S. J. Clarke, 1916.

Bakhtin, M. M. *The Dialogic Imagination: Four Essays*. Austin: University of Texas Press, 1981.

Baldwin, Rufus J. "Advent of the White Man." In Atwater, *History of the City of Minneapolis*, 21–27.

———. "Discovery." In Atwater, *History of the City of Minneapolis*, 11–17.

———. "Early Settlement." In Atwater, *History of the City of Minneapolis*, 29–48.

———. "French and American Occupation." In Atwater, *History of the City of Minneapolis*, 28.

———. "Indian Occupation and Wars." In Atwater, *History of the City of Minneapolis*, 18–20.

Banka, Ewelina. "'Homing' in the City: Sherman Alexie's Perspectives on Urban Indian Country." *European Review of Native American Studies* 20, no. 1 (2006): 35–38.

Barak, Julie. "Un-becoming White: Identity Transformation in Louise Erdrich's *The Antelope Wife*." *Studies in American Indian Literatures* 13, no. 4 (Winter 2001): 1–23.

Basso, Keith. *Wisdom Sits in Places: Landscape and Language among the Western Apache*. Albuquerque: University of New Mexico Press, 1996.

Bauerkemper, Joseph. "Introduction: Assessing and Advancing Tribalography." *Studies in American Indian Literatures* 26, no. 2 (Summer 2014): 3–12.

Bauman, John F., Roger Biles, and Kristin M. Szylvian. *The Ever-Changing American City: 1945–Present*. Lanham MD: Rowman and Littlefield, 2012.

Bean, Lowell John. Introduction to *The Ohlone Past and Present: Native Americans of the San Francisco Bay Region*, edited by Bean, xxi–xxx. Menlo Park CA: Ballena Press, 1994.

Beck, David. "The Chicago American Indian Community." In Straus, *Native Chicago*, 293–307.

———. "Developing a Voice: The Evolution of Self-Determination in an Urban Indian Community." *Wicazo Sa Review* 17, no. 2 (Fall 2002): 117–41.

Beebe, Maurice. *Ivory Towers and Sacred Founts: The Artist as Hero in Fiction from Goethe to James Joyce*. New York: New York University Press, 1964.

Beidler, Peter G. Review of *The Antelope Wife* by Louise Erdrich. *American Indian Research and Culture Journal* 23, no. 1 (1999): 219–21.

Beidler, Peter G., and Gay Barton. *A Reader's Guide to the Novels of Louise Erdrich.* Columbia: University of Missouri Press, 1999.

———. *A Reader's Guide to the Novels of Louise Erdrich: Revised and Expanded Edition.* Columbia: University of Missouri Press, 2006.

Bell, Michael Mayerfeld. "The Ghosts of Place." *Theory and Society* 26 (1997): 813–36.

Belin, Esther. *From the Belly of My Beauty.* Tucson: University of Arizona Press, 1999.

Benjamin, Walter. "The Storyteller." In *Illuminations,* translated by Harry Zohn, 83–109. New York: Schocken, 2007.

Bergland, Renée L. *The National Uncanny: Indian Ghosts and American Subjects.* Hanover NH: University Press of New England, 1999.

Berglund, Jeff, and Jan Roush, eds. *Sherman Alexie: A Collection of Critical Essays.* Salt Lake City: University of Utah Press, 2010.

Berkhofer, Robert F., Jr. *The White Man's Indian: Images of the American Indian from Columbus to the Present.* New York: Knopf, 1978.

Berman, Jessica. *Modernist Fiction, Cosmopolitanism, and the Politics of Community.* Cambridge: Cambridge University Press, 2001.

Bernardin, Susan. "Alexie-Vision: Getting the Picture." *World Literature Today,* July–August 2010, 521–55.

Berner, Robert L. Review of *The Jailing of Cecelia Capture* by Janet Campbell Hale and *Last Fall* by Bruce Stolbov. *American Indian Quarterly* 14, no. 2 (Spring 1990): 214–15.

Betty, Gerald. *Comanche Society: Before the Reservation.* College Station: Texas A&M University Press, 2002.

Bevis, William. "Native American Novels: Homing In." In *Recovering the Word: Essays on Native American Literature,* edited by Brian Swann and Arnold Krupat, 580–620. Berkeley: University of California Press, 1987.

Bhabha, Homi K. *The Location of Culture.* New York: Routledge, 1994.

Bierwert, Crisca. "Remembering Chief Seattle: Reversing Cultural Studies of a Vanishing Native American." *American Indian Quarterly* 22, no. 3 (Summer 1998): 280–304.

Biolsi, Thomas. "Imagined Geographies: Sovereignty, Indigenous Space, and American Indian Struggle." *American Ethnologist* 32, no. 2 (2005): 239–59.

Bird, Gloria. "The Exaggeration of Despair in Sherman Alexie's *Reservation Blues.*" *Wicazo Sa Review* 11, no. 2 (Fall 1995): 47–52.

Blackhawk, Ned. "I Can Carry On from Here: The Relocation of American Indians to Los Angeles." *Wicazo Sa Review* 11, no. 2 (Fall 1995): 16–30.

Blaeser, Kimberly M. *Absentee Indians and Other Poems.* East Lansing: Michigan State University Press, 2012.

———. "Like 'Reeds through the Ribs of a Basket': Native Women Weaving Stories."

In *Other Sisterhoods: Literary Theory and U.S. Women of Color*, edited by Sandra Kumamoto Stanley, 265–76. Urbana: University of Illinois Press, 1998.

———. "Sacred Journey Cycles: Pilgrimage as Re-turning and Re-telling in American Indigenous Literatures." *Religion and Literature* 35 (2003): 83–104.

Blauner, Robert. *Racial Oppression in America.* New York: Harper & Row, 1972.

Bogart, Michele H. *Public Sculpture and the Civic Ideal in New York City, 1890–1930.* Chicago: University of Chicago Press, 1989.

Bouzonviller, Elisabeth. "Cracks and 'Bricolage' in Louise Erdrich's *The Antelope Wife* or The Art of Hybridity." In *Hybridity: Forms and Figures in Literature and the Visual Arts*, edited by Vanessa Guignery, Catherine Pesso-Miquel, and François Specq, 147–57. Newcastle-upon-Tyne: Cambridge Scholars Publishing, 2011.

Boyd, Colleen, and Coll Thrush, eds. "Introduction: Bringing Ghosts to Ground." In Thrush and Boyd, *Phantom Past*, vii–xl.

Boyer, Lanada. "Reflections of Alcatraz." In *American Indian Activism: Alcatraz to the Longest Walk*, edited by Troy Johnson et al., 88–103. Urbana: University of Illinois Press, 1997.

Boyer, M. Christine. *The City of Collective Memory: Its Historical Imagery and Architectural Entertainments.* Cambridge MA: MIT Press, 1994.

Brant, Beth. "The Good Red Road: Journeys of Homecoming in Native Women's Writing." *American Indian Culture and Research Journal* 21, no. 1 (1997): 193–206.

———. *The Mohawk Trail.* Ithaca NY: Firebrand Books, 1985.

Breckenridge, Carol A., et al. "Cosmopolitanisms." In *Cosmopolitanism*, edited by Breckenridge et al., 1–15. Durham NC: Duke University Press, 2002.

Bremer, Sidney H. *Urban Intersections: Meetings of Life and Literature in United States Cities.* Urbana: University of Illinois Press, 1992.

Brennan, Timothy. *At Home in the World: Cosmopolitanism Now.* Cambridge MA: Harvard University Press, 1997.

Briggs, Laura, Gladys McCormick, and J. T. Way. "Transnationalism: A Category of Analysis." *American Quarterly* 60, no. 3 (2008): 625–48.

Brogan, Kathleen. *Cultural Haunting: Ghosts and Ethnicity in Recent American Literature.* Charlottesville: University Press of Virginia, 1998.

Broker, Ignatia. *Night Flying Woman: An Ojibway Narrative.* St. Paul MN: Borealis, 1983.

Bromley, Roger. *Narratives for a New Belonging: Diasporic Cultural Fictions.* Edinburgh: Edinburgh University Press, 2000.

Brown, Alanna K. "'Patterns and Waves Generation to Generation': *The Antelope Wife.*" In *Approaches to Teaching the Works of Louise Erdrich*, edited by Greg Sarris et al., 88–94. New York: Modern Language Association, 2004.

Brown, Michael F. *Who Owns Native Culture?* Cambridge MA: Harvard University Press, 2004.

Browner, Tara. *Heartbeat of the People: Music and Dance of the Northern Pow-Wow.* Urbana: University of Illinois Press, 2004.

Brozzo, Shirley. "Food for Thought: A Postcolonial Study of Food Imagery in Louise Erdrich's *The Antelope Wife.*" *Studies in American Indian Literatures* 17, no. 1 (Spring 2005): 1–15.

Buckley, Constance R. *Searching for Fort Dearborn: Perception, Commemoration, and Celebration of an Urban Creation Memory.* PhD diss., Loyola University, 2005. Ann Arbor: UMI, 2015.

Buell, Frederick. *National Culture and the New Global System.* Baltimore MD: Johns Hopkins University Press, 1994.

Buell, Lawrence. *The Environmental Imagination: Thoreau, Nature Writing, and the Formation of America.* Cambridge MA: Harvard University Press, 1995.

———. *Writing for an Endangered World: Literature, Culture, and Environment in the U.S. and Beyond.* Cambridge MA: Belknap–Harvard University Press, 2001.

Buff, Rachel. *Immigration and the Political Economy of Home: West Indian Brooklyn and American Indian Minneapolis, 1945–1992.* Berkeley: University of California Press, 2001.

Burke, Peter. "History as Social Memory." In *Memory: History, Culture and the Mind,* edited by Thomas Butler, 97–113. Oxford: Blackwell, 1989.

"Burke-Gilman History." www.seattle.gov. June 15, 2015.

Burnham, Michelle. "Sherman Alexie's *Indian Killer* as Indigenous Gothic." In Thrush and Boyd, *Phantom Past,* 3–25.

Burt, Larry W. "Roots of the Native American Urban Experience: Relocation Policy in the 1950s." *American Indian Quarterly* 10, no. 2 (1986): 85–99.

Buruma, Ian, and Avishai Margalit. *Occidentalism: The West in the Eyes of Its Enemies.* New York: Penguin, 2004.

Buse, Peter, and Andrew Stott. "Introduction: A Future for Haunting." In *Ghosts: Deconstruction, Psychoanalysis, History,* edited by Peter Buse and Andrew Stott, 1–20. New York: St. Martin's, 1999.

Butler, Judith, and Athena Athanasiou. *Dispossession: The Performative in the Political.* London: Polity, 2013.

Byrd, Jodi A. *The Transit of Empire: Indigenous Critiques of Colonialism.* Minneapolis: University of Minnesota Press, 2011.

Callahan, S. Alice. *Wynema: A Child of the Forest,* edited by A. LaVonne Brown Ruoff. 1891. Lincoln: University of Nebraska Press, 1997.

Camp, Gregory S. "Working Out Their Own Salvation: The Allotment of Land in

Severalty and the Turtle Mountain Chippewa Band, 1870–1920." *American Indian Culture and Research Journal* 14, no. 2 (1990): 19–38.

Carillo, Jo, ed. *Readings in American Indian Law: Recalling the Rhythm of Survival.* Philadelphia: Temple University Press, 1998.

Carocci, Max. "The Art of Chris Pappan and Debra Yepa-Pappan." In *First People, Second City.* Bristol: Rainmaker Gallery, 2014. Exhibition catalog.

———. "Living in the Urban Rez: Constructing San Francisco as Indian Land." In *Place and Native American Indian History and Culture*, edited by Joy Porter, 263–82. Oxford: Peter Lang, 2007.

Carpio, Myla Vicenti. *Indigenous Albuquerque.* Lubbock: Texas Tech University Press, 2011.

Carr, A. A. *Eye Killers.* Norman: University of Oklahoma Press, 1996.

Certeau, Michel de. *The Practice of Everyday Life.* Translated by Steven F. Rendall. Berkeley: University of California Press, 1984.

———. *The Writing of History.* Translated by Tom Conley. New York: Columbia University Press, 1988.

Chadwick, Whitney. "Reflecting on History as Histories." In *Art/Women/California: 1950–2000*, edited by Diana Burgess Fuller and Daniela Salvioni, 19–42. Berkeley: University of California Press, 2002.

Chavkin, Allan. "Vision and Revision in Louise Erdrich's *Love Medicine*." In *The Chippewa Landscape of Louise Erdrich*, edited by Allan Chavkin, 84–116. Tuscaloosa: University of Alabama Press, 1999.

Chicago Historical Society. *Ceremonies at the Unveiling of the Bronze Memorial Group of the Chicago Massacre of 1812.* Chicago: Chicago Historical Society, 1893.

Chopin, Kate. *The Awakening.* 1899. Reprint, Oxford: Oxford University Press, 2008.

Christie, Stuart. "Renaissance Man: The Tribal 'Schizophrenic' in Sherman Alexie's *Indian Killer*." *American Indian Culture and Research Journal* 25, no. 4 (2001): 1–19.

Clark, D. Anthony Tyeeme, and Malea Powell. "Guest Editors' Introduction: Resisting Exile in the 'Land of the Free': Indigenous Groundwork at Colonial Intersections." *American Indian Quarterly* 32, no. 1 (2008): 1–15.

Clayton, Jay. "The Narrative Turn in Recent Minority Fiction." *American Literary History* 2, no. 3 (1990): 375–93.

Clifford, James. "Mixed Feelings." In *Cosmopolitics: Thinking and Feeling beyond the Nation*, edited by Pheng Cheah and Bruce Robbins, 362–70. Cultural Politics, vol. 14. Minneapolis: University of Minnesota Press, 1998.

———. *Routes: Travel and Translation in the Late Twentieth Century.* Cambridge MA: Harvard University Press, 1997.

Cline, Irina. "The Hero of the Modern Mock Epic: Sherman Alexie's 'What You

Pawn I Will Redeem.'" In *The Image of the Hero II*, edited by Will Wright and Stephen Kaplan, 139–41. Pueblo: Colorado State University Press, 2010.

Cline, Lynn. "About Sherman Alexie." *Ploughshares* 26, no. 4 (2000–2001): 197–202.

Clingman, Stephen. *The Grammar of Identity: Transnational Fiction and the Nature of the Boundary*. New York: Oxford University Press, 2009.

Cole, Diane. Review of *The Jailing of Cecelia Capture* by Janet Campbell Hale. *Ms.*, April 1985, 14, 16.

Comer, Krista. *Landscapes of the New West: Gender and Geography in Contemporary Women's Writing*. Chapel Hill: University of North Carolina Press, 1999.

Cook-Lynn, Elizabeth. "The American Indian Fiction Writer: 'Cosmopolitanism, Nationalism, the Third World, and First Nation Sovereignty.'" *Wicazo Sa Review* 9, no. 2 (Fall 1993): 26–36.

———. *Then Badger Said This*. Fairfield WA: Ye Galleon Press, 1983.

Cooper, Brenda. *A New Generation of African Writers: Migration, Material Culture, and Language*. Oxford: Currey, 2008.

Cooper, Lydia R. "The Critique of Violent Atonement in Sherman Alexie's *Indian Killer* and David Treuer's *The Hiawatha*." *Studies in American Indian Literatures* 22, no. 4 (Winter 2010): 32–57.

Cornell, Stephen. "Discovered Identities and American Indian Supratribalism." In *We Are a People: Narrative and Multiplicity in Constructing Ethnic Identity*, edited by Paul Spickard and W. Jeffrey Burroughs, 98–123. Philadelphia: Temple University Press, 2000.

———. "That's the Story of Our Life." In *We Are a People: Narrative and Multiplicity in Constructing Ethnic Identity*, edited by Paul Spickard and W. Jeffrey Burroughs, 41–53. Philadelphia: Temple University Press, 2000.

Coulthard, Glen. *Red Skin, White Masks: Rejecting the Colonial Politics of Recognition*. Minneapolis: University of Minnesota Press, 2014.

Cox, James. *Muting White Noise: Native American and European American Novel Traditions*. Norman: University of Oklahoma Press, 2006.

———. "Muting White Noise: The Subversion of Popular Culture Narratives of Conquest in Sherman Alexie's Fiction." *Studies in American Indian Literatures* 9, no. 4 (Winter 1997): 52–70.

Cresswell, Tim. *In Place/Out of Place: Geography, Ideology, and Transgression*. Minneapolis: University of Minnesota Press, 1996.

Dailey, Tom. *Coast Salish Villages of Puget Sound*, June 16, 2015. http://coastsalishmap.org/storytelling_sites.htm.

Darby, Jaye T. "People with Strong Hearts: Staging Communitism in Hanay Geiogamah's Plays *Body Indian* and *49*." In *Native American Performance and*

Representation, edited by S. E. Wilmer, 155–70. Tucson: University of Arizona Press, 2009.

Davis, Fred. *Yearning for Yesterday: A Sociology of Identity*. New York: Free Press, 1979.

Davis, Mike. *City of Quartz: Excavating the Future in Los Angeles*. London: Verso, 1990.

Dean, Janet. "The Violence of Collection: *Indian Killer's* Archives." *Studies in American Indian Literatures* 20, no. 3 (Fall 2008): 29–51.

DeHay, Terry. "Narrating Memory." In *Memory, Narrative, and Identity: New Essays in Ethnic American Literatures*, edited by Amritjit Singh, Joseph T. Skerrett Jr., and Robert E. Hogan, 26–44. Boston: Northeastern University Press, 1994.

Deloria, Philip J. *Indians in Unexpected Places*. Lawrence: University Press of Kansas, 2004.

———. *Playing Indian*. New Haven CT: Yale University Press, 1998.

Deloria, Vine, Jr. *Custer Died for Your Sins: An Indian Manifesto*. 1969. Reprint, Norman: University of Oklahoma Press, 1988.

———. *God Is Red: A Native View of Religion*. 3rd ed. Golden CO: Fulcrum, 2003.

———. "Marginal and Submarginal." In *Indigenizing the Academy: Transforming Scholarship and Empowering Communities*, edited by Devon Abbott Mihesuah and Angela Cavender Wilson, 16–30. Lincoln: University of Nebraska Press, 2004.

Deloria, Vine, Jr., and Clifford M. Lytle. *The Nations Within: The Past and Future of American Indian Sovereignty*. New York: Pantheon, 1984.

DeLuca, Richard. "'We Hold the Rock!': The Indian Attempt to Reclaim Alcatraz Island." *California History* 62, no. 1 (1983): 2–22.

DeLugan, Robin Maria. "Indigeneity across Borders: Hemispheric Migrations and Cosmopolitan Encounters." *American Ethnologist* 37, no. 1 (2010): 83–97.

DeMallie, Raymond J., ed. *The Sixth Grandfather: Black Elk's Teachings Given to John G. Neihardt*. Lincoln: University of Nebraska Press, 1984.

Dennis, Helen May. *Native American Literature: Towards a Spatialized Reading*. London: Routledge, 2007.

Devens, Carol. *Countering Colonization: Native American Women and Great Lakes Missions, 1630–1900*. Berkeley: University of California Press, 1992.

Devereaux, Elizabeth. "*Love Medicine* Redux: New and Improved, but Why?" *Publishers Weekly*, November 23, 1992, 30.

Dimock, Wai Chee. "Deep Time: American Literature and World History." *American Literary History* 13 (2001): 755–75.

———. "A Theory of Resonance." *PMLA* 112 (1997): 1060–71.

Doerfler, Jill. "An Anishinaabe Tribalography: Investigating and Interweaving Conceptions of Identity during the 1910s on the White Earth Reservation." *American Indian Quarterly* 33, no. 3 (Summer 2009): 295–324.

Donovan, Kathleen M. *Feminist Readings of Native American Literature: Coming to Voice*. Tucson: University of Arizona Press, 1998.

Dreese, Donelle N. *Ecocriticism: Creating Self and Place in Environmental and American Indian Literatures*. New York: Lang, 2002.

Drury, Clifford Merrill. *Nine Years with the Spokane Indians: The Diary, 1838–1848, of Elkanah Walker*. Glendale CA: Arthur H. Clark, 1976.

Dubin, Lois Sherr. *The History of Beads: From 30,000 B.C. to the Present*. New York: Harry N. Abrams Publishers, 1987.

Duff, Andrew I. *Western Pueblo Identities: Regional Interaction, Migration, and Transformation*. Tucson: University of Arizona Press, 2002.

Dunn, Carolyn. "Deer Hunter." In *Outfoxing Coyote*. San Pedro CA: That Painted Horse, 2001.

DuPlessis, Rachel Blau. *The Pink Guitar: Writing as Feminist Practice*. New York: Routledge, 1990.

Ebott, Elizabeth, and Judith Rosenblatt. *Indians in Minnesota*. 4th ed. Minneapolis: University of Minnesota Press, 1985.

Egawa, Keith. *Madchild Running*. Albuquerque: University of New Mexico Press, 1999.

Ellis, Mel. *Sidewalk Indian*. New York: Holt, 1974.

Erdrich, Louise. *The Antelope Wife*. New York: Harper, 1998.

———. *The Antelope Wife: New and Revised Edition*. New York: Harper, 2012.

———. *Antelope Woman*. New York: Harper, 2016.

———. "The Art of Fiction No. 208." Interview with Lisa Halliday. *Paris Review* 195 (Winter 2010): n.p. www.theparisreview.org/interviews/6055/the-art-of-fiction-no-208-louise-erdrich.

———. *The Bingo Palace*. 1994. Reprint, New York: Harper, 2001.

———. *Books and Islands in Ojibwe Country*. Washington DC: National Geographic, 2003.

———. *Four Souls: A Novel*. New York: HarperCollins, 2004.

———. *Jacklight*. New York: Holt, 1984.

———. *Last Report on the Miracles at Little No Horse*. New York: HarperCollins, 2001.

———. *Love Medicine: New and Expanded Version*. New York: Harper, 1993.

———. *Love Medicine: Newly Revised Edition*. New York: Harper, 2009.

———. *Love Medicine: A Novel*. New York: Harper, 1984.

———. *Shadow Tag*. New York: Harper, 2010.

———. *Tales of Burning Love*. 1996. New York: Harper, 1997.

———. *Tracks*. 1988. New York: Harper, 1989.

———. "Two Languages in Mind, But Just One in the Heart." *New York Times*, May 22, 2000, E-1+. Reprinted in *North Dakota Quarterly* 67 (2000): 213–16.

————. "Where I Ought to Be: A Writer's Sense of Place." *New York Times*, July 28, 1985, 1.

Erkkila, Betsy. *Mixed Bloods and Other Crosses: Rethinking American Literature from the Revolution to the Culture Wars*. Philadelphia: University of Pennsylvania Press, 2005.

Evers, Larry. "Notes on the Deer Woman." *Indiana Folklore* 1, no. 11 (1978): 35–45.

Eyre, Chris, dir. *Smoke Signals*. Miramax, 1998. DVD, 89 minutes.

Fazio, Michele. "Homeless in Seattle: Class Violence in Sherman Alexie's *Indian Killer*." In *Critical Approaches to American Working-Class Literature*, edited by Michelle M. Tokarczyk, 141–58. New York: Routledge, 2011.

Ferrari, Rita. "'Where the Maps Stopped': The Aesthetics of Borders in Louise Erdrich's *Love Medicine* and *Tracks*." *Style* 33, no. 1 (1999): 144–64.

Finnegan, Jordana. "Refiguring Legacies of Personal and Cultural Dysfunction in Janet Campbell Hale's *Bloodlines: Odyssey of a Native Daughter*." *Studies in American Indian Literatures* 19, no. 3 (Fall 2007): 68–86.

Fisher, Lillian M. *The North American Martyrs: Jesuits in the New World*. Boston: Pauline Books, 2001.

Fisher, Philip. *Still the New World: American Literature in a Culture of Creative Destruction*. Cambridge MA: Harvard University Press, 1999.

Fitzgerald, Stephanie. "The Cultural Work of a Mohegan Painted Basket." In *Early Native Literacies in New England: A Documentary and Critical Anthology*, edited by Kristina Bross and Hilary E. Wyss, 52–56. Amherst: University of Massachusetts Press, 2008.

————. *Native Women and Land: Narratives of Dispossession and Resurgence*. Albuquerque: University of New Mexico Press, 2015.

Fitzgerald, Stephanie, and Hilary E. Wyss. "Land and Literacy: The Textualities of Native Studies." *Early American Literature* 45, no. 2 (2010): 241–50.

Fixico, Donald L. *Termination and Relocation: Federal Indian Policy, 1945–1960*. Albuquerque: University of New Mexico Press, 1986.

————. *The Urban Indian Experience in America*. Albuquerque: University of New Mexico Press, 2000.

Fogelson, Raymond D. "Perspectives on Native American Identity." In *Studying Native America: Problems and Prospects*, edited by Russell Thornton, 40–59. Madison: University of Wisconsin Press, 1998.

————. "The Red Man in the White City." In Straus, *Native Chicago*, 137–155.

Folsom, Ed. *Walt Whitman: Whitman Making Books, Books Making Whitman*. Iowa City: Obermann Center for Advanced Studies, 2005.

Forbes, Jack D. "The Urban Tradition among Native Americans." *American Indian*

Culture and Research Journal 22 (1998): 15–42. Reprinted in Lobo and Peters, *American Indians and the Urban Experience,* 5–25.

Forte, Maximilian C., ed. *Indigenous Cosmopolitans: Transnational and Transcultural Indigeneity in the Twenty-First Century.* New York: Peter Lang, 2010.

Fortunate Eagle, Adam. *Alcatraz! Alcatraz! The Indian Occupation of 1969–1971.* Berkeley CA: Heyday Books, 1992.

———. *Heart of the Rock: The Indian Invasion of Alcatraz.* Norman: University of Oklahoma Press, 2002.

Francis, Peter, Jr. *Beads and Discovery of the New World.* Occasional Papers of the Center for Bead Research No. 3. Lake Placid NY: Center for Bead Research, 1986.

Franke, Katherine M. "The Uses of History in Struggles for Racial Justice: Colonizing the Past and Managing Memory." *UCLA Law Review* 47 (2000): 1673–88.

Frazier, Gregory W. *Urban Indians: Drums from the Cities.* Denver: Arrowstar, 1993.

Fritsch, Esther, and Marion Gymnich. "'Crime Spirit': The Significance of Dreams and Ghosts in Three Contemporary Native American Crime Novels." In *Sleuthing Ethnicity: The Detective in Multiethnic Crime Fiction,* edited by Dorothea Fischer-Hornung and Monika Mueller, 204–23. Madison NJ: Fairleigh Dickinson University Press, 2003.

Fuller, Diana Burgess, and Daniela Salvioni, eds. *Art/Women/California: 1950–2000.* Berkeley: University of California Press, 2002.

Furlan, Laura M. "'Look for the Color Red': Recovering Janet Campbell Hale's *The Jailing of Cecelia Capture.*" *Intertexts* 14, no. 2 (2010): 53–71.

———. "Remapping Indian Country in Louise Erdrich's *The Antelope Wife.*" *Studies in American Indian Literatures* 19, no. 4 (Winter 2007): 54–76.

Furtwangler, Albert. *Answering Chief Seattle.* Seattle: University of Washington Press, 2012.

Gamber, John Blair. *Positive Pollutions and Cultural Toxins: Waste and Contamination in Contemporary U.S. Ethnic Literatures.* Lincoln: University of Nebraska Press, 2012.

Gansworth, Eric. *Breathing the Monster Alive.* Treadwell NY: Bright Hill, 2006.

———. *A Half-Life of Cardio-Pulmonary Function.* Syracuse NY: Syracuse University Press, 2008.

Gardner, Susan. Introduction to *Waterlily* by Ella Cara Deloria, v–xxviii. 1988. Reprint, Lincoln: University of Nebraska Press, 2009.

Garfield, Viola F., and Pamela T. Amoss. "Erna Gunther (1896–1982)." *American Anthropologist* 86, no. 2 (1984): 394–99.

Garroutte, Eva Marie. *Real Indians: Identity and the Survival of Native America.* Berkeley: University of California Press, 2003.

Geiogamah, Hanay. *New Native American Drama: Three Plays*. Norman: University of Oklahoma Press, 1980.

George, Rosemary Marangoly. *The Politics of Home: Postcolonial Relocations and Twentieth-Century Fiction*. Berkeley: University of California Press, 1999.

Gidley, Mick. *Edward S. Curtis and the North American Indian, Incorporated*. Cambridge: Cambridge University Press, 1998.

Giles, James. "The Return of John Smith: Sherman Alexie's *Indian Killer*." In *The Spaces of Violence*, 128–44. Tuscaloosa: University of Alabama Press, 2006.

Gilman, Charlotte Perkins. *The Yellow Wallpaper*. 1899. Edited by Thomas L. Erskine and Connie L. Richards. New Brunswick NJ: Rutgers University Press, 1993.

Gilroy, Paul. *The Black Atlantic: Modernity and Double Consciousness*. London: Verso, 1993.

Glancy, Diane. *Pushing the Bear: A Novel of the Trail of Tears*. San Diego: Harcourt, 1996.

Glassberg, David. "Public History and the Study of Memory." *Public Historian* 18, no. 2 (Spring 1996): 7–23.

Goeman, Mishuana R. "Disrupting a Settler-Colonial Grammar of Place: The Visual Memoir of Hulleah Tsinhnahjinnie." In *Theorizing Native Studies*, edited by Audra Simpson and Andrea Smith, 235–65. Durham NC: Duke University Press, 2014.

———. *Mark My Words: Native Women Mapping Our Nations*. Minneapolis: University of Minnesota Press, 2013.

———. "Notes toward a Native Feminism's Spatial Practice." *Wicazo Sa Review* 24, no. 2 (Fall 2009): 169–87.

Goodrich, Albert M. "Early Dakota Trails and Settlements at Centerville, Minn." In *Collections of the Minnesota Historical Society*, vol. 15. St. Paul: Minnesota Historical Society, 1915.

Goodvoice, Ed. "Relocation: Indian Life on Skid Row." In Straus, *Native Chicago*, 173–90.

Goody, Jack. "Memory in Oral Tradition." In *Memory*, edited by Patricia Fara and Karalyn Patterson, 73–94. Cambridge: Cambridge University Press, 1998.

Gordon, Avery F. *Ghostly Matters: Haunting and the Sociological Imagination*. Minneapolis: University of Minnesota Press, 1997.

Gould, Janice. *Earthquake Weather*. Tucson: University of Arizona Press, 1996.

Gramsci, Antonio. "The Intellectuals." In *Selections from the Prison Notebooks*, translated and edited by Q. Hoare and G. N. Smith, 3–23. New York: International Publishers, 1971.

Grassian, Daniel. *Understanding Sherman Alexie*. Columbia: University of South Carolina Press, 2005.

Green, Rayna. "Native American Women." *Signs: Journal of Women in Culture and Society* 6 (1980): 248–67.

———. "The Pocahontas Perplex: The Image of Indian Women in American Culture." *Massachusetts Review* 16 (1975): 698–714. Reprinted in *Unequal Sisters: A Multicultural Reader in U.S. Women's History*, edited by Ellen Carol DuBois and Vicki L. Ruiz, 15–21. New York: Routledge, 1990.

———, ed. *That's What She Said: Contemporary Poetry and Fiction by Native American Woman*. Bloomington: Indiana University Press, 1985.

———. "The Tribe Called Wannabee: Playing Indian in America and Europe." *Folklore* 99, no. 1 (Winter 1988): 30–55.

Grinde, Donald A., Jr. "Historical Narratives of Nationhood and the Semiotic Construction of Social Identity: A Native American Perspective." In *Issues in Native American Cultural Identity*, edited by Michael K. Green, 201–22. New York: Lang, 1995.

Guerrero, Marie Anna Jaimes. "Civil Rights versus Sovereignty: Native American Women in Life and Land Struggles." In *Feminist Genealogies, Colonial Legacies, Democratic Futures*, edited by M. Jacqui Alexander and Chandra Talpade Mohanty, 101–21. New York: Routledge, 1997.

Guillemin, Jeanne. *Urban Renegades: The Cultural Strategy of American Indians*. New York: Columbia University Press, 1975.

Gutiérrez-Jones, Carl. *Critical Race Narratives: A Study of Race, Rhetoric, and Injury*. New York: New York University Press, 2001.

Hafen, P. Jane. "Indigenous People and Place." In *A Companion to the Regional Literatures of America*, edited by Charles L. Crow, 154–70. Malden MA: Blackwell Publishing, 2003.

Hagemann, Fran. "Artistic Imagery of Indians on Public View in Chicago." In Straus, *Native Chicago*, 247–56.

Hale, Frederick. "Dreams and Vision Quests in Janet Campbell Hale's *The Owl's Song*." *Studies in American Indian Literatures* 12, no. 1 (Spring 2000): 69–82.

———. "In the Tradition of Native American Autobiography? Janet Campbell Hale's *Bloodlines*." *Studies in American Indian Literatures* 8, no. 1 (Spring 1996): 68–80.

———. *Janet Campbell Hale*. Boise ID: Boise State University, 1996.

———. "The Perils of Native American Urbanization and Alcoholism in Janet Campbell Hale's *The Jailing of Cecelia Capture*." *Journal of American Studies of Turkey* 8 (1998): 51–63.

Hale, Janet Campbell. *Bloodlines: Odyssey of a Native Daughter*. Tucson: University of Arizona Press, 1993.

———. *Custer Lives in Humboldt County and Other Poems*. Greenfield Center NY: Greenfield Review Press, 1978.

————. *The Jailing of Cecelia Capture*. Albuquerque: University of New Mexico Press, 1985.

————. *The Owl's Song*. Albuquerque: University of New Mexico Press, 1974.

————. *Women on the Run*. Moscow: University of Idaho Press, 1999.

Hale, Mary Thayer. *Early Minneapolis*. Minneapolis: Private printing, 1937.

Hall, Stuart. "Ethnicity: Identity and Difference." *Radical America* 23, no. 4 (October–December 1989): 9–20.

Harjo, Joy. *In Mad Love and War*. Middletown CT: Wesleyan University Press, 1990.

————. *She Had Some Horses*. New York: Thunder's Mouth Press, 1983.

Harlan, Theresa. "Indigenous Visionaries: Native Women Artists in California." In *Art/Women/California: 1950–2000*, 187–200.

Harvey, David. "Social Justice, Postmodernism, and the City." *International Journal of Urban and Regional Research* 16, no. 1 (December 1992): 588–601.

Hayden, Dolores. *The Power of Place: Urban Landscapes as Public History*. Cambridge MA: MIT Press, 1995.

Hedge Coke, Allison Adelle. *Blood Run*. Cambridge: Salt, 2006.

————. Interview with Julia Monczunski. *Food for Thought*. South Dakota Public Broadcasting. January 4, 2008.

Henry, Gordon. *The Light People: A Novel*. Norman: University of Oklahoma Press, 1994.

Herman, Matthew. *Politics and Aesthetics in Contemporary Native American Literature: Across Every Border*. New York: Routledge, 2010.

Hernández-Ávila, Inés. "Relocations upon Relocations: Home, Language, and Native American Women's Writings." *American Indian Quarterly* 19, no. 4 (Fall 1995): 491–507.

Hickerson, Harold. *The Chippewa and Their Neighbors: A Study in Ethnohistory*. New York: Holt, 1970.

Hightower-Langston, Donna. "American Indian Women's Activism in the 1960s and 1970s." *Hypatia* 18, no. 2 (Spring 2003): 114–32.

Hilden, Patricia Penn. *When Nickels Were Indians: An Urban, Mixed-Blood Story*. Washington DC: Smithsonian Institute, 1995.

Hittman, Michael, and Don Lynch. *Wovoka and the Ghost Dance*. Expanded ed. Lincoln: University of Nebraska Press, 1997.

Hobsbawm, Eric. "Introduction: Inventing Traditions." In *The Invention of Tradition*, edited by Hobsbawm and Terence Ranger, 1–14. Cambridge: Cambridge University Press, 1983.

Hogan, Linda. *Dwellings: A Spiritual History of the Living World*. New York: Simon & Schuster, 1996.

————. *Savings: Poems*. Minneapolis: Coffee House Press, 1988.

Hollrah, Patrice. "'I'm Talking Like a Twentieth-Century Indian Woman': Contemporary Female Warriors in the Works of Sherman Alexie." In *"The Old Lady Trill, the Victory Yell": The Power of Women in Native American Literature*, 133–69. New York: Routledge, 2003.

Hom, Sharon K., and Erik K. Yamamoto. "Collective Memory, History, and Social Justice." UCLA *Law Review* 47 (2000): 1747–1802.

Howe, LeAnne. "Blind Bread and the Business of Theory Making, by Embarrassed Grief." In *Reasoning Together: The Native Critics Collective*, edited by Craig S. Womack, Daniel Heath Justice, and Christopher B. Teuton, 325–39. Norman: University of Oklahoma Press, 2008.

———. "The Story of America: A Tribalography." In *Clearing a Path: Theorizing the Past in Native American Studies*, edited by Nancy Shoemaker, 29–48. New York: Routledge, 2001.

———. "Tribalography: The Power of Native Stories." *Journal of Dramatic Theory and Criticism* 14, no. 1 (Fall 1999): 117–25.

Huang, Hsinya, et al. "Charting Transnational Native American Studies." *Journal of Transnational American Studies* 4, no. 1 (2012): n.p. http://escholarship.org /uc/item/3w4347p6.

Huhndorf, Shari M. "Indigenous Feminism, Performance, and the Politics of Memory in the Plays of Monique Mojica." In *Indigenous Women and Feminism: Politics, Activism, Culture*, edited by Cheryl Suzack et al., 181–98. Vancouver: University of British Columbia Press, 2010.

———. *Mapping the Americas: The Transnational Politics of Contemporary Native Culture*. Ithaca NY: Cornell University Press, 2009.

Huhndorf, Shari M., and Cheryl Suzack. "Indigenous Feminism: Theorizing the Issues." In *Indigenous Women and Feminism: Politics, Activism, Culture*, edited by Cheryl Suzack et al., 1–17. Vancouver: University of British Columbia Press, 2010.

Hunter, Carol. "A MELUS Interview: Wendy Rose." *MELUS* 10, no. 3 (Fall 1983): 67–87.

Hutcheon, Linda. *The Politics of Postmodernism*. London: Routledge, 1989.

Igawa, Keith. *Madchild Running*. Santa Fe NM: Red Crane, 1999.

Indians of All Nations. *Alcatraz Is Not an Island*. Edited by Peter Blue Cloud. Berkeley CA: Wingbow, 1972.

Jackson, Deborah Davis. *Our Elders Lived It: American Indian Identity in the City*. Dekalb: Northern Illinois University Press, 2002.

Jackson, Robert H. "The Dynamic of Indian Demographic Collapse in the San Francisco Bay Missions, Alta California, 1775–1840." *American Indian Quarterly* 16, no. 2 (Spring 1992): 141–56.

Jacobs, Connie A. *The Novels of Louise Erdrich: Stories of Her People*. New York: Peter Lang, 2001.

James, Meredith K. "'Indians Do Not Live in Cities, They Only Reside There':
Captivity and the Urban Wilderness in *Indian Killer*." In Berglund and Roush,
Sherman Alexie: A Collection of Critical Essays, 171–85.

———. *Literary and Cinematic Reservation in Selected Works of Native American
Author Sherman Alexie*. Lewiston NY: Mellen, 2005.

Jay, Paul. "Beyond Discipline? Globalization and the Future of English." *PMLA* 116,
no. 1 (January 2001): 32–47.

———. *Contingency Blues: The Search for Foundations in American Criticism*. Madison: University of Wisconsin Press, 1997.

Jaye, Michael C., and Ann Chalmers Watts, eds. *Literature and the Urban Experience: Essays on the City and Literature*. New Brunswick NJ: Rutgers University
Press, 1981.

Joe, Jennie R., and Dorothy Lonewolf Miller. "Cultural Survival and Contemporary
American Indian Women in the City." In *Women of Color in U.S. Society*,
edited by Maxine Baca Zinn and Bonnie Thornton Dill, 185–202. Philadelphia:
Temple University Press, 1994.

Johnson, E. Pauline. *The Moccasin Maker*. 1913. Reprint, Norman: University of
Oklahoma Press, 1998.

Johnson, Jan. "Healing the Soul Wound in *Flight* and *The Absolutely True Diary of
a Part-Time Indian*." In Berglund and Roush, *Sherman Alexie: A Collection of
Critical Essays*, 224–40.

Johnson, Jay. "Dancing into Place: The Role of the Powwow within Urban Indigenous Communities." In *Indigenous in the City: Contemporary Identities and
Cultural Innovation*, edited by Evelyn Peters and Chris Anderson, 216–30.
Vancouver: University of British Columbia Press, 2013.

Johnson, Kelli Lyon. "Writing Deeper Maps: Mapmaking, Local Indigenous
Knowledges, and Literary Nationalism in Native Women's Writing." *Studies
in American Indian Literatures* 19, no. 4 (Winter 2007): 103–20.

Johnson, Troy, ed. *Alcatraz: Indian Land Forever*. Los Angeles: American Indian
Studies Center, UCLA, 1994.

———. *The Occupation of Alcatraz Island: Indian Self-Determination and the Rise of
Indian Activism*. Urbana: University of Illinois Press, 1996.

Johnson, Troy, Joane Nagel, and Duane Champagne, eds. *American Indian Activism: Alcatraz to the Longest Walk*. Urbana: University of Illinois Press, 1997.

Jones, B. J. *The Indian Child Welfare Act Handbook: A Legal Guide to the Custody and
Adoption of Native American Children*. Chicago: American Bar Association, 1995.

Kaiser, Rudolf. "Chief Seattle's Speech(es): American Origins and European Reception." In *Recovering the Word: Essays on Native American Literature*, edited by

Brian Swann and Arnold Krupat, 497–536. Berkeley: University of California Press, 1987.

Kamalakanthan, Prashanth. "The Ohlone People Were Forced Out of San Francisco. Now They Want Their Land Back." *Mother Jones*, November 22, 2014. www.motherjones.com/mojo/2014/11/ohlone-san-francisco-cultural-center.

Kaplan, Caren. *Questions of Travel: Postmodern Discourses of Displacement*. Durham NC: Duke University Press, 1996.

Keating, Ann Durkin. *Rising Up from Indian Country: The Battle of Fort Dearborn and the Birth of Chicago*. Chicago: University of Chicago Press, 2012.

Kehoe, Alice Beck. *The Ghost Dance: Ethnohistory and Revitalization*. New York: Holt, 1989.

Keith, M., and Steve Pile, eds. *Place and the Politics of Identity*. London: Routledge, 1993.

Kelsey, Penelope Myrtle. *Reading the Wampum: Essays on Hodinöhsö:ni' Visual Code and Epistemological Recovery*. Syracuse NY: Syracuse University Press, 2014.

———. *Tribal Theory in Native American Literature*. Lincoln: University of Nebraska Press, 2008.

Kleiner, Elaine, and Angela Vlaicu. "Revisioning Woman in America: A Study of Louise Erdrich's Novel *The Antelope Wife*." FEMSPEC 2, no. 2 (2001): 56–65.

Kolodny, Annette. *In Search of First Contact: The Vikings of Vinland, the Peoples of the Dawnland, and the Anglo-American Anxiety of Discovery*. Durham NC: Duke University Press, 2012.

Korpez, Esra. "The Windigo Myth in *The Antelope Wife* and *Last Standing Woman*: The Evil Within and Without." *Comparative Critical Studies* 2, no. 3 (2005): 349–63.

Kotlowski, Dean J. "Alcatraz, Wounded Knee, and Beyond: The Nixon and Ford Administrations Respond to Native American Protest." *Pacific Historical Review* 72 (2003): 201–27.

Krech, Shepard. *The Ecological Indian: Myth and History*. New York: Norton, 1999.

Kroeber, Karl. Review of *The Jailing of Cecelia Capture* by Janet Campbell Hale. *Studies in American Indian Literatures* 9, no. 4 (Winter 1985): 158–60.

Krupat, Arnold. "Chief Seattle's Speech Revisited." *American Indian Quarterly* 35, no. 2 (2011): 192–214.

———. *Red Matters: Native American Studies*. Philadelphia: University of Pennsylvania Press, 2002.

———. *Voice in the Margin: Native American Literature and the Canon*. Berkeley: University of California Press, 1989.

Lace, Ed. "Native Americans in the Chicago Area." In Straus, *Native Chicago*, 23–27.

Ladino, Jennifer. "'A Limited Range of Motion'? Multiculturalism, 'Human Questions,' and Urban Indian Identity in Sherman Alexie's *Ten Little Indians.*" *Studies in American Indian Literatures* 21, no. 3 (Fall 2009): 36–57.

LaDow, Beth. *The Medicine Line: Life and Death on a North American Borderland.* New York: Routledge, 2001.

LaDuke, Winona. *Last Standing Woman.* Stillwater MN: Voyageur Press, 1997.

LaGrand, James B. *Indian Metropolis: Native Americans in Chicago, 1945–75.* Urbana: University of Illinois Press, 2002.

Landrum, Cynthia. "Shape-Shifters, Ghosts, and Residual Power: An Examination of Northern Plains Spiritual Beliefs, Location, Objects, and Spiritual Colonialism." In Thrush and Boyd, *Phantom Past,* 255–79.

LaPier, Rosalyn R., and David R. M. Beck. *City Indian: Native American Activism in Chicago, 1893–1934.* Lincoln: University of Nebraska Press, 2015.

Larson, Charles R. *American Indian Fiction.* Albuquerque: University of New Mexico Press, 1978.

Lavie, Smadar, and Ted Swedenburg. "Introduction: Displacement, Diaspora, and Geographies of Identity." In *Displacement, Diaspora, and Geographies of Identity,* edited by Smadar Lavie and Ted Swedenburg, 1–25. Durham NC: Duke University Press, 1996.

Lawrence, Bonita. *"Real" Indians and Others: Mixed-Blood Urban Native Peoples and Indigenous Nationhood.* Lincoln: University of Nebraska Press, 2004.

Lawson, Michael L. *Dammed Indians: The Pick-Sloan Plan and the Missouri River Sioux, 1944–1980.* Norman: University of Oklahoma Press, 1982.

Lefebvre, Henri. *The Production of Space.* Chicago: Blackwell, 1991.

———. *The Urban Revolution.* 1970. Translated by Robert Bononno. Minneapolis: University of Minnesota Press, 2003.

Leibman, Laura Arnold. "A Bridge of Difference: Sherman Alexie and the Politics of Mourning." *American Literature* 77, no. 3 (Fall 2005): 541–61.

Leonard, William Edwin. *Early Days in Minneapolis.* St. Paul: Minnesota Historical Society, 1915.

Lewis, G. Malcolm, ed. *Cartographic Encounters: Perspectives on Native American Mapmaking and Map Use.* Chicago: University of Chicago Press, 1998.

Limerick, Patricia Nelson. "The Adventures of the Frontier in the Twentieth Century." In *The Frontier in American Culture,* edited by James R. Grossman, 67–102. Berkeley: University of California Press, 1994.

———. *Something in the Soil: Legacies and Reckonings in the New West.* New York: Norton, 2000.

Lincoln, Kenneth. "Indians Playing Indians." *MELUS* 16, no. 3 (Fall 1989–90): 91–98.

———. "*MELUS* Interview: Hanay Geiogamah." *MELUS* 16, no. 3 (Fall 1989–90): 69–81.

————. *Native American Renaissance*. Berkeley: University of California Press, 1983.

Lindsay, Brendan C. *Murder State: California's Native American Genocide: 1846–1873*. Lincoln: University of Nebraska Press, 2011.

Lippard, Lucy. *Mixed Blessings: New Art in a Multicultural America*. New York: New Press, 2000.

Lischke, Ute. "'Blitzkuchen': An Exploration of Story-Telling in Louise Erdrich's *The Antelope Wife*." In *Interdisciplinary and Cross-Cultural Narratives in North America*, edited by Mark Cronlund Anderson and Irene Maria F. Blayer, 61–72. Studies on Themes and Motifs in Literature, vol. 73. New York: Peter Lang, 2005.

Lister, Rachel. "'Power from the In-Between': Dialogic Encounters in *The Antelope Wife* and *The Last Report on the Miracles at Little No Horse*." In *Studies in the Literary Achievement of Louise Erdrich, Native American Writer: Fifteen Essays*, edited by Brajesh Sawhney, 213–31. Lewiston NY: Edwin Mellen Press, 2008.

Little, Jonathan. "Beading the Multicultural World: Louise Erdrich's *The Antelope Wife* and the Sacred Metaphysic." *Contemporary Literature* 41, no. 3 (Fall 2000): 495–524.

Lobo, Susan, ed. *Urban Voices: The Bay Area Indian Community*. Tucson: University of Arizona Press, 2002.

Lobo, Susan, and Kurt Peters, eds. *American Indians and the Urban Experience*. Walnut Creek CA: Altamira, 2001.

Loew, Patty. *Seventh Generation Earth Ethics: Native Voices from Wisconsin*. Madison: Wisconsin Historical Press, 2014.

Louis, Adrian. "Elegy for the Forgotten Oldsmobile." In *Fire Water World*. Albuquerque: West End Press, 1989.

Lowe, John, and Paula Holley. "Treaty of Chicago—September, 1833." In Straus, *Native Chicago*, 95–110.

Lowe, Lisa. "The Intimacies of Four Continents." In *Haunted by Empire: Geographies of Intimacy in North American History*, edited Ann Laura Stoler, 191–212. Durham NC: Duke University Press, 2005.

Lyons, Scott Richard. *X-Marks: Native Signatures of Assent*. Minneapolis: University of Minnesota Press, 2010.

Mackenzie, Kent, dir. *The Exiles*. 1961. New York: Milestone, 2008. DVD, 72 minutes.

Maddox, Lucy. *Citizen Indians: Native American Intellectuals, Race and Reform*. Ithaca NY: Cornell University Press, 2005.

Madley, Benjamin. *An American Genocide: The United States and the California Indian Catastrophe, 1846–1873*. New Haven CT: Yale University Press, 2016.

Madsen, Deborah L., ed. *Native Authenticity: Transnational Perspectives on Native American Literary Studies*. Albany: SUNY Press, 2010.

Makepeace, Anne. *Edward S. Curtis: Coming to Light*. Washington DC: National Geographic Society, 2001.

Mankiller, Wilma, and Michael Wallis. *Mankiller: A Chief and Her People*. New York: St. Martin's, 1993.

Manyarrows, Victoria Lena. "Native Women/Native Survival: A Review of Janet Campbell Hale's *The Jailing of Cecelia Capture*." In *Looking at the Words of Our People: First Nations Analysis of Literature*, edited by Jeanette Armstrong, 151–59. Penticton BC: Theytus, 1993.

Maracle, Lee. *I Am Woman*. Vancouver BC: Write-On Press, 1988.

———. *Ravensong*. Vancouver BC: Press Gang Publishers, 1994.

Mariani, Giorgio. "From Atopia to Utopia: Sherman Alexie's Interstitial Indians." In *America Today: Highways and Labyrinths*, edited by Gigliola Nocera, 582–91. Siracusa, Italy: Grafia Editrice, 2003.

———. *Post-tribal Epics: The Native American Novel between Tradition and Modernity*. Lewiston NY: Edwin Mellen Press, 1996.

Marks, Laura U. *The Skin of the Film: Intercultural Cinema, Embodiment, and the Senses*. Durham NC: Duke University Press, 2000.

Martin, Biddy, and Chandra Talpade Mohanty. "Feminist Politics: What's Home Got to Do with It?" In *Feminist Studies/Critical Studies*, edited by Teresa de Lauretis, 191–212. Bloomington: Indiana University Press, 1986.

Marx, Doug. "Sherman Alexie: A Reservation of the Mind." *Publishers Weekly*, September 16, 1996, 39–40.

Massachusetts Historical Society. *Proceedings of the Massachusetts Historical Society*, vol. 20. Boston: Massachusetts Historical Society, 1883.

Massey, Doreen B. *For Space*. Thousand Oaks CA: Sage, 2005.

———. *Space, Place, and Gender*. Minneapolis: University of Minnesota Press, 1994.

Matchie, Thomas. "*The Antelope Wife:* Louise Erdrich's 'Cloud Chamber.'" *North Dakota Quarterly* 67, no. 2 (Spring 2000): 26–37.

McGlennen, Molly. *Tribal Alliances: The Transnational Designs of Indigenous Women's Poetry*. Norman: University of Oklahoma Press, 2014.

McLeod, Neal. "Coming Home through Stories." In *(Ad)dressing Our Words: Aboriginal Perspectives on Aboriginal Literatures*, edited by Armand Garnet Ruoffo, 17–36. Penticton BC: Theytus, 2001.

McManamon, Francis P. "Policy and Practice in the Treatment of Archaeological Human Remains in North American Museum and Public Agency Collections." In *Human Remains and Museum Practice*, edited by Jack Lohman et al., 48–59. London: Museum of London, 2006.

McMaster, Gerald. "Living on Reservation X." In *Reservation X: The Power of Place in Aboriginal Contemporary Art*, edited by Gerald McMaster, 19–30. Seattle: University of Washington Press, 1998.

McMillan, Christian W. *Making Indian Law: The Hualapai Land Case and the Birth of Ethnohistory*. New Haven CT: Yale University Press, 2007.

McNally, Michael D. *Ojibwe Singers: Hymns, Grief, and a Native Culture in Motion*. New York: Oxford University Press, 2000.

McNickle, D'Arcy. *Runner in the Sun*. 1954. Reprint, Albuquerque: University of New Mexico Press, 1987.

———. *The Surrounded*. 1936. Reprint, Albuquerque: University of New Mexico Press, 1994.

Medicine, Beatrice. "Lakota Star Quilts: Commodity, Ceremony, and Economic Development." In *To Honor and Comfort: Native Quilting Traditions*, edited by Marsha L. MacDowell and C. Kurt Dewhurst, 111–17. Santa Fe: Museum of New Mexico Press, 1997.

Meeker, Ezra. *Personal Reminiscences of Puget Sound: The Tragedy of Leschi*. Seattle: Lowman and Hanford, 1905.

Meldrum, Jeff. *Sasquatch: Legend Meets Science*. New York: Forge, 2007.

Meyer, Melissa L. "'We Cannot Get a Living as We Used To': Dispossession and the White Earth Anishinaabeg 1889–1920." *American Historical Review* 96, no. 2 (1991): 368–94.

Michaelsen, Scott, and David E. Johnson. *Border Theory*. Minneapolis: University of Minnesota Press, 1997.

Mihesuah, Devon Abbott. *Indigenous American Women: Decolonialization, Empowerment, Activism*. Lincoln: University of Nebraska Press, 2003.

Miller, Carol. "Telling the Indian Urban: Representations in American Indian Fiction." In Lobo and Peters, *American Indians and the Urban Experience*, 29–45.

Miller, Christopher L., and George R. Hamell. "A New Perspective on Indian-White Contact: Cultural Symbols and Colonial Trade." *Journal of American History* 73, no. 2 (September 1986): 311–28.

Miller, Mark Edwin. *Forgotten Tribes: Unrecognized Indians and the Federal Acknowledgment Process*. Lincoln: University of Nebraska Press, 2004.

Miller, Robert J. "Exercising Cultural Self-Determination: The Makah Indian Tribe Goes Whaling." *American Indian Law Review* 25, no. 2 (2000): 165–273.

Minh-ha, Trinh T. "Not You/Like You: Post-colonial Women and the Interlocking Questions of Identity and Difference." In *Making Face, Making Soul (Haciendo Caras): Creative and Critical Perspectives by Feminists of Color*, edited by Gloria Anzaldúa, 371–75. San Francisco: Aunt Lute, 1990.

Miranda, Deborah. *Bad Indians: A Tribal Memoir*. Berkeley: Heydey, 2012.

Momaday, N. Scott. *The Ancient Child*. New York: Harper, 1989.

———. *House Made of Dawn*. 1968. New York: Harper, 1999.

———. "The Man Made of Words." In *The Remembered Earth*, edited by Geary Hobson, 162–73. Albuquerque: Red Earth Press, 1979.

———. "Native American Attitudes to the Environment." In *Seeing with a Native Eye: Essays on Native American Religion*, edited by Walter Holden Capps, 79–85. New York: Harper and Row, 1976.

———. *The Way to Rainy Mountain*. Albuquerque: University of New Mexico Press, 1969.

Mooney, James. *The Ghost Dance Religion and the Sioux Outbreak of 1890*. 1896. Reprint, Lincoln: University of Nebraska Press, 1991.

Moore, David L. "Sherman Alexie: Irony, Intimacy, and Agency." In *Cambridge Guide to Native American Literature*, edited by Joy Porter and Kenneth M. Roemer, 297–310. Cambridge: Cambridge University Press, 2005.

Moore, John H. "Truth and Tolerance in Native American Epistemology." In *Studying Native America: Problems and Prospects*, edited by Russell Thornton, 271–305. Madison: University of Wisconsin Press, 1998.

Morgan, Lewis Henry. *Ancient Society*. 1877. Ed. Leslie A. White. Reprint, Cambridge MA: Belknap–Harvard University Press, 1964.

Morgan, Murray. *Skid Road: An Informal Portrait of Seattle*. 1951. Revised ed., New York: Viking, 1960.

Morris, Irwin. *From the Glittering World*. Norman: University of Oklahoma Press, 1997.

Morrison, George, and Margot Fortunato Galt. *Turning the Feather Around: My Life in Art*. St. Paul: Minnesota Historical Society Press, 1998.

Murray, David. *Indian Giving: Economies of Power in Indian-White Exchanges*. Amherst: University of Massachusetts Press, 2000.

Nagel, Joane. *American Indian Ethnic Renewal: Red Power and the Resurgence of Identity and Culture*. New York: Oxford University Press, 1996.

Naranjo-Morse, Nora. *Mud Woman: Poems from the Clay*. Tucson: University of Arizona Press, 1992.

Neihardt, John G. *Black Elk Speaks: Being the Life Story of a Holy Man of the Oglala Sioux*. 1932. Reprint, Albany: State University of New York Press, 2008; Lincoln: University of Nebraska Press, 2014.

Neils, Elaine M. *Reservation to City: Indian Migration and Federal Relocation*. University of Chicago Department of Geography Research Paper No. 131, 1971.

Nelson, N. C. "San Francisco Bay Shellmounds." In *The California Indians: A Source Book*, edited by R. F. Heizer and M. A. Whipple, 144–57. Berkeley: University of California Press, 1971.

Nelson, Robert M. *Place and Vision: The Function of Landscape in Native American Fiction*. New York: Lang, 1993.

Nelson, Robert S., and Margaret Olin, eds. Introduction to *Monuments and Memory, Made and Unmade*, edited by Robert S. Nelson and Margaret Olin, 1–10. Chicago: University of Chicago Press, 2004.

New England's First Fruits; In Respect, First of the Conversion of Some, Conviction of Divers, Preparation of Sundry, 2. Of the Progresse of Learning, in the Colledge at Cambridge in Massacusets Bay, With Divers Other Speciall Matters concerning that Countrey. London: R. O. and G. D. for Henry Overton, 1643.

Noodin, Margaret. *Bawaajimo: A Dialect of Dreams in Anishinaabe Language and Literature.* East Lansing: Michigan State University Press, 2014.

———. "Megwa Baabaamiiaayaayaang Dibaajomoyaang: Anishinaabe Literature as Memory in Motion." In *The Oxford Handbook of Indigenous American Literature*, edited by James H. Cox and Daniel Justice, 175–84. Oxford: Oxford University Press, 2014.

Noori, Margaret. "Louise Erdrich Anishinaabezhibiiaan." In *Louise Erdrich*, edited by Jane Hafen, 105–19. Ipswich MA: Salem Press, 2010.

Nora, Pierre. "Between Memory and History: Les Lieux de Mémoire." Translated by Marc Roudebush. *Representations* 26 (Spring 1989): 7–24.

Northrup, Jim. *Walking the Rez Road.* Stillwater MN: Voyageur Press, 1993.

Omi, Michael, and Howard Winant. *Racial Formation in the United States from the 1960s to the 1990s.* 2nd ed. New York: Routledge, 1994.

Ong, Aihwa. *Flexible Citizenship: The Cultural Logics of Transnationality.* Durham NC: Duke University Press, 1999.

Ortiz, Simon. "Hunger in New York City." In *Going for the Rain: Poems*, 48. New York: Harper & Row, 1976.

———. "More Than Just a River." In *Out There Somewhere*, 107–10. Tucson: University of Arizona Press, 2002.

———. "Relocation." In *Going for the Rain: Poems*, 37. New York: Harper & Row, 1976.

———. "The San Francisco Indians." In *Men on the Moon: Collected Short Stories*, 117–22. Tucson: University of Arizona Press, 1999.

Owens, Louis. *I Hear the Train: Reflections, Inventions, Refractions.* Norman: University of Oklahoma Press, 2001.

———. *Mixedblood Messages: Literature, Film, Family, Place.* Norman: University of Oklahoma Press, 1998.

———. Review of *The Jailing of Cecelia Capture* by Janet Campbell Hale. *Western American Literature* 20, no. 4 (Winter 1986): 375–76.

Paredes, J. Anthony, ed. *Anishinabe: Six Studies of Modern Chippewa.* Tallahassee: University Press of Florida, 1980.

Parker, Emma. "Introduction: Unsettling Women." *Contemporary Women's Writing* 3, no. 1 (2009): 1–5.

Parker, Robert Dale. *The Sound the Stars Make Rushing through the Sky: The Writings of Jane Johnston Schoolcraft*. Philadelphia: University of Pennsylvania Press, 2008.

————. "Who Shot the Sheriff: Storytelling, Indian Identity, and the Marketplace of Masculinity of D'Arcy McNickle's *The Surrounded*." *Modern Fiction Studies* 43, no. 4 (Winter 1997): 898–932.

Patell, Cyrus R. K. "The Violence of Hybridity in Silko and Alexie." *Journal of American Studies of Turkey* 6 (1997): 3–9.

Patterson, Thomas Carl. *Inventing Western Civilization*. New York: Monthly Review, 1997.

Pauketat, Timothy R. *Cahokia: Ancient America's Great City on the Mississippi*. New York: Penguin, 2009.

Paulides, David. *The Hoopa Project: Bigfoot Encounters in California*. Surrey BC: Hancock House, 2008.

Pearce, Roy Harvey. *Savagism and Civilization: A Study of the Indian and the American Mind*. Berkeley: University of California Press, 1988.

Pearson-Little Thunder, Julie. "Acts of Transfer: The 1975 and 1976 Productions of *Raven* and *Body Indian* by Red Earth Performing Arts Company." In *Querying Difference in Theatre History*, edited by Ann Haugo and Scott Magelssen, 114–25. Newcastle upon Tyne: Cambridge Scholars, 2007.

Pease, Donald E. "Introduction: Re-mapping the Transnational Turn." In *Re-framing the Transnational Turn in American Studies*, edited by Winfried Fluck, Donald E. Pease, and John Carlos Rowe, 1–46. Lebanon NH: University Press of New England, 2011.

Peeren, Esther. *The Spectral Metaphor: Living Ghosts and the Agency of Invisibility*. New York: Palgrave Macmillan, 2014.

Peltier, Jerome. *A Brief History of the Coeur d'Alene Indians: 1806–1909*. Fairfield WA: Ye Galleon, 1982.

Peters, Evelyn, and Chris Andersen, eds. *Indigenous in the City: Contemporary Identities and Cultural Innovation*. Vancouver: University of British Columbia Press, 2013.

Peters, Kurt. "Continuing Identity: Laguna Pueblo Railroaders in Richmond, California." In Lobo and Peters, *American Indians and the Urban Experience*, 117–26.

Peters, Pamela J., dir. *Legacy of Exiled NDNZ*. Los Angeles: Red Wind Entertainment, 2014. DVD, 14 minutes.

Peterson, Jacqueline. "The Founding Fathers." In Straus, *Native Chicago*, 31–66.

Peterson, Nancy J., ed. *Conversations with Sherman Alexie*. Jackson: University of Mississippi Press, 2009.

————. "History, Postmodernism, and Louise Erdrich's *Tracks*." *PMLA* 109, no. 5 (1994): 982–94.

Philp, Kenneth R. "Stride toward Freedom: The Relocation of Indians to Cities, 1952–1960." *Western Historical Quarterly* 16, no. 2 (April 1985): 175–90.

Pokagon, Simon. "Red Man's Rebuke." Hartford MI: C. H. Engle, 1893.

Porsche, Michael. "John Smith in the (Post-) Colony: Hybridity and Authenticity in Sherman Alexie's *Indian Killer*." In *Wandering Selves: Essays on Migration and Multiculturalism*, edited by Christian Berkemeier, 103–12. Essen: Verlag Die Blaue Eule, 2001.

Power, Susan. "The Attic: A Family Museum." In *Home: American Writers Remember Rooms of Their Own*, edited by Sharon Sloan Fiffer and Steve Fiffer, 158–71. New York: Vintage Books, 1995.

———. "Dakota Woman." In *Riding Shotgun: Women Write about Their Mothers*, edited by Kathryn Kysar, 143–46. St. Paul: Borealis, 2008.

———. *The Grass Dancer*. New York: Putnam's, 1994.

———. "Learning to Listen: An Interview with Susan Power," by Rachel Kadish. *Ploughshares Blog*, May 5, 2012. http://blog.pshares.org/index.php/learning -to-listen-an-interview-with-susan-power/.

———. *Roofwalker*. Minneapolis: Milkweed, 2002.

———. "Roofwalker." In *Grand Mothers: Poems, Reminiscences, and Short Stories about the Keepers of Our Tradition*, edited by Nikki Giovanni, 21–38. New York: Holt, 1994.

———. *Sacred Wilderness*. East Lansing: Michigan State University Press, 2014.

———. "Stone Women." In *Going Where I'm Coming From: Memoirs of American Youth*, edited by Ann Mazer, 35–43. New York: Persea, 1995.

———. "Vision." *Granta New Writing*, August 5, 2011. http://granta.com/vision/.

Pratt, Mary Louise. *Imperial Eyes: Travel Writing and Transculturation*. New York: Routledge, 1992.

Quimby, George Irving. *Indian Culture and European Trade Goods*. Madison: University of Wisconsin Press, 1966.

Rader, Dean. *Engaged Resistance: American Indian Art, Literature and Film from Alcatraz to the NMAI*. Austin: University of Texas Press, 2011.

———. "The Epic Lyric: Genre and Contemporary American Indian Poetry." In *Speak to Me Words: Essays on Contemporary American Indian Poetry*, edited by Dean Rader and Janice Gould, 123–42. Tucson: University of Arizona Press, 2003.

———. "I Don't Speak Navajo: Esther G. Belin's *From the Belly of My Beauty*." *Studies in American Indian Literatures* 12, no. 3 (Fall 2000): 14–34.

Raheja, Michelle H. *Reservation Reelism: Redfacing, Visual Sovereignty, and Representations of Native Americans in Film*. Lincoln: University of Nebraska Press, 2011.

Ramirez, Renya K. *Native Hubs: Culture, Community, and Belonging in Silicon Valley and Beyond*. Durham NC: Duke University Press, 2007.

———. "Race, Tribal Nation, and Gender: A Native Feminist Approach to Belonging." *Meridians: Race, Feminism, Transnationalism* 7, no. 2 (2007): 22–40.

Rasmus, S. Michelle. "Repatriating Words: Local Knowledge in a Global Context." *American Indian Quarterly* 26, no. 2 (Spring 2002): 286–307.

Ray, Arthur. *Indians in the Fur Trade: Their Role as Trappers, Hunters, and Middlemen in the Southwest of Hudson Bay, 1660–1870.* Toronto: University of Toronto Press, 1998.

Redman, Samuel J. *Bone Rooms: From Scientific Racism to Human Prehistory.* Cambridge MA: Harvard University Press, 2016.

Redroad, Randy, dir. *133 Skyway.* Toronto: Big Soul Productions, 2006. DVD, 22 minutes.

Revard, Carter. *Family Matters, Tribal Affairs.* Tucson: University of Arizona Press, 1998.

———. *Winning the Dust Bowl.* Tucson: University of Arizona Press, 2001.

Reyes, Lawney L. *Bernie Whitebear: An Urban Indian's Quest for Justice.* Tucson: University of Arizona Press, 2006.

Rice, David A. "Witchery, Indigenous Resistance, and Urban Space in Leslie Marmon Silko's *Ceremony.*" *Studies in American Indian Literatures* 17, no. 4 (Winter 2005): 114–43.

"Richard Ray (Whitman)." In *Eight Native American Artists.* 27, 42–43. Fort Wayne IN: Fort Wayne Museum of Art, 1987.

Riche, Maureen. "'Waiting Halfway in Each Other's Bodies': Kinship and Corporeality in Louise Erdrich's 'Father's Milk.'" *Studies in American Indian Literatures* 25, no. 4 (Winter 2013): 48–68.

Ricoeur, Paul. *Memory, History, Forgetting.* Translated by Kathleen Blamey and David Pellauer. Chicago: University of Chicago Press, 2004.

Riedy, James L. *Chicago Sculpture.* Urbana: University of Illinois Press, 1981.

Rifkin, Mark. *When Did Indians Become Straight? Kinship, the History of Sexuality, and Native Sovereignty.* New York: Oxford University Press, 2011.

Rivard, Paul E. *A New Order of Things: How the Textile Industry Transformed New England.* Hanover NH: University Press of New England, 2002.

Robertson, Robbie. "Rattlebone." *Contact from the Underworld of Redboy.* Capitol, 1998. CD.

———. *Testimony.* New York: Crown Archetype, 2016.

Roderick, Kevin. "Modernizing 'The Exiles' Experience in Los Angeles." *LA Observed,* January 2, 2014. www.laobserved.com/archive/2014/01/updating_the_exiles_exper.php.

Roland, Walter. "Pan-American (Re)Visions: Magical Realism and Amerindian Cultures in Susan Power's *The Grass Dancer,* Gioconda Belli's *La Mujer Habitada,*

Linda Hogan's *Power*, and Mario Vargas Llosa's *El Hablador*." *American Studies International* 37, no. 3 (1999): 63–80.

Rolo, Mark Anthony. Review of *The Hiawatha* by David Treuer. *Progressive* 63, no. 10 (1999): 43.

Rose, Wendy. *Lost Copper*. Banning CA: Malki Museum Press, 1980.

Rosenthal, Nicolas G. *Reimagining Indian Country: Native American Migration and Identity in Twentieth-Century Los Angeles*. Chapel Hill: University of North Carolina Press, 2012.

Rowe, John Carlos. "Buried Alive: The Native American Political Unconscious in Louise Erdrich's Fiction." *Postcolonial Studies* 7, no. 2 (2004): 197–210.

Rubenstein, Roberta. *Home Matters: Longing and Belonging, Nostalgia and Mourning in Women's Fiction*. New York: Palgrave, 2001.

Ruby, Robert H., and John A. Brown. *A Guide to the Indian Tribes of the Pacific Northwest*. Rev. ed. Norman: University of Oklahoma Press, 1992.

Rundstrom, Robert A. "American Indian Placemaking on Alcatraz, 1969–1971." *American Indian Culture and Research Journal* 18, no. 4 (1994): 189–212.

Ruppert, James. "The Urban Reservation: Narrative, Identity, and the Postmodern City in Contemporary Native American Literature." In *Imaginary (Re-) Locations: Tradition, Modernity, and the Market in Contemporary Native American Literature and Culture*, edited by Helmbrecht Breinig, 47–62. Tübingen: Stauffenburg Verlag, 2003.

Rushing, W. Jackson, III. "Street Chiefs and Native Hosts: Richard Ray (Whitman) and Hachivi Edgar Heap of Birds Defend the Homeland." In *Green Acres: Neo-colonialism in the U.S.*, edited by Christopher Scoates, 23–42. St. Louis: Washington University Gallery of Art, 1992.

Rushing, W. Jackson, III, and Kristin Makholm. *Modern Spirit: The Art of George Morrison*. Norman: University of Oklahoma Press, 2013.

Russow, Kurt. "'Gazing at Her Cloven Feats': Mythic Tradition and 'The Sacred Way of Women' in Paula Gunn Allen's 'Deer Woman.'" *FEMSPEC* 13, no. 2 (2013): 25–39.

Said, Edward W. "Reflections on Exile." In *Reflections on Exile and Other Essays*, 173–86. Cambridge MA: Harvard University Press, 2000.

Saldívar, José David. *Border Matters: Remapping American Cultural Studies*. Berkeley: University of California Press, 1997.

Sarkowsky, Katja. *AlterNative Spaces: Constructions of Space in Native American and First Nations' Literatures*. Heidelberg: Universitätsverlag Winter, 2007.

Saunt, Claudio. *West of the Revolution: An Uncommon History of 1776*. New York: Norton, 2014.

Schell, Rev. James Peery. *In the Ojibway Country: A Story of Early Missions on the Minnesota Frontier.* Walhalla ND: Chas. H. Lee, 1911.

Schwab, Gabriele. *Haunting Legacies: Violent Histories and Trangenerational Trauma.* New York: Columbia University Press, 2010.

Schweninger, Lee. "Myth Launchings and Moon Landings: Parallel Realities in Susan Power's *The Grass Dancer.*" *Studies in American Indian Literatures* 16, no. 3 (Fall 2004): 47–69.

—. *Listening to the Land: Native American Literary Responses to the Landscape.* Athens: University of Georgia Press, 2008.

Seaburg, William R. "Whatever Happened to Thelma Adamson? A Footnote in the History of Northwestern Anthropological Research." *Northwest Anthropological Research Notes* 33, no. 1 (1999): 73–83.

Seattle/King County Coalition for the Homeless. "The 24th Annual One Night Count of People Who Are Homeless in King County, Washington." March 2003. www.homelessinfo.org/.

Seeman, Carole. "The Treaties of Puget Sound." In *Indians, Superintendents, and Councils: Northwestern Indian Policy, 1850–1855,* edited by Clifford E. Trafzer, 19–36. Lanham MD: University Press of America, 1986.

Seidel, Michael. *Exile and the Narrative Imagination.* New Haven CT: Yale University Press, 1986.

Seyhan, Azade. *Writing Outside the Nation.* Princeton NJ: Princeton University Press, 2001.

Shanley, Kathryn. "The Thinking Heart: American Indian Discourse and the Politics of Recognition." In *Race, Ethnicity, and Nationality in the United States: Toward the Twenty-First Century,* edited by Paul Wong, 256–76. Boulder CO: Westview, 1999.

—. "'Writing Indian': American Indian Literature and the Future of Native American Studies." In *Studying Native America: Problems and Prospects,* edited by Russell Thornton, 130–51. Madison: University of Wisconsin Press, 1998.

Shepherd, Jeffrey P. "At the Crossroads of Hualapai History, Memory, and American Colonization." *American Indian Quarterly* 32, no. 1 (Winter 2008): 16–42.

Shoemaker, Nancy. "Urban Indians and Ethnic Choices: American Indian Organizations in Minneapolis, 1920–50." *Western Historical Quarterly* 19, no. 4 (1988): 431–47.

Silko, Leslie Marmon. *Almanac of the Dead.* 1991. Reprint, New York: Penguin, 1992.

—. *Ceremony.* 1977. Reprint, New York: Penguin, 1986.

—. "Language and Literature from a Pueblo Indian Perspective." In *Nothing but the Truth: An Anthology of Native American Literature,* edited by John L. Purdy and James Ruppert, 159–65. Upper Saddle River NJ: Prentice Hall, 2001.

————. *Storyteller*. New York: Arcade, 1981.

Simon, Rita James, and Howard Alstein. *Transracial Adoption*. New York: Riley, 1977.

Simpson, Leanne. *Dancing on Our Turtle's Back: Stories of Nishnaabeg Re-creation, Resurgence, and a New Emergence*. Winnipeg: Arbeiter Ring, 2011.

Singh, Amritjit. Introduction to *Memory, Narrative, and Identity: New Essays in Ethnic American Literatures*, edited by Amritjit Singh, Joseph T. Skerrett Jr., and Robert E. Hogan, 3–25. Boston: Northeastern University Press, 1994.

Slotkin, Richard. *The Fatal Environment: The Myth of the Frontier in the Age of Industrialization, 1800–1890*. New York: Atheneum, 1985.

Smith, Andrea. *Conquest: Sexual Violence and American Indian Genocide*. Boston: South End Press, 2005. Reprint, Durham NC: Duke University Press, 2015.

————. "Native American Feminism, Sovereignty, and Social Change." *Feminist Studies* 31, no. 1 (Spring 2005): 116–32.

Smith, Linda Tuhiwai. *Decolonizing Methodologies: Research and Indigenous Peoples*. London: Zed Books, 1999.

Smith, Paul Chaat, and Robert Allen Warrior. *Like a Hurricane: The Indian Movement from Alcatraz to Wounded Knee*. New York: New Press, 1996.

Smoak, Gregory E. *Ghost Dances and Identity: Prophetic Religion and American Indian Ethnogenesis in the Nineteenth Century*. Berkeley: University of California Press, 2006.

Soja, Edward. *Postmodern Geographies: The Reassertion of Space in Critical Social Theory*. London: Verso, 1989.

Sorkin, Alan L. "Some Aspects of American Indian Migration." *Social Forces* 48, no. 2 (December 1969): 243–50.

————. *The Urban American Indian*. Lexington MA: Lexington, 1978.

Spahr, Clemens. "Sherman Alexie and the Limits of Storytelling." In *Native American Studies across Time and Space: Essays on the Indigenous Americas*, edited by Oliver Scheiding, 145–63. American Studies, vol. 191. Heidelberg: Universitätsverlag Winter, 2010.

Spickard, Paul, and W. Jeffrey Burroughs. "We Are a People." In *We Are a People: Narrative and Multiplicity in Constructing Ethnic Identity*, edited by Paul Spickard and W. Jeffrey Burroughs, 1–19. Philadelphia: Temple University Press, 2000.

St. Clair, Janet. "Fighting for Her Life: The Mixed-Blood Woman's Insistence upon Selfhood." In *Native American Writers*, edited by Harold Bloom, 151–59. Philadelphia: Chelsea, 1998.

Stanbury, W. T. *Success and Failure: Indians in Urban Society*. Vancouver: University of British Columbia Press, 1975.

Standing Bear, Luther. *My People the Sioux*. 1928. New ed. Lincoln: University of Nebraska Press, 2006.

Stillinger, Jack. *Coleridge and Textual Instability: The Multiple Versions of the Major Poems*. New York: Oxford University Press, 1994.

Stirrup, David. *Louise Erdrich*. Manchester: Manchester University Press, 2010.

Stokes, Karah K. "'Was Jesus an Indian?': Fighting Stories with Stories in Sherman Alexie's *Indian Killer*." *Kentucky Philological Review* 16 (2002): 44–47.

Strange, Carolyn, and Tina Loo. "'Holding the Rock': The Indianization of Alcatraz Island, 1969–1999." *Public Historian* 23, no. 1 (2001): 27–54.

Straus, Terry. "Founding Mothers." In Straus, *Native Chicago*, 67–77.

———, ed. *Native Chicago*. 2nd ed. Chicago: Albatross, 2002.

Stromberg, Ernest. "*The Jailing of Cecelia Capture* and the Rhetoric of Individualism." *MELUS* 28, no. 4 (Winter 2003): 101–23.

Suzack, Cheryl. "Land Claims, Identity Claims: Mapping Indigenous Feminism in Literary Criticism and in Winona LaDuke's *Last Standing Woman*." In *Reasoning Together: The Native Critics Collective*, edited by Craig S. Womack, Daniel Heath Justice, and Christopher B. Teuton, 169–92. Norman: University of Oklahoma Press, 2008.

Tapahonso, Luci. *Blue Horses Rush In: Poems and Stories*. Tucson: University of Arizona Press, 1997.

———. *A Radiant Curve: Poems and Stories*. Tucson: University of Arizona Press, 2008.

———. *Sáanii Dahataa, The Women Are Singing: Poems and Stories*. Tucson: University of Arizona Press, 1993.

Tatonetti, Lisa. "Dancing That Way, Things Began to Change." In Berglund and Roush, *Sherman Alexie: A Collection of Critical Essays*, 1–24.

———. *The Queerness of Native American Literature*. Minneapolis: University of Minnesota Press, 2014.

Tax, Sol. "The Impact of Urbanization on American Indians." *Annals of the American Academy of Political and Social Science* 436 (1978): 121–36.

Teuton, Christopher B. "The Cycle of Removal and Return: A Symbolic Geography of Indigenous Literature." *Canadian Journal of Native Studies* 29, no. 1–2 (2009): 45–64.

Teuton, Sean Kicummah. *Red Land, Red Power: Grounding Knowledge in the American Indian Novel*. Durham NC: Duke University Press, 2008.

Tharp, Julie. "Windigo Ways: Eating and Excess in Louise Erdrich's *The Antelope Wife*." *American Indian Culture and Research Journal* 27, no. 4 (2003): 117–31.

Thornton, Russell. *The Urbanization of American Indians: A Critical Bibliography*. Bloomington: Indiana University Press, 1982.

Thrush, Coll. "Hauntings as Histories." In Thrush and Boyd, *Phantom Past*, 54–81.

———. *Native Seattle: Histories from the Crossing-Over Place*. Seattle: University of Washington Press, 2007.

Thrush, Coll, and Colleen E. Boyd, eds. *Phantom Past, Indigenous Present: Native Ghosts in North American Culture and History*. Lincoln: University of Nebraska Press, 2011.

Tohe, Laura. "There Is No Word for Feminism in My Language." *Wicazo Sa Review* 15, no. 2 (Fall 2000): 103–10.

Torrey, E. Fuller. *American Psychosis: How the Federal Government Destroyed the Mental Illness Treatment System*. New York: Oxford, 2014.

Treuer, Anton. *Ojibwe in Minnesota*. Minneapolis: Minnesota Historical Society, 2010.

Treuer, David. *The Hiawatha*. New York: Picador, 1999.

———. *Native American Fiction: A User's Manual*. Minneapolis: Graywolf Press, 2006.

———. "Reading Culture." *Studies in American Indian Literatures* 14, no. 1 (Spring 2002): 51–64.

———. "Smartberries: Interpreting Louise Erdrich's *Love Medicine*." *American Indian Culture and Research Journal* 29, no. 1 (2005): 21–36.

A Tribe Called Red. "Woodcarver." *A Tribe Called Red*. Radicalized Records, 2012. CD.

Tuan, Yi-Fu. *Topophilia: A Study of Environmental Perception, Attitudes, and Values*. Englewood Cliffs NJ: Prentice-Hall, 1974.

TuSmith, Bonnie. *All My Relatives: Community in Contemporary Ethnic American Literatures*. Ann Arbor: University of Michigan Press, 1993.

Two-Rivers, Ed. "Red Path Theater." In Straus, *Native Chicago*, 335–36.

Two-Rivers, E. Donald. *Briefcase Warriors*. Norman: University of Oklahoma Press, 2001.

———. *Pow Wows, Fat Cats, and Other Indian Tales*. Lawrence KS: Mammoth, 2009.

———. *Survivor's Medicine: Short Stories*. Norman: University of Oklahoma Press, 1998

Upham, Warren. *Minnesota Geographic Names: Their Origin and Historic Significance*. Vol. 17. Minneapolis: Minnesota Historical Society, 1920.

United States, Department of Commerce, Census Bureau. The American Indian and Alaska Native Population, 2000.

———. DP-1. Profile of General Demographic Characteristics: 2000. Geographic Area: Minneapolis City, Hennepin County, Minnesota.

United States, Department of State, Bureau of Foreign and Domestic Commerce. *Commercial Relations of the United States with Foreign Countries*. Vol. 1. Washington DC: Government Printing Office, 1886.

Valaskakis, Gail Guthrie. "Indian Country: Negotiating the Meaning of Land in Native America." In *Disciplinarity and Dissent in Cultural Studies*, edited by Cary Nelson and Dilip Parameshwar Gaonkar, 149–169. New York: Routledge, 1996.

Van De Mark, Dorothy. "The Raid on the Reservations." *Harpers* 212 (March 1956): 45–55.

Van Dyke, Annette. "Encounters with Deer Woman: Sexual Relations in Susan

Power's *The Grass Dancer* and Louise Erdrich's *The Antelope Wife.*" *Studies in American Indian Literatures* 15, no. 3/4 (Fall 2003/Winter 2004): 168–88.

Van Ginkel, Rob. "The Makah Whale Hunt and Leviathan's Death: Reinventing Tradition and Disputing Authenticity in the Age of Modernity." *Etnofoor* 17, no. 1–2 (2004): 58–89.

Van Styvendale, Nancy. "The Trans/Historicity of Trauma in Jeannette Armstrong's *Slash* and Sherman Alexie's *Indian Killer.*" *Studies in the Novel* 40, no. 1–2 (Spring–Summer 2008): 203–23.

Vaughan, Alden T. *New England Frontier: Puritans and Indians 1620–1675.* Boston: Little, Brown, 1965.

Velie, Alan R. "The Rise and Fall of the Red Power Movement." *European Review of Native American Studies* 13, no. 1 (1999): 1–8.

Viejo-Rose, Dacia. "Memorial Functions: Intent, Impact, and the Right to Remember." *Memory Studies* 4, no. 4 (2011): 465–80.

Vizenor, Gerald. "Aesthetics of Survivance: Literary Theory and Practice." In *Survivance: Narratives of Native Presence,* edited by Gerald Vizenor, 1–24. Lincoln: University of Nebraska Press, 2008.

———. *Dead Voices: Natural Agonies in the New World.* Norman: University of Oklahoma Press, 1992.

———. *Fugitive Poses: Native American Indian Scenes of Absence and Presence.* Lincoln: University of Nebraska Press, 1998.

———. "Literary Transmotion: Survivance and Totemic Motion in Native American Indian Art and Literature." In *Twenty-First Century Perspectives on Indigenous Studies: Native North America in (Trans)Motion,* edited by Birgit Däwes et al., 17–30. New York: Routledge, 2015.

———. *Manifest Manners: Narratives on Postindian Survivance.* Lincoln: University of Nebraska Press, 1999.

———. *Native Liberty: Natural Reason and Cultural Survivance.* Lincoln: University of Nebraska Press, 2009.

———. *Wordarrows: Indians and Whites in the New Fur Trade.* Minneapolis: University of Minnesota Press, 1978.

Waddell, Jack O., and O. Michael Watson, eds. *The American Indian in Urban Society.* Boston: Little, Brown, 1971.

Walker, Deward E., Jr. *Indians of Idaho.* Moscow: University Press of Idaho, 1978.

Walker, James R. *Lakota Belief and Ritual.* Edited by Raymond J. DeMallie and Elaine A. Jahner. Lincoln: University of Nebraska Press, 1980.

Walsh, Dennis. "The Place of Janet Campbell Hale and Sherman Alexie in American Indian Literature." *Tough Paradise: The Literature of Idaho and the Intermountain West* (1995): 24–26.

Walters, Ana Lee. *Ghost Singer*. Albuquerque: University of New Mexico Press, 1988.

Warren, William W. *History of the Ojibway People*. 1885. Reprint, St. Paul: Minnesota Historical Society, 1984.

Warrior, Robert. "Native American Studies and the Transnational Turn." *Cultural Studies Review* 15, no. 2 (September 2009): 119–30.

Watson, Julia. "Writing in Blood: Autobiography and Technologies of the Real in Janet Campbell Hale's *Bloodlines*." In *Haunting Violations: Feminist Criticism and the Crisis of the "Real,"* edited by Wendy S. Hesford and Wendy Kozol, 111–36. Urbana: University of Illinois Press, 2001.

Wax, Murray T., and Robert W. Buchanan, eds. *Solving "The Indian Problem": The White Man's Burdensome Business*. New York: New York Times Book Company, 1975.

Weaver, Jace. *That the People Might Live: Native American Literatures and Native American Community*. New York: Oxford University Press, 1997.

Weibel-Orlando, Joan. *Indian Country, L.A.: Maintaining Community in Complex Society*. Rev. ed. Urbana: University of Illinois Press, 1999.

Welch, James. *The Death of Jim Loney*. New York: Penguin, 1979.

———. *The Heartsong of Charging Elk*. New York: Anchor, 2001.

———. *The Indian Lawyer*. 1990. Reprint, New York: Norton, 2007.

———. *Winter in the Blood*. New York: Harper & Row, 1974.

White, Richard. *The Roots of Dependency: Subsistence, Environment, and Social Change among the Choctaws, Pawnees, and Navajos*. Lincoln: University of Nebraska Press, 1983.

———. "What Is Spatial History?" *The Spatial History Project*, 2010, http://web.stanford.edu/group/spatialhistory/cgi-bin/site/pub.php?id=29.

White Hat, Albert, Sr. *Reading and Writing the Lakota Language*. Salt Lake City: University of Utah Press, 1999.

Whitman, Richard Ray. Interview by Larry Abbott, *A Time of Visions*, June 20, 2016, http://www.britesites.com/native_artist_interviews/rwhitman.htm.

Whitt, Laurie Anne. "Indigenous Peoples and the Cultural Politics of Knowledge." In *Issues in Native American Cultural Identity*, edited by Michael K. Green, 223–72. New York: Lang, 1995.

"Why Did Gloria Die?" *Bill Moyers Journal*. PBS, 1973. Videocassette.

Wildcat, Daniel R. "Indigenizing the Future: Why We Must Think Spatially in the Twenty-First Century." In *Destroying Dogma: Vine Deloria, Jr. and His Influence on American Society*, edited by Steve Pavlik and Daniel R. Wildcat, 131–56. Golden CO: Fulcrum, 2006.

Willard, William. "Outing, Relocation, and Employment Assistance: The Impact of Federal Indian Population Dispersal Programs in the Bay Area." *Wicazo Sa Review* 12, no. 1 (Spring 1997): 29–46.

Wilson, Angela Cavender. "Reclaiming Our Humanity: Decolonization and the Recovery of Indigenous Knowledge." In *Indigenizing the Academy: Transforming Scholarship and Empowering Communities*, edited by Devon Abbott Mihesuah and Angela Cavender Wilson, 69–87. Lincoln: University of Nebraska Press, 2004.

Wilson, Michael D. *Writing Home: Indigenous Narratives of Resistance*. East Lansing: Michigan State University Press, 2008.

Wilson, Natalia. "The Chicago Indian Village, 1970." In Straus, *Native Chicago*, 212–19.

Woloson, Wendy A. *In Hock: Pawning in America from Independence through the Great Depression*. Chicago: University of Chicago Press, 2009.

Womack, Craig S. *Red on Red: Native American Literary Separatism*. Minneapolis: University of Minnesota Press, 1999.

Woolf, Virginia. "Professions for Women." In *The Death of the Moth, and Other Essays*, 235–42. New York: Harcourt Brace Jovanovich, 1942.

Wright, Neil H. "Visitors from the Spirit Path: Tribal Magic in Susan Power's *The Grass Dancer*." *Kentucky Philological Review* 10 (1995): 39–43.

Yeahapu, Thomas. *X-Indian Chronicles: The Book of Mausape*. Somerville MA: Candlewick, 2006.

Young, James E. *The Texture of Memory: Holocaust Memorial and Meaning*. New Haven CT: Yale University Press, 1993.

Young Bear, Ray A. *Black Eagle Child: The Facepaint Narratives*. Iowa City: University of Iowa Press, 1992.

Zitkala-Ša. *American Indian Stories, Legends, and Other Writings*. 1921. Reprint, New York: Penguin, 2003.

Žižek, Slavoj. *Looking Awry: An Introduction to Jacques Lacan through Popular Culture*. Rev. ed. Cambridge MA: MIT Press, 1992.

alcohol abuse, 6, 12, 40, 63, 65, 196, 207
Aleuts, 117–18
Alexie, Sherman, 1, 27; about, 77,
    238n2, 239nn12–13; *Absolutely*
    True Diary of a Part-Time Indian,
    76, 120, 150, 248n132, 251n192,
    252n224, 252–53n226; *Business*
    of Fancydancing, 76, 84–85, 129,
    250n156; class in works of, 24, 77,
    91, 239n14, 248n136; conclusions
    on, 127–30; divide between urban
    and reservation Natives and, 84–
    85, 241nn43–44; "Freaks," 75–76,
    105; Ghost Dance and, 85–86, 87,
    110–12, 121–22, 126, 130, 243n61;
    homelessness and, 75–77, 82–84,
    86, 87, 103, 239n8; *Lone Ranger and*
    Tonto Fistfight in Heaven, 84, 85,
    129, 238n2, 241n40; overview of
    writings of, 75–77, 82–89, 238n4;
    "Pawn Shop," 116–17, 129; polit-
    ical issues and, 83, 241n34; *Real*
    Change interviews of, 77, 239n8;
    Reservation Blues, 84, 85, 252n218;
    "Sasquatch Poems," 94; *Summer*
    of Black Widows, 94; *Ten Little*
    Indians, 76, 83, 112, 241n35. See
    also *Flight* (Alexie); *Indian Killer*
    (Alexie); "What You Pawn I Will
    Redeem" (Alexie)
Alfred, Taiaiake, 40, 73, 231n16,
    235n87
aliens, 195, 275n129
Allen, Chadwick, 25–26, 93, 120, 138–
    39, 234n73
Allen, John, 80
Allen, Paula Gunn, 2, 38, 46, 131, 217,
    223–24n8
Alley Allies (Whitman), 127, 128

All Tribes American Indian Center,
    176, 270n28
Almanac of the Dead (Silko), 264n129,
    275–76n145
Almost Soup (character), 133, 152,
    256n15, 258n30, 258n34
alternative histories, 177. *See also*
    reconstruction of histories
American Indian Association and
    Tepee Order Club, 137
American Indian Center: in Chicago,
    169, 270n28; in *Jailing*, 53, 54; in
    Los Angeles, 270n27; in Minneapo-
    lis, 141, 142, 163–64, 164, 267n190,
    267n192; in San Francisco, 44,
    235n78; in "San Francisco Indians,"
    52; in Susan Power works, 172, 177,
    186, 189–90, 274n100
American Indian Hearse Service, 151
American Indian Historical Society, 43
American Indian Movement (AIM), 18,
    34, 137, 138, 141, 166, 185, 259n45
American Indians, Inc., 138
American Indian Theater Ensemble, 5
The Ancient Child (Momaday), 231n5
Anderson, Eric Gary, 147, 201
Andersson, Rani-Henrik, 85
Angeline, Princess, 79, 108, 240n21,
    240n26
Anglicizing names, 48
"Angry Fish" (Power), 194–96, 197,
    202, 208
Anishinaabeg, 134–35, 148. *See also*
    Ojibwes
The Antelope Wife/The Antelope
    Woman (Erdrich): background and
    overview of, 34, 131–40, 254–55n1,
    256nn11–12, 257nn17–18, 257n21,
    257n25; bakery in, 143–44, 158;

cars, 3–4, 224n10

Catholics and Natives, 41, 64, 101

Cecelia Capture (character), 33, 37, 39, 72, 73; activism and, 63–64, 69; father's influences on, 65–67; home and, 46, 47–52, 55–56; identity and, 40–41, 56–57, 67; urban Natives and, 53–54; white people and, 67–68; womanhood and, 57, 58–63

Cecille (character), 152, 158

Ceremony (Silko), 21, 30–31, 110, 229n112

Certeau, Michel de, 12, 24, 76, 111, 210

Chadwick, Whitney, 37

Chapel of the North American Martyrs, 100–101

Charles Bad Holy McLeod (character), 207–8

Chavkin, Allan, 134, 166

Cheeshateaumuck, Caleb, 181–82, 271n51

Cheyenne River Reservation, 205

Chicago Arts Group, 169, 171

Chicago Historical Society, 34–35, 174, 182–83

Chicago IL: about, 169, 172–76, 209–10, 269n16, 270n25, 270n28; *Fort Dearborn Massacre* monument and, 182–85, 272nn64–65; in *Grass Dancer*, 172; Lake Michigan and, 173, 202–4, 206–7, 269n13; name of, 170, 268n2; Natives and, 195; in *Roofwalker*, 34, 172

Chicago Indian Village (CIV) movement, 176

Chicago Transit Authority (CTA), 198–200

Chicago Tribune, 182

"Chicago Waters" (Power), 203

Chief-of-All-Women totem pole, 80, 118, 240n25

Chief Seattle: bones and burial of, 98–99, 247n118, 247nn120; sculpture of, 80, 81, 82, 240n26; speech of, 34, 86–87, 112, 130, 230n120, 242–43n56, 243n58; Treaty of Point Elliott and, 108, 240n20

Chief Seattle Club, 78, 239n15

Chief Seattle Fountain (Wehn), 80, 81, 82, 240n26

Child Welfare League of America, 253n228

Chili Corn (Two-Rivers), 184–85, 272n67

Choris, Louise, 71

Chouart, Médard, 135

Christian Science Monitor, 12–13

Christie, Stuart, 92, 244–45n87, 248n139

chronology, lack of, 177, 201, 202

cinema, intercultural, 161–62

citizenship, 23, 65, 137–38

citizenship rights, tribal, 27, 228n94

City Indian (LaPier and Beck), 175

City of Quartz (Davis), 24

city space: activism and, 12, 16, 17, 18–19, 24–25, 31, 227n57; as a place of empowerment, 113, 251n189; destructiveness of, 30, 33; identity and, 7, 53; movement and, 132, 255n5; Native spaces in, 31–32, 230n116; studies on Natives in, 137, 259nn38–39; views on Natives not belonging in, 20–21

"civilizing" Natives, 20, 182

Clarence Mather (character), 96, 97–99, 110

DeLugan, Robin, 139, 178
Denny, David, 107
Des Groseilliers, Sieur, 135
de Soto, Hernando, 135
diaspora, 26, 27, 28, 40, 155, 219
Dimock, Wai Chee, 11, 132, 225n31, 256n12
disease, 41–42
displacement, 7, 13, 83, 126, 127. *See also* relocation of Natives
dispossession, 23, 24–25, 33, 76, 83, 130
diversity of urban experience, 7, 169, 172, 178, 211
divide between urban and reservation Natives, 84–85, 241n41, 241nn43–44
Dock 47, 118
Donovan, Kathleen, 57
Dorris, Michael, 133, 257n18
Double Woman, 193
Dubin, Lois Sherr, 159
Duhaut-Cilly, Auguste, 71
Dunn, Carolyn, 131
DuPlessis, Rachel Blau, 167
Duwamish, 79, 108–9, 111, 117, 240n20, 250n168, 252n209

Eagle Capture (character), 65
Edna Pontellier (character), 63
the El, 198, *199*
Eliot, John, 180
Eliot, S. A., 80
Eliot Tracts, 180
Elliott Bay, 244n84
Ellis, Mel, 231n8
employment program for Native veterans, 14–15
engaged resistance, 34, 127
Engler, Robert Klein, 184

En Route (Yepa-Pappan), 200, 275n144
Entering Zig's Reservation (Jackson), 230n2
Erdrich, Aza, 255n1, 267n198
Erdrich, Louise, 256n11, 256n15; *Beet Queen*, 158, 255n5; *Bingo Palace*, 255n5, 262n106, 263n110, 264n126; *Books and Islands in Ojibwe Country*, 152, 156, 162–63, 164–65; *Four Souls*, 133, 136, 142, 154, 166, 257nn16–17; *Last Report at Little No Horse*, 133; *Love Medicine*, 134, 148, 166, 255n5, 256n15, 257n17, 262n106, 263n110; *Master Butchers Singing Club*, 158, 255n5; *Round House*, 257n17; "Strange People," 131, 145; *Tracks*, 133, 142, 148, 154, 198, 257nn16–17; "Two Languages in Mind, but Just One in the Heart," 167; "Where I Ought to Be," 132. See also *The Antelope Wife/The Antelope Woman* (Erdrich)
Escape from the Planet of the Apes, 108
exile, definition of, 4, 224n12
The Exiles (Mackenzie), 5, 11, 31; about and overview of, 1–2, 3–5, 6–7, 9–11, 216, 223nn2–5, 224n9; embedded histories in, 9–11, 225n27; *Legacy of Exiled NDNZ* and, 213–14, 216–17; place in, 4–5, 7, 11

Fairey, Shepard, 214, *215*, 278n3
Fassler, Joe, 85
Father Duncan (character), 100–101, 248n128, 248n132
Fazio, Michele, 239n14, 244n75, 248n136
feminism, 46, 47, 55, 57–58, 233n55
Ferrari, Rita, 148, 167, 256n15

Field Museum, 175, 184, 185–86, 269nn20–21, 272n71, 272n74

fires: Great Chicago, 174, 203; in Seattle, 79; Standing Rock, 204–6

"First Fruits" (Power), 179–82, 185–86, 193–94, 204, 205, 206, 270–71n41

First Fruits album (Melvin), 271n45

First Fruits pamphlet, 180, 194

First People, Second City (Pappan and Yepa-Pappan), 210, 275n144

fishing, 105–6, 250n168

fish-ins, 18, 106, 138

Fitzgerald, Stephanie, 193

Fixico, Donald L., 15, 226n40, 259n39

Flaherty, Robert, 223n4, 223n6

Fleur Pillager (character), 133, 142, 143

Flight (Alexie), 120–26; bird in, 124, 254n240; conclusion of, 126; Ghost Dance in, 121–22, 126; homeless father episode in, 123–25; movement in, 125–26, 253–54n240; national story of, 123; overview of, 33–34, 76, 82, 86, 241n39; time travel in, 122–23, 125

fluidity of Native life, 148, 166

Folk-Tales of the Coast Salish (Adamson), 98

Folsom, Ed, 166

Ford Thunderbird, 3

Fort Dearborn, 173–74, 271n57

Fort Dearborn Massacre, 173–74

Fort Dearborn Massacre monument, 174, 182–85, 272nn64–65

Fort Lawton, 240n19

Fort Ross Colony, 42

Fort St. Anthony, 136

foster families, 121

Four Souls (Erdrich), 133, 136, 142, 154, 166, 257nn16–17

Four Winds Club, 44

Fragua, Jaque, 13

Franklin, L. B., 240n26

Franklin Avenue, 138, *142*, 143, 259n45, 260n63, 261n65

Frank Shawano (character), 133–34, 143–44, 150, 158–59, 261n69, 262n83, 265n159

"Freaks" (Alexie), 75–76, 105

Free Speech Movement, 44

fry bread, 158

Gakahbekong, 132, 141, 162, 256n11. *See also* Minneapolis MN

garbage, 154

García, René, 69, *70*

Geiogamah, Hanay, 5–7, 224n13

gender, 46, 57–63, 236n96

genocide of California Natives, 42, 232nn28–30

genres, crossing, 200–202, 204, 276n149

Georgiana Lorraine Shoestring (character), 179, 181–82, 186, 194, 204, 205

German prisoner (character), 158, 265n159

Germans and Ojibwes, 158

Geronimo, 4

Ghost Dance: about, 85, 242n49, 242n53; Alcatraz occupation and, 69; in *Roofwalker*, 187, 196–97; Wounded Knee and, 48, 68, 85, 187, 234n61. *See also* Ghost Dance in Sherman Alexie

Ghost Dance in Sherman Alexie, 77, 85–86, 87, 129–30; in *Flight*, 121–22, 126; in *Indian Killer*, 85–86, 89–90, 99–100, 110–12, 239n7; in "What You Pawn," 113, 119, 120

Ghost Dance shirt, 196–97, 207
Ghostly Matters (Gordon), 88
ghosts, 88, 102, 108, 242n54,
    249n143; in Chief Seattle speech,
    87, 130, 243n58. *See also* ghosts in
    Sherman Alexie
ghosts in Sherman Alexie, 86, 87–89,
    111, 130; in *Flight*, 86, 122–23, 126;
    in *Indian Killer*, 94–101, 104, 105,
    109–10, 112, 118–19; in "What You
    Pawn," 118–19, 120
Giizis (character), 134, 141, 149, 150
Gilman, Charlotte Perkins, 55
Gilman, Daniel, 92
Gilmore, Josephine Parkhurst, 191–92
Gilroy, Paul, 26
Glassberg, David, 179
Goeman, Mishuana, 91, 186, 244n82
Gordon, Avery, 88, 99
Gould, Janice, 56
graffiti, 69, 71, 141, *142*, 237–38n157,
    260n55
The Grass Dancer (Power), 153, 170–72,
    178, 203, 207–8, 210, 269n5–6,
    269n9, 272n74
grass dancing, 170, 269n6
"Gravity" (Alexie), 129
Great Fire of 1871, 174, 203, 207
Great Northern Railroad, 260n62
Green, Rayna, 46, 60–61
Green Acres: Neo-colonialism in the U.S.
    show, 127
Greysolon, Daniel, 135
Guardian, 129
Gunther, Erna, 98, 247n115
Gus (character), 122–23

haircutting, 59
Hale, Frederick, 40

Hale, Janet Campbell. See *The Jailing
    of Cecelia Capture* (Hale)
Hall, Stuart, 167, 210
Hank Storm (character), 122–23
Hansen, Cecille, 109
Harjo, Joy, 38, 58, 131
Harlan, Theresa, 38
Harris, Tim, 77
Harvard, John, 179–80
Harvard College, 179–82, 186, 194
Harvey, David, 24
Haudenosaunee artists, 193
Heap of Birds, Hock E Aye Vi Edgar,
    80, *81, 82*, 86, 87, 240n26
Hedge Coke, Allison, 22, 228n70
Hennepin, Louis, 135
Henry Bullhead (character), 188, 204,
    273n87
Hernández-Avila, Inés, 46
hero plot, 45
Herring's House, 79
heyokas, 204
The Hiawatha (Treuer), 136–37, 143,
    260n63
Hickerson, Harold, 135
Hillaire, Joe, 80
Hill X, 1, 4–5, *5*
hippies, 52–53, 59
historical convergence in *Roofwalker*,
    186–92, 273n80, 273n93
Hobsbawm, Eric, 264n132
Hollywood Reelism (Raheja), 223n6
home, 7, 8–9; diaspora and, 27–28;
    in *Jailing*, 32, 45–52, 54–55, 72;
    in *Roofwalker*, 205; in Sherman
    Alexie, 81, 123, 126, 129
homelessness, 33–34, 80–81; in *Ante-
    lope Wife*, 145, 146–47; in *Flight*,
    121, 124–25; humanizing, 83–84,

Indigenous cosmopolitanism, 178
Indigenous Peoples' Day, 238n160, 239n13
indis, 151–52, 263nn117–18, 273n93
intercultural cinema, 161–62
interstice, 249n140
intertribal coalition, 5, 16–17, 19, 102, 109, 226n50
Intertribal Friendship House, 17, 44
intertribalism, 7, 16–17, 44, 54, 226n50
in transit, 140
invisibility of urban Natives, 53, 91, 198
Irene Muse (character), 117

Jackson, Robert H., 41
Jackson, Zig, 230n2
Jackson Jackson (character), 33, 76–77, 81, 86, 113–16, 117, 118–20, 125
Jack Wilson (character), 91, 96–97, 103–4, 105
Jacobs, Melville, 98
The Jailing of Cecelia Capture (Hale): activism in, 63–64, 68–69, 71–73; body image in, 60; captivity in, 46–47, 48, 55, 60, 63, 69, 72; ethnic identity and, 56–57; home and, 46–52, 55–56; indictment of white people in, 67–68; law and law school in, 65–67; overview of, 32, 33, 39–41, 45–46, 72–73, 231n10, 234n64; place in, 47–49, 72–73; urban Natives and, 53–54; womanhood and, 57, 58–63
James, Meredith K., 239n7, 241n43
Jay, Paul, 27
Jay Treaty, 163
Jessie (character), 186–87, 273n80
Jesuits martyred by Indians, 100, 248n130

Jim Loney (character), 110, 250–51n177
Jimmy Badger (character), 145, 161
Jimmy the pilot (character), 122–23
John Harvard statue, 179–80
John James Mauser (character), 142–43, 260n62
John Smith (character): about, 89, 92–93, 101, 243n71, 244–45n87, 245n91, 248n132, 248n137, 248n139; compared to Zits, 121, 124, 125, 126; ghosts and, 100, 109; mobility and, 91; place and space and, 90, 93, 94
Johnson, E. Pauline, 30, 235n95
Junior (character), 115, 117, 118, 251n192
Justice (character), 86, 121

Kasota, 144
Keating, Ann Durkin, 184
Keep America Beautiful commercial, 21
Kelly, Colvin, 196–97
Kelsey, Penelope, 193
Kim, Haena, 71
King (character), 102, 104–5, 106
Kinzie, John, 174
Kinzie, Juliette, 174
Klaus Shawano (character), 144–45, 153, 154, 156–58, 161, 164, 262n83
Kroeber, Karl, 42
Krupat, Arnold, 29, 250n168, 251n181
Kuo, Alex, 101
Kwandibens, Nadya, 230n2

Ladino, Jennifer, 83, 241n35, 251n189
LaDuke, Winona, 131
Lagunas, 44
Lake Michigan, 173, 202–4, 206–7, 269n13
Lake Oahe, 205

Morgan, Lewis Henry, 8

Morrison, George, 163–64, *164,* 267nn188–90, 267n192

The Mother (Curtis), 37

motherhood, 57–60, 63

Mother's Kitchen, 115, 252n199

movement and mobility, 7, 30, 32, 39; in *Antelope Wife,* 131–32, 138–40, 143–44, 146–50, 164–65; in *Exiles,* 3–4, 5, 6, 7, 10; in *Flight,* 125–26, 253–54n240; in *Indian Killer,* 90, 91, 118, 120; in *Indian Land Dancing,* 170; Indigeneity and, 139–40; in *Legacy of Exiled NDNZ,* 217; transnationalism and, 25–26; in *Turning the Feather Around,* 164

Moyers, Bill, 12, 219

multigenre work, 201–9

murals: *Indian Land Dancing,* 169–70, *171,* 209–10, 268n1, 268n3, 270n28; *Turning the Feather Around,* 163–64, *164,* 267n190, 267n192; *We Are Still Here,* 214, *215,* 278n3

"Museum Indians" (Power), 184, 185–86, 191

Muwekma Ohlones, 43, 233n39

"My Encounters with the Homeless People of the Pacific Northwest" (Alexie), 77

Myer, Dillon, 14

My People the Sioux (Standing Bear), 30

names used as place names, Native, 91–92, 244n83

Nanook of the North (Flaherty), 223n6

"Narrating Memory" (DeHay), 177

Narrative of the Massacre at Chicago (Kinzie), 174

narrators: in Louise Erdrich works, 133, 256n15; in Susan Power works, 177

Nathan (character), 61, 62, 63, 66

Native American and Indigenous Studies Association (NAISA), 139

Native American Committee (NAC), 176

Native American Graves Protection and Repatriation Act (NAGPRA), 99–100, 247n127, 263n111

Native American Renaissance, 21, 72

Native Seattle (Thrush), 78–79, 87–88, 109, 111, 118, 243n61, 244n78, 244n83, 246n106, 247n111

Native urban writing. *See* literature of urban Natives

NDNZ, 216

Neihardt, John, 229n111

Nelson, Robert S., 21, 183

New England Frontier (Vaughan), 181, 271n48, 271n50

New England's First Fruits, 180

New Tomahawk, 138

"new tribal consciousness," 17, 19, 28, 35, 40

New Yorker, 112

New York Times, 29–30, 132, 229n109

Nicole (character), 67

Night Flying Woman (Broker), 136

No More Silence, 249n151

Noodin (character), 134, 141, 149, 150, 160

Noodin, Margaret, 255n5, 256n11, 263n117, 264n144

nostalgia: in *Jailing,* 47, 50, 52, 72; in "What You Pawn," 118–19, 120

Nygren, Åse, 85, 242n48

Oahe Dam, 205, 206–7, 277n173

Oakes, Richard, 18

Oakland Intertribal Friendship House, 17

Occidental Park, 86, 115

Oceti Sakowin Camp, 226n50

Office of Indian Ministry, 151, 263n113

Officer Williams (character), 115, 119

"off the reservation," 2, 223–24n8

Off the Reservation (Allen), 217, 223n7, 223n8

Ohlones, 42–43, 69–71, 232–33nn35–36, 233n39

Ojibway-Dakota Research Society, 138

Ojibway Tomahawk Band, 138

Ojibwemowin, 132, 134, 138, 146, 152, 163, 257n20, 260n64

Ojibwes: about, 135–36, 159, 173, 258n29, 259n34; Dakotas and, 141–42, 255n4; Germans and, 158; Louise Erdrich's representation of, 132, 140, 143, 162, 165, 255n7

Oklahoma, 127

Olin, Margaret, 183

"One Little Indian Boy" (Alexie), 241n34

133 Skyway (Redroad), 117

Ortiz, Simon, 22, 52–53

Osborne, Todd, 169, *171*

Other Side of the Earth (character), 145, 149

Outing Club, 44

Outing Program, 43

Owns, Louis, 39–40, 231n7, 231n10, 241n44

Pam and Paul (characters), 124–25

pan-Indian, term of, 16

pantribal, term of, 16

Pappan, Chris, 169, 210, 275n144

Paris Review, 134, 166

Pasadena Monthly, 217

Patell, Cyrus, 83, 92

pawning, 116–17

"Pawn Shop" (Alexie), 116–17, 129

pawnshops, 113, 116–17, 119

Peake, Frederick W., 137

Pease, Donald, 138

Peltier, Jerome, 58

Pembina band of Ojibwe Indians, 160, 266n171

Peters, Pamela J., 213–19, 278n1

Peterson, Nancy, 198

Phillips neighborhood of Minneapolis MN, 138, 143, 261nn65–66

photography, Native: of Debra Yepa-Pappan, 198–200, *199*, 275n144; of Edward Curtis, 3, 37, 79, 127, 213, 216, 240n21; of Hulleah Tsinhnah-jinnie, 37–38, *38*; in *Indian Land Dancing* mural, 169–70, 209; of Nadya Kwandibens, 230n1; of Pamela Peters, 213, 217; *Re-Membering: Dismembered Memories, San Francisco Historical Circle of the Displaced*, 69, *70*; of Richard Whitman, 127, *128*, 254n247; of Zig Jackson, 230n2

Pike, Zebulon M., 135–36

Pillager band of Ojibwe Indians, 135, 257n25

Pioneer Square, 80, *81*, *82*, 115, 130, 240n25

place, 214; in *Antelope Wife*, 132–33, 137, 141–44, 165, 255n5; in *Exiles*, 4–5, 7, 11; histories, 111, 117–18, 120, 179–86; history and, 12; homeless-ness and, 81–82; identity and, 17, 21, 23–24, 28, 31–32, 198; in *Jailing*, 47–49, 72–73; memory and, 11, 22, 219; relationship between people

place (*continued*)
and, 8–9, 19–23, 45–46; in Sherman Alexie, 77, 90–92, 97, 107–8, 111, 123–24, 129. *See also* displacement; place-stories; spatial practice; spatiohistory
Place and Vision (Nelson), 21
place-histories, 111, 117–18, 120, 179–86
place-stories, 80, 88, 97, 112, 118, 130, 179
Planet of the Apes, 108
Ploughshares interview, 200, 276n147
poetry, urban, 7, 224n17
Pokagon, Charles, 203
Pokagon, Simon, 30, 173, 175, 203
population of urban Natives, 225n20
Port of Tacoma, 254n244
Potawatomis, 173, 203
Potlatch Meadows, 107
Powell, Peter, 176
Power, Susan, 153; about, 169, 170, 268–69n5, 271n42, 273–74n96, 277n179; autobiographical influences on works of, 170, 177, 193, 196, 200, 204, 271n42; *Grass Dancer*, 153, 170–72, 178, 203, 207–8, 210, 269nn5–6, 269n9, 272n74; on Lake Michigan, 202–3; Natives as transformers and, 192; reconstruction of histories and, 178–79, 180, 192–93, 210; *Sacred Wilderness*, 197, 205, 273n93, 275n138; *War Bundles*, 170, 268n5, 269n17. See also *Roofwalker* (Power)
Power, Susan Kelly (mother), 176, 184, 185–86, 190–92, 205–7
powwows, 153–54, 264n130, 264nn132–33

The Practice of Everyday Life (Certeau), 210
Pratt, Mary Louise, 12
Princess Angeline, 79, 108, 240n21, 240n26
The Problem of Indian Administration, 136
protest of *Fort Dearborn Massacre* monument, 183–85, 272n64
puberty ceremonies, 59
Public Law 959, 14
Puget, Peter, 92, 244n84
Puget Sound, 90, 91–92, 96, 244n84
Pullman, George L., 182
Pumpkin (character), 170–72, 203–4, 263n114, 268–69nn5–6
Puritan-Indian relations, 181, 194, 271n45, 271n48, 271n50
Puyallups, 126, 254n244

Quantum Leap, 120, 253n226
Queen Anne Hill, 107
quests, urban, 113, 114, 119
quilts, star, 186, 187, 273n79

racial unrest, 16, 108, 109
racism, 60, 66, 137
Rader, Dean, 121, 132, 204, 253n227; engaged resistance and, 34, 127; on genres, 201–2
Radio Free Alcatraz, 18
Radisson, Pierre-Esprit, 135
Raheja, Michelle H., 223n6
"Raid on the Reservations" (Van de Mark), 223n5
railroads, 6, 44, 92, 143, 203, 260n62
Ramirez, Renya, 26, 38, 102, 132, 140, 155, 233n36
"Rattlebone" (Robertson), 230n122

sunrise ceremony on Alcatraz, 71, 238n160
Suquamish, 79, 96, 108, 117, 240n20
The Surrounded (McNickle), 30
survival schools, 18
survivance, 31–32, 111, 129–30, 132, 139–40, 260n50
Suzack, Cheryl, 46, 233n55
Sweetheart Calico (character), 131, 134, 137, 144, 145–47, 160–62, 261nn80–81
Sweet Lu (character), 93–94

Tacoma WA, 126, 254n244
Tatonetti, Lisa, 57, 85, 111
Tayo (character), 31, 110, 250–51n177
Ten Little Indians (Alexie), 76, 83, 112, 241n35
termination policy, 15, 42
Teuton, Chris, 229n106
Teuton, Sean, 31, 231n10, 237n152
textual instability, 134, 166
Tharp, Julie, 157
theories of urban Native literature, 19–29; city images, 24–25; crossing borders, 23–24, 25–27; identity, 23–24; relationship between people and place, 19–23; transnationalism, 25–26, 228n87; tribal cosmopolitanism, 26–29, 229n98
There and Back Again (Yepa-Pappan), *199*, 200, 275n144
"There is No Word for Feminism in My Language" (Tohe), 58
"This Is Indian Land" (Fragua), 13
Thrush, Coll: on *Flight*, 123; on *Indian Killer*, 87–88, 111, 243n61; on Seattle, 78–79, 82, 109, 118, 244n78
thunderbirds as a symbol, 3–4, 224n11

Tilikum Place, 240n26
time: in *Antelope Wife*, 160; deep, 11, 132–33, 134–35, 165, 207, 214, 225n31, 256n12; in *Exiles*, 10; in *Roofwalker*, 181–82, 202
time travel, 120–21, 122–23, 125, 253n226
Tlingit totem pole, 80, 118, 240n25
tobacco, 155, 156–57, 264n144
Tobasonakwut, 163
Tohe, Laura, 46, 58
Toppenish, 117. *See also* Yakamas
"To Some Few Hopi Ancestors" (Rose), 38–39
Toughest Indian in the World (Alexie), 77
Tracks (Erdrich), 133, 142, 148, 154, 198, 257nn16–17
trade, 10, 28, 116, 135, 159, 160–61, 162
Trail of Broken Treaties, 18, 138
"Transient" (Alexie), 76
transit (Yepa-Pappan), 200, 275n144
transmotion, 139, 260n50
transnationalism, 19, 25–26, 120, 139–40, 228n87
Treaty of Chicago, 173
Treaty of Fort Laramie, 18, 237n156
Treaty of Greenville, 173
Treaty of Medicine Creek, 126
Treaty of Neah Bay, 106
Treaty of Point Elliott, 79, 94, 97, 108, 240n20
Treaty of Prairie du Chen, 135
Treuer, David, 136–37, 143, 260–61nn63–64
tribal consciousness, 17, 18, 19, 28, 40, 69
tribal cosmopolitanism, 9, 17, 27–29, 229n98
tribalism, 30, 122, 132, 253n236

CPSIA information can be obtained
at www.ICGtesting.com
Printed in the USA
LVOW08*0858080917

548034LV00005B/26/P